PERSONNEL SELECTION AND ASSESSMENT

Individual and Organizational Perspectives

SERIES IN APPLIED PSYCHOLOGY

Edwin A. Fleishman, George Mason University
Series Editor

Psychology in Organizations: Integrating Science and Practice
Kevin R. Murphy and Frank E. Saal

Teamwork and the Bottom Line: Groups Make a Difference
Ned Rosen

Patterns of Life History: The Ecology of Human Individuality
Michael D. Mumford, Garnett Stokes, and William A. Owens

Work Motivation
Uwe Kleinbeck, Hans-Henning Quast, Henk Thierry, and Hartmut Häcker

Contemporary Career Development Issues
Robert F. Morrison and Jerome Adams

Human Error: Cause, Prediction, and Reduction
John W. Senders and Neville P. Moray

Personnel Selection and Assessment: Individual and Organizational Perspectives
Heinz Schuler, James L. Farr, and Mike Smith

Justice in the Workplace: Approaching Fairness in Human Resource Management
Russell Cropanzano

PERSONNEL SELECTION AND ASSESSMENT

Individual and Organizational Perspectives

Edited by

Heinz Schuler
Universität Hohenheim, Germany

James L. Farr
The Pennsylvania State University

Mike Smith
University of Manchester Institute of Science and Technology, United Kingdom

LEA LAWRENCE ERLBAUM ASSOCIATES, PUBLISHERS
1993   Hillsdale, New Jersey   Hove and London

Lawrence Erlbaum Associates, Inc., Publishers
365 Broadway
Hillsdale, New Jersey 07642

Library of Congress Cataloging-in-Publication Data

Personnel selection and assessment : individual and organizational
  perspectives / edited by Heinz Schuler, James L. Farr, Mike Smith.
      p. cm. — (Series in applied psychology)
    Includes bibliographical references and indexes.
    ISBN 0-8058-1034-X (alk. paper)
    1. Employee selection. 2. Personnel management. I. Schuler,
Heinz. II. Farr, James L. III. Smith, Mike (J. Mike) IV. Series.
HF5549.5.S38P44 1993
658.3'112—dc20   93–19170
                                                    CIP

Books published by Lawrence Erlbaum Associates are printed on acid-free
paper, and their bindings are chosen for strength and durability.

Printed in the United States of America
10 9 8 7 6 5 4 3 2

Contents

Foreword

There is a compelling need for innovative approaches to the solution of many pressing problems involving human relationships in today's society. Such approaches are more likely to be successful when they are based on sound research and applications. This *Series in Applied Psychology* offers publications which emphasize state-of-the-art research and its application to important issues of human behavior in a variety of societal settings. The objective is to bridge both academic and applied interests.

A longstanding application of psychology has been in the area of personnel selection. Applied psychologists have developed a variety of assessment instruments, all designed for the purpose of measuring the extent to which job candidates possess skills, abilities, knowledges, and other characteristics relevant to successful performance of the job in question. For the most part, the application of such selection instruments, and the more basic psychological research underlying their use, has been directed toward organizational objectives, such as increasing the productivity of the workforce, reducing turnover, and minimizing training costs. The perspective of the job candidates has received little attention from researchers concerned with organizational selection systems.

This volume argues for the inclusion of the individual perspective in personnel selection and assessment and contains a number of chapters that provide examples of such perspectives as they apply to specific topical areas within this general domain. However, the organizational perspective is not ignored. The volume as a whole provides a useful balance to the important concerns of the employing organization and the individual job candidate.

Adding further variety to the perspectives expressed in these chapters is the international nature of the volume editors and chapter authors. There are contributors from Canada, Germany, the Netherlands, Spain, the United Kingdom, and the United States. The contributors include many distinguished researchers and practitioners who successfully bridge in their own careers the academic and applied interests that this book series strives to serve.

Personnel Selection and Assessment: Individual and Organizational Perspectives provides insights into the ways that industrial and organizational psychology can help organizations to develop human resource management systems that allow them to be both competitive and humane. As more and more organizations recognize their reliance on their human resources, such management systems become vital for organizational survival.

Edwin A. Fleishman, Editor
Series in Applied Psychology

Preface

The impetus for this volume came from the editors' belief that most current research and thinking about personnel selection and assessment in organizations considered only the perspective of the employer (or organization). The job applicant seeking to join the organization or the employee being considered for promotion or reassignment was typically given little attention from the designers of employment or assessment systems.

We believed that this imbalance had several negative implications. First, and foremost to us, organizational selection and assessment appeared to be the principal area within work and organizational psychology that had forgotten a basic tenet of the profession of psychology, namely, that the welfare of the individual is paramount. Second, a lack of concern for the individuals who were being assessed could result in additional criticisms of psychological assessment in employment settings. Third, the acceptability of selection and assessment devices and systems may impact in (largely) unknown ways on the decisions of individuals to apply for jobs or transfers, thus affecting the selection ratio and potential utility of such systems. Fourth, individual reactions to the characteristics of assessment and selection devices could affect the accuracy of the information obtained about those individuals, adversely affecting the reliability and validity of resulting personnel decisions.

We informally discussed these concerns with our professional colleagues and found that others were similarly troubled. Our next response to these concerns was to organize a 3-day conference held at Hohenheim University, Stuttgart, Germany, that brought together a number of researchers in applied psychology from North America, Europe, and Israel to present papers and participate in discussions related to balancing individual and organizational needs in selection and assessment. The papers presented at this conference form the core of this volume, but this book is not simply a conference proceedings. All presentations at the conference that appear here have been extensively revised. Several presentations made at the conference do not appear for various reasons, including an editorial decision to tighten the domain of the volume to employment selection and assessment. In addition, in order to fill what we perceived as gaps in conference coverage, we commissioned several chapters from individuals who did not participate in the conference.

We thank a number of individuals and organizations that have supported us while we have worked to produce this volume. The Symposienprogramm der Stiftung Volkswagenwerk provided generous support for the conference at Hohenheim University. The following staff and students at Hohenheim University contributed to the success of the conference: Heike Fricke, Rüdiger Fruhner, Michael Donat, and Uwe Funke. The Center for Applied Behavioral Sciences (Frank J. Landy, Director) at the Pennsylvania State University provided support for Jim Farr to attend planning and editorial meetings related to the conference and the volume. Finally, we acknowledge the help of support staff at the Manchester School of Management.

Heinz Schuler
James L. Farr
Mike Smith

List of Contributors

David Bartram Department of Psychology, The University of Hull, Hull, United Kingdom HU6 7RX.

Terry L. Dickinson Department of Psychology, Old Dominion University, Norfolk, VA 23529-0267.

James L. Farr Department of Psychology, The Pennsylvania State University, 615 Bruce V. Moore Building, University Park, PA 16802.

Barbara J. Finnegan Department of Management, University of Washington, Seattle, WA 98195.

Rüdiger Fruhner Hamburger Sparkasse, Postfach 11 15 49, D-2000 Hamburg 11, Germany.

Daniel R. Ilgen Department of Psychology, Michigan State University, East Lansing, MI 48824-1117.

Thomas Kirchenkamp Bodan Software GmbH, Postfach 13 49, D-7778 Markdorf, Germany.

Frank J. Landy Center for Applied Behavioral Sciences, 207 Research Bldg. D, The Pennsylvania State University, University Park, PA 16802.

Gary P. Latham Faculty of Management, University of Toronto, 246 Bloor Street West, Toronto, Ontario, Canada M5S1V4.

Michael Pearn Pearn Kandola Downs, 76 Banbury Road, Oxford, United Kingdom OX2 6JT.

José M. Prieto Department of Work Psychology, Complutense University, Somosaguas, E-28023 Madrid, Spain.

Wiebke Putz-Osterloh Lehrstuhl für Psychologie, Universität Bayreuth, Postfach 101251, D-8580 Bayreuth, Germany.

Sara L. Rynes College of Business Administration, Department of Management & Organizations, University of Iowa, Iowa City, IA 52242.

Paul R. Sackett Industrial Relations Center, University of Minnesota, 271 19th Ave. South, Minneapolis, MN 55455.

Neal Schmitt Department of Psychology, Psychology Research Building, Michigan State University, East Lansing, MI 48824-1117.

Heinz Schuler Lehrstuhl für Psychologie, Universität Hohenheim, Institut 430, Postfach 70 05 62, D-7000 Stuttgart 70, Germany.

Nicolás Seisdedos TEA Ediciones, S.A., c/o Fray Bernardino Sahagún 24, E-28036 Madrid, Spain.

Mike Smith Department of Management, University of Manchester Institute of Science and Technology, P.O. Box 88, Manchester, United Kingdom M60 1QD.

George C. Thornton III Department of Psychology, Colorado State University, Fort Collins, CO 80523.

Günter Trost Institute for Test Development and Talent Research, Koblenzer Strasse 17, D-5300 Bonn 2, Germany.

John P. Wanous College of Business, Hagerty Hall, Ohio State University, Columbus, OH 43210.

Alexandra K. Wigdor National Research Council, Washington, DC.

Charles J. de Wolff University of Nijmegen, Department of Work and Organizational Psychology, P.O. Box 9104, NL–6500 HE Nijmegen, The Netherlands.

The Individual and Organizational Sides of Personnel Selection and Assessment

Heinz Schuler
Universität Hohenheim
Stuttgart, Germany

James L. Farr
Pennsylvania State University

Mike Smith
University of Manchester
United Kingdom

In many areas of their professional interests, industrial and organizational psychologists are used to taking both sides of a problem into consideration—the organizational side and the individual side. When it comes to personnel selection, however, they seldom optimize more than cost-benefit relationships for the organization. The principle of giving open and accurate information to all involved individuals is canceled, in this way preserving the competitive character of the selection situation.

Porter, Lawler, and Hackman (1975) wrote:

> The ideal situation would look quite different from the one which typically exists. The organization would describe the job it has to offer in realistic terms, pointing out both the satisfactions and the frustrations that the job presents. It might present the results of job attitude surveys carried out with people in the job. If relevant, the individual might be given a chance to interview job holders. Tests would be administered and the individual would be presented with results to help him decide whether he wants the job. He would be told how likely people with his scores are to succeed on the job. The individual, on the other hand, would present as accurate a picture of himself as he could. He would talk openly about his strengths and weaknesses, and he would respond to selection instruments as candidly as possible. (p. 157 f.)

This field of activities being questioned so radically is what 40% of the articles in the four main journals of our discipline deal with (Cooper & Robertson, 1986)—personnel selection and assessment. Many advances have been made in personnel selection within the last 15 years or so. But all these advances lie in the "technical" (psychometric) or organizational (economic) side of the process. Only a few research studies, on the other hand, have been devoted to the individual side or to the interaction of both perspectives, although there are multiple reasons for such research and its reflection in practice.

Despite many demonstrations of selection utility (Boudreau, 1989), in large segments of the public a critical attitude toward methods of personnel psychology has taken place. In the United States, the ongoing discussion of test fairness demonstrates that reduction of procedural justice to statistical terms is not accepted by many who conceive it rather as a social–political problem.

In most European countries, fairness is not as prominent an issue as in the United States, but there has been a critical attitude against personnel selection, and especially against psychological tests, common in the last two decades. Among the aspects of this critique are:

- Selection is only in the interest of the organization.
- Selection is an untimely expression of differences in social power: Applicants are forced to undergo procedures arbitrarily imposed on them if they do not want to lose their chance to get the job.
- Selection and assessment situations are nontransparent, that is, candidates are not given the relevant information about what is measured and what conclusions are made.
- Selection and assessment is stressful to the candidate.

In many cases, this critique or skepticism is not openly uttered but is hidden behind or enforced by the argument that selection methods are invalid. It reflects changing societal values—a changing attitude toward science, demanding legitimization of scientifically based technology; skepticism against secret lore and growing requests for transparency or openness of methods and decision principles; and sensitization toward invasions of privacy and fear of misuse of personal data.

Criticism of this kind seldom found its counterpart in a systematic, theoretically based, and empirically convincing argument. Certainly, we do know reasons for individuals to deal with selection in a constructive way (e.g., to get information about job requirements, to gain a realistic view of own competencies and potentials, to avoid excessive demands—over or underload, or to profit from the advantage that working for an organization with an efficient (high-utility) selection system should be more competitive and thus provide a more secure and socially recognized employment setting).

Needless to say, for the organization there are also reasons to consider the individual's perspective. For example, the organization with a selection system that is viewed as valid and fair may find it easier to recruit qualified applicants; knowing which kind of information reduces later turnover of qualified people is of high value, the changing labor market making these aspects even more important; and not disturbing a positive organizational climate by an unacceptable

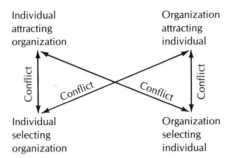

FIG. 1.1. The attraction–selection situation (from Porter, L. W., Lawler, E. E. III, & Hackman, J. R. (1975). *Behavior in organizations*. New York: McGraw-Hill, Inc. Reprinted with permission.

system of performance assessment. But, beyond utility calculation, there is also an ethical dimension in treating applicants and employees in the same responsible and humane manner that is characteristic of most other psychological practices in organizations (i.e., requirements to pursue fair and considerate principles and procedures in selection and assessment).

Porter, Lawler, and Hackman (1975) suggested a heuristic that makes plausible the advantages that exist for organizations as well as for individuals to consider the other's perspective. They present an attraction–selection framework in which individuals and organizations are both attempting to attract the other and to select from those attracted to them (Fig. 1.1).

From the individual's point of view, the selection process is not simply a matter of choosing a job in a given organization and gathering relevant information; the individual is, at the same time, interested to behave in such a way that will lead the organization to offer him or her a job. These intentions may get in conflict (e.g., asking some questions applicants are interested in may lower their chance to get a job offer).

The same is true for the organization. The selection process may attract potential employees, but it may also stand in contrast to the goal of attraction and repel the most qualified individuals. Especially if a low selection rate is intended, the effect may be to frustrate even a large number of qualified persons and result in unexpected effects for the organization's image.

A separate and almost ubiquitous kind of conflict for both of the contracting parties lies in the intention to be attractive to the other party. So, an individual's desire to attract the organization may lead to a kind of impression management that lowers the validity of the personnel decision. Or, the organization's desire to attract individuals by addressing their assumed occupational desires may stand in contrast to the individuals' interest to optimally choose an organization.

Of the four parameters of the Porter et al. model, only the selection of individuals by the organization is researched intensively. This is not true for the other three components, let alone the interactions (i.e., the conflicts among these goals). Although there is a vast amount of knowledge from basic research in different psychological disciplines that could be utilized, there is not even sufficient data at hand to support premises we have been relying on for decades. For example, the argument that rational selection is also in the interest of the individual as it protects the ill-suited applicant from potential stress or underutilization was forwarded by Münsterberg (1912), but although there are some indirect indicators for this, there are no studies to investigate this relationship directly. As long as we do not define and measure well-being indicators as validation criteria, our arguments can be viewed as being one-sided in favor of the organization.

Whether or not Porter, Lawler, and Hackman's (1975) vision of selection as a perfectly cooperative effort has a chance to be realized is open to question. Frustration of applicants can hardly be avoided if there are more qualified applicants than job openings, and the organization's interest in selecting the highest ranking person among them in many cases will lead to a conflict of interest. Furthermore, Porter et al. seem to take for granted that each rejected applicant can find a better fitting job. Among other things, our knowledge from validity generalization (Schmidt & Hunter, 1981) makes these assumptions questionable even in times of a labor market favoring applicants.

Consequently, this approach, taken literally, will be realistic only in a situation where at least one of the interaction partners is in a neutral position (e.g., the consultant in occupational counseling as it is institutionalized in the German Office of Labor). But there should also be possibilities to reach the goal to behave cooperatively at least partly or in essential components in organizational assessment and selection. Crucial for this is a better knowledge of participants' perceptions of and reactions to selection and assessment situations and of the relationships between individual and organizational perspectives.

This is the content of this volume. The authors of the following chapters summarize research and some theory related to this field and report recent investigations of special topics. The first section is devoted to individual perceptions. Included are chapters that describe how individuals—mostly applicants, but also representatives of the organization and others—perceive different selection methods and procedures; which parameters of assessment and selection situations have been shown or can further be expected to influence perceptions of the methods, of the persons acting, and of the organizations; and what can be done to improve those impressions.

The second section deals with individual reactions to personnel procedures, including job analysis, selection, assessment, and feedback. Although there is a certain body of research on motivational distortion in selection situations (which is represented here by an extensive study on personality questionnaires), there is less information on individual differences in responding to job analyses and job evaluations. In both cases, it may be useful to recognize and take into account such tendencies. Other contributions report emotional and cognitive reactions to selection situations (e.g., individual differences in stress and coping, and effects on participant's self-esteem). Two chapters on performance evaluation and feedback report that there are a number of factors determining reactions to appraisal. Most chapters in this section try to give advice for improving selection and assessment situations in regard to individual reactions. This is especially true for one chapter that takes pain to improve newcomer orientation programs by learning from patient preparation programs for medical operations.

In the third section individual and organizational perspectives are considered in a wider social context. Fairness is discussed in its different aspects and changing conceptions. According to different relevant issues in public policy, fairness turns out to have a different status in the United States and in Europe. The changing role of the psychologist in personnel selection is reflected in a review covering the last two decades, and some standard procedures in selection as well as in performance appraisal are questioned in favor of new orientations.

The last section includes a sample of contemporary approaches to selection and assessment. Computer-assisted assessment is one of the major trends in personnel selection, and an overview is given of the major steps and implications of automating assessment procedures from selecting an instrument to final decision making. Another chapter presents an approach that makes use of the special possibilities of personal computers in order to implement principally new task or test concepts in complex problem solving. Possibilities, but also problems, of planning and decision making in computer-simulated scenarios are discussed. A longitudinal study reports relationships between aptitude measures and self-report data on the one hand and occupational choice and satisfaction on the other hand. The final chapter offers evidence whether fairness of assessment center ratings is restricted by group composition effects.

REFERENCES

Boudreau, J. W. (1989). Selection utility analysis: A review and agenda for future research. In M. Smith & I. T. Robertson (Eds.), *Advances in selection and assessment* (pp. 227–257). New York: Wiley.

Cooper, C. L., & Robertson, I. T. (1986). Editorial foreword. In C. L. Cooper & I. T. Robertson (Eds.), *International review of industrial and organizational psychology 1986* (pp. ix–xi). Chichester: Wiley.

Münsterberg, H. (1912). *Psychologie und Wirtschaftsleben*. Leipzig: Barth.

Porter, L. W., Lawler, E. E., III, & Hackman, J. R. (1975). *Behavior in organizations*. New York: McGraw-Hill.

Schmidt, F. L., & Hunter, J. E. (1981). Employment testing: Old theories and new research findings. *American Psychologist, 36*, 1128–1137.

I

Individual Perceptions of Personnel Procedures: Introductory Comments

It is logical to start a book on the Individual and Organizational Perspectives of Selection and Assessment with a section on Perception. Unless the individual perceives the selection process, he or she can have no views or reactions to it—the perceptions form the basis for subsequent psychological processes. If the perceptions are positive, it augers well for latter stages such as commitment, participation, and acceptance. If the perceptions are negative, the prognosis is poor and there is a clear danger that the selection process will end in failure because the individual breaks the chain of events that could lead to his or her engagement by the company.

This section brings together four chapters focused on the perceptions of job candidates. These chapters have a great deal in common. For example, they all provide data on what candidates think about various selection methods, such as interviews, and they all report data on attitudes toward selection devices. However, they tackle this task in quite different ways so that the section as a whole gives a very rounded picture.

The first chapter by Heinz Schuler is unique in that it puts forward a clear model that aims to predict whether positive or negative perceptions will be formed. In essence, this model says that positive perceptions will result when (a) the candidate is given good information; (b) the candidate is not passive but is active and exerts some control (i.e., the candidate participates); (c) the situation is transparent to the candidate, and he or she can see the reasons for the methods and procedures used; and (d) the candidate receives feedback about his or her performance.

Schuler calls the positive perceptions that result from the presence of these factors *Social validity*. It should be noted that the use of the word validity in this context is slightly different from the present technical meaning that "validity is the correctness of the inferences which are drawn from a score," adding qualities of the selection process that makes it acceptable to participants. By this concept, the social impact of selection technology on participants is considered.

Schuler's use of model building is important because it clearly demonstrates that model building is possible. It also demonstrates how effective models can be in organizing and clarifying a myriad of empirical results. Having set up the model, Schuler then systematically explores its application to a wide range of selection methods that includes tests, work samples, and self-descriptions. One of the major accomplishments of this chapter is that it brings together many studies written in German and that are largely unavailable to those who are only proficient at reading English.

Schuler's chapter deals, in part, with the way that the information given out by an organization influences the perceptions of applicants. This issue forms the major theme of the chapter by Sara Rynes, which focuses entirely on the perceptions formed during recruitment. Ryne's chapter is also different in tone. Although it includes many references, the chapter is notable for the many quotations from actual candidates. These quotations serve to add "flesh and blood" to the statistical findings given elsewhere in the book. A major conclusion is that recruitment practices commonly fall far short of applicant expectations, and the shortfall can be attributed to four main reasons: (a) unrealistic applicant expectations, (b) conflicting objectives, (c) administrative complexities, and (d) surplus induced complacency.

Rynes is not content with leaving the analysis at this point. She suggests some potential solutions. In particular, she suggests that, from the individual perspective, assessment and selection could be improved by viewing applicants as customers and by better management of the recruitment process. The last recommendation, at least, will be music to the ears of software companies who are producing computer packages to streamline and improve the administrative aspects of recruitment!

Latham and Finnegan's chapter also focuses on perceptions of a limited area of selection and assessment—interviews. But the chapter has a much wider importance because it compares and contrasts applicants' perceptions with the perceptions of managers (potential users) and attorneys (who may advise those contemplating equal opportunity litigation). Thus, the focus is widened beyond the perceptions of the candidates themselves. In general, the results bode well for the use of the structured interview, which is usually regarded as the most accurate type of interview: Both managers and attorneys saw the situational interview as the most practical and the most valid type of interview. Interestingly, however, student applicants preferred unstructured interviews because they felt it allowed them to relax, to say what they wished, and to be able to influence the course of the interview—especially by showing their motivation. To an extent, this underlines the point made by Rynes—conflict of objectives between applicant and employer may often be expected.

The final chapter in this section further widens the focus. Thornton looks at the way in which a wide range of selection practices affect applicant perceptions. The chapter deals with some of the aspects such as recruiter behavior and selection procedures that were considered in previous chapters. However, Thornton also addresses such human resource practices as affirmative action programs, and to this extent useful links can be drawn with the chapter by Latham and Finnegan. Thornton also reminds us that perceptions of the selection process are influenced by factors outside the process. In particular, he mentions environmental factors such as the labor market and factors internal to the candidate such as self-confidence or mood. The last point is very important. This section was intended to concentrate on aspects of the selection procedure. But, this does not mean we can ignore other sources of influence. Indeed, a major research question waiting to be answered is: "What percentage of variance in perceptions is due to the selection procedure and what percentage of variance is due to other sources?" Most of the chapters in this book make the assumption that a large, possibly the major, part of the variance is due to the procedures adopted. It could be, however, that the biggest influence is exerted by the outcome (job offer or rejection), the characteristics of the applicant, or labor market conditions. Research on this issue is clearly needed, but in practice it will be very difficult to obtain a research design that measures the characteristics of a large sample of applicants and then tracks their perceptions as they apply for a number of jobs.

Thornton's chapter also attempts to differentiate the nature of individual perceptions. Many writers take a global and undifferentiated approach; perceptions can simply be either positive or negative. Thornton identifies at least four domains of applicant perception: (a) perceptions of the interviewer, (b) perceptions of the organizational climate (c) anticipated commitment, and (d) perceptions of the likelihood of accepting a job offer.

Some interesting questions then arise. Are these the main domains or are there other domains of applicant perceptions awaiting identification? Are the domains clustered or configured in certain ways? Do aspects of the selection procedure influence all the perceptual domains in the same way? As yet, we have few, if any, answers. They are research questions awaiting attention.

Finally, Thornton leads us on to the next section by indicating that matters do not cease at the perceptual level, and that perceptions can have important influences on outcomes such as job performance, turnover, and job satisfaction.

Social Validity of Selection Situations: A Concept and Some Empirical Results

Heinz Schuler
Universität Hohenheim, Stuttgart

GROWTH IN INTEREST IN CANDIDATE PERSPECTIVE

Personnel psychologists, in research as well as in practice, are often accused of being oriented only toward the organizational viewpoint of selection. Presumably, this is not exactly true. What they are interested in most of all are the methodological aspects of this task, and as methods have affinity to the organizational side of the task, the result may well look like ideological partisanship. Validity is a concept referring to large numbers of individuals, and utility calculations have not yet been successful except in economic terms for an organization.

During the last decade, however, interest has grown in considering the other side of this social process, the impact of selection situations on applicants, their well-being, their decision, and their behavior. Remarkably, this new orientation seems largely independent of the fairness discussion that has been led more by statistical, judicial, and social–political categories than by psychological terms (Schmitt & Noe, 1986).

One source of this new interest may be the labor market's changing power structures—at least for some occupations. Another source may be public criticisms of tests stressing, among other topics, the unequal power relationship and the opaqueness of assessment situations that evoke test anxiety and perhaps invade privacy (Spitznagel, 1982). In many cases, these criticisms come under the cover of assumed technical insufficiency of test methodology or of adverse impact (Haney, 1981). Further reasons for the orientation toward participants' reactions may be the growing emphasis on ethical considerations (Pulver, Lang, & Schmid, 1978) or a genuine scientific interest in reactions of subjects. Of specific interest are situations where there is a basic divergence in interests and goals of the selectors and the applicants, which then provokes corresponding behaviors on both sides (Tedeschi, 1981). Orientation toward applicants' perspectives can be seen from many viewpoints:

- Graham (1976) investigated the reasons for organizational choice.
- Wanous (1980) demonstrated the effects of realistic job previews.
- Herriot (1989) conceptualized the employment decision as social processes.
- Schmitt and Coyle (1976) found that interviewers are important determinants of applicants' decisions to accept a job offer.
- Martin and Nagao (1989) examined the effects of computerized interviewing on applicant responses.
- Nevo and Jäger (1986) discussed several aspects of the examinee perspective in psychological testing.
- Brandstätter (1982) suggested understanding the employment decision as a common problem-solving situation.

Schuler and Stehle (1983, 1985) asked which parameters make selection the last isle of opaqueness and nonparticipation in today's understanding of organizational functioning; and which are the characteristics of those selection situations that are seen as open, fair, respectful, and rational. They also asked what influences applicants' acceptance of a selection process (which surely is more than face validity).

A MODEL OF SOCIAL VALIDITY

Schuler and Stehle (1983) suggested that four components make selection situations socially acceptable: relevant *information* about task requirements and characteristics of the organization (including social psychological characteristics); direct or representative *participation* in the development and the execution of assessment programs; *transparency* of the situation, the assessment tools, and the judgmental evaluation; and content as well as method of communicating the results (i.e., *feedback* in an honest, considerate, and understandable manner).

As a succinct expression, the term *social validity* was chosen for the whole of those situational characteristics. It indicates a counterpoint to the traditional concept of validity as a technical term. (For the sake of terminological purism, the term *social quality* would do almost as well.) Figure 2.1 summarizes the concept of social validity.

The components or parameters of social validity are to be understood as in-

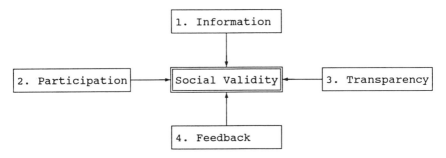

FIG. 2.1. The concept of social validity.

dependent variables which are presumed to influence participants' experience of and reactions to selection situations. The four components are not yet completely operationalized but—slightly developing the original concept—can be understood to include the following aspects:

1. Information.
- on the task domains of the job.
- on critical task requirements.
- on main organizational characteristics and goals.
- on organizational culture and style (e.g., interaction, leadership).
- on chances of personal and career development and other aspects that have been shown to influence performance and well-being for the respective group of persons and to enable informed self-selection.

2. Participation.
- in a narrower sense, participation is involvement in the development or choice of the selection situation or the selection instruments, or in the decision process (in either a direct or representative manner; e.g., by union members).
- in a wider sense, participation is the possibility to exert control over the situation or one's own behavior or the behavior or decision of relevant others, or freedom of coercion by others.

3. Transparency.

Transparency is the degree to which an applicant can clearly see or deduce the objectives of various facets of a selection situation. There are four main facets:
- the *selection situation*, including the acting persons, their roles, intentions, and competencies, as well as the behavioral expectations directed to the applicant.

- the *organizational importance* and *task relevance* of the diagnostic instruments (this aspect is closely related to face validity).
- the *evaluation process* and principles (i.e., of judgmental criteria, standards, principles of diagnostic conclusion, and the aggregation of data to judgments or of judgments to decisions).
- the *measurement process* in a form that allows self-assessment (and in consequence self-selection; e.g., as it is provided by work samples or by social comparison in an assessment center).

4. Feedback.

Feedback is the degree to which applicants receive information about their performance in a selection situation. The two main aspects of feedback that are responsible for a socially valid communication of assessment results are:

- *content:* open, honest, veridical, including probabilities of failures and chances for future development.
- *form:* comprehensible (semantically and pragmatically), considerate, supportive; facilitating self-insight, integration in the candidate's self-concept and an informed decision.

Whereas the components or parameters of social validity, the independent variables, allow themselves to some extent to be dimensionally ordered, the dependent variables are still rather vague. When we say social validity is what makes a selection situation a socially acceptable situation, we should be prepared to measure individual reactions, such as acceptance, well-being, feeling of control, comfort, nondefensiveness, of being fairly and respectfully treated, and not being unjustly subjected or dominated. It will also cover the impression of being informed about future tasks, demands and roles, possibilities and difficulties, and the likelihood of gaining insight into own strengths and weaknesses, thus facilitating an informed decision on the side of the applicant.

Social validity is not a concept for a single study but more for an extended research program. What has *not* yet been done is a comprehensive listing of research questions and designs. What *has* been done is a number of single studies, just loosely connected, mostly in the form of master's theses from several universities. As yet, they surely do not form anything more than some first tentative empirical realizations.

Here, a summary is given that includes most of these single studies. The concept cannot really claim to be a testable model but can only be seen as a heuristic. Most of the following studies cannot be viewed as theory testing in a global sense because they investigate only single aspects or hypotheses. It is not in every case easy to classify them unambiguously according to the four dimensions outlined earlier. This is attempted nonetheless.

EMPIRICAL FINDINGS RELATING TO THE MODEL

Information About Task and Organizational Characteristics

The question concerning the aspects of the job and the organization about which applicants especially want to be informed was investigated by Krauss (1985) and by Groepler (1988). Krauss asked applicants for management trainee positions what information they preferred and about the information they actually were supplied with. Unfortunately, the number of subjects in the main part of this study was only 19. What appeared rather clearly, however, were especially large differences between desired and received information, with "feedback concerning success and failure," "tasks and task demands," and "personal development and career" having high importance for the applicants. Definitely less importance was given to the aspects "starting salary" (not "future development of income," however, which was ranked highly), positional status, and working hours.

Groepler (1988) compared importance and credibility of informational sources for 75 graduates in business administration. Importance and credibility were highly correlated ($rs > +.50$), personal sources like interviewers and colleagues receiving higher credibility scores than sources of written information. This was in general also true for a second sample of 62 job incumbents in business administration. For this group, occupational values turned out to moderate the information desired. Given an occupational change, people with materialistic and intellectual values preferred information about the task and the organization (including social psychological aspects). Persons high in contact orientation preferred information on income, leisure time, and location.

In a study by Tachler (1983), 52 applicants for traineeships as administrators in a publishing company were asked what general information they preferred to be given at an interview as well as information relevant to the job. Table 2.1 shows that for those aspects that can easily be communicated sufficient

TABLE 2.1
Percentage of Respondents Asking for More Information About Task
or Organizational Characteristics

Task or Organizational Characteristic	Respondents Asking for More Information
Organizational climate	37
Leadership style	31
Chances of professional development	27
Professional image	10
Products	10
Details of traineeship	0

information was given, but the needs concerning climate, leadership, and development are only partly fulfilled.

After participating in a selection procedure comprised of several tests and work samples, the same subjects were asked for the amount of information the tests and work samples provided them about their future work. Results (Table 2.2) show that work sample tests have far higher informational content than traditional psychological tests. The counterpart of an assessment tool that is job related and informs about tasks is not only an uninformative instrument, but also one that is not restricted to job relevant characteristics, that does not respect privacy. Answers to these questions are also given in Table 2.2. It shows that work samples and to a certain degree achievement tests fulfill this requirement, but personality tests do not.

Participation and Control

As a step in the construction of a biographical inventory, Stehle (1983) asked 26 members of the target group and seven union members to rate each item of information obtained during selection according to its acceptability when put in oral or in written form. Generally, more items were rated as acceptable when put in oral than in written form. The most frequently rejected items were those questioning the areas of "family" and "childhood." Later statistical analyses suggested that elimination of these items did not diminish validity more than would be expected by lowered reliability for a reduced number of items. So the biographical inventory can be "filled up" by items of the acceptable categories and thus improved in terms of social validity, whereas not being diminished in the technical sense of validity.

TABLE 2.2
Percentages of Respondents Satisfied with Informational Characteristics
of Selection Instruments

	The Test has Informed me About my Future Work	The Test Respects My Privacy	The Test is Restricted to Job Relevant Characteristics
Self-description	0	7	21
Vocational interests	0	14	0
Concentration	0	57	21
Intelligence	7	35	21
Personality inventory	8	6	0
Vocabulary	11	47	26
Spelling	21	47	63
Work sample I	50	42	78
Work sample II	57	35	71

Ninety-six student subjects rated their impressions of directive or nondirective taped employment interviews in a study by Zehelein (1985). One variable connected with the concept of social validity is the feeling of control the interviewees have in these two interview styles. Results showed that nondirective interviewers were preferred in different respects. Nondirective interviewers were seen as more competent in their roles and more accurate in their assessments; subjects indicated that most people would like to be interviewed by nondirective interviewers, that they had a favorable impression of them, that it would be easy to talk to them, and that they would feel comfortable in this kind of situation (see Chapter 4, this volume, for similar results obtained in the United States by Latham and Finnegan). The nondirective interviewers were more in accordance with the applicant's perception of an ideal interviewer than the directive interviewers. Finally, nondirective interviewers were seen as easier to influence, the chances to get a job offer being higher in this case.

With a sample size of 48 applicants for an apprenticeship in a publishing company, Herberger (1984) tested the hypothesis that representative participation would enhance acceptance of the selection process and improve the image of the organization. The experimental group was informed that other apprentices participated in the control of the selection process, whereas the control group received neutral information. The results showed an expected and an unexpected effect. At first, participants' satisfaction with different aspects of the situation—test, psychologist, behavioral possibilities, organization—was somewhat higher in the participation condition—at least when the extent of participation was subjectively rather than objectively defined (for several members of the subgroup of internal applicants, the participation information seemed to be incredible).

But more interesting was the unexpected result that applicants in the participation condition performed worse in the tests than the control persons did. This effect amounted to half a standard deviation in average, being higher again for subjectively in contrast to objectively defined participation and higher for the performance factors Verbal and Knowledge in contrast to Number.

Transparency of the Situation and Evaluation

Borchers (1986) tested the hypothesis that acceptance of a personality questionnaire should increase when there is more information available about the test in use. A total of 82 applicants for middle management jobs were divided into three groups and given different information about the test. Group 1 received no information, Group 2 received "standard information" as used within the consulting firm cooperating in this investigation, and Group 3 was given more detailed information about the construction, use, and interpretation of this test. Acceptance was measured by a 30-item inventory focusing on four factors: validity, emotional reaction, positive impression management, and stress. Results show small effects in the direction of the hypotheses for all comparisons.

However, only the difference between Groups 1 and 3 (no information vs. detailed information) reaches an effect size of approximately half a standard deviation and an α level of at least .10. Experiencing personality questionnaires does not seem to enhance their acceptance. Experienced subjects rejected this type of test more than unexperienced subjects did. These attitudes were moderated by personality factors: Neuroticism was negatively correlated and diplomacy positively correlated with test acceptance.

Factors determining attitudes toward an assessment center were investigated by Lülsdorf (1986). One hundred and twenty former participants of a development-oriented assessment center were asked about affective, cognitive, and behavioral components of their attitudes toward this method. The better the explanation about the assessment center, the more positive were the participants' reactions on all three dimensions (total $r = .50$; unfortunately, independent and dependent variables were collected at the same time, retrospectively).

In Tachler's (1983) study (already mentioned in the information context), applicants were asked whether they could imagine how their suitability can be assessed by the respective instruments, how the scores are interpreted, and related questions (examples in Table 2.3).

The transparency comparisons show lower scores for self-evaluation and for the personality and interest inventories than for achievement tests and work samples.

TABLE 2.3
Percentage of Respondents Agreeing with Transparency-Related Statements

	SD	VI	CO	IN	PI	VO	SP	WI	WII
clear which traits and abilities are explored	35	57	64	85	33	58	76	85	78
unclear what to do to make a good impression	28	35	14	7	12	3	0	21	7
cannot imagine how qualification can be assessed in this way	21	7	28	7	31	18	5	0	0
have no idea how this test is interpreted	35	35	28	14	46	13	11	14	14
is especially important for the decision	28	14	21	50	8	26	44	21	28

Note: SD = Self-description; VI = Vocational interests; CO = Concentration; IN = Intelligence; PI = Personality inventory; VO = Vocabulary; SP = Spelling; WI = Work sample I; WII = Work sample II.

Feedback of Assessment Results

Relatively little empirical data have been collected until now on the communication of results. There are several American studies reporting positive responses of assessment center participants (cf. Kraut, 1973). Especially, the practitioner literature reports very positive attitudes to feedback even of a critical nature. But sometimes the impression remains that some of these reports are overly optimistic. On the other hand, the communication skills of the interviewers could be a critical variable. There are a number of reports from organizations indicating demotivation and other detrimental effects of performance feedback. However, most of those reports are of an anecdotal nature.

Lülsdorf (1986), in her study already mentioned, found that among the several components included in multiple regression the positivity of assessment results contributed little to participants' impressions of the assessment process. This means that feeling an assessment center is "alright" is actually widely independent of the individual's level of achievement at the assessment center.

This may be a function of the usual characteristics of assessment center participants—male, career oriented, self-assured persons. Quite a different result was shown for female apprentices in mechanical–technical occupations. In a study done by Schuler, Barthel, and Fünfgelt (1984), 32 girls in these unusual roles were compared to 31 boys in the same occupations. Among other aspects of achievement and well-being, the consequences of performance assessments for the young peoples' self-concepts were examined. The results are shown in Fig. 2.2 (the numbers indicate path coefficients). Whereas boys' job-related self-concept (self-assessments) at Time 2 was completely unaffected by their performance or performance assessment, girls' self-concept was to a large extent a function of preceding achievement.

GLOBAL EVALUATIONS

Schuler and Stehle (1983) suggested that the assessment center was an assessment situation that potentially allows a high degree of social validity in all or most of its different aspects. Referring to this suggestion, Harburger (1987) developed a questionnaire to measure reactions according to these aspects and used it to examine the qualities of an assessment center widely used by a consulting firm. Although, as a rough summary, the results were only moderately positive, they gave plenty of advice for improvement of this assessment center. As hypothesized by Schuler and Stehle, performance feedback by assessors, as well as the possibilities for social comparison during the assessment process, turned out to be especially highly valued. Further, it could lead to the effect that the assessors' actual feedback cannot match the high expectations. Concerning participants' personality variables, cognitive abilities were not related to their reactions, nor were persistence or general interest.

A large number of subjects ($N = 1,207$ students from different fields of study) was asked by Fruhner, Schuler, Funke, and Moser (1991) to compare and evaluate different selection instruments. As a general ranking of preferences, the

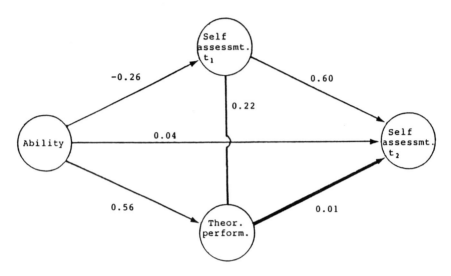

FIG. 2.2a. Dependence of self-concept from performance (boys).

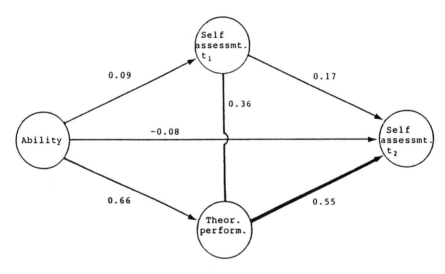

FIG. 2.2b. Dependence of self-concept from performance (girls).

following sequence turned out to be quite stable for different groups: Interview, Work sample, Internship, School grades, Psychological tests, Curriculum vitae, Handwriting, and Chance. Special consideration was given to the comparison of tests and interviews. Rating their qualities on a semantic differential scales resulted in the emergence of three factors: general evaluation, stress, and transparency.

Additionally, separate ratings were obtained for interviews and tests. Interviews were rated much more positively than tests. Whereas 84% of the experienced respondents would agree to take an interview once more, only 45% of test participants would agree to take a test again. Moreover, the interview was seen to be more informative concerning job demands and to be a more suitable measure of the relevant abilities. Respondents judged their achievements as good in both instruments with a slight advantage for the interview, although the difference was substantial again for the presumed possibility to influence one's own result (i.e., to exert situational control). One of the moderators was experience. Experienced subjects rated the interview higher than unexperienced ones (although there was no difference for tests in overall evaluation). Gender was also a moderator: Unexperienced women expected more stress in test situations than experienced ones.

In a multiple regression, the suitability for measuring the relevant (own) abilities and the possibility of influencing one's own result turned out to be sufficient predictors of global evaluation in the case of the tests. But, for the interview two additional components were needed: presumed own achievement and information about job demands.

With a questionnaire similar to the one used by Fruhner et al. (1991), Schmidt (1988) asked 31 applicants in three companies for their experience with employment interviews. Results indicated generally positive attitudes toward interviews. Multiple regression analysis showed that subjective control of the situation was the most important determinant of the evaluation of interviews as a selection method.

Finally, an assessment center experiment was conducted by Schuler and Fruhner (see chapter 8, this volume) with 96 participants. It included a variety of usual assessment center tasks. In addition to construct validation, the goal was to examine participants' evaluations of the instruments. A central question was how the variety of diagnostic information participants receive in this intense kind of situation (stemming from observation of own performance, from social comparison, and from feedback) would influence the self-concept and expectations of later occupational success. The results showed that simulation tasks were experienced as more stressful than the interview, but more transparent. Intelligence tests were rated less positively than simulations, but similar insofar as they were experienced as being transparent, stressful, and positive in general. In comparison to this, personality tests were seen as being less transparent, less stressful, and less positive in general. The effects of the assessment center on participants' self-concept turned out to be rather subtle and not consistent over several repeated measures. However, as a general tendency, improvement of self-ratings after feedback could be observed.

SUMMARY AND DISCUSSION

Focusing on the four aspects of social validity, the following impressions can be drawn.

Information

For this factor, relatively unambiguous empirical evidence has been collected. The data reviewed here stand with knowledge resulting from research presented, among others, by Wanous (1980) and by Rynes (chapter 3, this volume). The hypothesis that applicants are especially interested in the "social psychological" characteristics of organizations is well supported. Schmitt and Coyle's (1976) result that employment interviewers are important determinants of applicants' decisions to accept a job offer may well mean that the interaction initiated by the interviewer is interpreted by the candidate as a typical sample of the interaction in the given organization.

A comparison of the relative strength of needs, however, has to deal with a methodological problem common in motivation and satisfaction research. Needs are in principle measured in comparison to their present fulfillment and to that of the competing needs. This should also be the same way in our case: When our results show that applicants are more interested in the interaction style and in their developmental changes than in salaries and products, this may not mean that the latter information is principally irrelevant, but that it is—at present, in most organizations—given in a sufficient manner and so is taken for granted.

What has to be emphasized, however, is that information is a very important and a relatively easily fulfilled aspect of selection situations. Whereas giving the relevant information, communication mode as well as style is important.

Participation

Relating to this aspect, only few studies can be found that were conducted directly within this context. Relevant literature can be found only when participation is understood in the wider sense as the possibility to exert situational control. In this case, much social psychological research can be seen as relevant (e.g., Lacey, 1979). In this sense, participation undoubtedly belongs to man's basic needs and may be one of the reasons why selection situations are threatening for many people and make them feel uncomfortable and powerless. Interpreting the results reported here, situational control could have been responsible for the reliable preference of work samples and similar assessment tools over traditional psychological tests as work samples, tend to measure present and intentionally performed competencies, and by their very character often are presented in a relatively cooperative manner. Also, the preferences for interviews may be partly determined by the feeling of situational control (in spite of being a control illusion in some cases).

Concerning the narrower sense, as involvement in the development or choice of the selection situation or selection modes, some possibilities for participation could be demonstrated. So it is possible in principle to be included via representative participation (e.g., by union members or by members of the same group assessing acceptability and fairness of selection processes or instruments). However, if the "lulling effect of participation" that may have led to lower performance in one of the studies should be confirmed in further investigations, this problem has to be kept in mind in designing selection processes.

Transparency

A number of studies that were concerned with task acceptance can be connected to the factor transparency. Rather consistently it was shown that tasks that inform about job contents and requirements—what is usually the case with work samples—were better accepted by applicants than other tasks (e.g., Robertson & Kandola, 1982) and facilitated self-selection (Downs, Farr, & Colbeck, 1978). Also, the wide acceptance of assessment centers might be partly due to this factor. The studies reported here showed that transparency was a remarkable factor in multiple regression whenever these calculations were conducted. Additionally, it is probably a moderator of stress effects: Stress was negatively experienced only when processes and consequences were not transparent; combined with high transparency, participants tended to experience stress as activating. This may be one reason why ability and achievement tests were better accepted than personality and interest inventories.

Feedback

Effects of feedback can be assumed to depend on many characteristics of situations, of possible consequences, and of persons (Farr, 1991). Moreover, persons can be distinguished by their tendency to approach assessment situations. So effects of feedback tend to be moderated by roles of the individual and his or her personality variables such as gender, self-esteem, and experience. The generally positive reactions to detailed assessment center feedbacks suggest that feedback indeed belongs to the variables that can substantially contribute to the design of assessment processes as socially acceptable situations.

In combination, the reported studies may give some illustrations of the operational meanings of the concept of social validity. Of course, they are merely fragments, mostly resulting from a certain attraction the basic idea had for students. They now can give some basis for a more serious operational formulation of the components of this—hitherto rather loose and informal—framework. Related concepts and empirical work have to be compared and integrated. The consequences and extensions could also be considered (e.g., an attempt could be made to calculate utilities of selection processes for applicants).

Moreover, the importance of this cluster of situational characteristics called social validity is not necessarily restricted to applicants but could apply to all parties affected by a selection program, that is, to all members of an organization or of consulting agencies who should understand, accept, and make use of a selection system. A special target group are the assessors of an assessment center who might be enabled to play their roles better in situations where there is high social validity. Social validity may not only play a critical role in the selection process. It may also play a critical role in other forms of evaluation, especially in performance assessment.

REFERENCES

Borchers, M. (1986). *Zur akzeptanz von persönlichkeitsverfahren in der personalberatung* [Acceptance of personality inventories in personnel consultancy]. Unpublished diploma thesis, Universität Göttingen.

Brandstätter, H. (1982). Psychologische grundlagen personeller entscheidungen [Psychological methods of personnel decisions]. In H. Schuler & W. Stehle (Eds.), *Psychologie in Wirtschaft und Verwaltung. Praktische Erfahrungen mit organisationspsychologischen Konzepten* (pp. 19–48). Stuttgart: Poeschel.

Downs, S., Farr, R. M., & Colbeck, L. (1978). Self-appraisal: A convergence of selection and guidance. *Journal of Occupational Psychology, 51,* 271–278.

Farr, J. L. (1991). Leistungsfeedback und arbeitsverhalten [Performance feedback and work behavior]. In H. Schuler (Ed.), *Beurteilung und Förderung beruflicher Leistung* (pp. 57–80). Göttingen: Verlag für Angewandte Psychologie/Hogrefe.

Fruhner, R., Schuler, H., Funke, U., & Moser, K. (1991). Einige Determinanten der Bewertung von Personalauswahlverfahren [Some determinants of the evaluation of selection methods]. *Zeitschrift für Arbeits- und Organisations-psychologie, 35,* 170–178.

Graham, W. K. (1976). Commensurate characterization of persons, groups and organizations: Development of the Trait Ascription Questionnaire (TAQ). *Human Relations, 29,* 607–622.

Groepler, C. (1988). *Der informationsbedarf zur stellensuche bei wirtschaftswissenschaftlern: Vorstellungen und erfahrungen* [Informational needs of economists for job search]. Unpublished diploma thesis, Universität Bielefeld.

Haney, W. (1981). Validity, vaudeville, and values. A short history of social concerns over standardized testing. *American Psychologist, 36,* 1021–1034.

Harburger, W. (1987). *Psychologische eignungsdiagnostik, unter dem aspekt der sozialen validität als ergänzendes gütekriterium zur technisch-empirischen validität, überprüft am beispiel eines selektions-assessment-centers* [Social validity in personnel selection]. Unpublished diploma thesis, EWH Landau.

Herberger, J. (1984). *Partizipation und eignungsdiagnostik. Ein empirischer beitrag zum konzept der sozialen validität* [Participation in personnel selection. An empirical contribution to the concept of social validity]. Unpublished diploma thesis, Universität Erlangen-Nürnberg.

Herriot, P. (1989). Selection as a social process. In M. Smith & I. T. Robertson (Eds.), *Advances in selection and assessment* (pp. 171–187). New York: Wiley.

Krauss, D. (1985). *Bewerberzentriertes informationsverhalten von organisationen. Ein aspekt sozial akzeptabler eignungsdiagnostik* [Applicant-centered informational behavior in organizations]. Unpublished diploma thesis, EWH Landau.

Kraut, A. J. (1973). Managerial assessment centers in international organizations. *Industrial Relations, 12*, 172–182.

Lacey, H. M. (1979). Control, perceived control, and the methodological role of cognitive constructs. In L. C. Perlmuter & R. A. Monty (Eds.), *Choice and perceived control* (pp. 5–16). Hillsdale, NJ: Lawrence Erlbaum Associates.

Lülsdorf, C. (1986). *Einstellung ehemaliger teilnehmer zur assessment-center-methode und determinanten dieser einstellung* [Attitudes of assessment center participants]. Unpublished diploma thesis, Universität Bonn.

Martin, C. L., & Nagao, D. H. (1989). Some effects of computerized interviewing on job applicant responses. *Journal of Applied Psychology, 74*, 72–80.

Nevo, B., & Jäger, R. (Eds.). (1986). *Psychological testing: The examinee perspective*. Göttingen: Hogrefe.

Pulver, U., Lang, A., & Schmid, F. W. (Eds.). (1978). *Ist psychodiagnostik verantwortbar?* [Is psychological assessment justifiable?]. Bern: Huber.

Robertson, I. T., & Kandola, R. S. (1982). Work sample tests: Validity, adverse impact and applicant reaction. *Journal of Occupational Psychology, 55*, 171–183.

Schmidt, R. (1988). *Das Vorstellungsgespräch aus der sicht des stellenbewerbers* [The employment interview from the applicant's view]. Unpublished diploma thesis, Universität Bielefeld.

Schmitt, N., & Coyle, B. W. (1976). Applicant decisions in the employment interview. *Journal of Applied Psychology, 61*, 184–192.

Schmitt, N., & Noe, R. A. (1986). Personnel selection and equal employment opportunity. In A. Cooper & I. T. Robertson (Eds.), *International review of industrial and organizational psychology 1986* (pp. 71–115). Chichester: Wiley.

Schuler, H., Barthel, E., & Fünfgelt, V. (1984). Erfolg von mädchen in gewerblich-technischen ausbildungsberufen: Ein modellversuch [Girls' success in technical traineeship]. *Zeitschrift für Arbeits- und Organisationspsychologie, 28*, 67–78.

Schuler, H., & Stehle, W. (1983). Neuere entwicklungen des assessment center-ansatzes—beurteilt unter dem aspekt der sozialen validität [Recent developments in assessment centers—evaluated under the aspect of social validity]. *Zeitschrift für Arbeits- und Organisationspsychologie, 27*, (N.F.1), 33–44.

Schuler, H., & Stehle, W. (1985). Soziale validität eignungsdiagnostischer verfahren: Anforderungen für die zukunft [Social validity of selection methods: Future requirements]. In H. Schuler & W. Stehle (Eds.), *Organisationspsychologie und Unternehmenspraxis. Perspektiven der Kooperation* (pp. 133–138). Göttingen: Verlag für Angewandte Psychologie/Hogrefe.

Spitznagel, A. (1982). Die diagnostische situation [The assessment situation]. In K. J. Groffmann & L. Michel (Eds.), *Grundlagen psychologischer diagnostik. Enzyklopädie der psychologie, B/II/I* (pp. 248–294). Göttingen: Hogrefe.

Stehle, W. (1983). *Zur konzeption eines personalauswahlverfahrens auf der basis biographischer daten* [Construction of a personnel selection instrument on the basis of biographical data]. Unpublished doctoral thesis, Universität Hohenheim.

Tachler, E. (1983). *Empirischer beitrag zur erforschung der sozialen validität* [Empirical contribution to social validity research]. Unpublished manuscript, Universität Hohenheim.

Tedeschi, J. T. (Ed.). (1981). *Impression management theory and social psychological research*. New York: Academic Press.

Wanous, J. P. (Ed.). (1980). *Organizational entry*. Reading, PA: Addison-Wesley.

Zehelein, A. (1985). *Students' judgments of interviewers: The influence of gender and communication style*. Unpublished diploma thesis, Universität Erlangen-Nürnberg.

3

When Recruitment Fails to Attract: Individual Expectations Meet Organizational Realities in Recruitment

Sara L. Rynes
Department of Management & Organizations
University of Iowa

A recent study of recruitment experiences in an Ivy League university produced the following accounts from job applicants (Rynes, Bretz, & Gerhart, 1991):

> Some interviewers were really obnoxious. I wouldn't want to work for a company whose recruiters come off as a real pain in the _____. I immediately eliminated (Company A, Company B and others) because the recruiters were just stuck on themselves. I just didn't want to deal with them. I wanted to leave, but out of politeness, I didn't. (Male arts undergraduate)

> The recruiter was talking about the great presentational skills that Bank X teaches you, and the woman was barely literate. She was embarrassing. If that was the best they could do, I did not want any part of them. (Female minority arts undergraduate)

> I didn't want to talk to one firm initially, but they called me and asked me to. So I did, and then the recruiter was very, very rude. Yes, *very* rude, and I've run into that a couple of times. (Female engineering graduate)

> (I was looking forward to the interview because I) . . . had gotten exposed in a computer class to some advanced things this company was doing. The campus interview went really well, but they got back to me (with a second interview invitation) 7 months later! (Male industrial relations undergraduate)

> When I was done with the interview, they said, 'You can get a cab downstairs.' Well, there was a snowstorm and there weren't any cabs. I literally had to walk 12 or 14 blocks with my luggage, trying to find some way to get to the airport. They didn't book a hotel for the night of the snowstorm so I had to sit in the airport for eight hours trying to change my flight. I wound up being late to my next

interview because of the delay, and had to buy new clothes. They wouldn't even reimburse me for the additional plane fare. (Female management graduate)

Recruitment experiences (e.g., campus interviews and receptions) often represent the first direct contact applicants have with a potential employer. Because applicants frequently have limited information about a company at early stages, many rely heavily on recruitment experiences as signals of what a potential employer is "really" like (Rynes, Heneman, & Schwab, 1980):

There were a lot of companies where all I knew was what (product) they made. I generalize a lot about the company from their representative. If that person is not very sharp, does not seem to be particularly interested in me, or asks the same questions as every other recruiter, then I am not impressed. (Industrial relations undergraduate with four job offers; from Rynes et al., 1991)

I think a lot of people look at recruiting practices as reflective of the company, and in many cases that's absolutely accurate. Despite the fact that other factors matter, people do make choices based on how they're treated and how they feel about what's happening. If people feel they've been treated badly, even if it's just one person who is screwing up all along the way, I think that sways their decision. (Graduate student with 5 years' experience in a placement office)

Organizations have many reasons to design effective recruitment programs. For example, Murphy (1986) has formally demonstrated how the overall utility of a selection system can be dramatically reduced when organizations fail to attract their most desired candidates. Boudreau and Rynes (1985) have similarly shown that differences in recruitment costs, yields, and average service value have important impacts on overall selection utilities. Moreover, recruitment has a substantial public relations element, whereby impressions created in recruitment can extend beyond the immediate applicant to others, as well as beyond job choice to consumption.

Given the apparent importance of recruitment to overall selection utility, one would expect employers to try to create a positive impression during recruitment. Indeed, evidence suggests that employers often present *too* optimistic a picture, even at the expense of subsequent disenchantment and premature turnover (Schneider, 1976; Wanous, 1980). For example, surveys show that a large majority of human resource professionals view recruitment as a marketing activity, wherein "customers" (applicants) are attracted by surveying their needs and designing *messages* (but not necessarily jobs) to address those needs (e.g., Krett & Stright, 1985; Stoops, 1984, 1985).

Nevertheless, despite most organizations' intentions to create positive applicant impressions, favorable recruitment messages are sometimes negated by unimpressive recruiters, poor follow-up, and other recruitment features. In fact, although little research has aimed directly at assessing recruitment effectiveness, the limited evidence that does exist suggests that recruitment may *repel* nearly as often as it attracts (e.g., Downs, 1969; Fisher, Ilgen, & Hoyer, 1979; Gerstner, 1966; Luck, 1988).

Of course, organizations do not want to hire every applicant they interview, and some "unimpressed" applicants are undoubtedly "unimpressive" as well. Nevertheless, even applicants who eventually receive offers from firms (i.e., who are "desired" by them) report negative recruitment experiences with those same firms (Rynes et al., 1991).

Why do recruitment programs so often fall short of applicants' expectations, and what might be done about it? This chapter examines these questions through the following sequence. First, characteristics of an "ideal" recruitment process are described from the applicant's perspective. Second, actual organizational practices are summarized and compared against the ideal. Finally, underlying causes of discrepancies between expectations and realities are discussed, and possible ways of reducing them are explored.

IDEAL RECRUITMENT:
THE APPLICANT'S PERSPECTIVE

Not all applicants are alike. Some are looking for the best long-term career, others for the best short-term stepping stone (Rousseau, 1990). Some prefer rigorous selection procedures that allow them to "show their stuff," whereas others hope for "warm smile" interviews (Janz, Hellervik, & Gilmore, 1986) that favor charm over substance.

Nevertheless, applicants seem to have fairly consistent ideas about what constitute "good" and "bad" recruitment practices, at least in the context of college recruitment. Although empirical evidence from other contexts is sparse, we would expect many of the present generalizations to apply to other contexts as well, largely because they accord both with psychological theories and common sense. Preferred recruitment characteristics include the following.

Timing to Minimize Anxiety. Research suggests that most job applicants, even those in favorable labor markets, feel considerable anxiety about the job search process and their likely job prospects (Deutschman, 1990; Rynes et al., 1991; Soelberg, 1967). One side effect of this anxiety appears to be that applicants are very eager to obtain their first job offer. Soelberg (1967) has speculated that, because search failure can have such dramatic consequences, applicants distort their evaluations in favor of early offers, making it more difficult for latecomers to create a positive impression. More recent interviews with job applicants lend support to this hypothesis (Rynes et al., 1991):

> After I had an offer, I started judging more. In the beginning, it was just, 'Like me, *please* like me!' (Male undergraduate)

(The delay between the campus interview and second interview invitation) caused me to look deeper at certain parts of the company, to look more at the planning, to see if there was something I missed, or if it was something that just happened in my case . . . it suggested that I had to look at certain things about the company a little more closely than I might otherwise have done. (Male undergraduate)

The preceding comments suggest that recruiting advantages accrue to companies that attract attention early and then maintain it. Early attention can be facilitated by having a strong presence on campus, offering internships or co-op experiences, and holding information sessions early in the recruiting season. In contrast, *maintaining* attention seems to require keeping applicants' hopes alive through prompt follow-ups at each stage of the process: "within 2–3 weeks they should be giving some response. (When there was a delay), I assumed either that they had a disorganized staff, or (that) they were pulling my chain. In either case, I was not impressed . . . I just eliminated them from my list" (Male undergraduate with Japanese language skills and six job offers).

Although applicants seem to prefer early contacts, prompt follow-ups, and early offers, most do not want to be pressured into making quick decisions. Although there are wide individual differences in tolerance for prolonged search (e.g., Glueck, 1974; Sheppard & Belitsky, 1966), most applicants seem to want time to generate at least two offers so that there can be a "real" choice (i.e., something to reject, as well as something to accept; Glueck, 1974; Soelberg, 1967). Then, once offers are in hand, most want time to rationalize their decisions, which almost always involve accepting some suboptimal features along with the desirable ones (Soelberg, 1967; Vroom, 1966). For these reasons, most applicants regard pressure to reach a quick decision as at best unappealing, and at worst coercive.

From the applicant's perspective, the ideal recruitment program produces an early expectation of being in contention for an offer, maintains that expectation through prompt follow-ups, extends an early offer, and then waits long enough for the applicant to persuade her or himself that the best possible choice has been made.

Feedback to Optimize Scarce Job Search Resources.   Closely related to the issue of timing is that of feedback. Because job search is a costly activity (psychologically, monetarily, and time wise), most individuals ration their search resources toward alternatives where they stand at least a reasonable chance of receiving an offer (e.g., Schwab, Rynes, & Aldag, 1987).

Initially, judgments of offer expectancies are probably based on general notions of organizational selectivity as compared against the applicant's (perceived) rank in the applicant queue (Thurow, 1975). Once initial contact has been made, however, applicants begin to look for more personalized feedback regarding chances of receiving an offer.

When explicit information is not forthcoming, many applicants try to estimate their chances *indirectly* by interpreting other aspects of the recruitment process. For example, both field (e.g., Schmitt & Coyle, 1976) and laboratory (Rynes & Miller, 1983) research suggest that recruiter personality and informativeness can be important cues for estimating the likelihood of receiving an offer.

Another common source of indirect expectancy information is the length of time between recruitment contacts. Rynes et al. (1991) found that most applicants interpret long delays to mean that they are no longer being considered or are not the preferred candidate for a position. Correctly or not, most applicants view lack of direct contact as a recruiter's way of evading negative feedback. The assumption that organizations dislike communicating rejection is also evidenced by the belief that bad news travels via "ding letters," whereas good news travels by phone.

Although no one likes to be rejected, most of the applicants in Rynes et al. (1991) gave the impression that they would prefer direct rejection to no feedback. Lack of information prevents applicants from efficiently allocating their limited search resources. As such, withholding of negative feedback is often interpreted as "stringing applicants along" to preserve complete freedom of *organizational* decision making.

Information that Makes Distinctions.   Attempting to determine precisely what information is "most important" to applicants in job choice is an exercise fraught with difficulties (e.g., Lawler, 1971; Rynes, Schwab, & Heneman, 1983). As such, no attempt is made here to delineate the precise *content* of vacancy information desired by the "typical" applicant.

Nevertheless, compiling clues from various sources, it appears that applicants want information that (a) is detailed, specific, and relevant, (b) distinguishes one vacancy from others, and (c) includes some negative as well as positive information (e.g., Behling, Labovitz, & Gainer, 1968; Downs, 1969; Fisher et al., 1979; Wanous, 1980). Presumably, these characteristics not only help applicants make better choices but also prepare them to cope with the challenges they encounter as new employees. (The desire for detailed, relevant, credible information probably explains apparent preferences for certain *sources* of information as well—e.g., interviews rather than brochures, potential co-workers rather than recruiters, line rather than staff representatives.)

However, at the same time that applicants want thorough "differentiating" information, they also want to generate offers they feel good about and can describe enthusiastically to friends and family (Soelberg, 1967). According to some hiring managers, applicants have a limited tolerance for complete honesty and may "tune out" negative information transmitted during recruitment. Alternatively, they may reject the offer, particularly if they have an alternative where the downside is less apparent.

Applicants want detailed realistic information about vacancies, but they also prefer that information be largely positive. Although realistic job preview experiments have typically been silent about the precise favorability of the information presented—particularly in relation to competing offers (Rynes, 1991)—logic and limited data suggest that, at some point, the more that "detailed and specific information" translates into "bad news," the less likely an applicant will be to receive it positively.

Enthusiastic, Informative, and Credible Representatives. Although the precise role of organizational representatives in job choice remains unclear (see Rynes et al., 1991), there is nevertheless a fair consensus about what applicants *like or dislike* in recruiters. In particular, research indicates that applicants prefer warm enthusiastic recruiters who are able to discuss how applicant desires and qualifications relate to job requirements and career opportunities (e.g., Powell, 1991; Rynes et al., 1980; Schmitt & Coyle, 1976). By comparison, recruiter demographics such as age, race, or gender seem to have little consistent impact on applicants (Rynes & Barber, 1990).

Although most studies have focused on recruiter personality and informativeness, functional areas and status levels of organizational representatives also seem to make a difference (e.g., Rogers & Sincoff, 1978; Rynes et al., 1991):

> The best plant visit I had was with _____. The people made the difference. *I only met with people at the manager level and above.* (Minority graduate student with prior experience as a recruiter and eight job offers)

> Best visit was at _____. Their treatment and their attitude made the difference; always checking to see if anything was needed. *I was interviewed by the top people at corporate headquarters.* (Undergraduate with three offers)

> My best visit was at _____. *A lot of what I did was talk to people in operations and production, rather than in human resources (her own field).* (Graduate student with four offers)

> My worst interview was with _____, where they had about 2½ hours dead time for me. *They just left me with this secretary* who was in charge of scheduling people to come into town. She was kind of ditzy, and *I even had to spend lunch with her.* I would ask her questions that just flew over her head. . . . (In contrast, with the best company) . . . I got along with everyone. *I even got a personal phone call from the Vice President of my functional area.* (Graduate student with the highest grade point in the sample; accepted this offer on-the-spot because it dominated all others)

Prior research also suggests that applicants like to have contact with potential peers and co-workers (not just supervisors and recruiters), and with current employees who have similar educational or work histories. These preferences reflect applicants' beliefs that potential co-workers are more honest and credible than "formal" recruiters (Fisher et al., 1979; Rynes et al., 1991), as well as a tendency to extrapolate from the career experiences of prior applicants who were once "just like myself" (e.g., Alderfer & McCord, 1970).

From the applicant's perspective, "ideal" organizational representatives possess (a) warm outgoing personalities, (b) detailed information about how applicant skills and interests fit in with job and career opportunities, (c) high status and "line" credibility, and (d) personal and background similarities to the applicant.

IDEALS MEET REALITY: RECRUITMENT IN ACTION

Little research has been published over the past 10 to 20 years assessing either the procedural or bottom-line effectiveness of organizational recruitment efforts (Boudreau & Rynes, 1985; Murphy, 1986; Rynes & Barber, 1990). As such, it is difficult to ascertain (a) the extent to which typical recruitment practices deviate from the preceding ideal, and (b) how much difference such deviations make in terms of applicants' job choices and subsequent adjustment.

Nevertheless, various pieces of evidence suggest that recruitment practices commonly fall far short of applicant expectations. For example, descriptive research prior to 1980 reached very pessimistic conclusions about recruiter preparedness, informativeness, and credibility (Rynes et al., 1980). Hilgert and Eason (1968) reported that 55% of their applicant sample believed less than half of campus recruiters ever bothered to look at their resumes. Applicants also complained that recruiters were ill prepared to discuss vacancies in anything but the most general terms (Downs, 1969). Fisher et al. (1979) found that recruiters were regarded as a far less credible source of job information than friends, professors, or potential co-workers.

Although one might expect recruitment practices to have improved since the 1960s and 1970s, there is little evidence that this is actually the case. For example, in a 1986 survey of college recruiting practices of Fortune 1000 corporations, Rynes and Boudreau found that less than half the respondents offered training to recruiters, and, of those, less than half required that recruiters actually participate. Even where training was offered, only 1.3 hours (on average) were spent instructing recruiters on what to tell applicants about the organization. As such, it seems likely that today's applicants feel just as frustrated as those of earlier decades in terms of receiving specific information to help them differentiate one organization from another.

Other evidence similarly suggests that applicants are likely to be disappointed with the average campus recruiter. For example, whereas applicants appear to prefer high-status line recruiters, half the recruiters in Rynes and Boudreau's (1986) sample were staff employees who were described as only "moderate" in status. Moreover, responding firms rarely bothered to assess applicant reactions to their recruiters; if recruiters were evaluated at all, it was most commonly on procedural bases (e.g., whether they kept appointments, reported results, and took notes). Finally, respondents indicated that performance as a recruiter was of little consequence to overall performance evaluations and merit awards.

Few organizational activities appear to be directed at improving the impressions created by recruiters and recruitment programs, with somewhat predictable results. For example, in a recent series of applicant interviews, recruiters were variously described as "incompetent, obnoxious, boring, rude, embarrassing, illiterate, full of themselves, overbearing, and just plain assholes." In addition, excessive delays between recruitment phases were experienced by nearly 95% of the same sample (Rynes et al., 1991).

Although negative (or positive) impressions of recruitment do not necessarily translate into job rejections (or acceptances), a substantial proportion of both Glueck's (1973) and Rynes et al.'s (1991) subjects mentioned recruitment as at least *part* of the reason for their job choices. This is important in light of Boudreau and Rynes' (1985) and Murphy's (1986) demonstrations of recruitment impacts on overall selection utility.

SOURCES OF "REAL-VERSUS-IDEAL" DISCREPANCIES

Perhaps because descriptive recruitment research has been very limited in recent years, there has been little discussion of *why* recruitment practices so often fall short of applicant expectations. Nevertheless, it is important to examine this question so that appropriate remedies might be constructed.

Unrealistic Applicant Expectations. One reason experiences fall short of expectations lies in the sometimes naive nature of those expectations. For example, the typical applicant wants organizations to make early contact, but not at the expense of meaningful feedback about employment chances or detailed information about what vacancies will look like 6 months down the road. Similarly, the ideal recruitment program should be quick in reaching its own decisions, but slow in demanding the applicant's.

Moreover, the anxieties associated with job search can cause even minor violations of expectations (e.g., a 2-week follow-up delay or a misremembered fact from the resume) to take on inflated importance. To the applicant, job search is often a highly unique and life-central event, whereas to recruiters, recruitment can sometimes become numbingly routine. (One training manual for a Fortune 500 firm has a list of suggestions for recruiters on how to maintain a show of interest when they find themselves "drifting away" in an interview.)

It should be noted, however, that although anxiety translates into high expectations and close scrutiny for many job applicants, others give employers considerable leeway: "If the recruiter is very bad . . . I just chalk it up. There are always going to be 'bad apples' and that is just a bad apple" (Female arts undergraduate). "I didn't worry too much (about delays) . . . They're in business, and things happen in business that we don't know about" (Minority female labor relations undergraduate).

Conflicting Objectives. One of the more obvious sources of divergence between applicants' expectations and organizational behaviors is that applicant and organizational objectives do not always coincide. For example, although applicants may want feedback that permits early elimination of low-probability alternatives, organizations may not want to discourage "second choices" before receiving answers from their "firsts." Similarly, although applicants may want maximal time to feel comfortable with their job choices, organizations may need to press for decisions so as not to lose other candidates. Nevertheless, conflicting objectives seem inadequate to explain the substantial number of cases where applicants are kept dangling for months with no feedback, or those where recruiters come off not just as ineffective but as hostile, arrogant, embarrassing, or worse.

Administrative Complexities. College recruitment is a complex activity, particularly for large organizations. Applicants from diverse majors at multiple schools must be prescreened and contacted by a variety of organizational representatives, interviewed and evaluated, and then either informed of rejection or scheduled for subsequent interviews. These second interviews then take place with a new set of (mostly line) individuals who are often widely dispersed throughout the organization.

As a result, there are literally hundreds of "moments of truth" (Carlzon, 1987), in which applicants can either be won or lost by an organization. Interactions become particularly important in later stages, when applicants have narrowed their options and finally meet their potential colleagues. Because the potential for creating good (or poor) impressions is widely dispersed across individuals (e.g., potential supervisors, co-workers, staff support), it becomes very difficult to administratively control impression formation.

A second complexity involves juggling potential advantages of early contact against potential losses due to insufficient information about vacancies, inability to provide timely follow-up, or possibilities of alienating or losing preferred candidates due to unrealistically early deadlines. Unfortunately, there is virtually no research to help different types of organizations determine when to enter the market, when to extend offers, and when to impose (or extend) deadlines on candidates' decisions.

Surplus-Induced Complacency. Since World War II, most organizations have had a relatively easy time filling vacancies. Under labor surplus conditions, most organizations act as satisficers with respect to recruitment. In the face of adequate recruiting "base rates," employers see little reason to conduct systematic research on the costs and benefits of alternative recruitment activities (e.g., recruiter training; visiting new campuses) or existing programs (e.g., Miner, 1979; Rynes & Boudreau, 1986). Lack of formal experimentation and evaluation, in turn, prevents organizations from recognizing the potential magnitude of the benefits to be obtained from improved procedures (Boudreau & Rynes, 1985). The result is generally suboptimal recruitment practices, with vacancies getting filled, but not always by preferred candidates, and with applicants being none too impressed in the process.

In contrast, recruitment experimentation and monitoring are far more common in labor-shortage environments (e.g., Hanigan, 1987; Malm, 1954; Merrill, 1987). For example, considerable attention has been paid to recruitment in the armed services since the abolition of conscription, particularly with respect to the most highly qualified prospects (e.g., Asch, 1990; Hanssens & Levien, 1983; Tannen, 1987). Recruiting programs are also carefully designed and monitored in low-wage markets (e.g., Merrill, 1987) and markets where positions generate large sums of revenue, and talented individuals are both scarce and easy to observe (e.g., executives, professional sports; Wolff & Keteyian, 1990).

POTENTIAL SOLUTIONS

Despite a considerable literature on how recruitment might be improved, actual recruitment practices have been rather impervious to recommendations arising from research and theory: no surveys, experiments, or utility models have had a noticeable impact on practice. In a world of scarce resources and competing demands, it seems unlikely that most recruitment programs will make significant strides toward greater effectiveness until applicants become increasingly scarce and recruiting base rates plunge below a satisfactory level. Still, if the authors of *Workforce 2000* are correct, that time may not be far away (Johnston, 1987). The following principles are likely to prove useful in times of intensified competition for labor.

Viewing Applicants as "Customers." Just as American businesses have been criticized for not keeping close to their customers, neither have many stayed close to their applicants. Few companies seek systematic applicant feedback, and many design recruitment positions as rotational responsibilities from which individuals move on after only a few seasons (Asch, 1990; Rynes & Boudreau, 1986). These practices give a transitional flavor to recruitment, rather than a sense of long-term commitment and accountability.

Organizations wishing to improve recruiting effectiveness would do well to impose the applicant's perspective on all recruitment activities. In the case of college recruitment, this would mean continually reminding recruiters, managers, and administrative staff that job seekers are frequently anxious about their prospects; that most are trying to juggle interviews, plant visits, and full college courseloads; that most applicants are typically being "wooed" by multiple competitors; that applicants become increasingly judgmental as their alternatives solidify; that applicants sometimes make assumptions about an entire organization based on a single interaction, and that they generally make negative assumptions when the "courting" ceases for even short periods of time.

Managing the Recruitment Process. Many of the attraction and public relations failures of recruitment result from inadequate attention to program administration. Successful recruiting efforts require effective participation from many individuals, not just from recruitment support staff. And yet the vast majority of individuals who are counted on to impress applicants have never been trained to do so, have never been consulted about how to "sell" jobs or generate applicants, and receive no feedback on how well they do at any of the tasks surrounding recruitment and selection.

A well-managed recruitment process would commence at a carefully chosen time that takes into account the organization's unique costs and benefits of early versus late entry into the market. Initial campus representatives would be selected on the basis of their personalities, organizational knowledge, and credibility with line managers. These representatives would receive training, not just in procedural requirements, EEO, and interpersonal skills, but also in what to tell applicants about jobs, careers, the organization in general, and the recruitment process. Performance would be evaluated on substantive as well as procedural bases through monitoring of applicant impressions, line manager opinions, job offer and acceptance rates, and posthire success of a recruiter's referrals.

Hiring managers and administrative staff (not only recruiters) would also be trained to appreciate the applicant's perspective—to understand the importance of providing timely information, exercising flexibility in scheduling, and ensuring prompt follow-up. Where applicant expectations cannot be met (e.g., when a delay must be longer than desirable), prompt explanations would be offered and compensatory actions taken to minimize negative fallout. All organizational representatives throughout the process would be mindful of the fact that even rejected applicants can have an impact on the company through their roles as future consumers, and as "storytellers" to other applicants and consumers.

CONCLUDING COMMENTS

This chapter has focused mainly on negative aspects of recruitment: frequent discrepancies between applicant expectations and organizational realities, conflicts between individual and organizational objectives, and so on. But it is important to remember that applicants can also be "won" through effective recruitment. Although excellent recruiters and well-run procedures cannot overcome strong applicant job preferences or substandard employment offers, they can cause applicants to end up in organizations they did not initially favor (or even consider).

For example, Rynes et al. (1991) observed cases where applicants interviewed with companies where they had no real interest (e.g., for interview practice, or because placement directors asked them to fill empty slots) but ended up accepting a job because the interview generated interest that was sustained through later stages. Important elements in these scenarios were dynamic recruiters who were enthusiastic about their companies, quick invitations to site visits, well-organized visits with no "down time," opportunities to talk with high-ranking managers and people from other areas, and, again, continued contact and quick turnaround following the visit.

In the end, however, there are limits to the ability of recruitment planning, recruiter selection and training, and other formal recruitment activities to attract applicants. These activities are likely to be most successful in shaping experiences at the front end of the process (e.g., campus interviews), and hence to generate initial interest and site visit acceptances.

In contrast, the most important interactions in terms of ultimate job choices are likely to occur at the back end of the recruiting process. Because the final stages of recruitment are highly decentralized and controlled primarily by line managers and employees, it is difficult to create a good impression through formal "policies" if an organization is, in fact, poorly managed or has low morale, menial work, or poor career opportunities. Thus, in the final stages, true characteristics of the unit—both people and jobs—are more likely to reveal themselves to applicants and to stand on their own merits.

ACKNOWLEDGMENTS

The author thanks Karin Ash and Judy Olian for helpful comments on an earlier version of this chapter. Background research for this chapter was carried out with support from the U.S. Army Research Institute, Contract SRFC MDA903-87-K-001. However, the views, opinions, and findings reported in this chapter are those of the author and should not be construed as official Department of the Army policy.

REFERENCES

Alderfer, C., & McCord, C. (1970). Personal and situational factors in the recruitment interview. *Journal of Applied Psychology, 54,* 377–385.
Asch, B. J. (1990). Do incentives matter? The case of Navy recruiters. *Industrial & Labor Relations Review, 43,* 89–106-S.

Behling, O., Labovitz, G., & Gainer, M. (1968). College recruiting: A theoretical base. *Personnel Journal, 47*, 13–19.

Boudreau, J. W., & Rynes, S. L. (1985). Role of recruitment in staffing utility analysis. *Journal of Applied Psychology, 70*, 354–366.

Carlzon, J. (1987). *Moments of truth.* New York: Harper & Row.

Deutschman, A. (1990, August 27). What 25-year-olds want. *Fortune, 122*(5), 42–50.

Downs, C. W. (1969). Perceptions of the selection interview. *Personnel Administration, 32*, 8–23.

Fisher, C. D., Ilgen, D. R., & Hoyer, W. D. (1979). Source credibility, information favorability, and job offer acceptance. *Academy of Management Journal, 22*, 94–103.

Gerstner, L. V. (1966). College recruiting: Why the good ones get away. *Management Review, 55*, 4–12.

Glueck, W. F. (1973). Recruiters and executives: How do they affect job choice? *Journal of College Placement, 34*, 77–78.

Glueck, W. F. (1974). Decision making: Organizational choice. *Personnel Psychology, 27*, 77–93.

Hanigan, M. (1987). Campus recruiters upgrade their pitch. *Personnel Administrator, 32*, 55–58.

Hanssens, D. M., & Levien, H. A. (1983). An econometric study of recruitment marketing in the U.S. Navy. *Management Science, 29*, 1167–1184.

Hilgert, R., & Eason, L. (1968). How students weigh recruiters. *Journal of College Placement, 28*, 99–102.

Janz, J. T., Hellervik, L., & Gilmore, D. C. (1986). *Behavior description interviewing: New, accurate, cost effective.* Newton, MA: Allyn & Bacon.

Johnston, W. B. (1987). *Workforce 2000: Work and workers for the 21st century.* Indianapolis: Hudson Institute.

Krett, K., & Stright, J. F. (1985). Using market research as a recruitment strategy. *Personnel, 62*(11), 32–36.

Lawler, E. E., III. (1971). *Pay and organizational effectiveness.* New York: McGraw-Hill.

Luck, R. (1988, September 26). How industrial recruiters sell themselves short. *Wall Street Journal,* Manager's Journal.

Malm, F. T. (1954). Recruiting patterns and the functioning of labor markets. *Industrial & Labor Relations Review, 7*, 507–525.

Merrill, P. (1987). Sign of the times. *Personnel Administrator, 32*, 62–65.

Miner, M. G. (1979). *Recruiting policies and practices.* Washington, DC: Bureau of National Affairs.

Murphy, K. R. (1986). When your top choice turns you down: Effects of rejected job offers on selection test utility. *Psychological Bulletin, 99*, 133–138.

Powell, G. N. (1991). Applicant reactions to the initial employment interview: Exploring theoretical and methodological issues. *Personnel Psychology, 44*, 67–84.

Rogers, D., & Sincoff, M. (1978). Favorable impression characteristics of the recruitment interviewer. *Personnel Psychology, 31*, 495–504.

Rousseau, D. M. (1990). New hire perceptions of their own and their employer's obligations: A study of psychological contracts. *Journal of Organizational Behavior, 11*, 389–400.

Rynes, S. L. (1991). Recruitment, job choice, and post-hire consequences: A call for new research directions. In M. D. Dunnette (Ed.), *Handbook of Industrial and Organizational Psychology* (2nd ed., pp. 399–444). Palo Alto, CA: Consulting Psychologists' Press.

Rynes, S. L., & Barber, A. E. (1990). Applicant attraction strategies: An organizational perspective. *Academy of Management Review, 15*, 286–310.

Rynes, S. L., & Boudreau, J. W. (1986). College recruiting in large organizations: Practice, evaluation, and research implications. *Personnel Psychology, 39*, 729–758.

Rynes, S. L., Bretz, R., & Gerhart, B. (1991). The importance of recruitment in job choice: A different way of looking. *Personnel Psychology, 44*, 487–521.

Rynes, S. L., Heneman, H. G., & Schwab, D. P. (1980). Individual reactions to organizational recruiting: A review. *Personnel Psychology, 33*, 529–542.

Rynes, S. L., & Miller, H. E. (1983). Recruiter and job influences on candidates for employment. *Journal of Applied Psychology, 68*, 147–154.

Rynes, S. L., Schwab, D. P., & Heneman, H. G., III. (1983). The role of pay and market pay variability in job application decisions. *Organizational Behavior and Human Performance, 31*, 353–364.

Schmitt, N., & Coyle, B. (1976). Applicant decisions in the employment interview. *Journal of Applied Psychology, 61*, 184–192.

Schneider, B. (1976). *Staffing organizations*. Santa Monica, CA: Goodyear.

Schwab, D. P., Rynes, S. L., & Aldag, R. J. (1987). Theories and research on job search and choice. In K. Rowland & G. Ferris (Eds.), *Research in personnel and human resource management* (Vol. 5, pp. 129–166). Greenwich, CT: JAI Press.

Sheppard, H. I., & Belitsky, A. H. (1966). *The job hunt*. Baltimore: Johns Hopkins Press.

Soelberg, P. (1967). Unprogrammed decision making. *Industrial Management Review, 8*, 19–29.

Stoops, R. (1984). Reader survey supports marketing approach to recruitment. *Personnel Journal, 63*(3), 22–24.

Stoops, R. (1985). Nursing poor recruitment with a marketing approach. *Personnel Journal, 64*, 92–93.

Tannen, M. B. (1987). Is the Army college fund meeting its objectives? *Industrial and Labor Relations Review, 41*, 50–62.

Thurow, L. (1975). *Generating inequality*. New York: Basic Books.

Vroom, V. H. (1966). Organizational choice: A study of pre- and postdecision processes. *Organizational Behavior and Human Performance, 1*, 212–225.

Wanous, J. P. (1980). *Organizational entry*. Reading, MA: Addison–Wesley.

Wolff, A., & Keteyian, A. (1990). *Raw recruits*. New York: Pocket Books.

Perceived Practicality of Unstructured, Patterned, and Situational Interviews

Gary P. Latham
University of Toronto, Canada

Barbara J. Finnegan
University of Washington

THE IMPORTANCE OF PRACTICALITY

Techniques for improving the reliability and validity of selection interviews are now known (Arvey & Campion, 1982; Gatewood & Feild, 1987). However, such techniques are of value only to the extent that they are used in organizations to select employees. Thus, there is a strong need for researchers to take into account the practicality (Thorndike, 1949) of the interview in addition to its reliability and validity. Practicality can be defined as the extent to which the interview is perceived by users as enabling them to achieve their objectives. By understanding how different types of selection interviews are perceived by the people who use them, researchers can study ways in which the reliability and validity of the interview can be improved without sacrificing those qualities that make it attractive to users. There are at least three groups of users who should be considered in determining the practicality of an interview procedure, namely, managers or interviewers, applicants or interviewees, and the attorneys who are called on by clients to defend an interview procedure.

The need for researchers to consider the practicality of the interview from the interviewer's perspective was cogently pointed out by Dreher and Sackett (1983). An industry consortium had commissioned the development and validation of a battery of selection tests for a given job. After the validation of the battery had been demonstrated, it was not used because aspects of the tests did not "make sense" to the key decision makers in those companies.

From the applicant's perspective, the extent to which any selection device is perceived as fair and appropriate has implications for the filing of lawsuits in the United States under Title VII of the 1964 Civil Rights Act (Arvey & Faley, 1988), and under the 1965 Race Relations Act in Great Britain (see Pearn, chapter 13, this volume). This is particularly an issue with the interview due to the frequent findings of low reliability and validity (Ulrich & Trumbo, 1965; Wagner, 1949). This problem can be exacerbated if applicants learn that different people were asked different questions, or that applicants were asked the same questions but their responses to the questions were evaluated differently (e.g., answers from females were evaluated differently than those from males).

The need to consider the applicant's perspective is also important because of the role the interview plays as a recruiting device. In a study of college recruitment interviews, Schmitt and Coyle (1976) found that applicants' acceptance or willingness to accept a job offer was best predicted by factors related to the way in which the interview was conducted, such as the type of questions asked and the amount of information the interviewer was able to give on the nature of the job itself, as well as by the interpersonal skills of the interviewer. Thus there is a need for researchers to know how selection instruments are perceived by applicants, as well as by the managers who are conducting the interviews. Similarly, there is a need for researchers to know how selection techniques are perceived by the legal community, as attorneys have the ability to persuade a client to use or not use them.

Interview Methods

Three interview methods are the unstructured, the structured or patterned, and the situational interview. The unstructured interview generally takes the form of a free-flowing conversation. Consequently, the same questions are not asked of each applicant. The structured or patterned interview is sometimes characterized as an orally administered questionnaire (Gatewood & Feild, 1987). Thus each interview follows the same pattern in that all the applicants are asked the same questions. Because of this structure, the reliability of a patterned interview is usually higher than that of an unstructured interview (Gatewood & Feild, 1987; Schmitt, 1976). The criterion-related validities of each method, however, are generally low (Arvey & Campion, 1982; Arvey & Faley, 1988).

The situational interview consists of a series of hypothetical situations that are derived from a job analysis known as the critical incident technique (Flanagan, 1954). The method has been described in detail by Latham (1989). A European perspective has been provided by Tissen (1989). Applicants are asked what they would do in each situation. As is the case with a patterned interview, each person is asked the same questions. Unique to the situational interview is a behavioral scoring guide that is developed for the interviewer to use when evaluating applicant responses.

The reliability and validity of the situational interview have been demonstrated with regard to both the race and gender of employees (Latham, Saari, Pursell, & Campion, 1980). Maurer and Fay (1988) found that it had higher interrater reliability than the patterned interview, regardless of whether the interviewers had been trained to avoid rating errors. In addition, the validity of the situational interview has been demonstrated with both behavioral (Latham & Saari, 1984) and hard criteria (Weekley & Gier, 1987).

Unstructured interviews usually lack both reliability and validity. Patterned interviews usually have higher reliabilities than structured interviews, but low reliability remains an issue. The situational interview has acceptable reliability and validity. However, the psychometric improvements obtained in the patterned and situational interviews are useful only to the extent that these interview methods are in fact used in organizations to select employees. Therefore, it is necessary to know the extent to which the three interview formats are perceived as practical by interviewers, and as fair by applicants. The purpose of the present study was to examine the practicality of the unstructured, patterned, and situational interviews as perceived by managers, applicants, and attorneys, and to identify the reasons for their perceptions. Practicality was defined as the likelihood that an objective important to each respective group was perceived as attainable with each interview method.

METHOD

Sample

The study was conducted in the United States. The subjects consisted of five groups: (a) managers who had experience in using all three interview methods to hire people; (b) managers who had used only the unstructured and patterned interviews ("potential users" of the situational interview); (c) student applicants who had little interviewing experience of any kind; (d) employees who had experienced all three interview methods at one or more times in their careers; and (e) attorneys who practice Title VII litigation.

The first group of managers included line vice presidents and personnel managers ($n = 59$) in three international companies. Each manager had experience in using each interview method to hire people. Of these 59 people, 49 were male and 15 were under 40 years of age.

The second group of managers ($n = 33$) had no experience with the situational interview but had experience in conducting both unstructured and patterned interviews. Therefore, they were categorized as "potential users" of the situational interview. These managers were included in the study to determine the salability (Smith, 1976) of the situational interview relative to the two alternatives. All were members of an Executive MBA program who were employed as upper level managers (e.g., vice presidents, division directors) in their respective companies. Of these people, 22 were male and 27 were under 40 years of age.

The applicants also consisted of two groups. College students (n = 31) in a senior-level management class at the University of Washington participated in the study because they would be interviewing for jobs upon graduation. These subjects had very little interviewing experience of any kind. In addition, the class they attended was an organizational theory class that did not include selection or interviewing as part of the course curriculum. Therefore, these students had not been exposed to any discussion of the three interviewing methods. Of these 31 student applicants, 17 were male and all but 1 were under 40 years of age.

Because the student applicants had relatively little experience in interviewing, a second group of applicants was included in the study. This group of applicants, defined as *employee hires*, consisted of 24 people who, during their career, had experienced as an applicant each of the interview methods. Of the 24 people in this group, 17 were male and 18 were under 40 years of age.

Attorneys (n = 41) who specialize in Title VII litigation were identified in the Seattle, Washington, metropolitan area. Perceptions of attorneys were collected because they are called on by clients to defend the method that is used to make a selection decision when the decision is challenged by an applicant. Of the 41 attorneys who participated in the study, 31 were male and 21 were under 40 years of age.

Because reading a description of an interview procedure is arguably not the same as experiencing it, the interviewer and interviewee samples were balanced between groups who had and had not used all three interview techniques. Experience in conducting selection interviews was not an issue for the sample of attorneys because the norm is for them to present a case based on descriptions of events (e.g., depositions), rather than having participated in them.

Materials

Questionnaires.   Three respective questionnaires were developed for the managers, applicants, and attorneys. The procedure for developing the three questionnaires was as follows.

First, managers (n = 9) and employees (n = 10) at a local company were asked by the second author to name the things they thought were particularly good or bad about interviews. From this, two lists of items—one for interviewers and one for applicants—were generated. These items were supplemented by statements on what constitutes an acceptable selection method that were taken by the second author from undergraduate textbooks (Cherrington, 1983; Dessler, 1984; Klatt, Murdick, & Schuster, 1985; Mathis & Jackson, 1985). This procedure resulted in the generation of approximately 40 items for the interviewer and applicant questionnaires. These items were then reduced in number by sorting and combining them so that each idea on the original list was represented only once. In this way, overlap in items was eliminated so that items that may have favored any one interview approach were not over-represented.

A similar procedure was followed in developing the attorney's questionnaire. The second author and a labor law professor independently developed lists of items thought to be important to attorneys when defending clients' use of the selection interview. The two lists were compared and combined into a single list of 12 items. The lists were combined because 9 of the 12 items were the same, and there was agreement that the other 3 items should be included.

After the items on the respective questionnaires had been developed, each was converted into a two-part question. The first part was a manipulation check on the relevancy of the items. It asked the respondents to identify on a 5-point Likert-type scale the importance of the item to them personally. The second part requested the respondents to rate on a 5-point scale the likelihood that each interview method would meet the objective defined by each respective item. For example, managers were asked:

How important is it to you that you feel relaxed when you interview someone:

Not Important at All   1   2   3   4   5   Extremely Important

How likely is it that you would feel relaxed if you used a(n):

Patterned Interview?   Not Likely at all 1 2 3 4 5 Very Likely
Situational Interview?   Not Likely at all 1 2 3 4 5 Very Likely
Unstructured Interview? Not Likely at all 1 2 3 4 5 Very Likely

To counterbalance for possible order effects, the order in which the interview methods were listed was varied on each questionnaire. Consequently, an equal number of questionnaires had each of the three interview methods listed as first, second, or third.

The questionnaire for managers contained 16 items: 5 on the extent to which the interview enables the interviewer to identify applicants who are truly qualified for the job, 5 on the extent to which the interview format could be successfully defended against a lawsuit, and 6 on the extent to which the interview is easy and comfortable for the interviewer to use. Examples include "determining how well the applicant would fit in with the other people on the job," "whether the applicant can perform the job," "whether the interview procedure is legal," "ease of preparing for the interview," and "appearing organized to the applicant."

The applicant questionnaire contained 15 items: 4 on the extent to which the interview gives the applicants an opportunity to present their qualifications for the job in the best possible light, 7 on the extent to which applicants will be hired or rejected fairly on the basis of their qualifications for the job, and

4 on the extent to which the interview will enable applicants to learn enough about the job to decide if they want it. Examples include "that the same topics that were discussed with you were discussed with every other applicant who interviewed for the job," "ability to say everything you wanted to say about your qualifications for the job," "to feel relaxed during the interview," and "that your performance during the interview be determined by your abilities rather than by the skill of the interviewer."

The questionnaire for attorneys contained 12 items. Examples include "that both the questions and the interviewers' evaluations were stated in behavioral terms, not in terms of personality traits," "the evaluation of the applicant correlated significantly with subsequent job performance," "the questions in the interview were a representative sample of the types of occurrences that the applicant would encounter on the job," "the questions were based on a job analysis," and "two or more interviewers reached the same conclusion about the applicant."

Questionnaire Development. Because the names of the interview methods (unstructured, patterned, and situational) are not used uniformly in organizational settings, descriptions of the three interview methods were prepared to ensure that the subjects referred to the interview methods by the correct names when they completed the questionnaire. The procedure for writing the interview descriptions was as follows.

First, information about the three interview methods was located in undergraduate textbooks (Cherrington, 1983; Dessler, 1984; Klatt et al., 1985; Mathis & Jackson, 1985). This information was compiled into descriptions of the three interview methods. The descriptions were written in five sections: (a) preparation required prior to the start of the interview, (b) number of interviewers, (c) interview format (i.e., the procedure that is followed in a typical interview), (d) types of questions (with examples), and (e) how applicants are evaluated. This was done to ensure that all three descriptions contained comparable information and to facilitate comparisons among them.

Second, a pilot study was conducted to determine the objectivity of the three descriptions. Human resource-organizational behavior faculty ($n = 8$), who were familiar with the three interview formats, rated each description on its readability, factualness, neutrality, accuracy, and comprehensiveness. Suggestions were requested. The revised descriptions were then administered to 34 senior-level human resource management students who rated each on a series of five 5-point Likert-type scales to determine, again, the accuracy, factualness, neutrality, comprehensiveness, and readability of the descriptions. None of these students participated further in this study.

A score of perfect objectivity on the descriptions would have been 25 (based on the five 5-point scales). The actual means and standard deviations for the unstructured, patterned, and situational interviews were 20.34 (SD = 3.49),

21.54 (SD = 2.62), and 20.99 (SD = 3.23), respectively. A repeated measures analysis of variance revealed no significant differences among these means, thus indicating that the descriptions were not biased in favor of any one method.

Procedure

The Directors of Human Resources in the three companies that participated in this study distributed the questionnaires, along with a letter supporting the project, by company mail to the managers who had experience in using each interview method. The completed questionnaires were returned to the respective Directors, who then returned them to the authors. Of the 40 managers who were asked to participate in the study, 39 (98%) returned the questionnaire.

The Executive MBA ("potential user" interview) and student applicant groups completed the questionnaires anonymously in the classroom. All the students in both classes agreed to participate in the study, and all received extra credit for doing so.

The employee hires were mailed a copy of the questionnaire and interview descriptions, with a letter explaining the purpose of the study and a stamped envelope for returning the completed questionnaire to the authors. The names and addresses of the employee hires had been supplied by their companies' Human Resource Directors, who chose only those people who had experience with all three interview methods. Of the 30 employee hires contacted, 24 (80%) responded.

Eighty-five attorneys who specialize in Title VII litigation were contacted. To ensure an adequate sample size from a group of professionals who might not be inclined to take the time to respond to a mailing, the second author arranged meetings with 17 attorneys, at which time they completed the questionnaire. In addition, questionnaires were mailed to the remaining 68 attorneys, with a letter explaining the purpose of the study and a stamped envelope for returning the completed questionnaire. Of the 68 attorneys thus contacted, 24 (35%) responded, for a total response of 41 (48%).

The design of the questionnaire, the implementation of the study, and the analysis of the data were done solely by the second author. This was done to minimize possible biases of the first author, who was one of the original developers of the situational interview.

RESULTS

Reliability of Questionnaires

Cronbach's alphas were calculated for the practicality ratings given by each group of respondents to the unstructured, patterned, and situational interviews. The alphas were .86, .81, and .78, respectively, for the managers; .82, .74, and

.68, respectively, for the "potential users"; .67, .80, and .62, respectively, for the student applicants; .76, .83, and .68, respectively, for the employee hires; and .79, .70, and .70, respectively, for the attorneys.

Interviewers' Perceptions

The average importance ratings given to the questionnaire items by the managers and "potential users" were 4.09 (SD = .40) and 3.83 (SD = .35), respectively, on a 5-point scale. Thus it was concluded that the items on the questionnaire were of importance to both groups of interviewers.

The means and standard deviations of the practicality ratings by the managers who had actually used the unstructured, patterned, and situational interview methods were 2.65 (SD = .61), 3.67 (SD = .43), and 3.98 (SD = .43), respectively. A repeated measures analysis of variance revealed that these differences were highly significant (F [2,106] = 124.21, $p < .01$). Planned paired t-tests showed that the patterned interview was rated as significantly more practical than the unstructured interview (t [53] = 11.90, $p < .01$), and the situational interview was rated as significantly more practical than the patterned interview (t [53] = 4.56, $p < .01$).

An additional item requested the managers to indicate on a 5-point scale the extent to which they had experience in using each method. The respective means and standard deviations were 3.89 (1.22), 3.84 (1.24), and 3.95 (.99) for the unstructured, patterned, and situational interviews. A repeated measures F test was not significant. Thus the results were not biased by the managers having had more experience with one method relative to another.

The average ratings of practicality by the managers who had no experience with the situational interview (i.e., the potential user group) were 2.77 (SD = .55), 3.47 (SD = .40), and 3.75 (SD = .38) for the three respective methods. A repeated measures analysis of variance revealed that these differences too were highly significant (F [2,64] = 42.66, $p < .01$). Planned paired t-tests showed that the patterned interview was rated as significantly more practical than the unstructured interview (t [32] = 6.08, $p < .01$), and the situational interview was rated as significantly more practical than the patterned interview (t [32] = 3.54, $p < .01$). These findings occurred despite the fact that none of the potential users had ever used a situational interview. Moreover, the item requesting level of experience revealed a mean of 3.85 (SD = 1.25) for the unstructured as opposed to a mean of 2.45 (SD = 1.28) for the patterned interview (t [32] = 4.63, $p < .01$). Thus, it appears that the situational interview is salable to managers who have not used it despite their relatively high degree of experience with the unstructured interview.

An independent F test revealed that the difference in the responses for the two managerial groups was not statistically significant. The results were thus collapsed to determine whether there were differences in the responses from males (n = 51) and females (n = 18), or between those under 40 years of age (n = 37) and those 40 years or older (n = 39). Neither of these differences was statistically significant.

That manager and potential user interviews were indeed concerned that the way the interview is conducted be legal was evident from their responses to that item ($\bar{X}$ = 4.81, SD = .39 for managers; $\bar{X}$ = 4.30, SD = 1.02 for potential users). Other items of great importance (i.e., $\bar{X}$ greater than 4.0) to both groups of interviewers included appearing organized and prepared to the applicant, determining whether the applicant has the ability to perform the job, being able to compare the applicants on an objective basis, and being able to hire or reject the applicant on solely job-related reasons. In each instance the situational interview was rated higher than the alternative methods.

The situational interview received the lowest rating on one item, ease of preparation. The means and standard deviations for the unstructured, patterned, and situational interviews on that item were 3.36 (SD = 1.44), 3.40 (SD = 1.10), and 2.89 (SD = 1.37) respectively, for the managers who had used all three interview methods, and 4.52 (SD = .94), 3.03 (SD = 1.05), and 2.18 (SD = 1.10), respectively, for the managers who had used the unstructured and patterned, but not the situational, interviews.

Applicant Perceptions

The average importance ratings given to the questionnaire items by the student applicants and employee hires were 3.89 (SD = .36) and 4.11 (SD = .33), respectively. Thus it was concluded that items on the questionnaire were of importance to both groups of applicants.

The means and standard deviations of the practicality ratings by the student applicants were 3.27 (SD = .43), 3.40 (SD = .47), and 3.14 (SD = .43) for the unstructured, patterned, and situational interviews, respectively. A repeated measures analysis of variance revealed that these differences were not significantly different. However, two items on the questionnaire were rated less than 3.0 only by the students, namely, "how important would it be to you that only job-related topics were discussed by the interviewer" ($\bar{X}$ = 2.44, SD = 1.19), and "how important would it be to you that the same topics that were discussed with you were discussed with every other applicant who interviewed for the job" ($\bar{X}$ = 2.95, SD = .97). Because practicality was defined as the likelihood that an objective important to the user is perceived as attainable by each interview method, these two items that were rated as unimportant were deleted and the analysis was repeated.

The subsequent student ratings of the unstructured, patterned, and situational interviews were 3.51 (SD = .47), 3.34 (SD = .51), and 2.95 (SD = .49), respectively. A repeated measures analysis of variance revealed that these differences were highly significant (F [2,60] = 10.12, p < .01). Planned paired t-tests again showed no difference between the ratings given to the unstructured and patterned interviews, but the patterned interview was rated significantly higher than the situational interview (t [30] = 3.16, p < .01). The student applicants' experience with the unstructured interview ($\bar{X}$ = 2.93, SD = 1.21) was not significantly higher than their experience with the patterned interview ($\bar{X}$ = 2.47, SD = 1.14). None of the student applicants had ever experienced a situational interview.

An additional item requested the student applicants to indicate which of the three interview methods would most favorably influence them to accept a job offer. The number of people who chose the unstructured, patterned, and situational interviews were 17, 11, and 2, respectively. This difference in frequencies was highly significant (χ^2 [2,30] = 11.40, p < .01).

Another question was worded as follows: "If you were the type of person who would file a lawsuit against a company if you felt you had been rejected unfairly, which interview format would make you the most optimistic of winning your case?" The responses to the unstructured, patterned, and situational was highly significant in favor of the unstructured interview (χ^2 [2,30] = 10.92, p < .01). None of these results changed when the data were reanalyzed on the basis of male (n = 15)/female (n = 14) and White (n = 30/non-White (n = 6).

The employee hires who had been exposed to each interview method at one or more times in their career did not view one method as more advantageous to them than another. The average practicality ratings given to the unstructured, patterned, and situational interviews by the employee hires were 3.27 (SD = .43), 3.51 (SD = .47), and 3.50 (SD = .40), respectively (F [2,40] = 2.21, NS). However, as with the student applicants, the employee hires perceived that the likelihood of their winning a lawsuit was highest with the unstructured interview. The respective frequencies of 15, 2, 3 for the unstructured, patterned, and situational interviews were highly significant (χ^2 [2,20] = 15.68, p < .01).

In response to the question "Which interview format would most favorably influence your decision to accept a job offer?," the difference in frequencies with which people chose the unstructured, patterned, or situational interviews was not statistically significant.

Attorney Perceptions

The average importance ratings given to the questionnaire items by the attorneys was 3.87 (SD = .50). Thus it was concluded that the items on the questionnaire were judged by them to be important.

Practicality for attorneys was defined in terms of their ease of defending a client in court. The means and standard deviations of the practicality ratings given by attorneys to the unstructured, patterned, and situational interviews were 2.31 (SD = .50), 3.56 (SD = .37), and 4.18 (SD = .36), respectively. A repeated measures analysis of variance revealed that these differences were highly significant (F [2,72] = 226.97, p < .01). Planned paired t-tests showed that the patterned interview was rated as significantly more practical than the unstructured interview (t [36] = 16.50, p < .01), and the situational interview was rated as significantly more practical than the patterned interview (t [39] = 8.14, p < .01).

Attorneys especially valued the importance of their being able to show that the questions asked in the interview were based on a job analysis ($\bar{X}$ = 4.02, SD = .84), were a representative sample of the types of occurrences that the applicant would encounter on the job ($\bar{X}$ = 4.07, SD = .82), that the evaluation of the applicants was unaffected by the biases of the interviewers ($\bar{X}$ = 4.59, SD = .82), and that all the applicants were asked the same questions ($\bar{X}$ = 4.00, SD = .96). The situational interview was rated significantly higher than the two alternative interview methods on all these items. On no item was the situational interview rated by attorneys as less practical than the other interview methods.

DISCUSSION

Overall, the results of this study bode well for the future of the selection interview. Managers and attorneys, the two groups of people who have the greatest influence in determining which interview format a company will use, rated the situational interview as the most practical, followed by the patterned and unstructured interviews. This ranking of the three interview formats is in keeping with their psychometric rankings (i.e., the interviews with the highest reliability and validity were also rated as most practical by these two groups of users). It appears that for potential users, the battle of the selection interview may be half won—these people want to use the most psychometrically and legally defensible interview method. The reason that they do not is that they lack the knowledge of how to develop situational interviews. This could be corrected through seminar training and publications in practitioner-oriented journals.

From the applicants' perspective, the fact that the "employee hires" did not prefer one interview method over another suggests that employers can use the most reliable and valid techniques available when interviewing people with previous work experience. There is nothing in the experienced applicants' responses to indicate that doing so would in any way be perceived as detrimental to them. However, the fact that the "employee hires" did not prefer one interview method over another may have reflected their self-efficacy in obtaining a job regardless of the type of interview. Subsequent studies should measure perceptions of people who were rejected by different interview methods.

A potential problem regarding the perceptions of the college student applicants is that they rated two of the items on which the situational interview is particularly effective as being unimportant to them. Specifically, they did not feel that it is important for the interviewer to ask only job-related questions, nor did they think it is important that the same questions be asked of each applicant. These two items are, of course, necessary before an interview can be reliable and valid. The student applicants did acknowledge that the situational interview was the best of the three techniques on these two dimensions. Similarly, the students acknowledged that the situational interview was highest on the likelihood of their being evaluated objectively, and on the likelihood that two or more interviewers would reach the same decision to hire or reject them. Thus it is not surprising that they are optimistic of winning a court case should they challenge a selection decision that is based on an unstructured rather than a situational interview.

Another reason why the student applicants preferred the unstructured interview is that they saw the unstructured interview as allowing them to say everything they wanted to say, as enabling them to feel relaxed, as allowing the outcome to be based on their abilities rather than on the skill of the interviewer, and as enabling them to show the interviewer that they are highly motivated. These data suggest a desire on the part of the student applicants to control the interview. This may reflect the pressure that students feel when searching for their first "real" job, and the emphasis that is placed in magazine articles and college placement centers for the student to "come across well in the interview" (referring almost always to the unstructured or patterned interview). Because the student applicants had had very little interviewing experience of any kind, it may be natural that they would feel most comfortable with the methods they had been exposed to through the magazines and placement centers.

These findings support those obtained by Schuler in Germany (see chapter 2, this volume). Ninety-six college students rated their impressions of structured versus unstructured interviews. The results showed that interviewers who used an unstructured format were seen as more competent in their roles and more accurate in their assessments than interviewers who used a structured format. In addition, the German students indicated that they had a more favorable impression of those interviewers who used the unstructured format, that it would be easier to talk to them, and that they would feel more comfortable with them than they would with interviewers who used a structured technique. In short, interviewers who use an unstructured format were perceived as fulfilling the picture of an ideal interviewer. Finally, and highly supportive of the findings obtained in the present study involving American students, the students in Germany report that interviewers who used the unstructured format "were seen as easier to influence, the chances to get a job-offer being higher in this case" (chapter 2, this volume).

That student applicants in Germany and the United States prefer the unstructured interview has important implications for the efforts that are being made by researchers to improve the psychometric characteristics of the selection interview as it is used in actual practice. The student applicants indicated that the use of an unstructured interview would most favorably influence them to accept a job offer. Consequently, in times of high employment employers may sacrifice the benefits of psychometrically sound interview methods in order to minimize the risk of losing potential employees. Ways need to be found in which psychometrically sound interviews will be viewed positively by inexperienced applicants.

One solution may be for college placement centers, as well as other centers of instruction in interviewing, to emphasize the need for applicants to secure a job that is truly a good match for them, thereby strengthening applicants' perceptions of the need for interviews to be valid predictors of job performance. Thus research is needed on effective orientation procedures for applicants who are about to be exposed to various selection techniques so as to increase their understanding of them.

A second solution can be inferred from the social influence literature. White and Mitchell (1979) found that positive cues from others about a task were more important in influencing a person's job satisfaction than were the actual task characteristics. Interviewers should therefore find ways to introduce the situational interview to inexperienced applicants in a positive way.

Anecdotal support for this approach can be found in an American company that uses the situational interview. The personnel manager stated in a conversation with the second author that the employees at her company "love the situational interview because, having gone through it themselves, they know the people who are hired here are the best qualified for the job." She added that there is a spoken pride among the unionized employees of being the best for having passed the situational interview. This pride is conveyed to the new employees right from the first day and is probably responsible in large part for the positive perceptions the employees in the company have of the situational interview. Although the applicants in this particular company are seldom college students and not necessarily first-time applicants, a similar orientation to the situational interview may have similar results when used with inexperienced applicants.

The practical significance of this study is that it addresses two important issues that are under-represented in the scientific literature. First, it suggests ways in which the selection interview can be improved from the vantage point of its users without sacrificing the advances that have already been made in its reliability and validity. Such suggestions are important because the interview is here to stay, regardless of the admonitions of researchers who collect evidence on the low reliability and validity of the traditional (i.e., unstructured) interview. Second, this study addresses the question of what those who are most directly affected by interviews think of existing methods. Answers to this question are important as they affect actual use of selection methods (Dreher & Sackett, 1983).

Such answers are especially important in Europe. As Schuler and Funke (1989) said:

> The task of devising a suitable employment interview is complicated in West Germany by the legal emphasis (i.e., codetermination by staff councils) and social expectation that employer selection techniques must first and foremost be acceptable to applicants. . . . West German courts consider acceptability of selection procedures and the presumed reactions of applicants towards the selection tests to be most important. At the same time, comparatively lower importance is given to test validity and fairness. (p. 185)

As de Wolff (see chapter 16, this volume) has noted, Europeans are as much, if not more, interested in humanistic concerns for applicants as they are with issues of reliability and validity. The bias in the present chapter is that Thorndike's (1949) four criteria for evaluating psychometric instruments, namely, validity, reliability, freedom from contamination, and practicality, are of equal importance. North American scientists have been guilty of ignoring the latter in favor of the other three. Studies similar to the one described in this chapter will hopefully allow European scientists to emphasize the other three in addition to the latter.

ACKNOWLEDGMENTS

Support for this article was provided by a grant from the Social Sciences and Humanities Research Council of Canada to the first author.

REFERENCES

Arvey, R. D., & Campion, J. E. (1982). The employment interview: A summary and review of recent research. *Personnel Psychology, 35,* 281–322.

Arvey, R. D., & Faley, R. H. (1988). *Fairness in selecting employees* (2nd Edition). Reading, MA: Addison-Wesley.

Cherrington, D. J. (1983). *Personnel management: The management of human resources.* Dubuque, IA: Wm. C. Brown.

Dessler, G. (1984). *Personnel management* (3rd ed.). Reston, VA: Reston.

Dreher, G. F., & Sackett, P. R. (1983). *Perspectives on employee staffing and selection.* Homewood, IL: Irwin.

Flanagan, J. C. (1954). The critical incident technique. *Psychological Bulletin, 51,* 327–358.

Gatewood, R. D., & Feild, H. S. (1987). *Human resource selection.* New York: The Dryden Press.

Klatt, L. A., Murdick, R. G., & Schuster, F. E. (1985). *Human resource management.* Columbus, OH: Merrill.

Latham, G. P. (1989). The reliability, validity, and practicality of the situational interview. In R. W. Eder & G. R. Ferris (Eds.), *The employment interview: Theory, research, and practice* (pp. 169–182). Newbury Park, CA: Sage.

Latham, G. P., & Saari, L. M. (1984). Do people do what they say? Further studies on the situational interview. *Journal of Applied Psychology, 69*, 569–573.

Latham, G. P., Saari, L. M., Pursell, E. D., & Campion, M. A. (1980). The situational interview. *Journal of Applied Psychology, 65*, 422–427.

Mathis, R. L., & Jackson, J. H. (1985). *Personnel: Human resource management* (4th ed.). St. Paul, MN: West.

Maurer, S. D., & Fay, C. (1988). Effect of situational interviews, conventional structured interviews, and training on interview rating agreement: An experimental analysis. *Personnel Psychology, 41*, 329–344.

Schmitt, N. (1976). Social and situational determinants of interview decisions: Implications for the employment interview. *Personnel Psychology, 2*, 79–101.

Schmitt, N., & Coyle, B. W. (1976). Applicant decisions in the employment interview. *Journal of Applied Psychology, 61*, 184–192.

Schuler, H., & Funke, U. (1989). The interview as a multimodal procedure. In R. W. Eder & G. R. Ferris (Eds.), *The employment interview: Theory, research, and practice* (pp. 183–190). Newbury Park, CA: Sage.

Smith, P. C. (1976). Behaviors, results and organizational effectiveness: The problem of criteria. In M. D. Dunnette (Ed.), *Handbook of industrial organizational psychology* (pp. 745–775). Chicago: Rand McNally.

Thorndike, R. L. (1949). *Personnel selection: Test and measurement technique.* New York: Wiley.

Tissen, R. (1989). *Selection and Human Resource Management.* Paper presented at the Hohenheim conference, Stuttgart, Germany, Universitat Hohenheim.

Ulrich, L., & Trumbo, D. (1965). The selection interview since 1949. *Psychological Bulletin, 63*, 100–116.

Wagner, R. (1949). The employment interview: A critical summary. *Personnel Psychology, 2*, 17–46.

Weekley, J. A., & Gier, J. A. (1987). Reliability and validity of the situational interview for a sales position. *Journal of Applied Psychology, 72*, 484–487.

White, S. E., & Mitchell, T. R. (1979). Job enrichment versus social cues: A comparison and competitive test. *Journal of Applied Psychology, 64*, 1–9.

5

The Effect of Selection Practices on Applicants' Perceptions of Organizational Characteristics

George C. Thornton III
Colorado State University

Organizations and applicants go through a complex and sometimes conflicting process of gathering information about each other and attempting to appear attractive to each other (see Fig. 5.1; Porter, Lawler, & Hackman, 1975). The organization gathers information about the applicant to make employment decisions, and it strives to attract the applicant by providing favorable information about job opportunities and benefits from employment. At the same time, applicants are trying to show evidence of knowledge, skills, and other characteristics that make them suitable for employment. In addition, applicants are gathering information about the organization to make a decision about whether to accept a job offer. The purpose of this chapter is to explore the effects of organization recruitment and selection practices on applicant impressions of the organization and attitudes toward working there.

Conflicts may arise among the four processes just outlined. Two conflicts are particularly germane to the present chapter. First, the organization's attempts to gather in-depth information about the applicant may appear intrusive to the applicant and cause negative attitudes toward the organization. Second, the organization's desire to appear attractive to applicants may lead it to portray only positive information and thus interfere with the applicant's ability to obtain complete information on which to make a decision to join the organization.

It is important to study applicants' early impressions and decision-making processes about organizations for several reasons. Whereas an organization wants to obtain the best labor inputs, it must recognize that applicants are making choices about whether or not to join the organization. Better applicants may

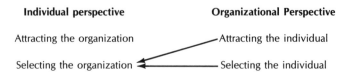

FIG. 5.1. Attraction-selection model. Adapted from Figure 5.1 in Porter, L. W., Lawler, E. E., III, & Hackman, J. R. (1975). *Behavior in organizations*. New York: McGraw-Hill. Reproduced with permission.

choose to go elsewhere if they develop negative impressions during the selection process. Murphy (1986) has demonstrated that the utility of a selection test is curtailed dramatically if top applicants do not accept a job offer. It is especially important to understand applicant reactions in a tight labor market where applicants have choices among job alternatives. The general unemployment rate in the United States is relatively low, hovering around 5% or 6%. The unemployment rate is even lower in certain regions of the country and in certain occupational fields. Actual labor shortages currently exist in some fields such as nursing and are projected to increase in other fields in the future. When a "sellers' market" exists, qualified applicants are in a position to make choices among alternative organizations. Thus, organizations must be sensitive to how applicants are reacting to recruiting and selection practices.

It is important to understand applicant perceptions even if applicants do not have numerous choices among organizations. Initial impressions form the basis for later impressions of the organization, job satisfaction, organization commitment, turnover, and performance (Premack & Wanous, 1985). A theoretical model of the dynamics of early organizational and newcomer interactions is provided by Wanous (1980).

In the following sections, research conducted by the author and his students into several factors that influence applicant perceptions of organizations is reported. These new studies extend our understanding of the processes whereby applicants form opinions about organizations and make decisions about job offers. Figure 5.2 shows a model of some of the factors investigated. Organization practices such as interviewer behavior and selection procedures are hypothesized to influence applicant perceptions. It is further hypothesized that these relationships are moderated by environmental factors (e.g., labor market conditions) and individual factors (e.g., applicant personality).

RECRUITER–INTERVIEWER BEHAVIOR

Traditionally, interviewers' decision-making processes have been studied. Excellent summaries of how interviewers gather, integrate, and evaluate information about applicants are available (Eder & Buckley, 1988; Gatewood & Feild, 1987). On the other hand, Webster (1982) pointed out that there has been less

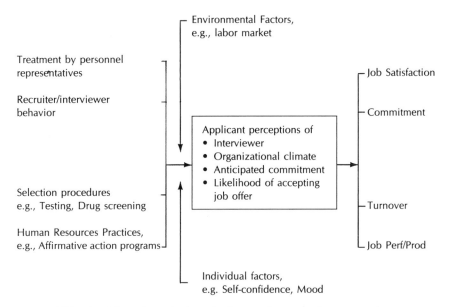

FIG. 5.2. Effect of organization selection practices on applicant perceptions.

research on the analogous process of interviewees gathering information, evaluating interviewers, and making decisions about the organization. Existing research shows conflicting evidence about the importance of interviewer behaviors on interviewee's perceptions of the organization.

Considerable research shows that the applicants' impressions of the recruiter have an effect on their perceptions of the organization (Boudreau & Rynes, 1985) and their willingness to pursue a job with the company (Alderfer & McCord, 1970). Less definitive research has been conducted to show the processes that explain such effects and the relative impact of the interviewer in comparison with other factors in the organizational choice process. For example, Harris and Fink (1987) called for research to help understand more specifically what behaviors of the interviewer–recruiter influence applicant perceptions: "What behaviors, mannerisms, or other characteristics do recruiters evidence that in turn lead them to be perceived as thoughtful, socially perceptive, and cooperative?" (p. 780).

The evidence of the relative importance of the recruiter in comparison with job attributes is quite mixed. On the one hand, some research has demonstrated that job attribute information is more important than recruiter behavior (Powell, 1984; Rynes & Miller, 1983; Taylor & Bergman, 1987). On the other hand, other research shows that the recruiter has an influence on the formation of impressions of the organization even when job attribute information is considered (Harris & Fink, 1987). Clearly, more research is needed to understand the role of recruiter–interviewer on formation of impressions of organizations and choice.

Our research from the interviewee's viewpoint has shown that the interviewer's behavior in conducting the interview affects the interviewee's perceptions of several important organizational characteristics. In a field study, Harn and Thornton (1985) found that college students in a university recruiting office could identify specific recruiter behaviors (e.g., frequent eye contact, self-disclosing remarks, and comments acknowledging feelings) that led to perceptions that the recruiter was "warm and thoughtful," a generalized variable found in previous studies to affect applicant perceptions of the organization (Schmitt & Coyle, 1976). These interviewer behaviors were related to a willingness to pursue further interviews with the organization and the likelihood of accepting a job offer if one were extended. In addition, it was found that, if the recruiter was perceived as representative of other people in the organization, the relationship of recruiter behavior and recruitee impressions was even stronger.

Three experimental studies were conducted to follow up the findings from the field study. These studies provide partial evidence sought by Rynes (1989), who called for controlled laboratory studies into the effects of interviewer behavior on specific perceptions. They show that interviewer treatment generalizes widely and powerfully to a variety of perceptions about the organization and work.

Interviewer behavior was manipulated on videotapes depicting an interview with a standardized interviewee. Specific behaviors displaying warmth and thoughtfulness (e.g., warm greeting, reflecting feelings and content of applicant's comments, frequent eye contact, approving response to statements) were contrasted with a realistic portrayal of a recruiter who lacked these behaviors. The first experimental study (Harn & Thornton, 1986) found an interaction between interviewer behavior and the amount of information the recruiter gave about the job. In the high job-related information condition, the recruiter gave the recruit specific information concerning type of work performed, amount of overtime work, first-year training, advancement possibilities, growth of the company, benefits, and the background of people the applicant would work with, if hired. In the low job-related information condition, the recruiter provided only general information concerning these topics. Subjects who saw a recruiter displaying warm and thoughtful behaviors reported more favorable impressions of the recruiter and organization, more willingness to be candid with the recruiter, more willingness to make further contacts with the organization and accept job offers, and higher estimates of recruiter willingness to recommend a job offer. When these warm and thoughtful behaviors were not displayed, the subjects were more willing to pursue further contacts with the organization only when the interviewer presented a high level of information. The recruiter interaction style had a considerable impact on applicants' reactions, especially when critical job-related information was *not* covered.

In the second study, Adams (1987) manipulated interviewee affect (i.e., being in a good mood or bad mood). A positive, neutral, or negative mood was induced by giving subjects false feedback about performance on a spatial relations test they had just taken. Subjects were told they did very well, about average, or below average. Mood had only minimal impact, but interviewer behavior clearly had a major impact on perceptions of the organization. Subjects who were treated in a warm and thoughtful manner by the interviewer had more positive impressions of organization climate and anticipated higher commitment to the organization, regardless of their mood.

In the third study, Kendrick (1987) manipulated labor market factors (i.e., whether there were many or few job opportunities available). Although there is considerable theoretical basis for expecting that the labor market will affect perceptions generated by organizational practices, the results of this study showed that interviewer behavior predominates. Engineering students were presented one of two fact sheets describing the labor market as either a "buyer's market" (i.e., high unemployment, many graduates in similar fields, and a weak industry and economy) or a "seller's market" (i.e., low unemployment, few graduates in similar fields, and a strong industry and economy). A manipulation check showed that these descriptions led students to believe they would have few or many job opportunities, respectively. Labor market conditions did not influence perceptions of the job, organizational climate, or treatment by co-workers and supervisors directly, nor did they interact with interviewer behavior. As before, interviewer behaviors did influence several of these perceptions of the job, organization, and future co-workers. Intentions to accept a job offer were not affected in this study.

In all three studies, interviewer behavior had a significant effect on the subjects' perceptions of the interviewer and other impressions of the organization. When the interviewer demonstrated behaviors reflecting warmth and thoughtfulness, the subject saw the interviewer more favorably, had more positive perceptions of the job and organization, and expected better treatment from supervisors and co-workers. Intentions to accept a job offer were usually not affected.

None of the other independent variables in these studies (i.e., recruiter knowledge of specific jobs, interviewee affect, or labor market conditions) had an effect on interviewee perceptions. Whereas negative results do not provide conclusive support that these variables are not important, the studies as a whole show the robustness and large power that interviewer treatment has on interviewee perceptions of the organization.

ATTRIBUTE CHARACTERISTICS

Rynes (1989) has called for more research on the characteristics of attributes that influence applicant decision processes about organizations along the lines of her earlier study (Rynes, Schwab, & Heneman, 1983). In response, Harn

(1987) demonstrated that the *range* of an attribute affects the importance attached to that attribute when choosing among job alternatives. Thirty-seven advanced undergraduate students in electrical engineering examined profiles of jobs reflecting different ranges of three attributes: salary, job content, and location. Pretesting of individuals allowed the experimenter to identify five levels of desirability of each job attribute for each individual student. The wide-range manipulation included job profiles presenting the "best," "fair," and "worst" levels of one of the attributes with a narrow range of "good," "fair," and "poor" levels of the other two attributes. In one session, a narrow range of all attributes was presented; in another session, one attribute was presented in the wide range and the other two in the narrow range. The students were asked to rate their willingness to accept the job offer represented by each profile. The results indicated that the attribute importance weights increased with the range of attribute levels available (i.e., students placed more weight on salary, content, and location when a wide range of alternatives were available).

TESTING PROCEDURES

The procedures used by organizations to test applicant characteristics may have an influence on applicant perceptions of the organization. Warrenfeltz (1982) studied the reactions of 96 high school students enrolled in vocational–technical education programs to different types of selection procedures. One testing procedure involved only a general mental ability test (the Wonderlic Personnel Test), whereas the other procedure involved specific tests constructed on the basis of job analysis information to be content-valid work sample tests. For example, students enrolled in auto maintenance who would be applying for a position as an auto mechanic received a test assessing skill in that area. Students exposed to the more content-valid tests expressed more favorable attitudes toward the organization, held more favorable initial impressions of the supervisors and peers they would work with, and demonstrated higher levels of anticipated commitment to the organization.

In a field study, Adams and Thornton (1987) surveyed applicants at three stages of a multiple hurdle selection process with regard to their reactions to the selection procedures. Applicants for positions as flight instructors were administered a series of paper-and-pencil tests (including a general reasoning test, a job knowledge test, and a test of instructional principles), interviewed jointly by two persons (including a personnel representative and a line manager), and then were assessed in a miniassessment center consisting of three work simulation techniques. The general reasoning test was seen by these applicants as the most impersonal and least helpful in giving information about the job, co-workers, and job outcomes; it was also seen as least accurate in revealing the applicants' job-relevant knowledge and experience. By contrast, the interview was seen as most helpful in finding out about the job, organization, and outcomes on the job, and as most accurately reflecting the applicants' knowledge and experience for the job.

Direct comparisons of the reactions are difficult because the respondents became a more restricted group as the screening progressed. Nevertheless, the results show that what industrial psychologists would consider the most valid predictors, the general reasoning test, was the least preferred among the applicants; what we would often consider the least valid, the interview, was considered the most favorable by the applicants.

PERSONALIZED REALISTIC JOB PREVIEWS

Up to this point, the chapter has dealt with the conflict between the organization's attempt to gather selection information and its attempt to appear attractive to applicants. The next section covers a second conflict, the effect of the organization's attempt to appear attractive on the applicants' impressions of the organization.

Previous research has shown that providing positive or negative information about organization and job characteristics influences applicant perceptions and behavior. Premack and Wanous (1985) and McEvoy and Cascio (1985) have summarized much of this literature and concluded that realistic job previews (RJPs) tend to lower initial expectations and turnover, whereas increasing self-selection, organizational commitment, job satisfaction, and performance.

Two studies by Gaugler and Thornton (1990) have extended this research to investigate the effect of personalizing the RJPs so as to provide information about each individual's highly valued work needs. Theory (Chusmir, 1982; Gould, 1979; Vroom, 1964) and research (Hall & Schneider, 1972; Kanungo, 1982) have implied that the decision to join an organization and the extent to which an applicant expects to be committed to the organization are a function of the strength of the individual's work needs and whether he or she expects the organization to fulfill those needs.

To explore this hypothesis, two of our studies queried subjects with a questionnaire to measure the importance of needs such as autonomy, achievement, and stability. The content of the RJPs for the experimental subjects was then tailor made to address each individual's five most important needs. The control group received information about a generic set of work conditions. Thus, in contrast to a traditional job-oriented RJP, this study used an individually oriented RJP. As in much prior research, realism of the job previews was manipulated by presenting both negative and positive information to some subjects and only positive information to other subjects.

In both studies the 2×2 design showed that a realistic preview, negative as well as positive information, led subjects to have less favorable initial impressions of the organization. In addition, the effects on applicant perceptions spread from the factors for which they received information about to perceptions of factors for which they received no information. In other words, getting negative information about a few factors influenced initial impressions of many other facets of the organization.

On the other hand, the presentation of individualized information had no impact beyond the effects of the information about the generic factors. Contrary to professional opinion (Greenhaus, Seidel, & Marinis, 1983; Jurgensen, 1978), these findings suggest that organizations may not want to expend the extra time and effort to find out what an individual applicant values most and provide information about those aspects of the job and organization.

There are potential problems with the direct estimation procedures used in these studies to obtain information about the importance of job attributes (Schwab, Rynes, & Aldag, 1987), including lack of self-insight and social desirability in responses. These problems may be overcome only with more elaborate policy-capturing approaches that are probably not feasible in applied organizational settings in employment offices.

AFFIRMATIVE ACTION PROGRAMS

Mondragon and Thornton (1988) studied the effect of the presence of affirmative action practices on the perception of White male college students soon to graduate with degrees in business. Affirmative action practices in three personnel areas (recruitment, selection, and promotion) were varied in the description about an organization. Aggressive affirmative action included seeking minorities and women applicants, giving special consideration to minorities and women in selection, and establishing goals for promoting the protected classes. As hypothesized, aggressive recruitment did not affect applicant reaction toward the organization, but applicants did react negatively to affirmative action in selection and promotion. These White male students believed the organization's policies and practices were unfair and led to diminished chances of promotion. Furthermore, these negative impressions spread to perceptions that the organization climate was undesirable and that they would be treated unfairly by co-workers and supervisors. On the other hand, these students were not less willing to accept a job offer in the organization.

DISCUSSION

Organizational practices at time of recruiting and selection have effects on several initial impressions of the organization. These effects generalize from the specific practices to a wide range of perceptions and work-related attitudes. For example, applicants form impressions of general personnel practices, anticipated treatment by the supervisor, expected interactions with peers, perceptions of the organization climate, and, in some cases, the willingness to accept a job offer. The results show clear conflicts between the organization's interest in obtaining valid information and attracting the individual versus the individual's interest in gathering information for his or her own decision-making process.

The advantages of studying applicant reactions to recruiting and selection procedures have not been fully explored. For a long time, psychometricians (e.g., Nunnally, 1978) have pointed out the importance of "face validity" of measurement. What is needed now is to demonstrate the relevance of this concept to subsequent applicant behaviors and attitudes toward the organization. The research reported here provides a starting point. It shows that organizational selection procedures affect a broad range of attitudes toward the organization.

Nevo (1989) has argued persuasively that there are three reasons we need to gather information from examinees about their reactions to testing procedures: Morally, it is right to give examinees a chance to express their opinions; practically, it is useful to find out what they think; and, theoretically, it is interesting to learn about examinee's reactions. Nevo then described the development and structure of the Examinee Feedback Questionnaire, which asks about reactions to the physical conditions, behavior of examiners, adequacy of time to complete the test, face validity of the test, methods of preparation, and prior knowledge of the examination procedures. This methodology should help selection researchers study applicant reactions to test scores, as a potentially relevant source of variance in test scores.

The model in Fig. 5.2 depicting the relationship among variables in the selection process may need revision in that some of the proposed moderators between selection practices and applicant perceptions were not found to be operative in the studies reported here. Thus, more research needs to be done to determine why variables, such as market conditions, had no effect in some studies and did have an effect in others.

Further research is needed to understand applicant reactions to selection procedures in different situations. Further research into the variables mediating and moderating (Baron & Kenny, 1986) the relationships between organizational selection practices and applicants' reactions is needed. Applicants may have different beliefs about the appropriateness of a selection procedure when applying for different types of jobs. What is considered a fair procedure for a lower level job or a job requiring relatively little interpersonal interaction may be quite different from what is considered fair for a managerial or professional job requiring extensive interpersonal interaction. For example, Martin and Nagao (1989) found that subjects applying for a managerial job expressed more resentment when interviewed by a computer or paper-and-pencil procedure in comparison with subjects being interviewed by a live interviewer, although the procedures had no effect when subjects were applying for a lower level clerical job.

Additional theoretical work is also needed. At a very general level, the results of the new studies reported here support the critical contact theory of organizational choice (Behling, Labowitz, & Gainer, 1968). According to this theory, applicants do not have full information about all facets of organization life and must use information they obtain from critical contacts they encounter. Thus, information from interviewers, personnel representatives, and tests serve as surrogates of the other people and practices in the organization.

The processes whereby recruiting and selection practices affect organization choice are not fully understood. In terms of theoretical development, Harris (1989) has applied the Elaboration Likelihood Model (ELM), a theory of persuasion, to the process of the recruitment interview from the applicant's point of view. This theory suggests that the interviewee will elaborate on (i.e., carefully scrutinize and evaluate) information from the interviewer if the interviewee has the ability and motivation to do so. Motivation in this context is a function of the personal relevance of the information presented and the involvement of the interviewee; ability is affected by the breadth of information the person possesses and distractions in the setting. Harris (1989) hypothesized that recruits often have low motivation and ability to carefully process information. Thus, only peripheral and temporary processing will take place. The level of processing (i.e., elaborate or peripheral) is important because, according to the theory, only when a message is elaborately processed will it have a strong and lasting effect.

Harris derives several propositions from the model with regard to the process of recruitment activities. Our research provides evidence that addresses some of these propositions. Harris proposed that interviewees may have low motivation to process information carefully when the interviewer is not someone whom they will interact with on the job. In support of this idea, Harn and Thornton (1986) found that when student recruits believed that the recruiter was representative of people in the company, the recruiter's behavior had a stronger impact on perceptions of the organization and likelihood of accepting a job offer than when the recruiter was seen as nonrepresentative.

Harris further proposed that job applicants have low ability to process information and will not carefully process information in the interview. Our findings that students evaluate organizational characteristics beyond those addressed in the job preview (Gaugler & Thornton, 1990) suggest that students form a general halo impression about the organization. This halo or stereotype can be interpreted as evidence of peripheral processing and not careful processing that would allow the applicant to distinguish among organizational characteristics.

Level of anxiety of the applicant is among the individual factors that Harris posits may influence the type of processing. Adam's (1987) study of affect addressed a related variable. She found that the interviewee's mood did not interact with treatment of the interviewer in influencing impressions of the organization (i.e., interviewer behavior had the same effect on organizational perceptions when applicants were in a good or bad mood).

Message characteristics are also proposed by Harris to influence the type of processing, such that a highly informative interview is expected to result in more careful attention and elaboration. In support of this hypothesis, Harn and Thornton (1986) found that subjects were more willing to pursue further contact with the organization when recruiters displayed friendly behavior and also covered critical job-related information.

According to the ELM theory, in tight labor market conditions the recruit will see few job opportunities and will not process the information in the interview carefully. Kendrick's (1987) study suggested that the objective conditions in the labor market will not influence applicant impressions, whereas Liden and Parsons (1986) found that applicant perceptions of job opportunities are an operative variable. More research is needed to understand the relative influence of objective labor market conditions and other more individualistic personality characteristics, such as self-confidence or self-esteem.

Our research on applicant reactions to selection and recruiting practices can also be cast in terms of Schuler's (see Chapter 2, this volume) innovative concept of social validity. Social validity refers to a quality of a selection process that makes it acceptable to participants. It considers the social impact on applicants' well-being, decision making, and behavior. Schuler suggested that there are four components to social validity of a selection process: information about tasks, jobs, organizational characteristics, and chances for career advancement; participation by the applicant in the development and execution of the assessment; transparency of the situation such that participants understand the selection process and can see its relevance to organization requirements; and honest and considerate feedback. Our research certainly shows the importance of information provided in the interview, but the consequences are not necessarily positive. Providing more negative information in a job preview may lead to less favorable attitudes toward the organization. In addition, our research has shown that contextual factors may influence how information about task attributes affects applicants' judgments. The importance of transparency is also illustrated in our research on applicants' reactions to different types of assessment techniques. Procedures such as the interview, which have clear relevance, are perceived more positively than abstract tests.

Some of our research does not easily fit in one of the four components of Schuler's model of social validity. The considerable research on the importance of the personal relationship between the interviewee and interviewer does not seem to be easily subsumed in the model. The concept of social validity is the first broad notion of how individuals and organizations interact at time of selection; the new research reported here, and elsewhere, may help with revision or extension of the components affecting how applicants perceive and react to organization selection practices.

REFERENCES

Adams, S. R. (1987). *Influence of interviewer counselling behaviors and interviewee mood on applicant perceptions*. Unpublished masters thesis, Colorado State University, Fort Collins.

Adams, S. R., & Thornton, G. C., III. (1987). *Organizational impressions: The role the selection process plays*. Unpublished manuscript, Colorado State University, Fort Collins.

Alderfer, C. P., & McCord, C. G. (1970). Personal and situational factors in the recruitment interview. *Journal of Applied Psychology, 54*, 377–385.

Baron, R. M., & Kenny, D. A. (1986). The moderator–mediator variable distinction in social psychological research: Conceptual, strategic, and statistical considerations. *Journal of Personality and Social Psychology, 51*, 1173–1182.

Behling, O., Labowitz, G., & Gainer, M. (1968). College recruiting: A theoretical base. *Personnel Journal, 47*, 13–19.

Boudreau, J. W., & Rynes, S. L. (1985). Role of recruitment in staffing utility analyses. *Journal of Applied Psychology, 70*, 354–366.

Chusmir, L. H. (1982). Job commitment and the organization woman. *Academy of Management Review, 7*, 595–602.

Eder, R. W., & Buckley, M. R. (1988). The employment interview: An interactionist perspective. In G. R. Ferris & K. M. Rowland (Eds.), *Research in personnel and human resources management* (Vol. 6, pp. 75–107). Greenwich, CT: JAI Press.

Gatewood, R. D., & Feild, H. S. (1987). *Human resource selection*. Chicago: Dryden Press.

Gaugler, B. B., & Thornton, G. C., III (1990). Matching job previews to individual applicant's needs. *Psychological Reports, 66*, 643–652.

Gould, S. (1979). An equity-exchange model of organizational involvement. *Academy of Management Review, 4*, 52–62.

Greenhaus, J., Seidel, C., & Marinis, M. (1983). The impact of expectations and values on job attitudes. *Organizational Behavior and Human Performance, 31*, 394–417.

Hall, D. T., & Schneider, B. (1972). Correlates of organizational identification as a function of career pattern and organizational type. *Administrative Science Quarterly, 17*, 340–350.

Harn, T. J. (1987). *The effect of range of job attributes on their importance in job choice decisions*. Unpublished doctoral dissertation, Colorado State University, Fort Collins.

Harn, T. J., & Thornton, G. C., III (1985). Recruiter counselling behaviors and applicant impressions. *Journal of Occupational Psychology, 58*, 57–65.

Harn, T. J., & Thornton, G. C., III (1986). *Impact of recruiter counselling behaviors and job-related information on engineering applicants in campus interviews*. Unpublished manuscript, Colorado State University, Fort Collins.

Harris, M. M. (1989). *The recruitment interview as persuasive communication: Applying the elaboration likelihood model*. Paper presented at the national meeting of the Academy of Management, Washington, DC.

Harris, M. M., & Fink, L. S. (1987). A field study of applicant reactions to employment opportunities: Does the recruiter make a difference? *Personnel Psychology, 40*, 765–784.

Jurgensen, C. F. (1978). Job preferences (what makes a job good or bad?). *Journal of Applied Psychology, 63*, 267–276.

Kanungo, R. N. (1982). Measurement of job and work involvement. *Journal of Applied Psychology, 67*, 341–349.

Kendrick, K. L. (1987). *Impact of recruiter counselling behaviors and number of perceived job alternatives on engineering applicants in simulated campus interviews*. Unpublished manuscript, Colorado State University, Fort Collins.

Liden, R. C., & Parsons, C. K. (1986). A field study of job applicant interview perceptions, alternative opportunities, and demographic characteristics. *Personnel Psychology, 39*, 109–122.

Martin, C. L., & Nagao, D. H. (1989). Some effects of computerized interviewing on job applicant responses. *Journal of Applied Psychology, 74*, 72–80.

McEvoy, G. M., & Cascio, W. F. (1985). Strategies for reducing employee turnover: A meta-analysis. *Journal of Applied Psychology, 70*, 342–353.

Mondragon, N., & Thornton, G. C., III (1988, October 13–14). *Effects of affirmative action programs on perceptions of organizations among White male college students.* Proceedings of the 1988 Annual Conference of the Council on Employee Responsibilities and Rights, Virginia Beach, VA.

Murphy, K. R. (1986). When your top choice turns you down: Effect of rejected offers on the utility of selection tests. *Psychological Bulletin, 99*, 133–138.

Nevo, B. (1989, May 25–27). *The practical and theoretical value of examinee feedback questionnaires (EFeQ).* Paper presented at the conference, "The individual and organizational side of selection and performance evaluation and appraisal," Universitat Hohenheim, Stuttgart.

Nunnally, J. (1978). *Psychometric theory.* New York: McGraw-Hill.

Porter, L. W., Lawler, E. E., & Hackman, J. R. (1975). *Behavior in organizations.* New York: McGraw-Hill.

Powell, G. N. (1984). Effects of job attributes and recruiting practices on applicant decisions: A comparison. *Personnel Psychology, 37*, 721–732.

Premack, S. L., & Wanous, J. P. (1985). A meta-analysis of realistic job preview experiments. *Journal of Applied Psychology, 70*, 706–719.

Rynes, S. L. (1989). The employment interview as a recruitment device. In R. W. Eder & G. R. Ferris (Eds.), *The employment interview: Theory, research and practice* (pp. 127–141). Newbury Park, CA: Sage.

Rynes, S. L., & Miller, H. E. (1983). Recruiter and job influences on candidates for employment. *Journal of Applied Psychology, 68*, 147–154.

Rynes, S. L., Schwab, D. P., & Heneman, H. G., III (1983). The role of pay and market pay variability in job applicant decisions. *Organizational Behavior and Human Performance, 31*, 353–364.

Schmitt, N., & Coyle, B. (1976). Applicant decisions in the employment interview. *Journal of Applied Psychology, 61*, 184–192.

Schwab, D. P., Rynes, S. L., & Aldag, R. J. (1987). Theories and research on job search and choice. In K. M. Rowland & G. R. Ferris (Eds.), *Research in personnel and human resources management* (Vol. 5, pp. 129–166). Greenwich, CT: JAI Press.

Taylor, M. S., & Bergman, T. J. (1987). Organizational recruitment activities and applicant's reactions at different stages of the recruitment process. *Personnel Psychology, 40*, 261–286.

Vroom, V. H. (1964). *Work and motivation.* New York: Wiley.

Wanous, J. P. (1980). *Organizational entry: Recruitment, selection and socialization of newcomers.* Reading, MA: Addison-Wesley.

Warrenfeltz, R. (1982). *The effect of realistic and humanistic information on expectations, commitment, and organizational choice.* Unpublished manuscript, Colorado State University, Fort Collins.

Webster, E. C. (1982). *The employment interview.* Schomberg, Ontario, Canada: S.I.P. Publications.

II

Individual Reactions to Personnel Procedures: Introductory Comments

This section focuses on the individual's reaction to various elements of the employment process and to components of the human resource management system in work organizations.

In Chapter 6, Landy examines the research literature concerning the extent to which individual differences among respondents affect the results of job analyses and job evaluations. Both job analysis and job evaluation are intended to develop accurate descriptions of the tasks that comprise a given job and of the knowledges, skills, abilities, and other characteristics that incumbents must possess in order to perform these tasks successfully, although their final uses of such information differ. Job analysis results are most often used in the development of selection systems, training programs, and performance evaluation systems. Job evaluation results are used to determine compensation levels for a job. Thus, both job analysis and job evaluation are important because they are the foundation on which many other organizational personnel systems are based.

Landy argues that the data indicate that respondent differences, including demographic, cognitive, and motivational factors, do influence job analysis and evaluation results. He then presents some techniques for minimizing the impact of these effects. One implication of this chapter is that the organizational goal of accuracy of job analysis and evaluation results is unlikely to be achieved without consideration of the goals and likely behavior of various respondent groups.

The next two chapters in this section address issues that occur during the selection process. Seisdedos argues that intentional or motivated distortions that occur when candidates try to present themselves in the best possible light (e.g., on personality inventories) should not be viewed only as error, but also as a form of reasonable, perhaps "intelligent," adaptation; that is, for some jobs the individual who can infer the "correct" behavior or characteristics may be a better performer. Thus, Seisdedos suggests that the validity of such adaptation should be researched as a possible predictor of performance.

In Chapter 8 Schuler and Fruhner examine changes in self-concept as a result of experience in an assessment center. Their data show several consistent changes in specific elements of self-concept, namely, those elements that were well measured in the assessment center (e.g., related to mathematical ability, problem solving, and general intelligence). Self-concept related to these specific aspects exhibited a decline from baseline following their measurement but then increased following feedback (which was generally favorable for the subjects with regard to these dimensions). Reactions to specific components of the assessment center indicated that the most favorable responses were to exercises and the multimodal interview, whereas intelligence and personality tests were less favorably received.

Successful candidates for employment are the focus of Chapter 9. Wanous reviews what is known about newcomer orientation programs and offers suggestions for improving these programs and the newcomers' attitudinal and behavioral reactions to their new organization, work group, and job. His suggestions are founded on recent research concerned with the psychological preparation of patients for the stress of medical procedures. This innovative approach provides a new perspective for such orientation programs that have in most organizations been concerned with communicating factual information about organizational procedures and policies and socializing the new employee with regard to the culture of the organization.

The final two chapters of this section deal with performance evaluation and feedback in work organizations. Dickinson (Chapter 10) reviews the literature related to employee attitudes concerning performance appraisal. Thus, it focuses on the periodic (often annual), formal, performance review (or interview) conducted at a prearranged time by the employee's supervisor. Dickinson concludes that appraisal attitudes are influenced by characteristics of the appraisal system, the employee, and the organization. Of special importance is the finding that the degree of favorability of the appraisal is *not* the sole determining factor, although, not surprisingly, employees are more favorable if they receive positive evaluations. Also of importance is the finding that there is not a unitary attitude about performance appraisals but rather a set of attitudes concerned with appraisal acceptability, accuracy, satisfaction, and fairness. Dickinson also suggests how to design a performance appraisal system so as to improve employee reactions to it.

In Chapter 11 Farr addresses the processes of giving and seeking informal performance feedback, that is, the performance-related information that is communicated in the course of day-to-day interactions between a work performer and others in the work setting. Farr notes that the individual works within an information environment in which much potentially relevant data exist. The individual is motivated to seek and obtain this information through a variety of mechanisms whereas also inhibited from such feedback seeking by the potential costs of the information. At the same time, the manager is motivated to give such information to improve employee performance whereas also being inhibited from doing so in the case of negative feedback. Farr discusses the implications of this perspective for the design of feedback systems in organizations and for the training of managers to give, and employees to receive, informal performance feedback.

6

Job Analysis and Job Evaluation: The Respondent's Perspective

Frank Landy
Pennsylvania State University

It is common to consider the results of a job analysis or job evaluation from a substantive perspective. We are typically interested in the answers to questions such as: Which task categories appear to be most important? Which KSAs seem central to task performance? Which environmental characteristics seem to increase the difficulty of the work performed? In other words, we are usually analyzing job analysis results to find out something about the nature of the work performed. Seldom do we conduct analyses to identify potentially contaminating respondent influences on those results. Consider the issue of face validity of a test. If a test does not *appear* to measure a KSA, it is possible that the behavior of the test taker might be affected in a way that distorts the meaning of the measures derived from the test. Similarly, the characteristics of the job analysis process might affect the integrity of the data gathered in that process. In addition, although not as obvious as in the case of an ability test, the characteristics of the respondent might have a substantial influence on the results of a job analysis. In an ability testing situation, we hope that the characteristics of the test taker influence the scores—at least the characteristics defined by the ability we purport to measure. But in the arena of job analyses and job evaluation, less attention is paid to respondent attributes. In this chapter, I address issues related to process and respondent characteristics and the extent to which they might influence the data collected.

Before a consideration of the empirical and theoretical issues, it might be wise to define some terms. Job analysis is the systematic collection of data describing the tasks that comprise a job and the knowledge, skills, abilities, and

75

other characteristics that enable a person to carry out those tasks. Job analysis results can be used to develop training programs, test batteries, performance evaluation systems, and reward systems (Landy, 1989). An associated but distinct process is job evaluation. The purpose of job evaluation is to determine compensation levels for a job. In determining those compensation levels, job analysis may be used as a point of departure, but other information is added. This other information might include the training necessary to do the job, the monotony or danger of the job, and the level of responsibility for equipment or product that characterizes the job. Although I discuss both processes in the chapter, it is useful to remember that they are distinct and subject to different influences.

Job analysis was added to the tool kit of the industrial psychologist by Lipmann (1916) early in this century and further refined by Viteles (1932). The cornerstone of this earliest form of job analysis was a device known as the "job psychograph" (Viteles, 1932). This instrument consisted of a list of trait-like characteristics that the job analyst inferred were implicated in successful job performance of the position under study. In today's vernacular, it was a list of knowledge, skills and abilities, or KSAs. The analyst arrived at those KSAs through observations, interviews, and, most importantly, actually performing the tasks that comprised the job. Viteles, in particular, felt that he could not truly understand the requirements of a job unless he performed that job. In a recent interview, he described the frustrations of navigating a submarine through the Atlantic Ocean from North Carolina to Bermuda as part of a job analysis involving naval personnel. He missed Bermuda twice before he was advised to surface, look for a large cloud mass (that typically forms over the island), and steer toward it! He eventually found Bermuda using this primitive heuristic.

Viteles and his contemporaries were convinced that in order to form a good theory of the job, it was necessary to get the best first-hand evidence possible. They were concerned that information that came exclusively from the incumbent would be misleading for several reasons. First, they were concerned that incumbents might be misleading in a self-serving way, that they would inflate their positions in order to impress the observer or interviewer. In addition, they were concerned that the incumbent might not be aware of all the intricacies of the job, many of which had become automatic over years of performance. As a result, the incumbent might not identify all the important and frequently occurring tasks. Finally, they were concerned that the incumbents were untrained in the nature of human abilities and thus could not provide any meaningful information about the KSAs. The time during which people like Lipmann and Viteles practiced was a transition period. The laboratory methods of Wundt, including the central medium of introspection, were giving way to field research and the collection of "objective" data. Nevertheless, this affinity for actually "doing the job" may have been a holdover from the earlier structuralist principles of introspection. That is not to say that information obtained from performing the job tasks was misleading. On the contrary, even today, it is illuminating for a job analyst to carry out the tasks of a job under question when possible. It does enhance the emergent theory of performance. Of course, there was no guarantee then, nor is there one now, that the job analyst is not biased in a particular way. As you see later in the chapter, there has been some concern that male job analysts tend to emphasize the manner in which a male performs a job at the expense of successful female strategies. For example, a male might use upper body strength in carrying out a lifting task, whereas a female would depend more heavily on lower body strength to accomplish the same task. The male job analyst might be inclined to identify upper body strength as a KSA and ignore lower body strength. Introspection would not eliminate this possible bias.

Job evaluation is somewhat more "modern" as a concept and was driven by concepts of "parity" and "equity" that arose from union–management negotiations. The most common forms of job evaluation are the point or factor methods (Gael, 1988). But, as was the case with job analysis, it is common for incumbents or incumbent supervisors to make judgments about job characteristics.

Both job analysis and job evaluation have evolved into somewhat different processes at the close of the century. The varieties of job analysis and evaluation can be seen in a recent two-volume work edited by Gael (1988) entitled "the Handbook of Job Analysis." In those volumes one can discover a wide variety of procedures, instruments, and data-analytic techniques intended to illuminate the critical aspects of a job or to guide the assignment of compensation levels. Central to many of these techniques are the job incumbent and incumbent supervisor. These people are known as subject matter experts (SMEs) and play a pivotal role in the description of both duties and responsibilities and the KSAs that support job performance as well as the conditions under which the job is performed. In test construction, the SMEs may also play a role in item development and in establishing links between the tasks and the test.

The increasing use of subject matter experts in job analysis and job evaluation may result in the flaws and biases that Viteles and his contemporaries feared in the development of theories of job performance. This is the question that I address in this chapter: To what extent is it possible that respondent influences contaminate the results of a job analysis or job evaluation? This is just one facet of the larger issue addressed in this book. Various chapters deal with variables associated with the "subject" in the personnel study. This particular chapter examines the extent to which the results of a job analysis are influenced by the characteristics of the SME. The characteristics I consider include demographic characteristics, motivational characteristics, and miscellaneous individual-difference variables. I first consider the issue of whether such influences have been documented and then consider strategies for reducing or measuring those influences. There are two goals to this examination. The first goal is purely scientific—I examine the process of job analysis in a novel manner and attempt to understand its dynamics. The second goal is pragmatic—I want to identify methods for improving the reliability and accuracy of job analyses. Because a job analysis is central to many other activities such as training, performance evaluation, and selection, there is ample reason to pursue avenues that will improve the results of a job analysis.

RESPONDENT CHARACTERISTICS

Demographic

Demographic characteristics, in and of themselves, are of little or no interest to the psychologist. They have been called "box car" variables because they carry with them interesting elements but are not the interesting elements themselves. Thus, in the example described earlier of the male job analyst and upper body strength, the interesting psychological issue is not that male and female job analysts may produce different descriptions of the job, but that *all* job analysts may be vulnerable to certain cognitive heuristics such as the representativeness heuristic or the availability heuristic (Nisbett & Ross, 1980) that will bias the results of the job analysis. Thus, although I consider certain demographic characteristics in this chapter, remember that the demographic characteristic itself is not the central point of interest but rather the cognitive, emotional, or behavioral variables associated with that demographic characteristic.

Race. Despite the attractiveness of the variable, there have been few studies of the effect of race on job analysis and evaluation results. One such study, however, was recently completed by Landy and Vasey (1991). They examined the job analysis ratings of several hundred police officers and found no significant differences in frequency or importance ratings of Black officers compared to White officers. In court cases, Black plaintiffs often claim that the job they perform (or are assigned) is drastically different from the job assigned to their White counterparts, but this is often a dispute about task assignment, not about the relative importance or frequency of the task in some aggregate form.

Gender. The most common demographic characteristics examined have been gender and experience. Arvey (1986) has argued forcefully that the gender of the analyst should be examined in some detail as a possible influence of ratings in job evaluation procedures. He believes that one possible reason for the wage gap between male and female workers in America may be the result of biased job analyses. Let us consider some of the empirical data.

Arvey, Passino, and Lounsbury (1977) examined the differential performance of male and female job analysts using a structured job analysis instrument, the Position Analysis Questionnaire or PAQ (McCormick, Jeanneret, & Mecham, 1972). They found systematic depression of scores assigned by female analysts to 22 of 29 PAQ job dimensions. This depression was independent of the gender of the worker interviewed or observed. The main effect was an analyst main effect. The effect was particularly pronounced on the PAQ dimension associated with obtaining information from things. I can only speculate regarding explanations for this result. One explanation might be that the female analyst might think of how she might do the job and come to the conclusion that she would be more likely to seek information from other people than from devices such as gauges, meters, or other displays. Incidentally, it could also be hypothesized that male analysts provide *inflated* ratings of tasks associated with obtaining information from things rather than that the female ratings are depressed. Nevertheless, Arvey et al. were able to demonstrate a gender effect on job analysis results.

Gender effects have also been found in two more recent studies. Zebrowitz, McArthur, and Obrant (1986) conducted a laboratory study of the effect of job analyst gender on PAQ ratings. The job analysts were students and they viewed videotapes of males and females performing the same job. The task was to use the PAQ to describe what they saw on the tape. When males performed the job in question, it was seen by male job analysts as significantly less structured than when females performed the job. The female job analysts showed a similar pattern, but the effect was nonsignificant. The female analysts, on the other hand, rated the job as requiring more education and involving considerably more decision making than did their male counterparts when the person on the videotape was a male. Again, there is the strong suggestion that the observation or information-processing mechanisms are being influenced by gender. It would appear that there may be predispositions or stereotypes that are affecting the judgments of the analysts. The saying "I'll see it when I believe it" might describe this situation. It is interesting to note that dimensions such as "amount of structure" and "decision-making responsibilities" would be likely to have an impact on wages. Those whose jobs are less structured and those who make more decisions are likely to be paid more. In this case, then, if a female were the job analyst, the job would have been seen as worth more money than if a male were the job analyst. You must remember, however, that the subjects were college students, viewing actors performing a "job" on videotape and using a complicated and somewhat rigid instrument (the PAQ) to describe the job. The leap from this artificial situation to the "real world" is a substantial one.

Cellar, Durr, and Hassell (1989) also found differences in the accuracy of male and female college students acting as job analysts, with females providing higher levels of accuracy. This finding was somewhat confounded by the fact that higher field independence, a cognitive set variable, was also associated with greater accuracy. Because the female subjects in this study were more field independent, it is not clear if the results were due to field independence or some other underlying variable.

Schmitt and Cohen (1989) examined the responses of 411 civil service managers acting as SMEs in a job analysis in a field setting. They found differences between male and female SMEs in terms of reported involvement in budgetary activities with females reporting less involvement, but they could not determine if these differences reflected actual job activities or the tendency of the two different genders to focus on different activities when describing the job.

The gender effect in job analysis studies is far from uniform, however. For example, Arvey, Davis, McGowen, and Dipboye (1982), in another study of the PAQ, did not find any job analyst gender effects. Similarly, Landy and Vasey (1991), in a study of police officer SMEs, suggested that the minor gender differences found were due to confounded experience differences because the female SMEs in their study had significantly fewer years in the job than the male SMEs. In fact, this problem of confounding afflicts many of the studies of demographic characteristics. Because of the disproportionately small numbers of female and minority incumbents in many positions, it is difficult to get a good assessment of the effects of gender and race on SME judgments. Nevertheless, it would appear that the studies of gender suggest that job analysis ratings are subject to influence by factors other than task characteristics.

A recent study by McShane (1990) relates more directly to the issue of job evaluation. He asked undergraduate business majors to rate several jobs for the purpose of establishing pay rates on compensable factors. He manipulated job titles to make the jobs appear to be held by male or female incumbents. Thus, the title "special assistant—accounting" was hypothesized to have a "male" connotation whereas the title "senior secretary—accounting" was thought to be more "female." The results showed that the "female" job was rated lower than the "male" job title. In a "real" job evaluation, this would result in a lower pay for the female title, even though the duties remained the same. Unfortunately, McShane does not report what would be the most interesting analysis for purposes of this chapter—the difference between male and female subjects. Thus, although we know that respondents can be influenced by variables other than the task statements and job description (in this case the gender stereotype of the job title), we do not know if the gender of the subject played a role in the ratings.

Experience. Another commonly examined variable in studies of both job analysts and SMEs has been experience. As an example, in a study by Friedman and Harvey (1986), inexperienced (student) job analysts were compared to experienced (professional) analysts in using a standard job analysis technique, the PAQ. The experienced job analysts produced more accurate ratings. It is interesting to note that it did not seem to matter how much information about the jobs (e.g., detailed task statements) the students were given, their ratings were still less accurate. A study by DeNisi, Cornelius, and Blencoe (1987), as well as the earlier study by Friedman and Harvey (1986), confirm these results.

This suggests that there are some rather basic mechanisms involved. By extension, then, it might be useful to know what level of accuracy is to be expected from first-time SMEs. Is the issue age, job experience, job analysis experience, or possibly some other motivational variable (e.g., job commitment) that might influence job analysis ratings?

In the Landy and Vasey (1991) study described earlier, they were able to examine the effects of job experience within the subset of male SMEs. This analysis demonstrated rather clear effects of experience on the job analysis results. More experienced police officers described a job that was substantially different from that depicted by the less experienced officers. The more experienced officers reported heavier involvement in felony arrests, court appearances, and dispute resolution, whereas less experienced officers reported greater frequency of misdemeanor processing, traffic control, and report completion. Observations and objective indices (e.g., court appearances) suggest that these differences are real task differences rather than reporting bias. In contrast, a study by Schmitt and Cohen (1986) of civil service managers showed no experience effect.

In both the Landy and Vasey study and the Schmitt and Cohen study, the SMEs were first-time "job analysts." As a result, it is not possible to assess the effects of job analysis experience in these studies as had been done in earlier studies aforementioned (DeNisi et al., 1987; Friedman & Harvey, 1986). Nevertheless, it appears that any influences resulting from work experience (as opposed to job analysis experience) are related to actual task performance differences. It would, however, be interesting to determine if differences arise in field studies of job analysis as a result of the exposure of the SMEs to previous job analysis efforts. In many settings (e.g., police and fire departments), the work force is stable and job analyses are completed with some regularity. This would permit an examination of the effect of SME experience. Later in the chapter, I discuss techniques that might be used to minimize the influence of SME experience should it turn out to be a distorting influence.

Education. There does seem to be a consistent finding with respect to the educational level of SMEs. Several studies have failed to find any effect of education on the accuracy or reliability of task ratings (Landy & Vasey, 1991; Schmitt & Cohen, 1989; Wexley & Silverman, 1978).

Motivational Variables

It has been suggested that some SME job analysts are more careful than others. Green and Stutzman (1986) developed what was labeled a *carelessness index* by including in a list of task statements, some tasks that were clearly not part of the job in question. For example, a task statement such as "Make decisions about budget requests to City Council" could be included in the task list for a municipal patrol officer. If the SME indicates that this task is an important part of the patrol officer's job and that the task is performed frequently, there is something amiss.

Green and Stutzman discovered that those who claimed to perform tasks that were clearly not part of their job produced overall information that was less reliable and less accurate than that produced by their colleagues who did not claim to perform those tasks. Green and Stutzman labeled this carelessness. It is likely that these "errors" represent one of two influences. The first is most certainly carelessness, but the second is more likely a more intentional influence.

In using the carelessness index, Green and Stutzman suggested that an individual be labeled *careless* only if several of these target tasks were endorsed. It is reasonable to expect that some error is bound to creep in to the completion of a task list of 100 + items being rated on frequency and importance. But when three or four of these errors occur, it would appear that something more systematic is occurring. For that reason, it appears that *carelessness* is really a euphemism for *distorted*. It is sobering to learn that in the Green and Stutzman study 145 of 290 SMEs reported performing tasks that could not have been part of their job duties! There are several possible explanations for this finding. First, the level of carelessness was peculiarly high for that job. This might have been because of cognitive characteristics of the respondents. Alternatively, the list might have been too long or too confusing to complete accurately. Finally, there might have been a motive for the SMEs to inflate the nature of their job.

In practice, it is not uncommon for some SMEs to inflate both the number and the importance of the tasks they perform. This is most likely the result of either a desire to enhance their self-esteem or an attempt to influence compensation decisions. The latter strategy seems to be documented by the research of London (1976). In this study, employees were quizzed on their attitudes toward job reevaluation. A reevaluation is a request by an employee to review a job with an eye toward increasing the pay rate of that job based on tasks or KSAs that were added to the job since the last evaluation. London found that pay increases associated with reevaluations are typically much greater than pay increases associated with merit increases. In his study, merit increases averaged 6%, but reevaluation increases were considerably higher, running up to 25% in some cases. The people interviewed believed that perseverance and job success would affect the reclassification decision. Further, the data demonstrated that reclassification requests were increasing substantially.

The point of the London study is that many employees realize that a path to increased pay is through reevaluation and that during that reevaluation it is important to demonstrate both the complexity of tasks and the broadest requirement for KSAs. It is reasonable to assume that this may be a general pattern, and that most incumbents have a bias toward enhancing the nature of their job.

It is interesting to note that in conducting job analyses, it is common (although not universal) to find that incumbents rate each task higher in importance than their supervisors do. Most experienced job analysts are aware of this tendency and are careful in requiring documentation and confirmation of what might be exaggerated claims when conducting interviews. Such checks and balances are not as easily applied to SME questionnaires.

The point of reviewing the research on the carelessness index is to further explore the possibility that there are systematic biasing influences in the judgments of SMEs. As was the case with the gender studies described earlier, although the data are sparse, they do suggest the possibility of such a respondent influence. Further, these data do conform to what is often experienced by job analysts in assessing the results of incumbent interviews.

Other Influences

In addition to research on demographic variables and the carelessness dimension, other research has been done that further addresses the issue of potential bias in job analysis ratings. For example, Arvey, Davis, McGowen, and Dipboye (1982) examined the extent to which the ratings of an SME were influenced by the extent to which that individual exhibited interest in his or her work. Those who were more interested in their work provided more accurate ratings of several task categories. Again, we are left with several potential explanations. The most plausible is that those who have the highest interest also have the most knowledge about their job. It is also possible that those with the highest interest have the greatest investment in describing their job to an outside observer. In practice, the job analyst often finds SMEs who are motivated to provide clear and complete pictures of their jobs. Invariably, these people are those most committed to or interested in their work.

Mullins and Kimbrough (1988) studied the job of patrol officer using SMEs from 12 different police departments. As part of their analysis, they used multidimensional scaling to cluster SMEs and identified subgroups with labels such as *legalistic, humanistic, cautious*, and so on. They discovered that these different subgroups provided different descriptions of the job in question. Thus, officers who appeared in the cluster "humanistic" emphasized dealing with others, communications activities, and so forth. In their job analysis ratings, whereas those officers in the "legalistic" cluster tended to emphasize procedural and administrative tasks. It is not clear, however, if this is a behavioral difference or a rating difference. In other words, it may very well be that the humanistic officers actually spend more time in these interpersonal tasks and that the legalistic officer devotes more time to procedural tasks. But it is also possible that, even though both types of officers spend equal amounts of time on both types, they report different levels of task performance. Once again, we see the possibility that SME responses may be influenced by variables other than the tasks.

Summary

The research evidence suggests the possibility that SME ratings may be influenced by characteristics other than the tasks that are being described. Note that you cannot conclude, simply because there is variance to ratings, that there is a systematic error in the task ratings. In fact, the reason for using multiple SMEs randomly or purposively drawn is to allow for the natural variation in task frequency and judged importance. But when this variation covaries with other variables unrelated to task variation (e.g., cognitive, demographic, or motivational variables), then a different situation obtains. In fact, the situation is much like the performance rating situation that has been studied so extensively. Several models of the performance rating scenario have been developed in the last decade (e.g., Feldman, 1981; Landy & Farr, 1980, 1983; Murphy & Balzer, 1986). These models propose a host of potential influences on supervisory performance ratings. The incomplete data presented previously suggest that there may be some need to develop or adapt a model to account for variation in job analysis ratings. Until such models are developed, however, there are some suggestions that might be made for controlling these unwanted influences on job analysis and job evaluation ratings. The following section explores these possibilities.

CONTROLLING UNWANTED INFLUENCES IN JOB ANALYSIS AND EVALUATION RATINGS

There are several rather straightforward methods for controlling inappropriate influences on task, KSA, and job characteristic ratings. These include instrument development, SME training and motivation, administrative safeguards, and analytic techniques.

Instrument Development

When asking SMEs to complete a job analysis or evaluation instrument, credibility is crucial. If a SME looks at a task list and the list includes unfamiliar terms, obsolete tasks, or tasks that are too broad to clearly indicate what behavior is involved or what KSA is tapped to support that behavior, the SME will have little confidence in the integrity of the instrument. Similarly, in completing a job evaluation instrument, if critical characteristics such as heat or smoke are ignored or levels of education are unrepresentative of the job under examination, skepticism is likely to result.

As a result, care should be taken to enhance the face validity of such instruments. The simplest way to do that is to enlist a small group of SMEs in developing the actual task list or job evaluation parameters and level descriptions.

You can gather a group of 5 to 8 SMEs and simply ask them to describe what they do in a "typical" day, or what distinguishes between an effective and an ineffective incumbent, or what variations in education are likely to be required by the job. Alternatively, you can start with the existing job description and ask them to elaborate on the tasks listed in that description or the factors that affect performance. From this base, you can easily develop a list of 100 to 200 tasks or preliminary evaluation components for all but the simplest of jobs. Such an instrument can then be taken to a second group of SMEs and presented for further critique, rewording, modification, and so forth. Finally, you might take the results of that critique to still a third group of SMEs and ask them to "think aloud" as they fill it out, articulating confusions, misunderstandings, needs for clarification, and so on.

Although you need not go through all these steps, the point is that the final instrument needs to be carefully developed so that the SMEs who will provide the eventual ratings have faith in the instrument and the process. When a procedure such as that just described is used, SMEs are often pleasantly surprised at how much you know about their job. In fact, even though the SMEs who will do the rating might be invited to add tasks, levels, or factors not included in the list, they seldom have any to suggest if the final list was carefully prepared and screened. In contrast, if the SMEs who are to rate the tasks, KSAs, or factors believe that the list is incomplete, incorrect in some essential category, or superficial, the motivation to provide accurate and reliable information will be substantially diminished.

In addition to the substance of the instrument itself, we must also consider both the length and the instructions that accompany that instrument. I alluded to this possible problem in the earlier discussion of the "carelessness" index (Green & Stutzman, 1986). Length is seldom an issue in job evaluation but can become a problem in job analysis. Raters can become fatigued and frustrated if steps are not taken to reduce these reactions. An unbroken list of 400 task statements is more intimidating than the same list broken into homogeneous subgroups of tasks. Thus, the list of 400 tasks might actually be presented as 10 task groups with 40 tasks in each. This seems to be easier to deal with than randomly ordered tasks, particularly when the list is long. It is always possible to check the dimensionality in a later component or cluster analysis. If a long unordered list of tasks were presented to the SMEs, it would not be surprising to find that after an initial portion of the questionnaire had been completed the rater began assigning uniform ratings of "average" or "high" to all task statements. In fact, if a task list is particularly long or complex, it might be better to subdivide the list and have different subgroups of SMEs complete different task groups.

A second area of concern in instrument development is the rating scale that is used to judge the task statements or KSAs. Typical ratings include frequency and importance for both job analysis and job evaluation. SMEs are easily frustrated by ambiguous anchors. Thus, frequency anchors such as "once each day," "once each week," and "one each year" are more effective than "a good deal," "not so much," and "hardly ever." Raters are uneasy with ambiguous anchors and will often become quite vocal and resistant in group rating sessions. They are trying to do a good job but are prevented by vagueness of the anchors. As was the case with the task list or job factor list, if SMEs have little confidence in the anchors they are using, they will be unlikely to take the rating task seriously or to provide data that will be accurate and reliable.

There are other areas of potential confusion. For example, an SME might want to know if she is to rate the job as she does it or to rate the "average" job as "most people" experience it would. The job analyst or evaluator should be prepared to answer that and similar questions. If the analyst is vague in answering such a question or stumbles and provides contradictory answers, the SMEs will again lose confidence in the process. As suggested before, a good set of pilot tests, including a think-aloud session, should reduce this type of problem.

Training and Motivation

Many SMEs are "first-time" raters and have never been involved in a job analysis or job evaluation project before. They need to receive careful explanations of what they are doing and how the results will be used. In the case of a job analysis, they need to be assured that this is not a performance evaluation of them or a job evaluation of their position. They need to be convinced that they are the experts and that your task (or the task of the questionnaire) is to liberate that expert knowledge. If possible, it helps to guarantee anonymity to the SMEs by not asking to put their name or employee number on a form. It is still possible to gather appropriate demographic information such as gender, race, experience, and so forth. Without compromising the anonymity. The point is that the initial orientation can be critical in establishing the credibility of the request and the instrument. If pilot studies were done, it helps to let the SMEs know that their colleagues helped to develop the form they will see. They are less likely to criticize such a form and will be more likely to cooperate because it is clear that others have cooperated before.

With respect to the actual rating procedures that will be used, some training would be appropriate. Thus, the researcher might provide an example of a task and how that task would be considered on a frequency or an importance dimension. You could even give them a practice task or two to rate and then discuss those ratings in order to establish a clear understanding and agreement regarding the underlying dimension.

With respect to KSA ratings, there is a clear need for instruction. SMEs feel very uncomfortable dealing with knowledge, skill, and ability ratings because they have seldom considered their jobs in that light. They feel like "amateur" psychologists or consultants. What is needed is clear instruction in the meaning and scope of the KSA list as well as clear examples of how that list can be applied to representative tasks. As was the case with the task list, some "hands on" training will provide a good foundation for completing the ratings.

From the motivational perspective, influences can be substantial. As suggested in earlier sections, raters may very well see rating behavior as "instrumental": in obtaining valued rewards. Certainly, if the job can be made to appear more complex than is currently thought, the incumbent might receive additional compensation or at least increased respect from the supervisor. Similarly, some incumbents are likely to respond in terms of how they would *like* the job to be performed, not how it is *actually* performed. As is the case in performance evaluation, much of this error can be eliminated by simply apprising the rater of such influences. Further, because it is unlikely that respondents would all distort in exactly the same manner, many of these influences may introduce random rather than systematic error. If there is some concern about the possibility, it might be wise to recognize it explicitly and permit the raters to provide information on both how the job is currently performed and how it "should be" performed. This might extract the error variance from the "is now" ratings.

Administrative Issues

You are more likely to enhance the credibility of the job analysis instrument with a face-to-face data collection session as opposed to a mail survey. You can answer questions, provide an elaborate orientation discussion, and generally persuade the SMEs that what they are doing is valuable. Further, it is likely that your return rate will be considerably higher than expected with a mail survey. There is also the issue of the care with which the scales are completed. When the SME comes to a group session to complete a job analysis form, there is usually a commitment to complete the task in a responsible manner. Because others (peer SMEs) are "watching," the individual is likely not to rush or engage in distracting activities. At home or at a work site, you are seldom as lucky. Distractions are common and the task is usually put off until the last minute, increasing the possibility that the individual will rush through the ratings and provide less thoughtful responses. If at all possible, it would be a substantial advantage to gather job analysis and job evaluation ratings in a group setting on company time. Other collection strategies are compromises that might substantially reduce the value of the data.

Effect Sizes

Unfortunately, few of the studies reviewed in this chapter report means and standard deviations ratings disaggregated by the level of the antecedent variable. This is a good indication of fact that the question about influences on job analysis–job evaluation results has seldom been asked. We are still at the stage of determining if, in fact, *any* effect exists. If that is established, then one might expect a greater interest in the *size* of that effect. At present, it is difficult to get a handle on how large the actual effects of rater and rating process attributes might be. One exception is the Arvey et al. (1977) study of gender effects on job analysis. From their results, it is possible to compute effect sizes (i.e., mean differences divided by pooled standard deviations). They were in the order of one-half standard deviation. Future researchers in this area should be sensitive to this issue of effect size estimation and report means and standard deviations, in addition to the results of significance tests. At present, it is simply impossible to determine if the influences examined are "important" in addition to being "significant."

Analytic Strategies

As was discussed in an earlier section of the chapter, the carelessness index is one way to provide an opportunity to clean your job analysis data and eliminate those raters who are not behaving responsibly. This requires you to take some actions in advance, however. It is necessary to build into the task list a set of tasks that would not be part of the job under consideration but might be chosen by someone seeking to inappropriately enhance their job description. This is almost like a "lie scale" of a personality inventory or the "socially desirable" alternative of the forced choice inventory that does not discriminate in terms of true performance. If you were to include 5 such items, a decision rule might be to exclude from the job analysis any SME who responded positively to at least 3 of the 5 items. Although this may cut down on your sample considerably, there is no advantage of adding people to the sample who will distort reality for idiosyncratic reasons. The data are compelling with respect to the improvement of reliability and accuracy that is gained from the exclusion of these "careless" raters.

The best safeguard against the influences of single raters is sample size. Thus, you are always better off with larger rather than smaller sample sizes (assuming that those in the sample do not fulfill the "careless" criterion described earlier).

CONCLUSION

It is reasonable to assume that most SMEs will try to meet your expectation if the conditions permit. These conditions include a well-developed and face-valid set of instruments, a rating task that is understandable and feasible, a data collection procedure that does not create unnecessary obstacles to complete and accurate ratings, and an analytic technique that will eliminate obvious sources of distortion. It seems clear that whenever rating is done individual difference variables may influence the results.

Until we know more about these influences and when they are most likely to occur, we should take the necessary developmental, administrative, and analytic steps necessary to protect the integrity of these data.

ACKNOWLEDGMENT

Several of the studies that appear in the first part of this chapter were identified by Laura Shankster. Her assistance is gratefully acknowledged.

REFERENCES

Arvey, R. D. (1986). Sex bias in job evaluation procedures. *Personnel Psychology, 39*(2), 315–335.

Arvey, R. D., Davis, G. A., McGowen, S. L., & Dipboye, R. L. (1982). Potential sources of bias in job analytic processes. *Academy of Management Journal, 25*, 618–629.

Arvey, R. D., Passino, E. M., & Lounsbury, J. W. (1977). Job analysis results as influenced by sex of incumbents and sex of analyst. *Journal of Applied Psychology, 62*, 411–416.

Cellar, D. F., Durr, M. L., & Hassell, S. (1989). The effect of field independence, job analysis format, and sex of rater on the accuracy of job evaluation ratings. *Journal of Applied Social Psychology, 19*, 363–376.

DeNisi, A. S., Cornelius, E. T., III, & Blencoe, A. G. (1987). Further investigation of common knowledge effects on job analysis ratings. *Journal of Applied Psychology, 72*, 262–268.

Feldman, J. M. (1981). Beyond attribution theory: Cognitive processes in performance appraisal. *Journal of Applied Psychology, 66*, 127–148.

Friedman, L., & Harvey, R. J. (1986). Can raters with reduced job descriptive information provide accurate Position Analysis Questionnaire (PAQ) ratings? *Personnel Psychology, 39*, 779–790.

Gael, S. (1988). *The job analysis handbook for business, industry and government.* New York: Wiley.

Green, S. B., & Stutzman, T. (1986). An evaluation of methods to select respondents to structured job analysis questionnaires. *Personnel Psychology, 39*, 543–564.

Landy, F. J. (1989). *The psychology of work behavior.* Monterey, CA: Brooks-Cole.

Landy, F. J., & Farr, J. L. (1980). Performance rating. *Psychological Bulletin, 87*, 72–107.

Landy, F. J., & Farr, J. L. (1983). *The measurement of work performance.* New York: Academic Press.

Landy, F. J., & Vasey, J. (1991). Job analysis: The composition of SME samples. *Personnel Psychology, 44*, 27–50.

Lipmann, O. (1916). Zur psychologischen charakteristik des "mittleren" berufe. *Zeitschrift fur Angewandte Psychologie, 12*, 99–107 (original work in Viteles, 1932).

London, M. (1976). Employee perceptions of the job reclassification process. *Personnel Psychology, 29*, 67–77.

McCormick, E. J., Jeanneret, P., & Mecham, R. C. (1972). A study of job characteristics of job dimensions as based on the position analysis questionnaires (Monograph). *Journal of Applied Psychology, 36*, 347–368.

McShane, S. L. (1990). Two tests of direct gender bias in job evaluation ratings. *Journal of Occupational Psychology, 63*, 129–140.

Mullins, W. C., & Kimbrough, W. W. (1988). Group composition as a determinant of job analysis outcomes. *Journal of Applied Psychology, 73*, 657–664.

Murphy, K. R., & Balzer, W. K. (1986). Systematic distortions in memory based behavior ratings and performance evaluations: Consequences for rating accuracy. *Journal of Applied Psychology, 71,* 39–44.

Nisbett, R., & Ross, L. (1980). *Human inference: Strategies and shortcomings of social judgment.* Englewood Cliffs, NJ: Prentice–Hall.

Schmitt, N., & Cohen, S. A. (1989). Internal analyses of task ratings by job incumbents. *Journal of Applied Psychology, 74,* 96–104.

Viteles, M. J. (1932). *Industrial psychology.* New York: Norton.

Wexley, K. N., & Silverman, S. B. (1978). An examination of differences between managerial effectiveness and response patterns on a structured job analysis questionnaire. *Journal of Applied Psychology, 63,* 646–649.

Zebrowitz, J., McArthur, L., & Obrant, S. W. (1986). Sex biases in comparable worth analysis. *Journal of Applied Social Psychology, 16,* 757–770.

7

Personnel Selection, Questionnaires, and Motivational Distortion: An Intelligent Attitude of Adaptation

N. Seisdedos
TEA Ediciones, S.A., Madrid

With increasing use in many countries, the questionnaire has demonstrated its value in obtaining pertinent information about candidates. It can be used to gather personal data, such as background activities, academic curricula, present expectations and projects, specific attitudes, personality traits, and so on. These instruments are useful considering their low cost.

This type of instrument has several limitations, however. Ellis (1946) reported up to 28 criticisms on the questionnaires; the following three are most related to the present work: (a) Subjects may easily fake answers, and they frequently do so; (b) subject's motivational drives may vary between the different situational settings where psychological variables are measured; (c) when used for a selection purpose, these instruments offer the possibility of a self-overestimation.

In other words, one of the most common criticisms against questionnaire-type measures has been the possibility to "fake" answers in order to give a deliberately "good" or "bad" image.

However, we should not necessarily consider this behavior and attitude as a form of insincerity, lying, or deliberate faking. It is not necessarily negative from the subject's viewpoint to show the best "ego," because, in some settings, that could be the way to adapt to the circumstances. It may be something like going to a rendezvous wearing one's best dress or suit, or after having visited the hairdresser. There are praiseworthy aspects in this behavior, although the psychologist would like to measure the individual in "normal dress."

In the past, much has been written about dissimulation, variously called distortion or faking. Nevertheless, it is well accepted that questionnaires may still provide a valid measure of some traits: Conditions of anonymity do not produce large changes in personality scores, and there is evidence that under ordinary conditions subjects give relatively truthful answers about themselves.

Several methods have been tried to define and measure the variable and, if possible, to correct other measures. Originally, the main strategy was to measure the person's tendency to deceive using a number of personal questions that, according to Hartshorne and May (1928), "on the whole have rather widespread social approval, but which at the same time are rarely done." This approach was pioneered by Dahlstrom and Welsh (1960), the authors of the Minnesota Multiphasic Personality Inventory (with its well-known L scale). Buros (1970) lists many attempts to evaluate this construct: The "F–K" dissimulation index by Gough (1950), the social desirability Sd scale by Wiggins (1959), Edwards (1970), Crowne and Marlow (1964); Butcher's (1969) book contains 27 references about the answer bias and 69 concerning social desirability and acquiescence.

This type of measure was introduced in the Eysenck's EPI and EPQ (Eysenck & Eysenck, 1978, 1986) as well as in the Cattell's 16PF. Spanish adaptations of all these instruments (MMPI, EPQ, 16PF, etc.) attempted the same goals and have been well accepted by Spanish users.

The first versions of the 16PF, HSPQ, CPQ, and ESPQ had no measure of "motivational distortion" (MD). But some years later, Cattell, Eber, and Tatsuoka (1970) dedicated a whole chapter to this matter and pointed out that two-thirds of their 16 scales were influenced by the MD variable. As is shown later in the chapter, the Spanish adaptation of these instruments found a similar structure.

The present work has the following structure: (a) Our hypothesis about dissimulation; (b) a review of data already published elsewhere; (c) a more detailed exposition of recent studies, including the analyses of the dissimulation unit, the questionnaire item; (d) finally, the relationship between dissimulation and other variables (e.g., age, intellectual functioning, antisocial behavior and attitudes).

SOME HYPOTHESES ABOUT THE NATURE OF THE "FAKING" MEASURES

Several studies have pointed out that dissimulation might have a situational meaning from the point of view of personality structure.

Dicken (1959) suggested three possible reasons for a high score: deliberate "faking," response in terms of an ideal self-concept rather than a candid self-appraisal, and response in terms of an "honest" but inaccurate and uninsightful self-assessment. Eysenck adds a fourth possibility, also suggested by Hartshorne and May (1928), that a genuine conformity to social rules or mores may result in elevated L scores. A fifth possibility is defensiveness on the subject's part.

Another hypothesis has been phrased in terms of a personality dimension stressing such traits as conformity, orthodoxy, and conservatism, whereby the high scorer behaves in a more conforming way; the high scorer could be a conformist who puts his or herself in the best possible light to gain public approval.

Our hypothesis about the nature of faking is based on motivation. Paraphrasing the Spanish philosopher Ortega y Gasset (who said "man is himself and his circumstances"), this drive functions according to the individual personality as a whole and the environmental characteristics. In other words, when answering a questionnaire instrument the subject adapts to the surrounding demands with all capabilities (knowledge, intelligence, experiences, etc.) and moods. According to this hypothesis, faking might be an intelligent form of the subject's adaptation.

PREVIOUS RESEARCH AND RESULTS

Work on Spanish adaptation of the Eysenck's and Cattell's questionnaires as well as the MMPI quickly showed that dissimulation scores (L/S or MD) have significant relationships with personality traits.

The L scale of the Eysenck's EPQ measures was negatively related with Psychoticism and Neuroticism, and positively with age in adults. The correlations were also negative in children and young adolescents (EPQ-J).

We pointed out earlier that there is a cognitive component to dissimulation. This component is still maturing in older children and adolescents. This fact might explain the distribution of the phenomenon. A recent study of dissimulation in youngsters (Seisdedos, 1988) shows there is a curvilinear "U" effect from childhood to adulthood: (a) In the first part of the curve, the young child obtains a high L score that suggests high dissimulation, but this may simply be a pragmatic adjustment of her or himself to the adult's norms; (b) later, at adolescence (even young adulthood), rebellious and independent attitudes toward norms produce a drastic sincerity where it is slight social faults that constitute the L scales being readily admitted; the attitude is similar to the behavior of antisocial or delinquent youngsters (Seisdedos, 1979, Giorgi & Seisdedos, 1982); (c) at the end of the growing process, adulthood, the "superego" drive, and the need to adjust to the circumstances lead to a more frequent endorsement of the L items.

The MMPI studies follow a different methodology. The 15 items of L scale are independent of the other scales. An adaptation of the MMPI (Seisdedos, 1986) analyzed very different samples, and Table 7.1 gives the L correlation indexes with the other scales, in the seven groups.

L is systematically related to the validation F score (with negative sign) and

TABLE 7.1

L Relationships with Other MMPI Scales

Sample	?	F	K	HS	D	Hy	Pd	Mf	Pa	Pt	Sc	Ma	Si
A	06	-24	24	-08	-04	02	-24	-18	-25	-22	-24	-25	-16
B	-04	-26	54	05	-02	23	-08	00	-07	-17	-21	-10	-31
C	06	-02	46	01	08	15	03	-10	-09	-20	-13	-12	-14
D	02	-25	25	-12	12	04	-15	-10	-19	-22	-20	-21	-12
E	-08	-23	50	05	03	12	01	-03	03	-14	-22	-12	-13
F	09	-21	35	10	-04	17	-10	10	-00	-09	-24	-14	00
G	08	-25	42	-04	01	06	-10	-06	-07	-20	-23	-11	-17
Median r	*06*	*-24*	*42*	*05*	*01*	*12*	*-10*	*-06*	*-07*	*-20*	*-22*	*-12*	*-14*

Sample descriptions:

A/D : 200/200 males/females, students, 16/17 years old
B/E : 345/530 males/females, candidates (over 25 years old)
C/F : 256/125 males/females, university students
G : 244 females, students, 16/17 years old

to the correction K measure (with positive sign); both scales are included within the MMPI "validation scales" to measure subject attitudes when answering the test. Readers familiar with works of Gough (1950) and his scale to measure dissimulation will know that the score "F minus K" means a distortion toward a good or bad self-image. F minus K is better than L to measure distortion.

In samples B and E (obtained as a part of university selection), scores for the 16PF were also available, and we could cross-validate the L scores with the Cattell's motivational distortion score.

The procedure to obtain a Spanish MD scale from Form A followed Karson and O'Dell (1980). An experimental sample of 214 university students anonymously answered the questionnaire. After an interval of 1 week to 2 months, they did the test again, but this time they were instructed to fake (with a sentence like "You are supposed to be candidates for a job you are longing for or you like very much."). The item analysis shows that 15 questions were significantly influenced by these instructions. The resulting MD scale was cross-validated with two more samples: 400 subjects in a guidance setting and a similar group in a selection process.

Later, other adult samples in selection settings indicate that high MD scores correlate negatively with Anxiety (emotional instability, guilt proneness, frustration) and positively with Extroversion (warmth, impulsivity, group dependency, venturesomeness).

NEW RESEARCH FINDINGS

Recently, with larger samples and using other analysis and techniques, results have been replicated. Subjects and variables (var.) were as follows:

a. 422 young adults, candidates for a Spanish city police force, 29 var.:
   16PF Form C : 16 primary scales and MD
   CAQ, Clinical Analysis Questionnaire : 12 var.
b. 1,186 adults (20–40 years old), candidates for clerical jobs, 27 var.:
   16PF Form A : 16 primary scales, MD and Negative attitude
   Intelligence : 9-speed aptitude tests.
c. 3,558 adults (19–55 years), candidates for assistant clerical jobs, 26 var.:
   16PF Form D (parallel to Form C) : 16 scales and MD
   Intelligence : 9-speed aptitude tests.
d. 1,127 young adults, candidates for clerical jobs, 19 var.:
   16PF Form A, 16 primary scales, MD and Negative attitude
   Subtests AR, VR, and NA of DAT (Differential Apt. Tests)

e. 87 samples of 34 Spanish provinces (total n = 34,687), candidates for clerical and assistant jobs, 9 var.:
   EPI Form A : 3 scales, and 6 aptitude tests

f. 1,080 adolescents, pupils in several capital city schools, 8 var.:
   EPI Form A : 3 scales
   Antisocial-Delictive questionnaire : 2 scales
   Mores and habits questionnaire

g. 1,040 anonymous and heterogeneous adults, experimental sample, 13 var.:
   EPQ Form Adults : 4 scales
   Spanish Psychosocial Scale, 9 attitudes

The analyses carried out with these subjects have been very heterogeneous
and the amount of statistics gathered very large. Within the tables we discuss
we have tried to abbreviate and summarize those most related with the dissimulation construct and its implications for other variables.

In most of our analyses we have used the Cattell's and colleagues instruments. A major question is how well the different 16PF Forms measure distortion (MD) variables and how this is related to the other personality scales.

TABLE 7.2
MD Relationships with 16PF Scales in Several Samples

n Sca.	1,183 16PF-A	1,125 16PF-A	422 16PF-C	3,487 16PF-D
A	0.35	0.32	0.34	0.18
B	0.07	0.11	−0.12	−0.01
C	0.54 (0.07)	0.49	0.57	0.34
E	0.34 (0.07)	0.28	0.18	−0.04
F	0.27 (0.07)	0.29	0.32	0.17
G	0.28	0.33	0.20	0.16
H	0.63 (0.22)	0.62	0.42	0.26
I	−0.19 (0.08)	−0.32	−0.03	0.08
L	−0.14	−0.15	−0.25	−0.19
M	0.19	0.19	0.15	0.06
N	−0.01	0.04	−0.20	−0.09
O	−0.55	−0.50	−0.38	−0.21
Q1	0.08	0.09	0.03	−0.02
Q2	−0.15 (0.08)	−0.26	−0.32	−0.20
Q3	0.48 (0.24)	0.49	0.47	0.38
Q4	−0.62 (0.29)	−0.52	−0.48	−0.18
c. level	0.08	0.08	0.13	0.04
MD Mean	6.86	6.11	9.11	8.39
MD St.d.	3.42	2.97	3.29	2.40

Table 7.2 summarizes four analyses (Form B has not, for the moment, an MD scale).

The MD items of 16PF Form A were contained in the personality scales; so the first column of Table 7.2 also presents (in brackets) a contamination index (Guilford's formula).

Notice that the structure in all columns is very similar. The four personality traits most influenced by the dissimulation variables define subjects whose features are boldness, stability, self-assurance, self-control, and relaxation.

It seems that Forms A and C have a very similar MD structure, although the C raw mean is higher; this may be due to item weighting (0–1–2 in Form C; 0–1 in Form A). Form D (with a 0–1–2 weights) shows lower correlations, which might mean this form is less influenced by MD, or it might less credibly mean that the 3,500 subjects were less motivated to fake.

Thus, with all three Forms of 16PF, the MD + person seems to be subjectively adjusting to a more conforming pattern to the present social mores and stereotypes.

These features are normally and socially desirable from the point of view of the work and social relationships; probably, the subject knows that and adjusts when answering the personality questionnaires. Is that not a fair adjustment for an intelligent person, well-fitted to the environment? If so, should we start to interpret MD on this line?

These features agree with those found "desirable" or "ideal" by Meredith's (1968) subjects and are consistent with the hypotheses of Cattell et al. (1970).

But, do both genders behave with the same pattern? The 16PF Technical Manual points out that males have lower MD scores. Where the gender of the respondents is known, we reanalyzed the data for each. Mean MD scores for males are higher in Form A, but both genders had very similar scores on Form D. However, the relationship with personality is clearer in males. Thus we propose the following alternatives about the male behavior: (a) Men are more prone to employ the "distortion" construct in order to improve appearance; (b) men have fewer good social qualities and have recourse to MD for amending appearance; (c) we believe men risk more in the testing setting.

In order to explain further with another focus, we classified our large 16PF–A sample (n = 1,186) into five subgroups according to degree of faking (MD1 to MD5, from low to high) and calculated their statistics on the 16PF–A scales; then we transformed the subgroups' averages into scaled scores S (with a mean of 50 and an s.d. of 20), using as norms the whole sample statistic.

In the 16PF scales most influenced by the faking, the extreme subgroups (MD1 and MD5) obtained S scores more separated from the average of 50. For instance, the average MD1 and MD5 subjects (with extreme scores) defined themselves with a special pattern and obtained the following S scores:

		Low MD subjects		High MD subjects
Sc.	S	(MD1)	S	(MD5)
H	34	restrained	68	adventurous
C	35	emotion. unstable	65	emotionally stable
Q3	36	careless/social rules	63	socially precise
A	43	aloof	60	warmhearted
G	44	unconcerned	58	responsible
O	60	apprehensive	34	self-assured
Q4	68	frustrated	33	relaxed

This might suggest that in selection candidates behave in a "bright" manner, adjusting themselves to the setting and showing the "profile" they consider more appropriate. Similar findings were found when scores from Form D were analyzed.

So far, then, the faking pattern is confirmed in several analyses. The personality structure of someone with high MD scores agrees with what we have seen in the literature; that is, a person who, in order to show an adjusted personality, tries to hide anxiety characteristics.

To provide an analysis at the level of second-order factors, we took one of the samples (n = 1,183) using the 16PF Form A and calculated the 5 factor scores using the weights obtained by Seisdedos (1981). We also calculated the 5 regression estimated scores proposed by Cattell et al. (1970): psychoticism, neuroticism, leadership, creativity, and achievement. Then, the relationships between MD and these 10 secondary scores were analyzed.

The correlations indicate, at a secondary dimension level, the personality characteristics of the high MD scorer: well adjusted (low anxiety), extroverted, somewhat independent, without pathological problems (psychotic or neurotic), a good leader, and ready to do well in training.

Similar results were obtained from a larger sample using Form D, but the relationships were generally lower than those obtained with Form A.

The database with Form D was sufficiently large to permit isolating extreme groups of high and low scorers on the MD scale (n = 222 and n = 273, respectively). Each group contained approximately one-fifth of the total sample. A factor analysis was conducted on each sample.

The next step in our studies was to investigate the internal structure of the MD construct using multiple regression. In this case, we have employed the 16PF Form D sample (n = 3,487), and the analysis was done for both genders separately.

The results of the stepwise multiple regression are given in Table 7.3.

The R and CV% indexes are higher in males. However, it seems that each gender enlarges those variables that, from a subjective point of view, are more desirable. First, both genders show the feature of a controlled person, and this explains more than half of the common variance (CV%). Second, males show

TABLE 7.3
MD Beta Regression Weights of 16PD-D Scales

The Male is . . .	Sc.	Beta	.	Beta	Sc.	The Female is . . .
controlled	Q3+	0.40	.	0.35	Q3+	controlled
emotionally stable	C+	0.27	.	0.18	H+	socially bold
enthusiastic	F+	0.15	.	-0.15	Q2-	group dependent
warmhearted	A+	0.09	.	0.12	C+	emotionally stable
group dependent	Q2-	-0.08	.	0.10	A+	warmhearted
trusting	L-	-0.07	.	-0.08	L-	trusting
responsible	G+	0.07	.	0.05	E+	assertive
obedient	E-	-0.05	.	0.05	G+	responsible
low mental ability	B-	-0.05	.	0.05	M+	imaginative
self-assured	O-	-0.05	.			
socially bold	H+	0.05	.			
Multiple R		0.520	.	0.458.		
CV %		27.05	.	20.97.		

the characteristics of an emotionally stable (C +) but impulsive and enthusiastic person (F +), whereas females are prone to exhibit those features of social boldness (H +) but group dependence (Q2 –). We have to point out that, in our Spanish culture, the "boldness" is mainly a male characteristic, and we see now how females have used it to adapt themselves to the job requirements. After that, but still with a significant weight, we see that females show a higher ego strength (C +, also present with significant weight in the male column), and then in both genders there appears a participating warmth (A +).

The regression analyses was repeated using the secondary factors previously defined (Anxiety, Extraversion, Socialization, and Subjectivism).

The schema was implicit in previous analyses: Motivational Distortion was related to Anxiety avoidance, adherence to the social norms in order to show the Extravert features, and, when the subject is a female, to exhibit Subjectivism.

Investigation of the pathological correlates of motivational distortion was conducted using a sample of 422 adults (mainly males) who answered the 16PF Form C and the Clinical Analysis Questionnaire, CAQ (Krug, 1987). The CAQ is an instrument with seven scales to measure depression (D1 to D7) and another five scales whose titles resemble some MMPI clinical measures. Subjects were classified into three subgroups (according to their MD score; Table 7.4 shows the correlational study and the scores for three subgroups). The first column shows how most CAQ scales are related to the MD scale of 16PF Form C, significantly and negatively; that is, the subjects deny having these pathological traits. This is a convenient faking behavior, and the subjects use it to better adjust themselves to the selection requirements.

Table 7.4 shows that the only two scales with average scores are D3 (Agitation) and Pp (psychopathic deviation). The CAQ technical manual (Krug, 1987)

TABLE 7.4
MD Relationships with CAQ Scales and S Score of MD Subgroups

CAQ Scale		MD r	Score of Subgroups		
			MD1	MD2	MD3
D1	Hypochondriasis	−0.45	63	49	41
D2	Suicidal depression	−0.28	58	50	44
D3	Agitation	0.04	48	49	52
D4	Anxious depression	−0.48	64	50	39
D5	Low energy depression	−0.49	65	48	41
D6	Guilt an resentment	−0.36	60	52	40
D7	Boredom and Withdrawal	−0.41	62	49	42
Pa	Paranoia	−0.26	48	49	45
Pp	Psychopathic deviation	0.27	42	49	57
Sc	Schizophrenia	−0.51	65	49	39
As	Psychastenia	−0.24	56	51	43
Ps	Psychological inadequacy	−0.54	64	51	37
	n	422	114	182	126
Md	(Mean = 9.41 Sd. = 3.31) range		0–7	8–11	12–14

defines the high D3 scorer as "a person who would like adventurous jobs and jobs where he has to speak up and take charge, he craves excitement, adventure and risk" (p. 29), and these features are not depreciatory from the distortion point of view. On the other hand, it seems to us that in the Pp scale (that defines "a low inhibited individual who does not mind being the center of attention, can go without sleep, and enjoy emergencies and quarrels")) (p. 31), we may observe the oppositionist behavior we study later; the young MD + adult of our sample seems to boast of this endorsement of inhibition, both by the physical danger–pain and by the social criticism.

THE FAKING MEASURE UNIT: THE ITEM

In the preceding pages we have analyzed the MD construct in selection settings using raw scores in questionnaire scales. Now, we try to go farther, to the item level. In a work previously quoted (Seisdedos, 1988), we have studied the L scale structure of EPQ–J in adolescents; these analyses defined three content subscales (behaviors relating with other young subjects, with the adult world, and with social abstract rules). They were recently verified with three factor dimensions from the 20 questionnaire L items. One conclusion was that subgroups of different ages and gender obtain significantly different scores, and this seems to corroborate our hypothesis about the MD as an "intelligent attitude of adjustment."

The investigation used a sample of nearly 3,000 candidates for clerical jobs who answered the EPI Form A. The analyses focused on the nine items of its L scale. Table 7.5 gives the item endorsement percentage (End%) and its average (Av.), the item relationships with age and EPI personality traits, the corrected homogeneity index (HIc), and (at the bottom) our English version for each item.

The relationship of one L item with the L score (HI, homogeneity index) is contaminated because the same item is one of the nine components of the L score. To obviate this contamination, the HIc index (corrected) was estimated using the correlation of each item with the L score obtained by the other eight items. The conclusions of these analyses are: (a) The item endorsement averages are not far from the ideal 50%, lower in males (37%) than in females (43%); (b) in both genders, the item with highest frequency is a negative response to "speak sometimes about unknown matters." The lowest frequency is the negative answer to the existence of persons one does not like at all; (c) the L items are significantly and negatively related to Instability and positively to Extraversion; (d) only a few items are related to age.

The matrices of item intercorrelations of each gender were factor analyzed (MLFA, as in previous analyses); the oblique solution loadings (decimal point omitted), as well as the item communalities (h2) and the common variance (CV%), are in Table 7.6. The factorial structure is very similar in both genders, and the two factors are highly correlated (-0.51 in males and -0.39 in females), which corroborates the existence of one general L dimension, as defined by the authors (H. J. Eysenck & S. B. G. Eysenck, 1978).

The first subfactor includes behaviors that, in some form, involve another person: to be on time for an appointment, to gossip, to rest in bed after having heard the alarm clock (supposedly this relates to being on time in social contexts), and to like to be praised by others. The second subfactor seems to refer to the subject's insight: mood fluctuations, good habits, and having eaten too much. The 18th item (to refuse personal dislikes) has the lower communality; in males it is aligned with the social subfactor (I), but in females it is aligned with the insight connotations. Consequently, the 18th item was not used in our next step calculating factorial scores (L-1 and L-2) for subjects and correlating them with personality traits.

For this analysis Extraversion was separated into two components, Impulsivity (IM) and Socialization (SO) (Eysenck & Eysenck, 1963, 1977; Luengo Martin, 1986), and the results are in Table 7.7.

From the data of Table 7.7, it seems that for both genders the subscale L-1 has a higher negative correlation than a positive correlation with Extraversion. However L-2 has a higher correlation with Extraversion. Thus people with high "faking" scores tend to be more stable and better socialized.

TABLE 7.5
Item Analysis of L Scale in EPI-A*

It	918 Males						1,926 Females					
	End%	Age	N	E	L	HIc	End%	Age	N	E	L	HIc
1	18	0.04	-0.19	0.14	0.51	0.35	15	0.05	-0.21	0.11	0.46	0.29
2	19	0.10	-0.22	0.19	0.46	0.18	20	0.00	-0.21	0.20	0.45	0.26
3	9	0.05	-0.04	-0.11	0.31	0.17	15	0.04	-0.01	-0.10	0.30	0.14
4	57	0.05	-0.13	0.09	0.57	0.37	53	0.02	-0.18	0.09	0.61	0.40
5	63	0.05	-0.12	0.02	0.55	0.35	73	0.10	-0.14	-0.04	0.47	0.26
6	58	-0.03	-0.18	0.10	0.59	0.39	63	0.04	-0.21	0.08	0.60	0.39
7	59	0.11	-0.20	0.10	0.60	0.40	63	0.08	-0.17	0.10	0.55	0.34
8	34	0.07	-0.13	0.02	0.54	0.34	69	0.07	-0.16	-0.05	0.52	0.31
9	18	0.08	-0.21	0.14	0.50	0.35	15	0.03	-0.13	0.10	0.44	0.28
Average	37						43					

Wording of L Items

1. Does your mood often go up and down? (NO)
2. Are all your mores and habits good and desirable? (YES)
3. Between the persons you know, is there someone you do not like at all? (NO)
4. Have you ever been late for an appointment or for work? (NO)
5. Do you sometimes speak about matters you do not know? (NO)
6. Do you ever enjoy gossiping about other persons? (NO)
7. After having heard the morning alarm-clock, do you sometimes remain a little more on bed? (NO)
8. Do you sometimes like that the others praise what you have done? (NO)
9. Have you ever eaten more than you should? (NO)

*In relationships, critical levels (ϕ = 0.01) are 0.09 (M) and 0.06 (F).

TABLE 7.6
Factor Analyses of EPI-A'L Items

It.	918 males			1,926 females		
	I	II	h2	I	II	h2
6		−.74	.47		−.47	.24
12		−.41	.19		−.56	.31
18		−.19	.05	.19		.04
24	.57		.29	.51		.30
30	.48		.23	.38		.14
36	.60		.33	.55		.32
42	.42		.26	.37		.18
48	.31		.17	.48		.22
54		−.53	.29		−.56	.31

DISTORTION AND AGE

In the beginning of this chapter, we pointed out that the relationship between distortion and age is probably curvilinear. It decreases in children and adolescents and increases in adults. Adults are in the ascendant second half when they are in the selection situation.

An ideal study of this phenomenon would be longitudinal, but none has been conducted. However, we may get some information if we have a large sample, which can be subdivided into age groups. That was our case when we analyzed the EPI Form A scores in the 33,279 subjects from the same selection process; the testing was done the same day in all Spanish capital cities. First, they were classified by gender, and then the age subgroups were made with a 5-year range. Means and standard deviations of the L scale are given in Table 7.8.

The subgroup samples are large enough for small differences to become statistically significant. There is a similar pattern for males and females, but the female scores are higher in all age subgroups.

TABLE 7.7
Two L Subscales and Personality Traits

EPI	968 Males		2,112 Females	
	L-1	L-2	L-1	L-2
N	−0.24**	−0.28**	−0.27**	−0.25**
E	0.11**	0.22**	0.06*	0.19**
IM	0.16**	0.22**	0.11**	0.19**
SO	0.01	0.14**	−0.02	0.12**

*$p < 0.05$; **$p < 0.01$.

TABLE 7.8
Age Trend in Males/Females L Scores

Age	15,160 Males			18,119 Females		
	n	*Mean*	*S.d.*	*n*	*Mean*	*S.d.*
15–19	1,599	3.42	2.07	3,285	4.17	2.17
20–24	7,546	3.27	2.00	9,307	3.81	1.93
25–29	3,867	3.38	2.05	3,816	3.98	1.96
30–34	1,102	3.79	2.06	1,051	4.24	2.00
35–39	474	4.15	2.08	398	4.63	1.94
40–44	284	4.69	2.15	189	4.79	1.93
45–49	167	4.56	2.02	50	5.46	1.69
50–54	121	4.87	2.07	23	5.70	2.05

DISTORTION AND INTELLIGENCE MEASURES

In some of the preceding samples we had aptitude scores, which can be examined in relation to the distortion construct.

An earlier study by Seisdedos (1988) found a slight negative correlation between intelligence (factor "g") and L scores; perhaps the more gifted subjects are freer of "social norms" and they pay less attention to the adult rules. Consequently, their L endorsement is less frequent; that is to say, they are more "sincere."

In a selection context, we had a sample of 13,557 young adults, candidates for clerical jobs, who answered the EPI Form A, two intelligence tests (TIG–1 and Coins' measures of factor "g"), and an aptitude battery (BPA–T). Table 7.9 shows the intercorrelation indices.

In the total sample and in both genders we observe that there is a significant negative correlation between intelligence (g) and Neuroticism (N) and distortion (L). The gifted (g +) person seems to be more sincere (L –) and stable (N –).

TABLE 7.9
Intelligence, Sex, and Personality (N, E, & L)

Test	Total (N = 13,557)			Males (N = 4,267)			Females (N = 9,289)		
	N	*E*	*L*	*N*	*E*	*L*	*N*	*E*	*L*
TIG–1	−15	08	−11	−13	07	−09	−14	09	−09
COINS	−17	05	−12	−15	04	−09	−15	07	−09
BPA–T	−15	06	−12	−14	05	−12	−15	08	−11
EPI-N		−18	−29		−20	−31		−17	−32
EPI-E			06			08			05

A multiple correlation was conducted to determine the relation of the L score to personality, intelligence, and age. In the two analyses of Table 7.10 the dependent variable is distortion as measured by the EPI Form A.

The first analysis (using only the more discriminating intelligence test, Coins) obtained a multiple R of 0.34, which explains 12% of the L variance, and the main weight is Stability (N–).

The second analysis of Table 7.10 also includes the other intelligence test (TIG–1) and age; the explained variance from the enlarged multiple regression only increases to 14%. The larger contributor is also Stability (N–) and next is intelligence. The influence of age has been subsumed or diluted by the previous variables, and the Extroversion effect has disappeared.

The data again confirm the fact that, although the main distortion (L) relationship is with Stability (N–), intelligence has a significant weight. The L scorer tells us he or she is stable, a common characteristic in the gifted person.

DISTORTION AND PSYCHOSOCIAL ATTITUDES

One thousand and forty subjects of a sample used to standardized the Spanish Psychosocial Scale, SPS, also answered Eysenck's EPQ–A; both questionnaires were administered in a volunteer and anonymous settings (Giorgi & Seisdedos, 1982). We reanalyzed the data and related the L variable with the items and scales of the SPS.

A factor analyses of 82 original SPS items defined a tridimensional structure (replicated with different subsamples), and the 63 items of the final version defined three subscales (bipolar factors) that pointed to the following constructs: – RE: religious attitudes, including worry about the transcendental ideas and life after death, refusal of the discrepant liberties, and apology of the traditional norms of the Spanish culture (24 items); – DO: dogmatic attitudes, aggressive, radical, and tough views in the conduct with others (24 items); – HE: the hedonistic enjoyment of life pleasures and the search of more liberties (27 items).

TABLE 7.10
L Multiple Regression of Personality, Intelligence and Age

Variable	Beta	% expl.	Variable	Beta	% expl.
EPI-N	−0.33	10.62	EPI-N	−0.34	11.50
EPI-E	0.02		EPI-E	0.01	
Coins-1	−0.18	3.28	Coins-1	−0.10	1.00
			TIG-1	−0.08	0.69
			Age	−0.02	
Sq. multiple R		0.12	Sq. multiple R		0.14
Multiple R		0.34	Multiple R		0.37

Most of the negative correlations between L and SPS items were from the HE and RE dimensions, that is, high L scores tend to be associated with "the strict upbringing of children," "the censorship in certain journalistic articles," "the religious education in schools," and "the fulfillment of divine laws," and the rejection of statements such as "the freedom of the press in all subjects," "the right to take one's own life," or "sexual intercourse before marriage."

The subscale items were then classified according to content into the following three subgroups: general ideas or beliefs (G), the social aspects (S), and personal (P) aspects, including the family ones. This produced a total of nine subscales:

- REG, pure religious matters.
- RES, family and education religious aspects.
- REP, social religious themes.
- DOG, dogmatic matters about discipline and tough life views.
- DOS, dogmatism related to own personal superiority.
- DOP, corporal punishment and violence.
- HEG, hedonistic ideas about sex and marriage.
- HES, individual liberties and rights in society.
- HEP, peace to enjoy life and personal pleasures.

These attitude scores (nine subscales and three scales) have been correlated with the EPQ–L distortion scale, and the data clearly point out that distortion individuals (L+) significantly adhere themselves to the poles RE+ (0.40), DO+ (0.43), and HE− (−0.47) of the variables. The portrait of these poles is, at least in our Spanish culture, a socially approved image.

The "good image" of the person who answered the SPS attitude scale was of someone who tells us he or she has: assertion of the traditional religion, discipline, strict and self-sufficient mores, austere avoidance of leisures and liberties.

Going further in our analysis, we tried a multiple correlation index using the preceding nine SPS subscales, and Table 7.11 shows the beta weights, and the bivariate "r" correlations of each subscale with distortion.

Data of Table 7.11 shows that a 27% of the L total variance may be explained by six attitude subscales: all the three hedonistic ones, two dogmatic attitudes (general ideas and social aspects), and the social religious themes (REP). The portrait of the L+ person is again of someone trying to show a good image when relating with others (the social aspects of attitudes).

However, the reader must remember that SPS standardization data was obtained in a volunteer and anonymous setting, without a utilitarian context; so the question arises, why should dissimulation occur? Probably, what happens in our culture is that we groom our hair or wear a tie not only to please others but also to please ourselves (or to adjust ourselves to our inner ideal); we like

TABLE 7.11
L Multiple Regression of Attitudes

Subscale	Beta	% explained	r with L
HES	−0.14	6.30	−0.45
DOS	0.10	4.00	0.40
HEG	−0.11	4.73	−0.43
DOG	0.10	4.10	0.41
REP	0.12	4.56	0.38
HEP	−0.09	3.06	−0.34
Sq. multiple R = 0.27		Multiple R = 0.52	

to hide our "defects" (or what society shows to us as defects) even in the intimacy of home.

CONCLUSIONS

From the previous analyses, we may suppose that the distortion construct is an intrinsic characteristic of the candidate in selection processes, not only when answering questionnaire measures but also when being in a personal interview.

The high distortion subject defines himself with the adjectives more socially desirable: punctual, adventurous, emotionally stable, socially precise, warmhearted, responsible, self-assured, relaxed, assertive of the traditional religion, strict, self-sufficient, and austere.

Probably we might accept that this is an intelligent adjustment to the setting, and the subject uses all his capabilities. To run on the point made in the beginning of the chapter, these are praiseworthy aspects in this behavior, at least within human relationships.

The psychologist, who uses questionnaires within his or her selection battery, should bear in mind the aforementioned results and consider distortion measures as an interesting variable in its own right. It seems probable that, in some occasions, he or she may justifiably give the advice to fill the job with a person who knows how "to behave in the actual state of things."

REFERENCES

Buros, O. K. (1970). *Personality tests and reviews*. NJ: Gryphon Press.
Butcher, J. N. (1969). *MMPI: Research developments and clinical applications*. NJ: Gryphon Press.
Cattell, R. B., Eber, H. W., & Tatsuoka, M. M. (1970). *Handbook for the Sixteen Personality Factor Questionnaire (16PF)*. Champaign, IL: IPAT (Institute for Personality and Ability Testing).
Crowne, D., & Marlow, D. (1964). *The approval motive*. New York: Wiley.
Dahlstrom, W. G., & Welsh, G. S. (1960). *An MMPI handbook: A guide to use in clinical practice and research*. Minneapolis: University of Minnesota Press.

Dicken, C. F. (1959). Simulated patterns on the Edwards Personal Preference Schedule. *Journal of Applied Psychology, 43*, 373–378.

Edwards, A. L. (1970). *The measurement of personality traits by scales and inventories*. New York: Holt Rinehart & Winston.

Ellis, A. (1946). The validity of personality questionnaires. *Psychological Bulletin, 43*, 385–440.

Eysenck, H. J., & Eysenck, S. B. G. (1978). *EPQ A/J Cuestionario de personalidad para niños y adultos* [Technical Manual, 1st ed.]. Madrid: TEA Ediciones S.A.

Eysenck, H. J., & Eysenck, S. B. G. (1986). *EPQ A/J, Cuestionario de personalidad para niños y adultos* [Technical Manual, 4th ed.]. Madrid: TEA Ediciones S.A.

Eysenck, S. B. G., & Eysenck, H. J. (1963). On the dual nature of extroversion. *British Journal of Social & Clinical Psychology,*, 46–55.

Giorgi, B., & Seisdedos, N. (1982). *SPS, Escala Psicosocial Española* [Technical Manual]. Madrid: TEA Ediciones S.A.

Gough, H. G. (1950). The F minus K dissimulation index for the MMPI. *Journal of Consulting Psychology, 14*, 408–413.

Hartshorne, H., & May, M. A. (1928). *Studies in deceit*. New York: MacMillan.

Karson, S., & O'Dell, J. W. (1980). *A guide to the clinical use of the 16 PF*. Madrid: TEA Ediciones, S.A.

Krug, S. E. (1987). *Clinical analysis questionnaire* [Technical Manual, Spanish adaptation]. Madrid: TEA Ediciones S.A.

Luengo Martin, M. A. (1986). The extroversion dimension of the EPI: A comparative study. *Revista Psicologia General y Aplicada, 41*, 463–486.

Meredith, G. M. (1968). Stereotypic desirability profiles for the 16PF questionnaire. *Psychological Reports*, 1173–1174.

Seisdedos, N. (1979). Personality, adaptation, intelligence, and environment. *Revista Psicologia General y Aplicada*, 650–659.

Seisdedos, N. (1981). *16PF, Technical handbook*. Madrid: TEA Ediciones S.A.

Seisdedos, N. (1986). MMPI, Technical supplement [2nd ed.]. Madrid: TEA Ediciones, S.A.

Seisdedos, N. (1988). Studies of the 'Lie' scale in Spanish Adolescents. In D. H. Saklofske & S. B. G. Eysenck (Eds.), *Individual differences in children and adolescents, international perspectives* (Chapter 18, pp. 209–227). London & Toronto: Hodder & Stoughton.

Wiggins, J. S. (1959). Intercorrelationships among MMPI measures of dissimulation under standard and social desirability instructions. *Journal of Consulting Psychology, 23*, 419–427.

Effects of Assessment Center Participation on Self-Esteem and on Evaluation of the Selection Situation

Heinz Schuler
Universität Hohenheim, Stuttgart

Rüdiger Fruhner
Hamburger Sparkasse

The usefulness of assessment centers for personnel selection and development is well documented (e.g., Thornton, Gaugler, Rosenthal, & Bentson, 1987). But, past research primarily has examined methodological aspects like predictive and construct validity (Sackett & Dreher, 1982; Schmitt, Gooding, Noe, & Kirsch, 1984). However, the social components of the selection situation require as much emphasis as the methodological aspects. For instance, Schuler and Stehle (1983) compared psychological test methods and assessment centers with respect to "social validity" (cf. Schuler, chapter 1, this volume). The comparison showed that the assessment center is superior to psychological test methods with respect to the information, participation, transparency, and feedback these methods offer to the participants. If it is assumed that assessment centers and tests (especially ability tests) possess an approximately comparable predictive validity (Schuler & Funke, 1989), the assessment center receives applicants' greater acceptance because of its higher "social validity" (Bourgeois, Leim, Slivinski, & Grant, 1975; Dodd, 1977; Noe & Steffy, 1987).

Applicants' rejections of job offers can reduce the financial gain of selection methods (Murphy, 1986). At the same time, assessment situations serve as preview for the organization (Premack & Wanous, 1985; Robertson & Smith, 1989). Selection instruments can therefore be deliberately used as instruments of personnel marketing. The use of certain selection methods (e.g., personality tests, ability tests, interviews, or assessment centers) arouses applicants' presumptions concerning the company's culture.

Of course, the selection method is not only important in forming judgments about the organization. It may also influence the applicant's achievement in the test situation, and it may influence the individual's self-perception. Years ago, effects of the assessment center on the participants (e.g., MacKinnon, 1975) were already documented. MacKinnon especially emphasized the effects of the feedback after a developmental assessment center on the participants and called the detrimental effect of a rejection for an employee's job career a "kiss of death." Also Moses (1985) emphasized the efficiency of feedback and claimed careful dealing with participants during the conversation: "For many of these managers the feedback session is long remembered as a key life event in his or her career" (p. 189). The importance of the feedback session also is supported by the study of Bourgeois et al. (1975). In particular, demand-related tasks in the assessment center allow participants to become aware of their own potential. This will not only be apparent to the participants during the feedback session but also in the course of the assessment center where there is the possibility of social comparison (i.e., comparing one's own behavior and performance with that of other participants).

How do applicants experience a selection situation and what happens to them during this situation? From a variety of studies we know that certain methods are preferred and others are rejected. Cascio and Phillips (1979) emphasized applicants' high acceptance of "performance tests" compared with "paper-and-pencil tests." A review on positive reactions of applicants with "work sample tests" was given by Robertson and Kandola (1982). From our own investigation (Fruhner & Schuler, 1988), we know that in particular interviews work samples and internships are evaluated positively by applicants, whereas personality tests are judged rather critically. As the assessment center consists of a combination of different types of tasks (work samples, interviews, tests; Schuler & Stehle, 1987; Thornton & Byham, 1982), the question arises of how these different tasks in the assessment center are experienced by the participants.

But the acceptance of the assessment center is not only a relevant "dependent variable," but also it has an impact on the self-concept of the participants, or on their judgment of their own abilities. As already explained, the assessment center is considered to be an instrument that potentially gives realistic information concerning one's own abilities. But what happens if one's own expectancies (i.e., the wish for a job or of promotion) are not met because of poor assessment center performance? How does an applicant react to such a rejection? Does he or she thereby receive the "kiss of death"? A negative assessment center result presumably has consequences on self-perceptions of abilities, and repeated failure could lead to a changed self-evaluation (self-concept). As an example, Schmitt, Ford, and Stults (1986) found that assessment center participants showed significant changes in the perception of their own abilities after an assessment center. Bourgeois et al. (1975) reported on changes in individual career planning as a result of assessment center participation. By social comparison and by the final feedback, the applicants gain new information on their own performance and potential. So if an assessment center intends to assess management potential, by negative feedback or by a negative result of the comparison process, the applicant is indirectly shown that he or she is not suited for a management position. This information has possible consequences for the appraisal of one's own abilities and can effect changes in the self-concept. This consideration leads to two questions that shall be investigated empirically: (a) Do participants of an assessment center experience changes in their self-concept?; (b) How are the single tasks appraised by assessment center participants? Do their appraisals differentiate among single tasks? In order to examine these questions empirically, a number of experimental assessment centers were conducted.

METHOD

Participants and Assessors

Participants were 96 students of economics and business administration in their final semesters. Their average age was 24 years. The experimental groups included 48 persons (30 males and 18 females), as well as the control groups (30 males and 18 females). Assessors were senior personnel clerks of various banks and organizational psychologists. The assessors were trained for their task beforehand.

Experimental Design

Self-concept was measured at four different points of time—before the assessment center, after the first day, after all exercises and tests were run (second day), and after the feedback session. For the control of reactivity effects, the design shown in Table 8.1 was applied. The single assessment center exercises were evaluated by the participants immediately after their accomplishment.

Measurement Instruments

Self-concept. The self-concept questionnaire consisted of two parts. The first part was the German translation of the "Self-Description Questionnaire" (SDQ–III) of Marsh and O'Neill (1984), which is closely related to the concepts of Shavelson, Hubner, and Stanton (1976) and Shavelson and Bolus (1982). This instrument is conceived to measure hierarchically organized components of the self, changeable situation-specific concepts representing the basis, and more stable concepts representing higher levels. This stands in close relationship to

TABLE 8.1
Experimental Design

	Before ac Starts		1st Day	End of 1st Day		2nd Day		End of ac		Feedback		After Feed- back
A:	m1	-----	t	-----	m2	-----	t	-----	m3	-----	t	-----	m4
B:	m1	-----	t	-----		-----	t	-----		-----	t	-----	m4
C:	m1				m2				m3				m4
D:													m4

Note: m1–m4: points of measurement; t: treatment.
A: experimental group, N = 24
B: experimental group, N = 24
C: control group, N = 24
D: control group, N = 24
                        ——————
                         N = 96

the self-concept model of Epstein (1979). On top of this hierarchy stands the "general self," operationalized as general self-esteem. Apart from this there are 12 scales to measure hierarchically lower ordered aspects of the self.

Out of this questionnaire, the following seven scales were used:

- general self-esteem
- emotional self-concept
- academic self-concept
    mathematical self-concept
    verbal self-concept
    creativity and problem solving
- social self-concept
    relations to same-sex peers
    relations to other-sex peers

Eight-point scales were used, high scores indicating positive values.

In the second part, self-referring cognitions were measured at the state level (state self-concept; Schwarzer, Jerusalem, & Quast, 1986). Also, participants were asked for their intelligence self-ratings (Schwarzer et al., 1985). These scales use 4-point ratings. In addition, subjects were asked to rate their probability to reach a leading position (100% = most probable), in how many years this leading position will be reached, how high initial salary will be, and how high salary will be after 5 years of job experience.

As shown in Table 8.1, the self-concept questionnaire was answered by the Experimental Group A and the Control Group C at four times of measurement, Experimental Group B only answered it before the assessment center and after the feedback, and Control Group D only at Time 4. In order to demonstrate to the participants that this questionnaire was not a component of the appraisal process in the assessment center, the questionnaire was marked by colors and distributed by a "neutral" co-worker who also was the ombudsman but beside that was not involved in the assessment center process.

Evaluation of the Exercises and Tasks. For the appraisal of the tasks and tests, a questionnaire that was used before by Fruhner and Schuler (1988) was adapted for this investigation.

The following questions were asked:

- How do you feel in this moment? (FEELING)
- How do you evaluate this exercise–task? (EVALUATION)
- In your opinion, how did you come out in this exercise–task? (RESULT)
- Did you have any influence on the result? (INFLUENCE)
- Were your abilities fairly measured? (ABILITY)

This was a 5-point scale, with low scores signifying positive appraisal.

Additionally, each exercise was rated on a 20-item semantic differential (7 points). Again, low scores indicated positive appraisals. This questionnaire also was marked by colors to show that these statements were excluded from the assessment center appraisal.

Assessment Center Process

The method was a typical assessment center for trainee selection lasting 2 days and including the following exercises and tests. These exercises can be classified in four groups:

1. typical assessment center-exercises (Thornton & Byham, 1982)
    - structured group discussion
    - unstructured group discussion
    - in-basket
    - role playing "performance feedback"
    - presentation
    - time management task
2. Interview
    - structured multimodal interview
3. Intelligence test
    - WILDE-intelligence test (WIT; Jäger & Althoff, 1983)
4. Personality tests
    - FSK (social competence; Schuler & Funke, undated)

- IPC (locus of control; Krampen, 1981)
- LMT (achievement motivation; Hermans, Petermann, & Zielinski, 1978)
- CPI (management scales only; Gough & Weinert, in preparation)

After the assessment center the assessors discussed and aggregated their appraisals for each person. Afterwards, the feedback sessions were held.

RESULTS

In the first part, self-concept data are presented, followed by the results of the exercise appraisals. Statistical analyses were done by t-tests, analyses of variance, and single comparisons with the Scheffé test.

Self-Concept

There were no significant differences between the experimental and the control group for the first point of measurement (m1).

Differences Between m1 and m4. In a first step we compared the results of the experimental group (A + B) and the control group (C) for the points of measurement m1 and m4. Table 8.2 shows the self-concept measurements for these two points.

Notice in Table 8.2 that the experimental groups (A + B) showed significant increases for "emotional self-concept" ($t = 3.9$; $p < .01$) and "perceived intelligence" ($t = 2.24$; $p < .05$). For the control group (C) two scales were increasing: "general self-concept" ($t = 2.67$; $p < .05$) and "emotional self-concept" ($t = 5.10$; $p < .01$), which are effects of the instrument. All other scales did not show any significant differences.

Differences Between the Four Points of Measurement. As a next step we compared the trend of the four different points of measurement for the experimental group (A) and the control group (C).

With this presentation of results for reasons of visibility, scales "PROB," "YEARS," "SALARY1," and "SALARY2" are omitted as they did not show any differences. In the experimental group (A) there were no significant differences concerning the "general self-concept." The "emotional self-concept" showed a continuous increase from one measurement point to the next ($\Delta_{crit} = .31$; $p < .01$). The scales of the academic self-concept for "mathematical self-concept" between m1 and m4 showed no significant differences ($t = .63$; $p < .60$) but the trend of the whole measurement is very interesting. The scores

TABLE 8.2
Differences in Self-Concepts Between Measurement 1 and Measurement 4
(Paired t-Tests for Repeated Measurements)

Measurement Point:	Experimental Group (A + B) (N = 48) m1–m4	Control Group (C) (N = 24) m1–m4
*general self-concept	6.6–6.8	6.3–6.6**
*emotional self-concept	5.7–6.0***	5.6–6.1***
*academic self-concept		
mathematics	5.4–5.4	5.5–5.4
verbal	5.9–5.9	5.6–5.8
problem solving/creativity	5.4–5.4	5.4–5.4
*social self-concept		
relations to same-sex peers	6.0–6.2	6.0–6.1
relations to opposite-sex peers	6.2–6.2	6.0–6.0
*perceived intelligence	3.3–3.5**	3.3–3.3
*state self-concept	3.4–3.5	3.4–3.4
probability of reaching a leader position (%)	75.0–73.4	62.0–62.5
years to reach a leading position	5.6–5.6	6.9–6.4
first salary (DM/year)	49610–49660	49437–51208
salary after 5 years (DM/year)	77484–77100	71812–73000

$**p < .05; ***p < .01.$

decreased from m1 to m3 and increased after the feedback (m4) ($\Delta_{crit} = .34$; $p < .05$). The "verbal self-concept" remained constant. Within the scale "problem solving–creativity," first there also was a decrease (m1 to m2) ($\Delta_{crit} = .31$: $p < .10$) and then a slow increase to m4. Within the social self-concept, only the scale "relation to same-sex peers" showed a significant effect. The scores between m1 and m3 were constant and increased from m3 to m4 after the feedback ($\Delta_{crit} = .24$; $p < .10$).

Both scales "perceived intelligence" ($\Delta_{crit} = .22$; $p < .05$) and "state self-concept" ($\Delta_{crit} = .20$; $p < .05$) showed a significant increase between m2 and m4. All the other scales were constant between the four points of measurement.

Control group (C) showed a continuous increase of the "general self-concept" between m1 to m4, but only the differences between m1 and the other three points of measurement (m2, m3, m4) were significant ($\Delta_{crit} = .27$; $p < .05$). When exactly analyzed, the significant difference of "emotional self-concept" scores between m1 and m4 is reduced to an increase from m1 to m2 ($\Delta_{crit} = .31$; $p < .01$); from m2 to m4 the scores remained constant. All the other scales of the control group did not show any significant differences. Figure 8.1 demonstrates the changes in self-concept between the four points of measurement.

TABLE 8.3
Differences Between Points of Measurement for the Experimental
Group A (*N* = 24) and the Control Group C (*N* = 24)

	m1	m2	m3	m4	Sign. Diff.	
*general self-concept						
exp. group A	6.8	6.8	6.8	7.0		
contr. group C	6.3	6.5	6.6	6.6	1 2 3 4	**
					‾‾‾	**
					‾‾‾‾‾	**
*emotional self-concept						***
					‾‾‾	***
					‾‾‾‾‾	***
exp. group A	5.8	5.9	6.1	6.3	1 2 3 4	
contr. group C	5.6	6.0	6.0	6.1	1 2 3 4	***
					‾‾‾	***
					‾‾‾‾‾	***
*academic self-concept						
mathematics					‾‾‾	*
					‾‾‾‾‾	**
					‾‾‾	**
exp. group A	5.3	4.9	4.9	5.2	1 2 3 4	
contr. group C	5.5	5.4	5.4	5.4		
verbal						
exp. group A	6.0	5.8	5.9	6.0		
contr. group C	5.6	5.7	5.8	5.8		
problem solving/creativity					‾‾‾	*
					‾‾‾‾‾	*
exp. group A	5.7	5.4	5.5	5.7	1 2 4	
contr. group C	5.4	5.4	5.5	5.4		
*social self-concept						
relation to same-sex peers					‾‾‾‾‾	*
exp. group A	6.1	6.1	6.1	6.3	1 4	
contr. group C	6.0	6.0	6.1	6.1		
relations to opposite-sex peers						
exp. group A	6.3	6.2	6.4	6.3		
contr. group C	6.0	6.0	6.0	6.0		
*perceived intelligence					‾‾‾	**
exp. group A	3.4	3.2	3.3	3.5	2 4	
contr. group C	3.3	3.3	3.3	3.3		
*state self-concept					‾‾‾	**
exp. group A	3.4	3.4	3.5	3.6	2 4	
control group C	3.4	3.4	3.4	3.4		

*$p < .10$; **$p < .05$; ***$p < .01$.

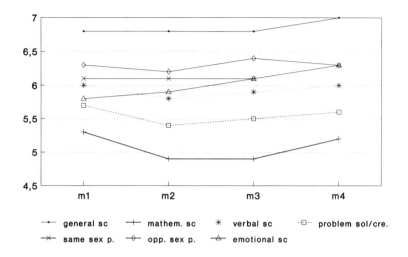

(1= very low ... 8 = very high)

FIG. 8.1. Self concept scores at different points of measurement for the experimental group A.

Evaluation of Exercises

As described before, all exercises and tests were grouped into four types of tasks: exercises (group discussions, in-basket, presentation, role playing, and "time management"); interview; intelligence test (WIT); personality tests (LMT, CPI, IPC, FSK).

Figure 8.2 shows the different evaluation of these four types of exercises–tests (tasks) for Questions 1 to 5 and the semantic differential. On the basis of their means, the appraisals in the semantic differential were summarized into three scales. These scales are called *general appraisal, stress,* and *transparency* (compare Fruhner, Schuler, Funke, & Moser, 1991).

If we first look at the results of Questions 1 to 5, it is striking that the typical AC-exercises and the interview in all questions are similarly evaluated, whereas the two types of psychological tests (personality tests and intelligence test) are seen more differently. When comparing the exercises and the interview, no difference was statistically significant.

Compared to the intelligence test, the personality tests are evaluated more negatively (Δ_{crit} = 0.43; p < .01), the applicant's possibility of influencing them is seen to be lower (Δ_{crit} = 0.54; p < .01), and own abilities came into play "only to a small extent" (Δ_{crit} = 0.49; p < .01). After the intelligence test, however, participants felt worse than after the personality tests (Δ_{crit} = 0.35; p < .01) and also, one's own performance is given a lower evaluation than with

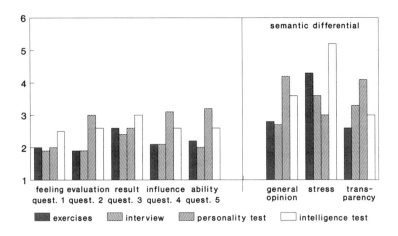

(1 = very good ... 5 = very bad; for the
semantic differential: 7 = very bad)

FIG. 8.2. Evaluations of exercises, interview, personality tests, and intelligence
test.

personality tests ($\Delta_{crit} = 0.35$; $p < .01$). In the semantic differential, the appraisal results in a general "similar opinion" to that expressed in Question 2 (evaluation). As expected, the personality tests received the most negative evaluation, followed by the intelligence test. The interview and the exercises were liked best. The scale "stress" gives an obvious ranking: The intelligence test was experienced as the most exhausting, followed by the exercises, then by the interview; the personality tests are rated as least stressful ($\Delta_{crit} = .64$; $p < .01$). The exercises, the interview, and the intelligence test were experienced as the most transparent instruments. Differences among them were not significant. In contrast, personality tests were experienced as very opaque ($\Delta_{crit} = .69$; $p < .05$). It can be said that the transparency is at its lowest with personality tests and at its highest with typical exercises. The subjective experience of stress was the strongest with the intelligence test and the smallest with personality tests. However, personality tests are evaluated the most negatively.

Table 8.4 shows the correlation between "evaluation" (Question 2) and the other items measuring individual reactions to the tasks (i.e., "feeling," Question 1, "result," Question 3, "influence," Question 4, and "ability," Question 5), as well as the three scales of the semantic differential for the four types of tasks. With the Questions 1 to 5 we find homogeneously high correlations for the interview, somewhat lower but still relatively homogeneous correlations for the exercises and the intelligence test, and very heterogeneous correlations for the personality tests. "Feeling" (Question 1) and "influence" (Question 4) are practically uncorrelated with the evaluation of personality tests. For the semantic differential, the correlations between "evaluation" and "general

TABLE 8.4
Correlations Between Task Evaluation (Question 2) and the Other Questions
and the Semantic Differential

| | Tasks-Evaluation (Question 2) | | | |
	Exercises	Interview	Personality Tests	Intelligence Test
question 1 (FEELING)	.56	.48	.01	.30
question 3 (RESULT)	.39	.70	.36	.36
question 4 (INFLUENCE)	.42	.50	−.11	.36
question 5 (ABILITY)	.35	.67	.52	.39
semantic differential				
general opinion	.67	.75	.76	.57
stress	.37	.59	.47	.21
transparency	.36	.71	.26	.32

Note: for $r > .29$, $p < .05$ (2-tailed).

opinion" are especially high. With interview, we again find relatively homogeneous and high correlations among all aspects, and for the exercises moderately high ones. The correlations between the general evaluation of personality tests and transparency ($r = .26$), as well as between the evaluation of the intelligence tests and stress ($r = .21$), are not significant.

DISCUSSION

The hierarchical model of self-concept postulates changes only at the lowest levels (Shavelson & Bolus, 1982; Shavelson et al., 1976; Shavelson & Marsh, 1986). Contrary to these assumptions, we found changes in the "general self-concept" for the control group. The four measurement points show an increase that is significant between m1 and m4. As no experimental treatment was applied to the control group, we can interpret this increase as an effect of the repeated measurements (reactivity). For the control group another change in the self-concept occurred on the "emotional" scale. This is a component localized at a lower hierarchical position than the "general self-concept." There is again a significant increase between m1 and m2. From m2 to m4 the mean score remained constant. Possibly, the increase can be interpreted as an effect of the different time of day. The first measurement took place in the morning, with the others in the afternoon or in the evening. If this reflects a general dependency of the emotional self-concept from the time of measurement, however, it is surprising that we did not find this increase within the experimental group A. Perhaps, there are other effects that concealed the increase of the "emotional self-concept" scale. Additionally, there was no change in "general self-concept" within the experimental group A.

However, some other aspects of the self-concept changed in reaction to the assessment center and the feedback. This was especially true for two scales of the "academic self-concept": "Mathematical" and "problem solving–creativity" decreased after the first point of measurement and increased after the feedback to the same level as m1. The scores of the scale "relations with same-sex peers" remained constant until m3 and increased after the feedback. A similar but not statistically significant trend emerged for the "verbal self-concept." In addition, "perceived intelligence" and "state self-concept" decreased after the first measurement and increased after the feedback, but only the differences between m2 and m4 were significant.

How can we explain such changes? Before the assessment center started, all participants evaluated their own abilities based on their previous experiences and their own performance appraisal (perhaps wishful thinking) (m1). This is the baseline. After the next measurement (after the first day of the assessment center), all participants took part in an intelligence test, an unstructured group discussion, an in-basket exercise, a presentation, and an interview. By then, they could compare their actual performances with their abilities evaluated by themselves, and also they could compare themselves directly with peers. Because of the perceived differences between self-evaluated abilities and the actual performances, parts of the self-concept decreased.

After the assessment center (m3) all participants could validate and if necessary revise their evaluations. Especially, two scales of the "academic self-concept" decreased. These abilities are measured very well by the assessment center. After the feedback (m4), which was positive for the majority of the assessees, these components of the self-concept were evaluated as more positive, and we observed an increase to the values of m1 again. So, by comparing m1 and m4 directly, there are no differences between these two measurements.

Comparing the two scales of the social self-concept, they showed a different trend between the four points of measurement. "Relations with same-sex peers" remained constant between m1 to m3 and increased after the feedback, whereas "relations with opposite-sex peers" showed no significant changes between the four measurements. Conceiving the assessment center as a competitive situation, the participants may have perceived especially the same-sex peers as competitors. This way, there is no change in their relationships during the assessment process. Then, at the feedback, the participants received information about their behavior toward their peers, and they reevaluated the competitive situation and thereby the relationships with the same-sex peers.

In contrast to this, attitudes toward opposite-sex peers could be characterized by greater role ambiguity, having the consequence that competition becomes less dominant. If it is true that the competition role becomes more salient in relation to same-sex peers than to persons of the opposite gender, then earlier experience with opposite-sex peers should determine the "relation to opposite-sex peers'' scores and result in higher stability of these scores during the assessment center.

The changes of the "emotional self-concept" are identical for the experimental and the control group. Thus, it cannot be ruled out that the observed improvements were basically an effect of the repeated measurements.

The scale "perceived intelligence" showed trends comparable to the scales of the "academic self-concept." We propose the same explanations. Self-description on the scale "state self-concept" is increasing from measurement to measurement. Perhaps this can be interpreted as a general description of what is going on in an assessment center. At the beginning (m1), participants had a skeptical attitude toward the assessment center that gradually decreased. After the feedback, self-concept had increased and attitudes toward this selection instrument were very positive. All the other questions ("probability of occupational success" to "salary after 5 years") showed no significant changes between the measurements. This could indicate that the respective aspects of the self-concept were sufficiently stable not to be influenced by the assessment center. However, this result could also be interpreted in a way that the expectations concerning future occupational success and income are relatively independent of present self-knowledge and instead are more influenced by average occupational chances.

Thus, the results of this study have shown specific changes in the self-concept of assessment center participants. These changes were of rather low magnitude, but viewing them graphically (Fig. 8.2), the same curvilinear shape can be recognized for all single aspects. Most markedly, the changes referred to the dimensions "mathematical self-concept," "creativity and problem solving," and "perceived intelligence," all of which are dimensions that are measured by the assessment center. In the light of these results, the usual confidence in positive reactions of participants can be modified: Essential for a positive reaction is a competent and considerate feedback procedure, as this seems to be the source of well-being after an assessment center. During the continuing assessment process, there are also times of doubts and lowered self-esteem.

Concerning the evaluation of the tasks, it is striking that the exercises and the interview are evaluated similarly with respect to Questions 1 to 5. These two types of tasks belong to the most preferred selection instruments both by assessees and organizations. The reason may be that, apart from obvious phenomenological differences, the main parameters of social validity are similar for these two selection tools and lead to positive evaluations: Participants have the impression that they can influence the situation, that their abilities can be measured, that they received good results based on present goal-oriented behavior. Finally they end up with positive well-being. Thus, only two dimensions of the semantic differential differentiated between the tasks. The assessment exercises are more stressful, but they are also more transparent than the interview. Contrary to this, the personality tests are less stressful, but they are also less transparent and less positively evaluated. Comparing the intelligence and personality tests, the intelligence test is the most stressful (more than exercises), but it is also as transparent as the exercises. The personality tests are not very transparent, yet the applicants' well-being is the same after the personality tests as after the interview or after the exercises. The concept of "social validity" assumes that transparency is one decisive variable for the acceptance of a selection instrument. Independent of a stressful task, selection instruments with high transparency are evaluated more positively than opaque instruments.

When computing multiple regression with the items of the semantic differential as predictors and the evaluation of the tasks (Question 2) as criteria, the exercises are described by the items "agreeable," "useful," "considerate," and "fair." The interview is described by the items "delightful" and "pleasant." The intelligence test is described as "positive" and "useful," whereas only the item "positive" seems to be characteristic for the personality tests. Moreover, all tasks except the personality tests are described by emotional or relevant (substantial) items.

These results support the impression that positive assessment center evaluations are primarily due to positive qualities of typical assessment center exercises, whereas the inclusion of tests may be a handicap from the perspective of social validity. The addition of a structured interview, on the other hand, should not diminish the social qualities of this multiple procedure, as interviews are experienced in a similar manner as typical assessment center exercises.

REFERENCES

Bourgeois, R. P., Leim, M. A., Slivinski, L. W., & Grant, K. W. (1975). Evaluation of an assessment centre in terms of acceptability. *Canadian Personnel and Industrial Relations Journal, 22,* 17–20.

Cascio, W. F., & Phillips, N. F. (1979). Performance testing: A rose among thorns? *Personnel Psychology, 32,* 751–766.

Dodd, W. E. (1977). Attitudes toward assessment center programs. In J. L. Moses & W. C. Byham (Eds.), *Applying the assessment center method* (pp. 161–183). New York: Pergamon Press.

Epstein, S. (1979). Entwurf einer integrativen Persönlichkeitstheorie [Outline of an integrative personality theory]. In S. H. Filipp (Ed.), *Selbstkonzeptforschung* (pp. 15–46). Stuttgart: Klett-Cotta.

Fruhner, R., & Schuler, H. (1988). Bewertung eignungsdiagnostischer Verfahren zur Personalauswahl durch potentielle Stellenbewerber [Evaluation of selection methods by potential applicants]. In G. Romkopf, W. D. Fröhlich, & I. Lindner (Eds.), *Forschung und Praxis im Dialog* (pp. 107–111). Bonn: Deutscher Psychologen Verlag.

Fruhner, R., Schuler, H., Funke, U., & Moser, K. (1991). Einige Determinanten der Bewertung von Personalauswahlverfahren [Some determinants of the evaluation of selection methods]. *Zeitschrift für Arbeits- und Organisationspsychologie, 35,* 170–178.

Gough, H. G., & Weinert, A. B. (in prep.). *Deutscher CPI* [German CPI]. Bern: Huber.

Hermans, H., Petermann, F., & Zielinski, W. (1978). *Leistungs Motivations Test (LMT)* [Achievement Motivation Test]. Amsterdam: Swets en Zeitlinger.

Jäger, A. O., & Althoff, K. (1983). *Der WILDE-Intelligenz-Test (WIT)* [WILDE Intelligence Test]. Göttingen: Hogrefe.

Krampen, G. (1981). *IPC-Fragebogen zur Kontrollüberzeugung* [Locus of control inventory]. Göttingen: Hogrefe.

MacKinnon, D. W. (1975). *An overview of assessment centers* (No. 1). Greensboro, NC: Center for Creative Leadership.

Marsh, H. W., & O'Neill, R. (1984). Self-description questionnaire III: The construct validity of multidimensional self-construct ratings by late adolescents. *Journal of Educational Measurement, 21,* 153–174.

Moses, J. L. (1985). Using clinical methods in a high-level management assessment center. In H. J. Bernardin & D. A. Bownas (Eds.), *Personality assessment in organisations* (pp. 177–192). New York: Praeger.

Murphy, K. A. (1986). When your top choice turns you down: Effect of rejected job offers on the utility of selection tests. *Psychological Bulletin, 99,* 133–138.

Noe, R. A., & Steffy, B. D. (1987). The influence of individual characteristics and assessment center evaluation on career exploration behavior and job involvement. *Journal of Vocational Behavior, 30,* 187–202.

Premack, S. L., & Wanous, J. P. (1985). A meta-analysis of realistic job preview experiments. *Journal of Applied Psychology, 70,* 706–719.

Robertson, I. T., & Kandola, R. S. (1982). Work sample tests: Validity, adverse impact and applicant reaction. *Journal of Occupational Psychology, 55,* 171–183.

Robertson, I. T., & Smith, M. (1989). Personnel selection methods. In M. Smith & I. T. Robertson (Eds.), *Advances in selection and assessment* (pp. 89–112). New York: Wiley.

Sackett, P. R., & Dreher, G. F. (1982). Constructs and assessment center dimensions: Some troubling empirical findings. *Journal of Applied Psychology, 67,* 401–410.

Schmitt, N., Ford, J. K., & Stults, D. M. (1986). Changes in self-perceived ability as a function of performance in an assessment centre. *Journal of Occupational Psychology, 59,* 327–335.

Schmitt, N., Gooding, R. Z., Noe, R. A., & Kirsch, M. (1984). Metaanalyses of validity studies published between 1964 and 1982 and the investigation of study characteristics. *Personnel Psychology, 37,* 407–422.

Schuler, H. (1989). Construct validity of a multimodal employment interview. In B. J. Fallon, H. P. Pfister, & J. Brebner (Eds.), *Advances in industrial organizational psychology* (pp. 343–354). North-Holland: Elsevier.

Schuler, H., & Funke, U. (1989). Berufseignungsdiagnostik [Personnel Selection]. In E. Roth (Ed.), *Organisationspsychologie. Enzyklopädie der Psychologie D/III/3* (pp. 281–320). Göttingen: Hogrefe.

Schuler, H., & Funke, H. (undated). *Fragebogen zur Messung sozialer Kompetenz* (FSK) [Social Competence Questionnaire]. Stuttgart: Universität Hohenheim.

Schuler, H., & Stehle, W. (1983). Neuere Entwicklungen des Assessment-Center-Ansatzes—beurteilt unter dem Aspekt der sozialen Validität [Recent developments in assessment centers—evaluated under the aspect of social validity]. *Zeitschrift für Arbeits- und Organisationspsychologie, 27,* 33–44.

Schuler, H., & Stehle, W. (Eds.). (1987). *Assessment center als methode der personalentwicklung* [Assessment center as an instrument of personnel development]. Göttingen: Verlag für Angewandte Psychologie/Hogrefe.

Schwarzer, R., Jerusalem, M., & Quast, H. H. (1986). Selbstkonzept als Zustand (SKZ) [Self-concept as a state]. In R. Schwarzer (Ed.), *Skalen zur befindlichkeit und persönlichkeit.* Freie Universität Berlin: Institut für Psychologie, Pädagogische Psychologie.

Shavelson, R. J., & Bolus, R. (1982). Self-concept: The interplay of theory and methods. *Journal of Educational Psychology, 74,* 3–17.

Shavelson, R. J., Hubner, J. J., & Stanton, G. C. (1976). Self-concept: Validation of construct interpretations. *Review of Educational Research, 46,* 407–441.

Shavelson, R. J., & Marsh, H. W. (1986). On the structure of self-concept. In R. Schwarzer (Ed.), *Self-related cognitions in anxiety and motivation* (pp. 305–330). Hillsdale, NJ: Lawrence Erlbaum Associates.

Thornton, G. C., & Byham, W. C. (1982). *Assessment centers and managerial performance.* New York: Academic Press.

Thornton, G. C., Gaugler, B. B., Rosenthal, D. B., & Bentson, C. (1987). Die prädiktive Validität des Assessment Centers—eine Metaanalyse [Predictive validity of assessment centers—a meta-analysis]. In H. Schuler & W. Stehle (Eds.), *Assessment center als methode der personalentwicklung.* Göttingen: Verlag für Angewandte Psychologie/Hogrefe.

9

Newcomer Orientation Programs That Facilitate Organizational Entry

John P. Wanous
The Ohio State University

The entry of new employees into organizations has been described as a dual-matching process between the individual and the organization (Wanous, 1980, 1992). One match-up concerns the individual's abilities–capabilities with the organization's job requirements. The primary consequence of this match-up is on job performance. A second match-up concerns the individual's needs–specific job wants with the organizational climates–culture. The primary consequence of this latter match-up is on employee retention-related attitudes such as job satisfaction and organizational commitment, and, ultimately, on retention itself. Recent research supports this model (Vandenberg & Scarpello, 1990).

In addition to being seen as a dual-matching process, organizational entry has been characterized as being fraught with conflicts between individuals and organizations (Porter, Lawler, & Hackman, 1975). The conflicts occur because the objectives of individuals and organizations in trying to attract and select each other are typically in opposition to one another. For example, organizations who try to maximize the number of qualified job candidates (for selection) may present positively biased information to job candidates (for their attraction), and vice versa for the candidates themselves. These "best foot forward" biases can lead to poor match-ups.

The preceding two views of the organizational entry process suggest that most staffing techniques can be classified in the 2 × 2 matrix shown in Fig. 9.1; that is, any particular technique for recruitment–selection–socialization can be categorized as primarily being used to achieve one or the other of the two

125

	Type of Individual-Organizational Match-up	
Effect on Individual-Organizational Conflict	Individual Abilities to Organizational Requirements	Individual Job Wants to Organizational Climates
Maintains Conflict	1 Testing	2 Work History, Biodata
Avoids Conflict	3 Assessment Center (Orientation Programs)	4 Realistic Job Previews (Orientation Programs)

FIG. 9.1. Staffing techniques that match individuals and organizations.

match-ups, and whether it maintains or tries to avoid the conflicts between individual and organization.

Figure 9.1 shows a representative example of each of the four cells defined by the two dimensions. Cell 1 may be best represented by traditional psychological testing for general–specific abilities and could also include drug–honesty testing as current examples. Cell 2 shows some traditional ways that organizations have gathered data on job candidates about their propensity to quit (i.e., examining work history and/or certain biodata factors related to retention). The assessment center method for selection is placed in Cell 3 because some of them have sufficiently realistic simulations of job situations as to be helpful in a candidate's decision to accept a job offer. Finally, Cell 4 contains the realistic job preview (RJP) as an example of a recruitment technique that avoids individual versus organizational conflicts and facilitates newcomer retention.

It is argued in this chapter that formal newcomer orientation programs have the potential to facilitate both match-ups and also avoid the conflict between individual and organization. Although this may seem to be a lofty claim, the key word is "potential." This is because it is also argued that current approaches to orientation have been based on the wrong paradigm. A new one is suggested here.

The reason for optimism about orientation programs comes from a parallel body of research on preparing medical patients for the stress of invasive medical–dental examinations, hospitalization, surgery, and chronic pain. In contrast to newcomer orientation, this body of research is distinctive in three ways, which are described in greater detail later. Briefly, however, the medical research is distinctive because it is based on different assumptions (i.e., it is a different paradigm), has been thoroughly studied, and is effective.

Although the preparation of medical patients may appear to have little relevance for organizational entry, the reality is that they have much in common. This is because both situations are examples of role transitions with considerable stress. The source of stress for medical patients may differ from that of organizational entry, but the amount of stress is actually quite similar in these two situations. A newcomer to a job may have left school or college and may have moved geographically, both of which cause considerable stress. According to one scheme for quantifying the level of stress experienced (Cochrane & Robertson, 1973), these two changes would combine for 88 points of stress, as compared to 65 points for an illness requiring hospitalization. If the newcomer also took out a mortgage to purchase a house in the new area (40 points), the total degree of stress can actually be greater than that experienced by many medical patients. Thus, the stress-coping techniques developed for medical patients can have applicability to newcomers, even though the source of high stress differs between these two situations.

The rest of this chapter proceeds as follows. First, newcomer orientation is defined and contrasted with two similar, but distinct, processes: realistic job previews and organizational socialization. Second, the existing research on newcomer orientation is summarized and evaluated. Third, the psychological preparation of medical patients is presented as a better paradigm for conducting future newcomer orientation programs. Finally, the chapter is concluded with an agenda for future research and suggestions for the design of future newcomer orientation programs.

DEFINING NEWCOMER ORIENTATION

Formal newcomer orientation programs appear to be a popular means to facilitate organizational entry. For example, one survey found that 64% of college graduates from East and West coast universities went through some kind of program (Louis, Posner, & Powell, 1983). The survey did not define what constituted such a program, however. In fact, there does not seem to be any agreed upon definition in the research literature. Thus, one is attempted here.

The three elements of a definition that should be addressed are: (a) the focal ("target") group, (b) the objectives, and (c) the methods used to achieve objectives. The people going through newcomer orientation are those who have just entered a new organization. In fact, formal orientation programs should probably be thought of as occurring during the first week of formal employment, preferably the first day. This aspect of the definition helps to distinguish them from socialization, which is usually considered to be a more encompassing and enduring process. For example, according to Van Maahen and Schein (1979), socialization has been called a "ubiquitous process of learning," and said to include "any and all passages . . . from beginning to end . . . (of a) person's career" (p. 213).

The broad objectives of an orientation program are to help newcomers become better "matched" to the organization in both meanings of the term. Thus, one would hope to see *both* performance *and* retention-related attitudes–behavior improved by an effective orientation program. This focus on both types of person–organizational matching means that orientation is more broadly aimed than the organization entry procedures shown in Fig. 9.1. In order to achieve the broad objectives of dual matching, the primary operational objective of an orientation program is to help newcomers cope with the stress of organizational entry.

There seems to be general agreement in the literature on stress (Ivancevich, Matteson, Freedman, & Phillips, 1990) that interventions to manage it fall into three categories: (a) those directly affecting the causes of stress (e.g., job design), (b) those that affect how people think about stress (e.g., stress inoculation training), and (c) those that help people cope with the physiological-psychological outcomes (symptoms) of stress (e.g., relaxation, exercise, or meditation). However, virtually all the organizational research on stress management has concerned the latter two categories (Ivancevich et al., 1990), as does the literature on stress coping for medical patients.

The basic method used thus far for newcomer orientation has been to create realistic expectations for the recruits. This suggests that previous newcomer orientation programs appear to be indistinguishable from the realistic job preview (RJP). Although this is true to an extent, the basic purpose of an orientation program is to help newcomers cope with entry stress, *not* to encourage them to withdraw from the entry process as is true for the RJP. Whereas these objectives were once thought to be compatible (Wanous, 1980), they now appear to be *in*compatible (Wanous, 1989, 1992); that is, presenting negative (albeit realistic) information to recruits may encourage self-selection, but it does not increase coping (Premack & Wanous, 1985).

Although orientation programs have sometimes relied on the presentation of realistic information to recruits, this is not the only method that should be used. One of the main points to be made here is that orientation programs need to adopt other methods, as can be found in the literature on medical patient preparation, which is summarized and discussed after a review of the existing research on newcomer orientation.

One way to summarize this definition of newcomer orientation is to compare it to both RJPs and organizational socialization. The most important difference between RJPs and newcomer orientation is the emphasis on self-selection in an RJP (i.e., encouraging job candidates to remove themselves from further consideration). In contrast, newcomer orientation programs are focused on helping new employees cope with the organizational entry transition.

A second difference is that the RJP is done to increase job survival, whereas newcomer orientation is designed to increase both job survival *and* job performance. Thus, newcomer orientation programs must be concerned with a wider range of issues than those included in the typical RJP, because the factors affecting performance are different from those affecting job survival (March & Simon, 1958).

Newcomer orientation can also be distinguished from organizational socialization. The first distinguishing characteristic of newcomer orientation is its relatively finite nature (i.e., it is a prominent event rather than a never-ending ubiquitous process such as socialization). Second, orientation programs are concerned with the entry transition along the inclusion dimension, not the other two dimensions (functional & hierarchical) that are also considered to be part of socialization (Schein, 1971). Third, only some of the inclusion dimension is relevant in orientation (i.e., the outsider to employee transition); that is, orientation is designed to prevent premature movement out of the organization along the inclusion axis. In contrast, socialization is aimed at facilitating movement inward on this axis. Fourth, there are usually far fewer people involved in orienting newcomers. In contrast, socialization can involve one's entire role set. Fifth, those conducting orientation may not be in authority over the newcomer, in contrast to socialization. Sixth, those conducting orientation may not be one's working peers, as is often the case in socialization where conformity pressures can be significant. The seventh, and last, difference is an important one that concerns the basic objectives of newcomer orientation, as contrasted with socialization. During an orientation program the newcomer can receive two types of support. One type is specific coping skills, which includes managing one's own anxieties and/or learning how to manage one's working environment. The other type can be general supportiveness not geared toward the prevention or solving of specific problems. Whereas these coping–supportive activities may be a part of some socialization experiences, the tenor of much writing on the subject suggests otherwise. Newcomers are often seen as being persuaded, being coerced, and subjected to conformity pressure during socialization. In contrast, the orientation programs reviewed in the next section include attempts to empower newcomers with ways to act on their environment.

RESEARCH ON NEWCOMER ORIENTATION

Five field experiments were found that evaluated newcomer orientation programs (Githens & Zalinski, 1983; Gomersall & Myers, 1966; Horner, Mobley, & Meglino, 1979; Meglino, DeNisi, Youngblood, & Williams, 1988; Novaco, Cook, & Sarason, 1983).[1] The criterion used to select these five studies is whether or not they represent the essence of newcomer orientation (i.e., a program designed to help newcomers cope with organizational entry stress). These five studies are reviewed in chronological order.

Gomersall and Myers (1966) developed an anxiety reduction orientation program at Texas Instruments in order to increase the rate at which newcomers

---

[1]One study (McGarrell, 1984) that is labeled newcomer orientation is excluded because it does not meet the definition used here. This study is more properly considered as socialization, because it involved a minimum of nine sessions spread over the first 6 months of employment.

learned their new jobs. The program developed by them was a 6-hour orientation session held on the first day at work, following the standard 2-hour orientation by Personnel. Those hired in the control groups received only the standard 2-hour orientation, which focused on hours of work, insurance programs, parking, work rules, various employee services, and warnings about the consequences of failing to live up to company expectations.

The experimental stress-coping orientation program emphasized four main points: (a) opportunities to succeed are very good; less than 1% fail to perform satisfactorily; (b) "hall talk" should be disregarded because "old-timers" liked to "play games" with the newcomers; (c) people should take the initiative in communication, particularly with supervisors; and (d) newcomers were told about the uniqueness of their own supervisor (e.g., Gomersall & Myers, 1966, said: "the supervisor is strict, but friendly; his hobby is fishing and ham radio operation; he tends to be shy sometime, but he really likes to talk to you if you want to; he would like you to check with him before you go on a personal break, just so he knows where you are"; p. 67).

Approximately 100 persons were randomly assigned to each of the newcomer groups. Descriptive (not inferential) statistics show there was greater productivity, less absenteeism, and less training needed for the experimental stress-coping group.

The second orientation program was developed for U.S. Marine Corps recruits at the Parris Island training facility (Horner et al., 1979). An 80-minute video called "The Beginning" was developed to show recruits all phases of basic training. The orientation video showed three different "models" (poor-average–good performers), so that recruits might be able to discriminate among the different levels of performance. It was also thought that it would be easier for recruits to identify with a particular model if a variety was shown, rather than showing only excellent performers. Besides showing models, the "voice-over" commentary from selected recruits explained how each model was trying to cope.

The research design included random assignment of recruits on a group basis (i.e., Platoons) to one of two groups. The experimental groups saw the orientation video and the control groups saw a set of three traditional Marine Corps videos, so that both groups were in a theater for the same length of time. Both groups completed questionnaires before and after seeing the videos. Attrition was monitored at 3, 6, and 12 months.

The results of this experiment are somewhat puzzling. None of the questionnaire measures used as manipulation checks showed the expected differences; that is, there were no significant differences in expectation levels, self-efficacy expectations, perceived ambiguity, initial commitment to the marines, and intentions to quit, among a host of questions asked. Furthermore, differences in attrition were not significantly different at either 3 or 6 months, although there was significantly lower turnover at 12 months for those seeing the stress-coping video. Thus, it is possible to question the effectiveness of this orientation program, and/or the validity of the randomization procedure.

The third orientation program (Novaco, Cook, & Sarason, 1983) showed stress-coping activities in a 35-minute videotape called "Making It." The video began with a short segment of realistic information but then focused on two main themes for the remainder: (a) self-control regulation of one's emotions, and (b) performing effectively on various tasks. These two themes are actually intertwined throughout, because focusing on effective task performance is one of the suggested ways to control one's own emotions. Control of emotions is achieved by first validating the recruits' own experiences of distress but then giving them understanding of why this occurs. For example, recruits are told that the drill instructors are doing a job and that they should not take yelling and criticism personally.

The experimental design of the Novaco et al. (1983) study involved a comparison of their own "Making It" video with "The Beginning" video used by Horner et al. (1979). Recruits were individually assigned to a treatment group, an unusual procedure in military research. They divided 530 recruits into five groups according to the type of orientation: (a) "Making It" (MI), (b) "The Beginning" (BG), (c) MI followed by BG, (d) BG followed by MI, and (e) no video at all.

Novaco et al.'s description of the results is brief, yet they do report results supporting the superiority of their own stress-coping orientation program. They report a significant main effect for their "Making It" (MI) video on increasing self-efficacy expectations, and that the MI group reported fewer problems adjusting to drill instructors. No data on the effects of these videos on attrition are reported, however, and this is an important omission.

The fourth study (Githens & Zalinski, 1983) used the same two orientation videos, "The Beginning" versus "Making It," randomly assigned to 83 platoons (approximately $N = 80$ per platoon). Again, there was a separate treatment group for each video, one that saw both, and a control group. There was no counterbalancing for order affects when both videos were shown. (It appears that "The Beginning" was shown prior to "Making It" for the group seeing both.) No questionnaire data were gathered as manipulation checks. Attrition was the only outcome measured, and there was no significant difference across the four groups.

The fifth experimental study of newcomer orientation was conducted for U.S. Army recruits in basic training. The study began in 1979 but was not published until 1988 (Meglino, DeNisi, Youngblood, & Williams, 1988). Two video previews were developed after extensive diagnostic research and revisions. Professional actors were used in the key roles, rather than the recruits themselves. The first video was originally called a "content preview" (Meglino, DeNisi, Youngblood, Williams, Johnson, Randolph, & Laughlin, 1983) but later referred to as a "reduction preview" (Meglino et al., 1988). This was a 27-minute video of the four phases in basic training (introduction, weapons training, individual tactics training, and necessary testing). It is a factual presentation without explicit coping material, thus a typical RJP. The second video was a 24-minute portrayal of the emotional side of adjusting to basic training. It was originally called a "coping preview" (Meglino et al., 1983) but later referred to as an "enhancement preview" (Meglino et al., 1988). According to my definition, this is a newcomer orientation video because it teaches coping skills.

The research design was a four-group experiment where one group saw the RJP video (content–reduction), another saw the newcomer orientation video (coping–enhancement), a third saw both (RJP followed by orientation), and a control group saw neither. The trainees ($N = 533$) were assigned to the four treatments in their platoons (about $N = 33$ per platoon). Questionnaires were administered three times: (a) prior to seeing a video, (b) immediately after a video, and (c) after 5 weeks of training. The questionnaire data were used to assess various explanations for why realistic expectations enhance job survival, but no data were gathered on how well coping strategies were learned, nor how confident recruits felt as a result of seeing coping strategies.

Attrition was defined as leaving before the end of the 7-week training period for other than involuntary reasons. The group seeing both RJP and orientation videos had significantly lower attrition than any other group. There were no significant attrition differences between the RJP-only and the orientation-only groups, and these two single treatment groups were significantly different from the control group only for those recruits whose commitment to the Army was in the top 50% of the distribution. In fact, the only time any of the experimental groups had significantly lower attrition than the control group was when the top 50% of the subjects in intelligence and/or in commitment were analyzed. Finally, the questionnaire data relevant for stress coping showed no significant differences among groups in terms of perceived role ambiguity. When 15 items about recruit worries were assessed, few significant differences emerged except that those in the RJP group sometimes worried more than those in the orientation group.

Summary of Research

The Gomersall and Myers (1966) study is the outlier in this group. It is the only one to use people (rather than videos) to present the newcomer orientation. Thus, it is the only one that clearly incorporated two-way communication between the new recruits and the organization. It also is the only one to report the explicit use of group discussion. Finally, at 6 hours it is by far the longest of any newcomer orientation program.

The results of the Gomersall and Myers study are reported to be the most positive of five experiments. However, their report lacks critical information about experimental procedures and does not present detailed results, so the authors' enthusiasm must be regarded with caution.

The four studies of basic training recruits are remarkably similar in methods and research design. All four used videos ranging in length from 24 to 80 minutes, and three of them used the same video, "The Beginning," developed by Horner et al. (1979). This particular video appears to be a borderline case between an orientation video and an RJP. It is included here because it does show role models handling various situations, although it may be weaker than other orientation videos in explicitly teaching recruits how to cope with specific stressors in basic training. When "The Beginning" is contrasted with a more explicit stress-coping program like "Making It" (Githens & Salinski, 1983; Novaco et al., 1983), it is more like the traditional RJP by comparison.

Three of the military studies used a two-treatment design in which a newcomer orientation program is directly compared to an RJP. Based on these comparisons, here is some indication that the newcomer orientation video produces more self-efficacy (Novaco et al., 1983) and slightly lower attrition (Githens & Zalinski, 1983; Meglino et al., 1988).

ORIENTATION OF MEDICAL PATIENTS

Research concerning the psychological preparation of medical patients to cope with stress of hospitalization, surgery, invasive diagnostic medical–dental procedures, and chronic pain has been reviewed at least eight times (Anderson & Masur, 1983; Auerbach & Kilmann, 1977; Ludwick-Rosenthal & Neufeld, 1988; MacDonald & Kuiper, 1983; Mumford, Schlesinger, & Glass, 1982; Posavac, 1980; Tan, 1982; Wilson-Barnett, 1984). These reviews, however, vary considerably in their usefulness. Most used the narrative review method; only two used meta-analysis (Mumford et al., 1983; Posavac, 1980), and neither of these used the Schmidt and Hunter (1977, 1990) method. Some (Auerbach & Kilmann, 1977; Posavac, 1980) reviewed only one method (information provision), so that direct comparisons about the relative effectiveness of alternative methods cannot be made.

Techniques for Psychological Preparation

The psychological preparation of medical patients has been done in five ways: (a) presenting information, (b) showing models, (c) doing stress inoculation, (d) conducting short psychotherapy, and (e) teaching self-control of one's thoughts and/or feelings.

Presenting Information.   One type of preparation is to convey realistic information about what will happen (e.g., what will be done, when it will begin, how long it will take, etc.). This has been called "what kind of event" information, as compared to "how you will feel" information about forthcoming physical and emotional sensations (Miller, 1981).

Modeling. Modeling (based on Bandura, 1977) is a familiar technique, because it has been used in various types of training programs in business (e.g., Goldstein & Sorcher, 1974). The same principles are used in medical research; that is, patients are first shown a model coping with the situation, followed by a discussion of what was observed, and practice in the particular technique.

Stress Inoculation. Stress inoculation has three essential steps (Janis, 1958, 1983): (a) Call attention to upcoming events—both gains and losses, (b) encourage the person to engage in self-reassurance and other coping techniques, and (c) give help in practicing the coping methods. The first of these steps is essentially information provision. The second step can include a rather wide variety of specific actions (e.g., various imagination strategies, "self-talk" about coping, and even physical actions to cope with pain such as deep breathing and relaxation exercises). During Step three patients can test out their newly acquired coping skills in various ways (e.g., talking, imagining, role playing, and even experiencing mild forms of pain under controlled conditions).

Short Psychotherapy. This type of therapy has been done both individually and in groups, ranging in duration from a 1-hour session to several sessions of ½ to 1 hour in length. Generally speaking, patients are encouraged to express their expectations, feelings, and coping plans. The therapy provider typically gives general reassurance and emotional support and may even provide information to make expectations more accurate (Mumford et al., 1982). Some therapists have even used hypnosis. Of all the categories, this one is the most diverse because it includes interventions aimed at thoughts (e.g., the Rational-Emotive Therapy of Ellis, 1962, 1970), feelings, and the unconscious (i.e., the use of hypnosis).

Self-Control: Thoughts and Feelings. Tan (1977) described six variations for cognitive coping with pain: (a) imaginative inattention (think about being at the beach); (b) imaginative transformation of pain (acknowledge it, but minimize it as either trivial or unreal); (c) imaginative transformation of context (acknowledge the pain but pretend it was caused by something else, e.g., a championship football game); (d) external attention–diversion (e.g., count ceiling tiles); (e) internal attention–diversion (e.g., do mental arithmetic); and (f) somatization (focus on the pain area in a detailed manner as if you were observing yourself).

A second form of self-control has focused on one's feelings rather than on one's thoughts. Two techniques have been used. The first is relaxation as a way to cope with stress (e.g., exercises in muscle flexing and breathing;

Jacobson, 1970). The second is desensitization, a familiar clinical technique for overcoming fear where one approaches the fearful situation in a series of increasingly realistic approximations (Machen & Johnson, 1974).

Effectiveness of Psychological Preparation

Two general conclusions seem warranted. First, the effects of psychological preparation of medical patients are strong. This conclusion is based largely on the two reviews of the medical research that did use meta-analysis to quantify effect sizes (expressed as d).[2] Posavac (1980) reported an overall $d = .74$, based on 104 effect sizes from 23 studies of information provision treatments. Mumford et al. (1982) reported an overall $d = .49$ for 210 measures obtained from 34 experiments.

The Mumford et al. (1982) review went further to translate meta-analysis effect sizes into practical terms. They estimated that patient preparation programs reduce the average hospital stay by slightly more than 2 full days.[3] Because hospitals are usually paid on a preset fee schedule, any intervention to speed up patient discharge can be quite beneficial in monetary terms.

A second general conclusion from the medical research is that complex techniques appear to be more effective than simpler ones. Mumford et al. (1982) reported that a combination of "educational" and "psychotherapeutic" programs is more effective ($d = .65$) than either education alone ($d = .30$) or psychotherapy alone ($d = .41$). This conclusion is further supported by several of the narrative reviews. For example, Ludwick-Rosenthal and Neufeld (1988) concluded that modeling and stress inoculation were more effective than relaxation training or information provision. Similarly, Tan (1982) concluded that simply providing information was not as effective as when information was combined with various stress-coping skills, as is typical of stress inoculation training.

LESSONS LEARNED
FROM THE MEDICAL RESEARCH

A first general lesson is that the appearance of stronger effect sizes in psychologically preparing patients versus newcomer employees may be due to the more complex methods used in the former context; that is, one would expect to find a complete stress inoculation or behavior modeling program to be more effective than just one of its components alone (e.g., information provision). None

---

[2]The d statistic refers to the degree of difference between experimental (stress coping) and control groups expressed in standard deviation units for the dependent variable.

[3]The standard deviation for length of hospital stay was 4.75 days; when a $d = .49$ is multiplied by 4.75, the estimated effect is 2.3 days.

of the five newcomer orientation experiments had a complete stress inoculation or behavior modeling program, compared to many of the medical patient studies.

A second lesson is that newcomer orientation programs need to incorporate more active participation by those exposed to them. Of the five newcomer orientation studies reviewed here, none had any rehearsal (mental or physical), compared to many of the medical orientation programs.

A third lesson is that newcomer orientation probably needs to be conducted in relatively small groups, perhaps even individually. One sharp contrast between the five studies reviewed here and virtually all the medical research is the size of groups being psychologically prepared. In the four military newcomer orientation programs, all the groups were quite large—a type of "collective" orientation (Van Maanen & Schein, 1979) carried to an extreme. In contrast, medical patients are rarely found in large cohorts like those in the military. This difference in size probably makes rehearsal easier, and it most likely increases a patient's feeling that special caring concern is being given.

A fourth lesson is that live models of effective coping behavior appear to be better than videotaped models (Anderson & Masur, 1983), but live models have yet to be used in newcomer orientation. This could be an important omission, because much of what newcomers need to learn is of an interpersonal nature. In fact, some empirical research in organizational socialization has found social aspects to be very important (Allen & Meyer, 1990; Jones, 1986). Using live models allows for greater flexibility in presenting a variety of situations without having to write a script and produce a formal vignette on videotape for every interpersonal learning point.

Finally, it may be possible to adopt self-control methods (particularly the cognitive type) to newcomer orientation, even though they appear to be more appropriate for the extremely threatening physical trauma typical of the medical studies. In order to do this, the newcomer orientation program would have to include a component devoted to *general* supportiveness and stress coping, rather than being exclusively concerned with organizationally specific problems. Newcomers would be taught how to cope with unforeseen stressors.

THE FUTURE OF NEWCOMER ORIENTATION PROGRAMS

The future of newcomer orientation programs is brighter than the past, but only if there is a paradigm shift. The future design of newcomer orientation programs must incorporate the basic goal and some of the methods of medical patient psychological preparation. In terms of goals, this means a shift away from the "RJP paradigm" of presenting information to help candidates make informed self-selection decisions at the point of entry into a new organization. The shift must go in the direction of helping newcomers to cope with entry-related stress.

Whereas the RJP may be thought of as a type of "decision aide" (Janis & Mann, 1977), once the decision has been made to enter a new organization, a different approach needs to be taken for orientation. Newcomer orientation programs should be concerned with thoughts, feelings, and behavior as they relate to *both* job survival and job performance.

The paradigm of stress coping for newcomer orientation is also a shift away from the organizational socialization paradigm. To the extent that socialization implies newcomers are primarily on the receiving end of influence attempts, newcomer orientation is distinctive in that the outcome of various methods should be the empowerment of newcomers to cope with entry stress.

The "medical model" described here seems to best fit the way orientation programs should be designed if they are to achieve the two basic individual-organizational match-ups. Of the specific techniques used to prepare medical patients, modeling and stress inoculation appear to be the most effective ones that can be transported to the newcomer orientation context. These techniques are sufficiently flexible as to permit their being geared toward both performance *and* retention-related stressors.

Despite my optimism for the potential of the medical paradigm to be applied to newcomer orientation, two final notes of caution must be sounded. First, the five studies reviewed here do not constitute much of an empirical base for this enthusiasm, which is driven more by the logical appeal of switching to a new paradigm than by the evidence accumulated to date. Second, some of the recommendations may be difficult to implement in certain organizational entry situations. For example, it may be difficult to "individualize" newcomer orientation for large cohorts of newcomers. Thus, my specific recommendations for increased discussion of learning points, actual rehearsal of coping methods, and the use of live models may all prove not feasible in such situations. The type of newcomer orientation programs likely to be successful are labor intensive from an organizational perspective. Those organizations that are unable or unwilling to commit sufficient resources for an orientation program modeled on the medical paradigm may not be able to reap the potential benefits. As always, however, only future research will give us the answers.

REFERENCES

Allen, N. J., & Meyer, J. P. (1990). Organization socialization tactics: A longitudinal analysis of links to newcomers' commitment and role orientation. *Academy of Management Journal, 33*, 847–858.

Anderson, K. O., & Masur, T. F. III. (1983). Psychological preparation for invasive medical and dental procedures. *Journal of Behavioral Medicine, 6*, 1–40.

Auerbach, S. M., & Kilmann, P. R. (1977). Crisis intervention: A review of outcome research. *Psychological Bulletin, 84*, 1189–1217.

Bandura, A. (1977). *Social learning theory.* Englewood Cliffs, NJ: Prentice–Hall.

Cochrane, R., & Robertson, A. (1973). The life events inventory: A measure of the relative severity of psycho-social stressors. *Journal of Psychomatic Research, 17*, 135–139.

Ellis, A. (1962). *Reason and emotion in psychotherapy.* New York: Lyle Stuart.

Ellis, A. (1970). *The essence of rational psychotherapy: A comprehensive approach to treatment.* New York: Institution for Rational Living.

Githens, W. H., & Zalinski, J. (1983). *An evaluation of realistic job preview and stress-coping films' effect on Marine Corps recruit training attrition* (Technical Rep. No. 83–78). Navy Personnel Research and Development Center, San Diego.

Goldstein, A. P., & Sorcher, M. (1974). *Changing supervisor behavior.* New York: Pergamon.

Gomersall, E. R., & Myers, M. S. (1966, July–August). Breakthrough in on-the-job-training. *Harvard Business Review*, 62–72.

Horner, S. O., Mobley, W. H., & Meglino, B. M. (1979). *An experimental evaluation of the effects of a realistic job preview on marine recruit affect, intentions & behavior* (Technical Report No. 9). Center for management and organizational research, College of Business, University of South Carolina, Columbia.

Ivancevich, J. M., Matteson, M. T., Freedman, S. M. & Phillips, J. S. (1990). Worksite stress management interventions. *American Psychologist, 45*, 252–261.

Jacobson, E. (1970). *Modern treatment of tense patients.* Springfield, IL: Charles C. Thomas.

Janis, I. L. (1958). *Psychological stress.* New York: Wiley.

Janis, I. L. (1983). Stress inoculation in health care: Theory and research. In D. Meichenbaum & M. E. Jaremko (Eds.), *Stress reduction and prevention* (pp. 67–99). New York: Plenum Press.

Janis, I. L., & Mann, L. (1977). *Decision making: A psychological analysis of conflict, choice, and commitment.* New York: Free Press.

Jones, G. R. (1986). Socialization tactics, self-efficacy, and newcomers' adjustments to organizations. *Academy of Management Journal, 29*, 262–279.

Louis, M. R., Posner, B. Z., & Powell, G. N. (1983). The availability and helpfulness of socialization practices. *Personnel Psychology, 36*, 857–866.

Ludwick-Rosenthal, R., & Neufeld, R. W. J. (1988). Stress management during noxious medical procedures: An evaluative review of outcome studies. *Psychological Bulletin, 104*, 326–342.

MacDonald, M. R., & Kuiper, N. A. (1983). Cognitive–behavioral preparations for surgery: Some theoretical and methodological concerns. *Clinical Psychology Review, 3*, 27–39.

Machen, J. B., & Johnson, R. (1974). Densensitization, model learning, and the dental behavior of children. *Journal of Dental Research, 53*, 83–87.

March, J. G., & Simon, H. A. (1958). *Organizations.* New York: Wiley.

McGarrell, E. J., Jr. (1984). An orientation system that builds productivity. *Personnel Administrator, October*, 75–85.

Meglino, B. M., DeNisi, A. S., Youngblood, S. A., & Williams, K. J. (1988). Effects of realistic job previews: A comparison using an "enhancement" and a "reduction" preview. *Journal of Applied Psychology, 73*, 259–266.

Meglino, B. M., DeNisi, A. S., Youngblood, S. A., Williams, K. J., Johnson, W. E., Randolph, W. A., & Laughlin, J. E. (1983). *Formulation and analysis of counter attrition strategies in the U.S. Army* (Technical report). Division of Research, College of Business, University of South Carolina, Columbia.

Miller, S. (1981). Predictability and human stress: Toward a clarification of evidence and theory. In L. Berkowitz (Ed.), *Advances in experimental social psychology* (Vol. 14, pp. 203–256). New York: Academic Press.

Mumford, E., Schlesinger, H. J., & Glass, G. V. (1982). The effects of psychological intervention on recovery from surgery and heart attacks: An analysis of the literature. *American Journal of Public Health, 72*, 141–151.

Novaco, R. W., Cook, T. M., & Sarason, I. G. (1983). Military recruit training: An arena for stress-coping skills. In D. Meichenbaum & M. E. Jaremko (Eds.), *Stress reduction and prevention* (pp. 377–418). New York: Plenum Press.

Porter, L. W., Lawler, E. E., III, & Hackman, J. R. (1975). *Behavior in organizations*. New York: McGraw-Hill.

Posavac, E. J. (1980). Evaluations of patient education programs. *Evaluation & the Health Professions, 3*, 47–62.

Premack, S. L., & Wanous, J. P. (1985). A meta-analysis of realistic job preview experiments. *Journal of Applied Psychology, 70*, 706–719.

Schein, E. H. (1971). The individual, the organization, and the career: A conceptual scheme. *Journal of Applied Behavioral Science, 7*, 401–426.

Schmidt, R. L., & Hunter, J. E. (1977). Development of a general solution to the problem of validity generalization. *Journal of Applied Psychology, 62*, 529–540.

Schmidt, F. L., & Hunter, J. E. (1990). *Meta-analysis*. Beverly Hills, CA: Sage.

Tan, S. Y. (1982). Cognitive and cognitive-behavioral methods for pain control: A selective review. *Pain, 12*, 201–228.

Vandenberg, R. J., & Scarpello, V. (1990). The matching model: An examination of the processes underlying realistic job previews. *Journal of Applied Psychology, 75*, 60–67.

Van Maanen, J., & Schein, E. H. (1979). Toward a theory of organizational socialization. In B. M. Staw (Ed.), *Research in organizational behavior* (Vol. 1, pp. 209–264). Greenwich, CT: JAI Press.

Wanous, J. P. (1980). *Organizational entry: Recruitment, selection, and socialization of newcomers*. Reading, MA: Addison-Wesley.

Wanous, J. P. (1989). Installing a realistic job preview: Ten tough choices. *Personnel Psychology, 42*, 117–134.

Wanous, J. P. (1992). *Organizational entry: Recruitment, selection, orientation, and socialization*. Reading, MA: Addison-Wesley.

Wilson-Barnett, J. (1984). Interventions to alleviate patients' stress: A review. *Journal of Psychosomatic Research, 28*, 63–72.

10

Attitudes About Performance Appraisal

Terry L. Dickinson
Old Dominion University

Performance appraisal is integral to the successful operation of most organizations. During this process, employees are evaluated formally and informally to determine the nature of their contributions to the organization. Appraisal occurs during time periods and in meetings that are scheduled to produce a reasoned consideration of contributions, but it also occurs informally as employee contributions are observed, or when an evaluation is brought to the attention of others.

Performance appraisal is instrumental in helping organizations and employees achieve a variety of important outcomes. These outcomes include rewards and sanctions defined by the organization, emotions experienced and knowledge gained by the employees, and goals and plans developed by the organization and its members. The importance of these outcomes suggests that employees often have strong attitudes about performance appraisal. Certainly, if negative attitudes prevail among members, performance appraisal will be unacceptable to many members, and its use may hinder rather than help achieve outcomes. Indeed, when a supervisor discusses the appraisal of a subordinate's performance, the setting of goals for performance improvement may be difficult or impossible. This is especially true if job security, self-esteem, or pay increases are believed to be threatened by the appraisal. Nonetheless, employees desire and often seek out information about their performance. This is particularly true if employees are new to their job or are uncertain about job duties or work assignments.

The purpose of this chapter is to examine employee attitudes about performance appraisal. Research and theory are reviewed to identify factors that positively or negatively influence these attitudes and to suggest issues to consider in future research efforts.

PERFORMANCE APPRAISAL ATTITUDES

In spite of the commonsense logic that attitudes about performance appraisal are crucial to its effective use, researchers only recently began to investigate the nature of these attitudes. In his seminal article, Lawler (1967) proposed a model of the factors that affect the validity of performance ratings. Central to the model is the proposition that attitudes concerning the fairness and acceptability of the performance appraisal system are the major determinants of rating validity. In turn, these attitudes are seen as due to organizational and individual characteristics, as well as characteristics of the system itself. An adaptation of this model is shown in Fig. 10.1.

As conceived by Lawler (1967), characteristics of the performance appraisal system include rater sources and the nature of the attributes that are rated by these sources. Individual differences include the incumbent's need for feedback and extent of authoritarian personality. Presumably, the greater the need for feedback and the less authoritarian the personality, the more an employee would find peer and subordinate sources of performance appraisal to be acceptable. With respect to organizational characteristics, peer, self-, and subordinate ratings are seen as more acceptable in organizations with a management style that encourages employees to participate in decision making.

Landy, Barnes, and Murphy (1978) were the first researchers to focus attention solely on the relation of attitudinal factors to performance appraisal. Using a single-item measure of perceived fairness and accuracy of the performance

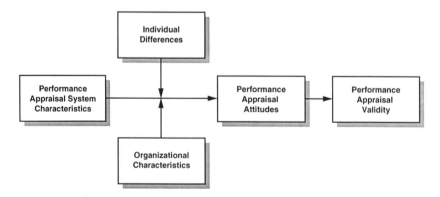

FIG. 10.1.   Factors that affect the validity of ratings (adapted from Lawler, 1967).

appraisal process, they identified five appraisal characteristics with regression analysis that accounted for 26% of the variance in this measure. Employees perceived greater fairness and accuracy when performance appraisal (a) was part of a program, (b) was done at least once a year, (c) was based on knowledge of the employee's performance, (d) allowed the employee opportunity to express feelings, and (e) led to an action plan for eliminating performance weaknesses.

In a follow-up study with another sample from the same organization, Landy, Barnes-Farrell, and Cleveland (1980) reported that fairness and accuracy perceptions were not related to the performance appraisal ratings received by the employees. This follow-up finding suggests that the appraisal process accounted for fairness and accuracy perceptions rather than the performance ratings. Thus, favorable attitudes about performance appraisal could not be explained simply as being due to the reception of a favorable performance rating.

In a similar investigation, Dipboye and de Pontbriand (1981) examined attitudes toward the performance appraisal system as well as the performance rating itself. Four characteristics were found with regression analysis that accounted for 56% of the variance in satisfaction with the rating and 40% in satisfaction with the system. These characteristics were (a) perceived level of the performance rating relative to expectations, (b) opportunity of employees to participate in a performance appraisal discussion, (c) relevancy of job appraisal dimensions, and (d) discussion of plans and objectives.

In contrast to the follow-up finding of Landy et al. (1980), Dipboye and de Pontbriand (1981) reported that perceived level of the rating relative to expectations was related strongly ($r = .52$) to satisfaction with the appraisal. More recently, Russell and Goode (1988) reported that employee satisfaction with their own performance appraisal interview correlated significantly with recalled ($r = .64$) and actual performance ratings ($r = .63$). However, employee perceptions that the interview had value for improvement were not correlated significantly with recalled ($r = .09$) and actual performance ratings ($r = -.03$). These contradictory findings suggest that the magnitude of the performance rating has complex relationships with attitudes about performance appraisal.

In a series of four studies, Kavanagh and his colleagues (Kavanagh & Hedge, 1983; Kavanagh, Hedge, Ree, Earles, & DeBiasi, 1985) extensively examined acceptability of a performance appraisal system. They maintained that Lawler's (1967) conception of acceptability had not been adequately measured in previous research, because that research focused primarily on a single aspect of acceptability and tended to utilize single-item measures. For example, Landy and his colleagues used the fairness and accuracy item to reflect the acceptability of performance appraisal, and the only system characteristic examined was frequency of appraisal.

In one study, Kavanagh et al. (1985) administered an 81-item survey to 5,770 civilian employees of the United States Air Force to measure acceptability of the appraisal system for promotion purposes. Seven factors were found to describe general attitudes about the system. These factors are defined in Table 10.1, and they clearly suggest that acceptability of a performance appraisal system is described by more than the fairness and accuracy of an appraisal. Nonetheless, in the Air Force study and the remaining three studies, regression analyses indicated that fairness and accuracy was the most potent predictor of the overall acceptability of the appraisal system. Other consistent predictors of overall acceptability included: (a) agreement that clear performance standards were communicated; (b) satisfaction with performance feedback; (c) satisfaction with the performance appraisal rating; and (d) agreement that the performance appraisal form distinguishes between good and poor employees.

Kavanagh et al. (1985) also explored the influence of the time since the last appraisal and organizational position on acceptability of the appraisal system. For a sample of 1,149 hospital employees, Kavanagh et al. found that employees who were evaluated within the last year (e.g., 1, 3, and 6 months) had significantly more correlates with their acceptability of the system than employees who were evaluated over a year ago. Only the fairness and accuracy of appraisals made over 1 year ago related to system acceptability. Apparently, attitudes about the acceptability of the performance appraisal system became less differentiated with increases in the time since the last appraisal; after the passing of more than a year, only a general impression remained of the system.

With respect to organizational position, the factors that explained overall acceptability varied by position. Managers had significantly more factors that were related to overall acceptability than employees in other positions. This finding is consistent with the effects of time since the last appraisal. Managers had the richer delineation of attitudes, because they had more experience with performance appraisals.

TABLE 10.1
Appraisal System Factors and Definitions[a]

Factor Name	Definition
Fairness and Accuracy	Performance appraisals fairly and accurately describe job performance
Supervisory Input	Supervisor is capable and can be trusted to make accurate appraisals
Clear Performance Standards	Employee has a clear idea of work standards
Adherence to Appraisal System Procedures	Appraisals are used and made according to policy
Co-worker Input	Co-workers are capable and can be trusted to make accurate appraisals
Dislike of Appraisals	Use self-appraisals or no appraisals
Use Other Measures	Use job knowledge tests, aptitude tests, or training performance

[a]Adapted from Kavanagh et al. (1985).

Finally, Kavanagh et al. (1985) compared the attitudes of two samples toward the appraisal form and the broader concept of the appraisal system. One sample consisted of nursing supervisors, who had a performance appraisal system that included (a) use of behaviorally anchored rating scales, (b) performance appraisal interviews, and (c) a two-day training workshop for supervisors in rating and interviewing. The second sample consisted of supervisors in a university setting. The university performance appraisal system was less sophisticated; it consisted of trait rating scales, no required appraisal interview, and no training in rating or interviewing.

Both the nursing and university supervisors were unable to distinguish between the performance appraisal form and the system. Virtually identical regression models were found for form and system acceptability. However, nursing supervisors in the more sophisticated appraisal system had significantly more appraisal correlates of acceptability. This latter finding suggests that the nature of the performance appraisal system influences the structural complexity of attitudes about performance appraisal.

Characteristics of the Performance Appraisal System

Rating Source.   The immediate supervisor is the most frequently used source for performance appraisals. In fact, Lazer and Wilkstrom (1977) estimated that immediate supervisors generate and communicate 95% of the appraisals made in organizations. However, other sources readily available in most organizations include peers as well as the incumbent. Most research on attitudes about performance appraisal has focused on supervisory appraisals. Only two studies bear directly on peer appraisals (Cederblom & Lounsbury, 1980; McEvoy & Buller, 1987), and none on self-appraisals.

McEvoy and Buller (1987) evaluated a peer-appraisal system for hourly employees, who worked in a food-processing plant. Employees attitudes toward the system were quite positive. They favored continuing the system that had been in place for a year, were satisfied with peers as a source for appraisal, and were satisfied with their last performance rating. In contrast, Cederblom and Lounsbury (1980) reported low acceptance by faculty members of peer appraisals. A difference between the two appraisal systems was that faculty members were provided with individual signed evaluations from peers, whereas the hourly workers received anonymous averaged peer ratings. It appears that acceptance of a peer-appraisal system is due partly to maintenance of rater confidentiality.

Rating Form.   Several studies bear on the effects that rating form has on performance appraisal attitudes. Forms that provide behavioral information about performance are viewed more favorably. For example, Dickinson and Zellinger (1980) compared behaviorally anchored rating scales to mixed standard scales and found that raters preferred the anchored scales, because they allowed raters to include written comments about their ratings.

Another unique feature of behaviorally anchored rating scales is the involvement of raters, and potentially, ratees in scale development. Although rater-ratee involvement is designed to improve the psychometric properties of rating scales (Friedman & Cornelius, 1976), it also apparently enhances attitudes toward the appraisal process. Silverman and Wexley (1984) compared the perceptions of employees who had and had not participated in the development of behaviorally anchored scales used in discussing performance in appraisal interviews. Those employees who participated in form development reported more satisfaction with their appraisal interview, more motivation to improve, and learning more from the interview. They also reported making more contributions, setting more goals, and having more opportunities to participate during the interview.

More recently, Hedge, Teachout, and Dickinson (1987) examined attitudes about several rating forms to be used in a research program for validating the Air Force's selection and classification test battery. For eight job specialties, four rating forms were used that measured employee performance at the task, dimensional, or global levels. Using all forms, job incumbents rated themselves, whereas supervisors and co-workers rated the incumbents. Factor analysis was used to identify factors of form acceptability, motivation to rate, job satisfaction, and rater trust of the researchers. Form acceptability involved perceptions of fairness and accuracy, clarity of instructions, and confidence in the obtained ratings. Regression analyses indicated that motivation to rate and trust of the researchers were highly predictive of the acceptability of each form. Mean comparisons indicated that the task-level rating form was significantly less acceptable to the raters. Although the task-level form allowed assessment of performance with greater detail, this form also required more effort to use. Apparently, raters disliked the task-level form, because it contained 25 to 40 items compared to the 6 to 9 items contained in the dimensional-level form and the 2 items in the global form.

The Appraisal Interview. Perhaps the most important aspect of a performance appraisal system is the performance appraisal interview. In the interview, performance is reviewed, usually by the employee's supervisor, and performance-related information is discussed that may affect the employee's future work behavior. As depicted in Fig. 10.2, structure and process characteristics influence outcomes from the performance appraisal interview.

The interview can serve a variety of purposes, including discussing performance ratings, solving performance problems, setting goals, and discussing administrative decisions (e.g., pay raises, promotion, and disciplinary actions). Meyer, Kay, and French (1965) were the first to suggest that a single interview session should not be used to accomplish multiple purposes. They maintained that interviews focusing on employee development should be held

FIG. 10.2. Characteristics of the performance appraisal interview.

separately from those focusing on administrative decisions. Meyer et al. argued that the two purposes force the interviewer into two conflicting roles (i.e., facilitator and judge). The interviewer's role for employee development requires acting as a facilitator, whereas that for administrative decisions requires acting as a judge. An interviewer attempting to accomplish both purposes in a single session typically emphasizes administrative decisions to the exclusion of development, and consequently, the interviewer must deal with an employee who feels threatened about job security or pay. Meyer et al. reported improvements in employee attitudes and performance when the two roles were split into separate interview sessions.

Other researchers have questioned the advantages of a strict separation of performance appraisal interviews by purpose (Dorfman, Stephan, & Loveland, 1986; Ilgen & Feldman, 1983; Prince & Lawler, 1986). For example, motivational theory suggests that developmental goals should be linked to feedback *and* rewards to increase the likelihood of goal achievement (Cummings, 1973). One strategy to consider is a separation of interviews based on relative emphasis. A 6-month interval could be used between an interview emphasizing employee development and another emphasizing rewards. This strategy would allow progress in solving problems and meeting goals that were identified in the first interview to be linked into administrative decisions made in the second interview. The suggestion is supported by Keaveny, Inderrieden, and Allen (1987), who found no effects on satisfaction with the interview when developmental and administrative functions were combined in the same interview. Further, employees were more satisfied with the interview when a linkage was perceived with performance goals that were set in a previous interview.

Of course, more than two interviews could be conducted annually (cf. Beer, Ruh, Dawson, McCaa, & Kavanagh, 1978). Although research (Landy et al., 1978; Kavanagh et al., 1985) suggests that employees who are evaluated at least once a year have more favorable attitudes about performance appraisal, no guidelines are available as to the optimal number of performance appraisal interviews. Very frequent interviews could be viewed as controlling and intrusive by supervisors and employees. As noted by Cederblom (1982), further research is needed on the effects of interview frequency.

The interview process has been extensively examined, and several characteristics appear to influence interview outcomes (cf. Burke, Weitzel, & Weir,

1978; Burke & Wilcox, 1969; Ilgen, Peterson, Martin, & Boeschen, 1981; Kay, Meyer, & French, 1965; Maier, 1958; Nemeroff & Wexley, 1979; Wexley, 1979). First, employees who report more participation in the appraisal interview also report more satisfaction with the interview, more motivation to improve, and more actual improvement. Second, the support shown by the interviewer for the employee has also been linked to positive outcomes from the interview. Interviewers are more effective when they listen to employee points of view, minimize criticisms, and acknowledge good performance. Third, solving problems that hinder employee performance has been linked to positive outcomes from the interview. Finally, mutual goal setting by the employee and interviewer is related to satisfaction with the interview, motivation to improve, and reports of actual job improvement.

Interviewing style has been used as a means to encourage employee discussion of job performance and, consequently, to obtain greater participation, minimization of threat, problem solving, mutual goal setting, motivation to improve, and satisfaction with the interview (e.g., French, Kay, & Meyer, 1966; Wexley, Singh, & Yukl, 1973). The classic tripartite description by Maier (1958) reflects important variations in interviewing style. The "tell and sell" style involves informing the employee about the interviewer's appraisal of strengths and weaknesses and then persuading the employee to follow the interviewer's suggestions for improvement. The "tell and listen" style adds to the interview the opportunity for the employee to express feelings about the appraisal. Finally, the "problem-solving" style emphasizes a nondirective discussion to encourage the employee to express ideas and feelings about strengths and weaknesses. This discussion leads to a mutual agreement about goals and plans for improving performance.

Although interviewing style is clearly important, attributes that the interviewer brings to the interview also influence the effectiveness of the interview. An interviewer who is perceived to be credible is more likely to provide performance-related information that is acceptable to the employee (Ilgen, Fisher, & Taylor, 1979). Credibility can be acquired, because the source is perceived to (a) be an expert with respect to job performance, (b) have formal power (e.g., the immediate supervisor), and (c) have trustworthy motives.

The highly sensitive nature of the appraisal interview makes employee trust of the interviewer especially critical to the acceptance of an appraisal. In a constructive replication of the Landy et al. (1978) research, Fulk, Brief, and Barr (1985) included a measure of the trust between supervisor and employee. Fulk et al. obtained correlations nearly identical to those reported in the original research. Further, they developed a causal model of supervisory effects on perceived fairness and accuracy. As shown in Fig. 10.3, significant direct and indirect paths were obtained from the supervisor's knowledge of the subordinate's performance to fairness and accuracy of appraisals. Direct paths were also obtained from trust in the supervisor and the development of action plans with the performance appraisal to fairness and accuracy.

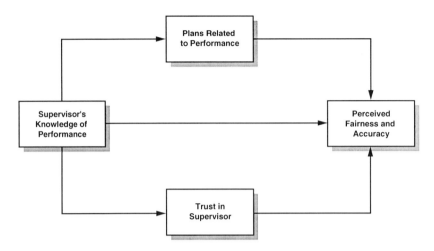

FIG. 10.3. Trust in the supervisor and performance appraisal attitudes (adapted from Fulk et al., 1985).

The findings of Fulk et al. (1985) were expanded by Secunda (1983), who hypothesized that acceptability of a performance appraisal system is determined by perceptions of fairness and accuracy, the supervisor, and the performance appraisal interview. In addition, the purpose for the appraisal (i.e., developmental vs. administrative) and the frequency of appraisal were hypothesized to influence perceptions of the performance appraisal interview. Notably, Secunda constructed multi-item scales to measure perceptions of fairness (e.g., ratings are fair in relation to others), accuracy (e.g., my rating represents my true performance), and acceptability (e.g., appraisal program is an acceptable way to evaluate performance).

Secunda (1983) used structural equation analysis to evaluate the hypothesized relations. His final trimmed model is depicted in Fig. 10.4. This model suggests that acceptability of the performance appraisal system is determined by several direct and indirect effects. Acceptability was directly influenced by perceptions of fairness and accuracy of the appraisal rating, and whether the performance appraisal system was used primarily for growth and development. Acceptability was indirectly influenced by the effects that attitudes about the supervisor and performance appraisal interview had on fairness and accuracy. Further, perceived fairness and accuracy were each directly determined by attitudes about the supervisor and appraisal interview as well as the actual performance rating. Finally, attitudes about the appraisal interview were determined by attitudes about the supervisor and the frequency of appraisal.

Another attribute that influences employee attitudes about performance appraisal is the content of the feedback provided by the supervisor during the appraisal (see Fig. 10.5). The most important aspect of content is the sign of

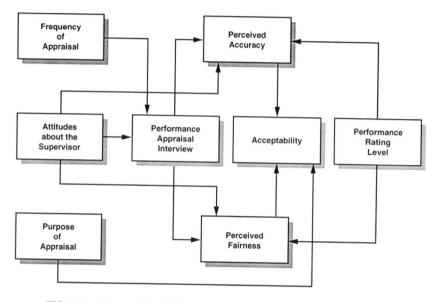

FIG. 10.4.   Structural model of attitudes about performance appraisal (adapted from Secunda, 1983).

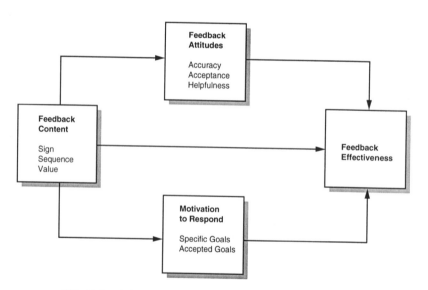

FIG. 10.5.   Attitudes about and motivation to respond to feedback.

feedback (Herold & Greller, 1977; Ilgen et al., 1979). Although positive feedback is more acceptable than negative feedback, and there is research evidence that supervisors distort feedback by making it more positive (Fisher, 1979; Ilgen & Knowlton, 1980), only giving positive feedback is not realistic. Many employees need improvements in their job performance.

The sequencing of feedback by its sign is a strategy for influencing attitudes about that feedback without distorting its content. A laboratory study by Stone, Gueutal, and McIntosh (1984) investigated the commonsense notion that a praise-first and criticize-later approach to feedback makes that feedback more acceptable to employees. Stone et al. found that a positive–negative sequence of feedback in a performance appraisal interview about in-basket performance was perceived as more accurate than a negative–positive sequence. Further, this sequence effect occurred only when the supervisor was perceived to have high expertise. Although these results need to be replicated in a field setting, they suggest that a praise-first approach in the appraisal interview by a credible supervisor increases the perceived accuracy and acceptance of feedback.

Another aspect of content is the specificity of feedback. French et al. (1966) cautioned that nonspecific feedback in the appraisal interview, even if positive, is of little value. The information value of the feedback (e.g., correctness of responses, goal appropriateness) probably enhances the credibility of the source and leads to more favorable attitudes (Steers & Porter, 1974). More important is the response value of the feedback (e.g., identifying goals, rewards, or appropriate responses), because it impacts on the motivation to respond (e.g., goal setting and the acceptance of specific goals) and ultimately on performance.

Aside from its content, feedback must be seen by the employee as helpful rather than being used to control work behavior (Deci, 1975; Ilgen et al., 1979). Perceptions of personal control are important for attaining a sense of competence and maintaining intrinsic motivation. Thus, feedback should be given in a manner to generate feelings of accomplishment (Fisher, 1978). Although no research is available, this probably requires a delicate balancing of the sign and information value of the feedback.

Individual Characteristics

Several personality theories support the notion that individuals distort performance information to maintain favorable attitudes about one's self. For example, self-esteem theories propose that individuals have the need to enhance their self-evaluation and to increase, maintain, or confirm feelings of personal satisfaction, worth, and effectiveness (Jones, 1973). Self-enhancement theory assumes that people have the basic desire to think favorably of themselves, and that the longer the drive is unsatisfied, the more it increases in strength (Shrauger, 1975). Further, self-concept theories predict that when skills, qualifications, or abilities can be or are negatively evaluated, the self-concept is threatened. Under these conditions, protection of self-concept would be a probable reaction (Wiener, 1973). In sum, performance appraisal information probably arouses desires to enhance self-esteem, think favorably of one's self, or protect self-concept.

Self-Esteem. Although several personality variables have been related to performance feedback (Ilgen et al., 1979), little research has been reported that relates these variables to performance appraisal attitudes. In the research by Ilgen et al. (1981), self-esteem was investigated as a correlate of subordinate reactions to their performance appraisal interviews. However, self-esteem was not related to overall satisfaction with the session or the extent to which the session was friendly, helpful, or focused on specific performance issues.

Two aspects of this research qualify the results. First, the organization had recently instituted a performance appraisal system oriented to Management by Objectives, and supervisors had been given extensive training in goal setting and conducting appraisal interviews. These organizational changes resulted in very positive attitudes about performance appraisal. Thus, there could have been a ceiling effect on the relationships between attitudes and self-esteem. Second, the outcome of the appraisal was not controlled. Personality theories suggest that the relationships of self-esteem with attitudes about an appraisal depend on the content of that appraisal.

In their laboratory study, Stone et al. (1984) controlled the feedback given to high and low self-esteem individuals. All individuals received the same appraisal feedback, except for its positive–negative sequencing. High self-esteem individuals perceived the feedback to be more accurate, and their perceptions were influenced by sequence. High self-esteem individuals perceived feedback to be more accurate when it was in the positive–negative sequence. No sequence effects were found for low self-esteem individuals. Apparently, the greater the self-esteem, the more likely an individual avoids or ignores the negative aspects of performance appraisal.

Age and Job Experience. These variables have been hypothesized to be inversely related to acceptance of performance feedback (Ilgen et al., 1979). The rationale is that older and more experienced employees would have accumulated knowledge of performance standards, and they would not need feedback or find it to be acceptable. Three studies relate to this hypothesis. Ilgen et al. (1981) reported positive but nonsignificant correlations of age and years with the company with attitudes about performance appraisal interviews. In contrast, McEvoy and Buller (1987) reported small negative correlations between attitudes toward the peer-appraisal system and years with the company. On postsurvey comments, more senior employees indicated that peers with less experience did not have a good understanding of job requirements. Steel (1985) also reported that more senior employees (i.e., 15 years plus service and 56 years plus in age) had less favorable attitudes toward a new performance appraisal system. Unfortunately, none of these studies measured curvilinear relations between employee attitudes and age and job experience.

Feedback Seeking. Finally, individuals often actively seek feedback from others about their own performance. This feedback-seeking behavior is thought to be tied to motivations for achieving competence as well as protecting and enhancing self-esteem (Ashford & Cummings, 1983). According to theory, individuals differ in their history and propensity for feedback-seeking behavior just as they differ in motivations related to competence and self-esteem. Ashford and Cummings suggest that acceptance and desire to respond to feedback is greater when the feedback is actively sought. Perhaps, individuals with a greater propensity for feedback-seeking behavior also have more favorable attitudes about performance appraisal.

Organizational Characteristics

Organizations can do much to create a favorable context for performance appraisal. Performance appraisal should be viewed as an integral part of a manager's organizational role (Katz & Kahn, 1978). Managers should be given adequate time to make appraisals, training, and rewards for the fairness and accuracy of their appraisals. Of course, employees attach the same degree of importance to performance appraisal as they perceive being attached by their superiors (Rowe, 1964). If performance appraisal has visible and continued support from all levels in the organization, employees should evaluate the appraisal process positively.

Policies. Kavanagh and Taber (1987) have argued that organizations should consider implementing policies that affirm employee rights in performance appraisal systems. These rights include fairness and accuracy of appraisals, privacy, use of performance standards, and supervisor competency for appraisal. Kavanagh and Taber hypothesized that organizations incorporating these rights would improve employee acceptance of the performance appraisal process. Unfortunately, no research has been conducted that directly bears on this hypothesis.

A theoretical rationale for establishing organizational policies for performance appraisal could be based on the concepts of justice developed in social psychology. Distributive justice refers to the perceived fairness of the outcomes of decision making, whereas procedural justice refers to the perceived fairness of the procedures used in decision making (Folger & Greenberg, 1985). Outcomes in organizational decision making include wage scales, labor-management agreements, performance appraisal ratings, and performance goals. Processes related to these outcomes include job evaluation systems, dispute-resolution procedures, performance appraisal interviews, and Management by Objectives, respectively. Most organizations already have policies concerning outcomes such as wage scales and labor-management agreements as well as the processes of job evaluation and dispute resolution used to attain these outcomes.

In support of the rationale, Greenberg (1986) has already demonstrated that perceived fairness in performance appraisal can be understood in terms of the notions of procedural and distributive justice. He had managers, who claimed to have had at least 30 experiences giving and receiving performance appraisals, describe incidents in which they received a particularly fair or unfair performance appraisal. A second group of managers was then asked to identify categories reflected in these incidents using the Q-sort technique. A final group of managers rated the categories for importance as determinants of fair appraisals. A factor analysis of the importance ratings yielded two factors that accounted for 95% of the rating variance. One factor dealt with procedural processes (e.g., soliciting input prior to making an evaluation and using it; two-way communication during the appraisal interview). A second factor dealt with the relation between the appraisal rating and subsequent administration action (e.g., recommendation for salary–promotion based on rating).

Programs.   Although most employees would welcome an appraisal that helps them to improve and leads to performance-based rewards, they could believe that the appraisal is based on inadequate or irrelevant information. Clearly, supervisors must be encouraged to attain first-hand knowledge of employee performance, an understanding of job duties, and the ability to conduct appraisals. Otherwise, performance appraisals would lead to few improvements and be unacceptable to employees.

Training programs have been shown to be effective for improving supervisory ability to make appraisals (DeCotiis & Petit, 1978; Dickinson & Baker, 1989; Landy & Farr, 1980). Effective training should illustrate and provide practice in observing performance, recording relevant information, and making performance ratings (Wexley & Latham, 1981). Training should also be provided in how to conduct performance appraisal interviews. Ivancevich (1982) reported a field study that examined employee attitudes toward appraisal interviews that were conducted by supervisors who received training in providing feedback and/or assigning performance goals (i.e., variations of the ''tell and sell'' style). These training programs increased employee perceptions of the fairness, accuracy, and clarity of the appraisal interview.

In some organizations, performance is constrained by factors in the work environment that are not under employee control (Eulberg, O'Connor, Peters, & Watson, 1984). For example, employees may receive services and help from others to do their job, or they may have to wait for previous stages of the work flow to be completed. In these situations, performance can be impeded by poor coordination of work activities or unplanned changes in work schedules. If supervisors do not consider performance constraints in conducting appraisals, employees may believe that the appraisals are unfair and inaccurate reflections of their contributions to the organization.

Dickinson and Davis (1984) used structural equation analysis to evaluate the influence of perceived performance constraints (e.g., my appraisal considers limitations imposed by others), rater ability (e.g., received training; is familiar with my performance), and appraisal purpose (e.g., used for development and promotion decisions) on the perceived utility of the performance appraisals (e.g., aid for setting goals). The results suggested that appraisal purpose and performance constraints had direct influences on perceived utility. However, rater ability was perceived to influence utility indirectly to the extent that raters considered performance constraints in making appraisals. Greater rater ability was perceived to lead to more consideration of performance constraints, and in turn this led to greater perceived utility for the appraisals.

The motivation of the managers who use a performance appraisal system is also critical to its acceptance. Unless managers perceive support from top management for the appraisal system, they may not be motivated to use that system. Beer et al. (1978) described a comprehensive appraisal system, whose acceptance by managers was still in doubt after several years of operation. The system included extensive training for most levels of management, an emphasis on goal setting and development, and the splitting of salary and developmental interviews. Although the system was highly accepted by those managers who did use it, this enthusiasm did not spread throughout the organization. Managers who did not use the system reported that they do not use it because top management had not endorsed the system. Apparently, nonusers were reluctant to engage in the time-consuming process of using the new system, unless they were encouraged to do so by top management.

Managers should not only be encouraged by top management to use a performance appraisal system, but they should also be rewarded for performance appraisal. In a unique study, Napier and Latham (1986) asked managers to describe the outcomes that they expected from conducting performance appraisals. The outcomes included "nothing," intrinsic satisfaction, financial reward, and promotion. Napier and Latham also found that a majority of managers expected "nothing" as the primary consequence of giving employees positive or negative appraisals. Importantly, appraisals were perceived not to depend on financial reward or the likelihood of promotion. Although managers did expect appreciation from employees and superiors for positive appraisals, they expected little appreciation for negative appraisals. Napier and Latham asserted that expectations of few positive outcomes from conducting performance appraisals explain why managers tend to make inaccurate ratings. Obviously, these outcome expectations also help in understanding managerial attitudes about performance appraisal.

Context. On the other hand, managers do engage in activities that support and enhance employee performance. These activities are important for managerial and organizational success, because they create the context for job performance. As suggested by Lawler (1967), organizations and managers differ in characteristics that determine not only the context for job performance, but also the context for performance appraisal.

Recently, Davis and Dickinson (1987) investigated the influence of contextual variables on attitudes about performance appraisal. State employees were surveyed from organizational units that provided mental health, mental retardation, and substance abuse services. Attitudes about performance appraisal were related to unit- and individual-level contextual variables. The unit-level variables represented differences between sets of supervisors and subordinates (e.g., member communications, enforcement of work policies), and the individual-level variables reflected aspects of managerial style.

Both unit- and individual-level variables accounted for unique variance in acceptability. Employees in units characterized by good lateral and vertical communications among members perceived performance appraisals to be more acceptable. Openness in unit communications apparently included open discussions about performance. Greater unit standardization also led to more acceptable performance appraisals. When operating rules and policies were strictly adhered to within the work unit, it probably resulted in greater clarity and consistency in performance standards, and subsequently, to favorable attitudes about performance appraisal. With respect to individual-level variables, several aspects of managerial style influenced attitudes. Performance appraisals were more acceptable to subordinates when they perceived their supervisors as trustworthy and supportive, receptive to change, and able to facilitate positive interactions among unit members.

CONCLUSIONS

The research on performance appraisal attitudes has supported Lawler's (1967) contention that these attitudes are determined by characteristics of the appraisal system, the individual, and the organization. A summary is shown in Fig. 10.6 of the characteristics that have been shown to influence various appraisal attitudes.

Early research focused on single-item measures (Dipboye & de Pontbriand, 1981; Landy et al., 1978), whereas later research attempted to develop and use multi-item scales (Davis & Dickinson, 1987; Kavanagh et al., 1985; Secunda, 1983). This is a desirable trend. The use of single-item measures restricts reliability and raises questions about the conceptualization of the constructs. For example, Landy et al. included several items that reflect goal setting in the performance appraisal interview, and several others that reflect the expression of emotion during that interview. In contrast, two studies used factor analysis

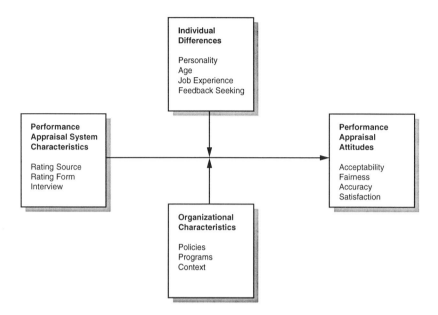

FIG. 10.6. Summary model of performance appraisal attitudes.

of their attitudinal items to develop different constructs for understanding the appraisal interview. Namely, Greenberg (1986) identified factors of procedural and distributive justice, whereas Russell and Goode (1988) identified factors of appraisal satisfaction and improvement value. Clearly, several constructs underlie attitudes about performance appraisal. Future research should delineate these constructs, develop adequate scales to measure them, and determine their usefulness for understanding performance appraisal.

Early research also viewed the performance-rating level as a parsimonious explanation for attitudes about performance appraisal. The argument was that the favorability of performance appraisal attitudes could be simply due to the performance rating per se rather than the nature of the processes that determined the rating. Although the principle of parsimony is useful in model building and verification, a broader perspective includes the performance rating and process measures in a nomological network for explaining appraisal attitudes. In this way, research evidence can accumulate to help in model building and verification. The model developed by Secunda (1983) illustrates that the level of the performance rating helps but does not *solely* explain attitudes about performance appraisal.

Perhaps the single most important determinant of employee attitudes about performance appraisal is the supervisor. When the supervisor is perceived as trustworthy and supportive, attitudes about performance appraisal are favorable. Specific attitudes about performance appraisal must be viewed as tied to the general issue of supervisory effectiveness (Ilgen et al., 1981). Supervisors often lack knowledge of their subordinates' job duties, and they are poorly trained in providing performance feedback, gauging employee reactions to that feedback, and setting improvement goals. A focus on supervisors must also include attention to the expectations that they have for conducting performance appraisals. If supervisors believe that performance appraisal is a negative and nonrewarding endeavor, their subordinates are likely to have attitudes that match these expectations.

Another focus for research is the influence of organizational differences on attitudes about performance appraisal. Appraisal attitudes are shaped by variables that are properly conceived at the organizational level. This level of research is difficult to conduct because it requires the sampling of organizations or the sampling of distinct units in very large organizations. However, attitudes about performance appraisal systems are formed in a milieu of other organizational subsystems and variables (McCall & DeVries, 1976). These subsystems and variables probably shape appraisal attitudes and the usefulness of the appraisal system to a much greater degree than is currently known.

Organizations also differ in their policies about performance appraisal, and the extent to which these policies are known and enforced by management. Policies can reflect that top management is serious about the importance of performance appraisal and its central role in organizational decision making. They help to foster widespread use of the performance appraisal system as well as favorable attitudes about that system. Mechanisms for establishing appraisal policies (e.g., procedural and distributed justice) and the effects of those policies on appraisal attitudes need to be considered in future research.

Another research issue to consider is the unsettling possibility that individuals who are exposed to sophisticated appraisal systems probably have more complex appraisal attitudes. For example, in organizational settings where appraisal is done infrequently, employee attitudes are probably not well differentiated and are strongly determined by performance-rating level. A related issue is that attitudes toward other job-related attributes (e.g., pay and benefits) probably determine the complexity of appraisal attitudes. Such possibilities suggest that models of appraisal attitudes will be exceedingly difficult to validate, because they may not readily generalize across organizations. Future research investigations should carefully describe the nature of the organizations, performance appraisal systems, and processes under investigation.

In summary, the broad categories suggested by Lawler (1967) must be considered a starting point for the development of models of appraisal attitudes. At a minimum, the models should be based on constructs that are measured with multi-item scales. The models should be sophisticated and include constructs about supervision and the appraisal process, performance ratings as determinants, and organizational context variables. When possible, these models should be compared across organizations to evaluate their generalizability for understanding attitudes about performance appraisal.

REFERENCES

Ashford, S. J., & Cummings, L. L. (1983). Feedback as an individual resource: Personal strategies of creating information. *Organizational Behavior and Human Performance, 32,* 370–398.

Beer, M., Ruh, R., Dawson, J. A., McCaa, B. B., & Kavanagh, M. J. (1978). A performance management system: Research, design, introduction and evaluation. *Personnel Psychology, 31,* 505–535.

Burke, R. J., Weitzel, W., & Weir, T. (1978). Characteristics of effective employee performance review and development interviews: Replication and extension. *Personnel Psychology, 31,* 903–919.

Burke, R. J., & Wilcox, D. S. (1969). Characteristics of effective employee performance review and development interviews. *Personnel Psychology, 22,* 291–305.

Cederblom, D. (1982). The performance appraisal interview: A review, implications, and suggestions. *Academy of Management Review, 7,* 219–227.

Cederblom, D., & Lounsbury, J. W. (1980). An investigation of user acceptance of peer evaluations. *Personnel Psychology, 33,* 567–579.

Cummings, L. L. (1973). A field experimental study of the effects of two performance appraisal systems. *Personnel Psychology, 26,* 489–502.

Davis, D. D., & Dickinson, T. L. (1987, August). Organizational and contextual determinants of the perceived utility of performance appraisals. In M. Secunda (Chair), *Beyond current performance appraisal research: Acceptability as a new paradigm.* Symposium conducted at the annual meeting of the American Psychological Association, New York.

Deci, E. L. (1975). *Intrinsic motivation.* New York: Plenum Press.

DeCotiis, T. A., & Petit, A. (1978). The performance appraisal process: A model and some testable propositions. *Academy of Management Review, 3,* 635–646.

Dickinson, T. L., & Baker, T. A. (1989, August). *Training to improve rating accuracy: A meta-analysis.* Paper presented at the annual meeting of the American Psychological Association, New Orleans.

Dickinson, T. L., & Davis, D. D. (1984, March). *The perceived utility of performance: A structural model and organizational analysis.* Paper presented at the annual meeting of the Southeastern Psychological Association, New Orleans.

Dickinson, T. L., & Zellinger, P. M. (1980). A comparison of the behaviorally anchored rating and mixed standard scale formats. *Journal of Applied Psychology, 65,* 147–154.

Dipboye, R., & de Pontbriand, R. (1981). Correlates of employee reactions to performance appraisals and appraisal systems. *Journal of Applied Psychology, 66,* 248–251.

Dorfman, P. W., Stephan, W. G., & Loveland, J. (1986). Performance appraisal behaviors: Supervisor perceptions and subordinate reactions. *Personnel Psychology, 39,* 579–597.

Eulberg, J. R., O'Connor, E. J., Peters, L. H., & Watson, T. W. (1984). *Situational constraints upon performance: A selective review of relevant literature* (AFHRL-TP-83-48, AD-A138 337). Brooks AFB, TX: Manpower and Personnel Division, Air Force Human Resources Laboratory.

Fisher, C. D. (1978). The effects of personal control, competence, and extrinsic reward systems on intrinsic motivation. *Organizational Behavior and Human Performance, 21,* 273–288.

Fisher, C. D. (1979). Transmission of positive and negative feedback to subordinates: A laboratory investigation. *Journal of Applied Psychology, 62,* 624–627.

Folger, R., & Greenberg, J. (1985). Procedural justice: An interpretive analysis of personnel systems. In K. M. Rowland & G. R. Ferris (Eds.), *Research in personnel and human resources management* (Vol. 3, pp. 141–183). Greenwich, CT: JAI Press.

French, J. R. P., Kay, E., & Meyer, H. H. (1966). Participation and the appraisal system. *Human Relations, 19,* 3–19.

Friedman, B. A., & Cornelius, E. T. (1976). Effects of rater participation in scale construction on the psychometric characteristics of two rating scale formats. *Journal of Applied Psychology, 61,* 210–216.

Fulk, J., Brief, A. P., & Barr, S. H. (1985). Trust in supervisor and perceived fairness and accuracy of performance evaluations. *Journal of Business Research, 13,* 301–313.

Greenberg, J. (1986). Determinants of perceived fairness of performance evaluations. *Journal of Applied Psychology, 71,* 340–342.

Hedge, J. W., Teachout, M. S., & Dickinson, T. L. (1987, August). User acceptance as a criterion for choosing performance measures. In M. Secunda (Chair), *Beyond current performance appraisal research: Acceptability as a new paradigm.* Symposium conducted at the annual meeting of the American Psychological Association, New York.

Herold, D. M., & Greller, M. M. (1977). Feedback: The definition of a construct. *Academy of Management Journal, 20,* 142–147.

Ilgen, D. R., & Feldman, J. M. (1983). Performance appraisal: A process focus. In B. M. Staw & L. L. Cummings (Eds.), *Research in organizational behavior* (Vol. 5, pp. 141–197). Greenwich, CT: JAI Press.

Ilgen, D. R., Fisher, C. D., & Taylor, M. S. (1979). Consequences of individual feedback on behavior in organizations. *Journal of Applied Psychology, 64,* 349–371.

Ilgen, D. R., & Knowlton, W. A., Jr. (1980). Performance attributional effects on feedback from superiors. *Organizational Behavior and Human Performance, 25,* 441–456.

Ilgen, D. R., Peterson, R. B., Martin, B. A., & Boeschen, D. A. (1981). Supervisor and subordinate reactions to performance appraisal sessions. *Organizational Behavior and Human Performance, 28,* 311–330.

Ivancevich, J. M. (1982). Subordinates' reactions to performance appraisal interviews: A test of feedback and goal-setting techniques. *Journal of Applied Psychology, 67,* 581–587.

Jones, S. C. (1973). Self- and interpersonal evaluations: Esteem theories versus consistency theories. *Psychological Bulletin, 79,* 185–199.

Katz, D., & Kahn, R. (1978). *The social psychology of organizations* (2nd ed.). New York: Wiley.

Kavanagh, M. J., & Hedge, J. W. (1983, May). *A closer look at correlates of performance appraisal system acceptability.* Paper presented at the annual meeting of the Eastern Academy of Management, Pittsburgh.

Kavanagh, M. J., Hedge, J. W., Ree, M., Earles, J., & DeBiasi, G. L. (1985, May). *Clarification of some issues in regard to employee acceptability of performance appraisal: Results from five samples.* Paper presented at the annual meeting of the Eastern Academy of Management, Albany, NY.

Kavanagh, M. J., & Taber, T. (1987, August). Employee acceptability and rights in performance appraisal: Directions for research. In M. Secunda (Chair), *Beyond current performance appraisal research: Acceptability as a new paradigm.* Symposium conducted at the annual meeting of the American Psychological Association, New York.

Kay, E., Meyer, H. H., & French, J. R. P. (1965). Effects of threat in a performance appraisal interview. *Journal of Applied Psychology, 49,* 311–317.

Keaveny, T. J., Inderrieden, E. J., & Allen, R. E. (1987). An integrated perspective of performance appraisal interviews. *Psychological Reports, 61,* 639–646.

Landy, F. J., Barnes, J. L., & Murphy, K. R. (1978). Correlates of perceived fairness and accuracy of performance evaluation. *Journal of Applied Psychology, 63,* 751–754.

Landy, F. J., Barnes-Farrell, J., & Cleveland, J. (1980). Perceived fairness and accuracy of performance evaluation: A follow-up. *Journal of Applied Psychology, 65,* 355–356.

Landy, F. J., & Farr, J. L. (1980). Performance rating. *Psychological Bulletin, 87,* 72–107.

Lawler, E. E. (1967). The multitrait–multirater approach to measuring managerial job performance. *Journal of Applied Psychology, 51,* 369–381.

Lazer, R. I., & Wilkstrom, W. S. (1977). *Appraising managerial performance: Current practices and future directions.* New York: The Conference Board.

Maier, N. R. F. (1958). *The appraisal interview: Objectives, methods and skills.* New York: Wiley.

McCall, M. W., Jr., & DeVries, D. L. (1976). *Appraisal in context: Clashing with organizational realities.* Paper presented at the annual meeting of the American Psychological Association, Washington, DC.

McEvoy, G. M., & Buller, P. F. (1987). User acceptance of peer appraisals in an industrial setting. *Personnel Psychology, 40,* 785–797.

Meyer, H. H., Kay, E., & French, J. R. P. (1965). Split roles in performance appraisal. *Harvard Business Review, 43*, 123–129.

Napier, N. K., & Latham, G. P. (1986). Outcome expectancies of people who conduct performance appraisals. *Personnel Psychology, 39*, 827–837.

Nemeroff, W. F., & Wexley, K. N. (1979). An exploration of the relationship between performance feedback interview characteristics and interview outcomes as perceived by managers and subordinates. *Journal of Occupational Psychology, 52*, 25–34.

Prince, J. B., & Lawler, E. E. (1986). Does salary discussion hurt the developmental performance appraisal? *Organizational Behavior and Human Decision Processes, 37*, 357–375.

Rowe, K. H., (1964). An appraisal of appraisals. *The Journal of Management Studies, 1*, 1–26.

Russell, J. S., & Goode, D. L. (1988). An analysis of managers' reactions to their own performance appraisal feedback. *Journal of Applied Psychology, 73*, 63–67.

Secunda, M. D. (1983). *Employee perceptions of performance appraisal systems: Causal determinants of fairness, accuracy, and acceptability.* Unpublished doctoral dissertation, Old Dominion University, Norfolk, VA.

Shrauger, J. S. (1975). Responses to evaluation as a function of initial self-perceptions. *Psychological Bulletin, 82*, 581–596.

Silverman, S. S., & Wexley, K. N. (1984). Reaction of employees to performance appraisal interviews as a function of their participation in rating scale development. *Personnel Psychology, 37*, 703–710.

Steel, B. S. (1985). Participative performance appraisal in Washington: An assessment of post-implementation receptivity. *Public Personnel Management, 14*, 153–171.

Steers, R. M., & Porter, L. W. (1974). The role of task-goal attributes in employee performance. *Psychological Bulletin, 81*, 434–452.

Stone, D. L., Gueutal, H. G., & McIntosh, B. (1984). The effects of feedback sequence and expertise of the rater on perceived feedback accuracy. *Personnel Psychology, 37*, 487–506.

Wexley, K. N. (1979). Performance appraisal and feedback. In S. Kerr (Ed.), *Organizational behavior* (pp. 241–259). Columbus, OH: Grid.

Wexley, K. N., & Latham. G. P. (1981). *Developing and training human resources in organizations.* Glenview, IL: Scott, Foresman.

Wexley, K. N., Singh, J. P., & Yukl, G. A. (1973). Subordinate personality as a moderator of the effects of participation in three types of appraisal interviews. *Journal of Applied Psychology, 58*, 54–59.

Wiener, Y. (1973). Task ego involvement and self-esteem as moderators of situationally devalued self-esteem. *Journal of Applied Psychology, 58*, 225–232.

Informal Performance Feedback: Seeking and Giving

James L. Farr
Pennsylvania State University

Information concerning one's performance on a task or job is an important factor in the learning of a new task or job, in the maintenance of performance levels on a previously learned task or job, and in the motivation of the individual toward improved performance levels. Such feedback can be given by the manager to the individual in a *formal* performance appraisal interview setting. Dickinson (this volume) has discussed the research related to individual attitudes about performance appraisal. Feedback can also be communicated in an *informal* manner in the course of day-to-day interactions between the manager and the employee, between the individual and the customers or clients, and among co-workers. A consideration of issues related to the *giving* of informal feedback by the manager to an employee and to the *seeking* of such feedback by the employee is the primary focus of this chapter.

The giving and seeking of informal feedback about work performance may not, at first glance, be related to the focus of this volume, individual and organizational perspectives related to personnel selection and assessment. However, if we consider that the informal feedback that an individual receives is likely to color his or her reaction to such personnel decisions as promotions, then relevance to the individual perspective is more apparent. Further, as is discussed later in this chapter in more detail, the active seeking of performance feedback by the work performer may alter the nature or favorability of the informal feedback that the individual receives from others. Thus, feedback seeking may indirectly affect the individual's expectations about and reactions to formal organizational assessments of performance effectiveness and related personnel decisions.

163

In examining informal feedback, it is useful to consider the work setting as an information environment (Hanser & Muchinsky, 1978). An information-environment framework implies that an individual not only receives performance-related information from various elements in the environment but also monitors the environment for such information and acts on the environment to create such information. This chapter begins with a more extended treatment of the information-environment approach to performance feedback. A consideration of the individual as an active seeker of feedback within this environment follows. Then, factors that affect the giving of feedback (primarily by the manager) to the individual performer are discussed. Finally, the implications of this perspective for feedback systems in organizations are examined.

FEEDBACK IN AN INFORMATION ENVIRONMENT

Thinking about the work setting as an information environment recognizes that the individual at work faces daily a large array of information that may have relevance for the individual's learning about how well he or she is performing at work. A major task for the individual is to make sense of this environment, to create a personal meaning for the environment relevant to the goals and purposes of the individual. Within the work setting it has been argued (e.g., Ashford & Cummings, 1983) that important goals for many individuals include the correction of performance errors, the reduction of personal uncertainty about the appropriateness of various work behaviors and how others perceive and evaluate one's performance, and the attainment and maintenance of feelings of self-competence with regard to job performance. Thus, performance-related information in the work environment should have considerable salience, and the individual is likely to be motivated to gain access to such information.

It is important to note that these personal goals may only partially overlap with organizational goals related to feedback. Organizational goals are usually concerned almost exclusively with performance improvement.

Performance-related information (hereafter simply called feedback) can be categorized along several dimensions. Three such dimensions are type of information, source of information, and information acquisition mode.

Types of Informal Feedback

There are two broad types of feedback: informative and evaluative. Informative feedback tells the performer what behaviors are necessary for successful performance of the job, and evaluative feedback informs the performer about whether he or she is performing successfully on the job (Greller & Herold, 1975; Hanser & Muchinsky, 1978). Both types of feedback are likely to be necessary for the performer to meet his or her goals. Greller and Herold (1975) and Hanser and Muchinsky (1978) have found that both informative and evaluative feedback are perceived by work performers, although the distinctiveness of the two types was not clear. Many feedback messages contain both informative and evaluative elements. Thus, it may be difficult for work performers to distinguish between them in actual work settings.

Other researchers have proposed different terms for the categorization of feedback that may be easier to distinguish than "informative" and "evaluative." For example, Earley, Northcraft, Lee, and Lituchy (1990) referred to *outcome* and *process* feedback. Outcome feedback is information concerning performance outcomes, whereas process feedback is information concerning the manner by which the work performer implements a work strategy. Process feedback is clearly more specific and informative with regard to how the individual might alter performance strategies, whereas outcome feedback primarily informs the individual about overall performance success and may impact more on motivation or effort level rather than on strategy.

Sources of Informal Feedback

Source refers to which element in the work environment supplies the feedback to the work performer. There are a variety of possible sources for informal feedback. These include: (a) higher hierarchical sources (immediate supervisor and higher management); (b) interpersonal sources not higher than the role performer in the formal organizational hierarchy (peers, subordinates, and customer–clients); and (c) the process of task–job performance itself (task–self).

Data obtained by Herold, Liden, and Leatherwood (1987) suggested strongly that feedback from the task and self is viewed most favorably by work performers with regard to personal usefulness. Feedback from supervisors was rated next most useful, followed by that from co-workers. Feedback that came from the formal organization was viewed as least useful by the work performers. The data of Herold et al. (1987) did not include an examination of the relationship of perceptions of the usefulness of feedback from different sources to actual job performance. A study by Becker and Klimoski (1989) did examine the relationship between the organizational feedback environment (as measured by the Job Feedback Survey of Herold and Parsons, 1985) and a composite performance measure developed from supervisory, peer, and self-ratings. Becker and Klimoski found that feedback from the supervisor and organization had the strongest relationship to performance. Higher frequencies of negative feedback from the supervisor and organization were associated with lower performance and more frequent positive feedback from these sources was associated with higher performance. Note that the correlational nature of these data preclude any statement about direction of causality.

Additional research that examines perceptions of usefulness of feedback from various sources, the amount of feedback provided from different sources, and

performance of the feedback recipients is needed to clarify the apparent incon-
sistency between the findings of Herold et al. (1987) and those of Becker and
Klimoski (1989). It should be noted that the Herold et al. study did obtain perceptions of frequency as well as usefulness of feedback from various sources.
These perceptions had a median correlation of about .55 across the five sources
(i.e., the more frequent the feedback from a given source, the more useful it
was judged). This may represent a confound in the measurement of these variables that partially explains their differences from the results of Becker and
Klimoski.

Modes of Informal Feedback Information Acquisition

Recent theory and research (e.g., Ashford, 1986; Ashford & Cummings, 1983;
Farr, 1991; Larson, 1989) have suggested that individuals attempt to obtain
performance-related information via several modes. However, most research
concerned with performance feedback has looked at such information as a special case of a one-way communication paradigm. From this perspective the work
performer is a relatively passive recipient of feedback information intentionally
transmitted by the source(s). The response of the recipient is generally evaluated in terms of whether it represents a behavioral change in the direction that
was advocated by the feedback message, that is, whether the recipient's performance is improved (at least in the view of the source). Thus, much of this
research on feedback has been concerned with how feedback leads to performance improvements and with what message and source factors lead to the
greatest amount of improvement. Psychological models of feedback developed
within this perspective tend to be focused on the characteristics of the recipient
that mediate the perception and acceptance of feedback messages and the intent to respond in accordance with feedback (e.g., Ilgen, Fisher, & Taylor, 1979).

Feedback information can be intentionally transmitted to the role performer
by a number of sources, such as supervisors, co-workers, subordinates, and
customers. For example, the supervisor may do this on a formal basis in an
appraisal interview such as described by Dickinson (this volume). As noted by
Ashford and Cummings (1983), these sources may also unintentionally provide
feedback to a work performer. Ashford and Cummings argued that work performers may actively seek more informal feedback about their performance via
two modes of information acquisition. First, the work environment may be monitored for performance-relevant information. The monitoring mode requires the
work performer to observe the work environment and the behavior of others
in that environment for cues that may be useful as feedback. These cues must
then be integrated by the individual performer and meaning relevant to performance derived. Second, the work performer may attempt to increase the amount
of available performance-relevant information by "creating" such information.
This may be done by directly asking others in the work setting for their evalua-

tions about the individual's performance (labeled as inquiry by Ashford and Cummings). For example, former Mayor Edward Koch of New York City frequently asked citizens on the street or at meetings: "How am I doing (as mayor)?"

Feedback may also be created (or stimulated) by performing in novel or innovative ways (at least in reference to the performer's past behavior; Farr, 1991). Changes in performance levels or styles are more likely than static levels or styles to elicit overt feedback information as well as behavioral cues that can be monitored and interpreted. A form of active seeking of informal feedback similar to inquiry, but less direct, has been labeled as prompting (Starnes & Farr, 1991). Prompting refers to the solicitation of informal feedback through behaviors that cue the source to provide feedback but do not directly ask for it.

Thus, four modes of feedback seeking have been suggested: inquiry, monitoring, innovative acts, and prompting. Miller and Jablin (1991) described some related tactics that organizational newcomers may use to seek information useful to them during their period of entry and assimilation into the organization. Most of the information-seeking tactics noted by Miller and Jablin fall under one of the four modes described earlier, although their terminology differs.

The several modes of actively seeking feedback can be arrayed in terms of their likely effort and cost to the individual performer (Ashford & Cummings, 1983). For example, monitoring typically requires less physical effort than innovation, prompting, or inquiry but may require more cognitive processing of many cues and more attentional effort if clear cues are not present in the work environment.

Three major types of costs exist: loss-of-face (or social costs in the terminology of Miller & Jablin, 1991; or desire to maintain a favorable self-presentation as noted by Northcraft & Ashford, 1990); negative impact on one's self-concept; and inferential. Loss-of-face refers to the fact that it may be embarrassing to ask others for feedback or to be known as desirous of feedback. Others may judge the work performer to be insecure, ingratiating, and so forth (Ashford & Cummings, 1983). The likelihood of face loss is clearly greatest for the inquiry mode and least for the monitoring mode with innovation and prompting in between.

Negative impact on self-concept is possible if negative feedback is received (Northcraft & Ashford, 1990). Because most individuals are motivated to enhance or maintain favorable views of themselves, any potential threat to such views will be perceived as very costly by the individual. Here, individual differences are likely to moderate the degree of cost associated with various modes of feedback seeking. Those with low self-concepts or performance expectations are likely to perceive greater costs with all modes of feedback seeking than those with strong self-concepts or high performance expectations (Northcraft & Ashford, 1990). Individuals with a learning goal orientation may view the potential of receiving negative feedback as less costly than those with a performance goal orientation (Dweck, 1986). Those with a learning goal orientation consider errors or negative feedback to be useful information about how to master a task or develop a skill and, consequently, do not react defensively to such feedback.

Inference costs refer to possible errors the work performer can make concerning the feedback information obtained. The less direct mode of monitoring is more likely to result in inferential errors about the meaning of a manager's smile or a co-worker's invitation to lunch than is the more direct mode of asking a supervisor or co-worker about one's work performance (i.e., inquiry). Prompting and innovation are likely to fall in between monitoring and inquiry in terms of inferential costs. For the individual performer there is generally a trade-off between face loss and inferential error costs. Ashford and Cummings (1983) suggested that the individual will actively seek feedback information only when the perceived anticipated value of the information to be obtained exceeds the negative aspects of effort and cost.

Feedback seeking is highly consistent with a view of work as an information environment and emphasizes the active, rather than the passive, role that the individual takes in the feedback process. It also suggests that a social information-processing or social-comparison component (e.g., Salancik & Pfeffer, 1978; Weiss & Shaw, 1979; Zalesny & Ford, 1990) is likely to be important to the understanding of how the role performer develops and interprets feedback information.

Although absolute standards of performance may exist for certain aspects of jobs, it would be unusual for job performance to be thoroughly, or even adequately, covered by such measures for the great majority of jobs. Instead, the assessment of performance level (by self and others) is done on a relative basis, that is, comparing the work performer's behavior with that of others in the same or similar jobs. Also, it is likely that the interpretation of indirect performance cues (obtained via monitoring, for example) is in part based on comparisons of such cues that other work performers have received.

Inferring the Meaning of Informal Feedback

Drawing on conceptual and empirical developments in attribution theory (e.g., Kelley & Michela, 1980), it seems reasonable that a work performer would use certain pieces of information about the feedback to draw inferences about its possible meaning. This information includes the dimensions of consensus, consistency, and distinctiveness. In the context of drawing inferences about possible performance cues, consensus can refer to two comparisons. First, consensus refers to whether a single source provides similar or identical feedback to other role performers when they perform in a way comparable to the target work performer. Second, consensus can refer to whether multiple sources provide similar feedback to the individual about job performance. Consistency refers to whether the cue is provided to the target role performer each time the individual performs in a similar way. Distinctiveness refers to whether the cue is not provided to the target performer when he or she performs in a manner quantitatively or qualitatively different from the initial performance.

If a cue is perceived to be contingently related to performance, then the cue would be seen as being consistent and distinctive. Thus, its perceived information value should be high. Further, if the cue is contingently provided to other work performers (that is, has consensus), then its perceived information value would be still higher. Finally, if different sources provide similar feedback to the individual, then its information value would be perceived as even higher. The most salient cue dimensions should be those related to one's own performance, not those concerned with the relation of cues to the behavior of other work performers. Consistency, distinctiveness, and consensus related to multiple feedback sources are only concerned with the relation of the possible performance cue to one's own behavior or performance. Consensus related to other work performers is concerned with the linkage of cues to the behavior of others and is less likely to affect perceived information value (Mitchell, Green, & Wood, 1981).

However, consensus related to other work performers should have more impact on the perceived information value of feedback to the extent that the job duties of other performers are similar to those of the target performer, the physical proximity of other performers, and the observability of others' work outcomes. These factors should facilitate the ease of comparisons of the links between feedback and the performance of others.

Liden and Mitchell (1985) found that recipients of feedback preferred feedback that contained attributional information to feedback without such information. In general, they also preferred feedback that implied an external attribution for poor performance rather than an internal one.

It should be noted that research suggests that there is a bias toward seeing more covariation between events in our environment than objectively does exist (e.g., Jennings, Amabile, & Ross, 1982). Individuals often have an "implicit theory" that predicts that elements in our environment are linked together in predictable ways. It is likely that most work performers would have a personal theory (implicitly even if not articulated) about the relationships between one's performance and the behaviors of others (that is, possible feedback cues). Thus, the tendency to believe that certain behaviors are diagnostic of others' evaluations of one's job performance may be widespread.

Use of Feedback Seeking in Work Settings

Studies by Ashford and Cummings (1985) and Herold and Parsons (1985) report data consistent with the view that proactive feedback seeking is a common and important method for obtaining performance-related information in work settings. Herold and Parsons conducted a series of factor analyses of responses to a feedback questionnaire. The resulting factors suggest that work performers use a variety of cues, both direct and indirect, when attempting to determine how well they are performing their jobs. Their data indicate that individuals do use self-generated feedback for obtaining both favorable and unfavorable information about performance.

Ashford and Cummings (1985) examined the relationship between feedback-seeking behavior and a variety of individual and situational characteristics. They found that those work performers with relatively short tenure with the organization were more likely to seek feedback than longer term employees (a finding compatible with the discussion of the information seeking of organizational newcomers by Miller & Jablin, 1991). Individuals who indicated higher levels of job involvement sought feedback to a greater extent than those with lower levels of involvement. Tolerance for ambiguity operated as a moderator of the effects of role ambiguity and contingency on feedback seeking. Only individuals who were relatively intolerant of ambiguity sought more feedback when their jobs were ambiguous in terms of behavioral requirements; those who could tolerate such ambiguity did not seek more feedback even if their jobs were ambiguous.

A similar effect was found for contingency uncertainty (defined as the individual's experienced uncertainty about the relationship between evaluations of current performance and the attainment of second-order rewards such as promotions and pay increases). Those individuals relatively intolerant of ambiguity sought more feedback when experienced contingency uncertainty was high, but those relatively tolerant of ambiguity did not. These findings support the argument that feedback should be treated as a resource for the individual work performer. Those individuals who should place greater value on feedback (that is, have a greater need for it) were more likely to seek it actively. Essentially, the data suggest that people seek feedback about their performance to the extent that they do not already possess internal standards of comparison and to the extent that such information is not forthcoming from external sources. There are likely to be individual differences (for example, intolerance for ambiguity) that affect the total amount of performance-related information that an individual desires or requires. These findings require replication before too much is made of them as such interactions are often unreliable.

Bennett, Herold, and Ashford (1990) reported a reanalysis of the Ashford and Cummings (1985) data that separated job-related and problem-solving tolerance for ambiguity; these two forms of tolerance for ambiguity had been aggregated in the earlier article. Further, Bennett et al. assessed the relationship of these two forms of tolerance for ambiguity with several specific forms of feedback seeking, namely: (a) inquiry from manager, (b) inquiry from co-worker, and (c) monitoring the feedback environment, for two different types of information, information regarding current performance and information regarding advancement potential. Results indicated that individuals with low job-related tolerance for ambiguity queried managers and monitored the environment more for feedback about both current performance and advancement than those high in such tolerance. There was no relationship between job-related tolerance for ambiguity and feedback queries to co-workers. Neither did problem-solving tolerance for ambiguity correlate with feedback seeking, except for an unexpected finding that those with low tolerance for such ambiguity sought less feedback from supervisors about advancement potential than those with high tolerance. This study also suggests that the delineation of modes of feedback seeking is desirable in research, at least until more is known about the relationships among the various modes.

Additional data consistent with the view that feedback seeking is related to its relative costs and benefits were obtained by Ashford (1986). She found that longer tenure employees sought less feedback than those with shorter time in the organization or in their current position. Employees in the organization for a longer period saw greater risk in feedback seeking and those in their current job for a longer time placed less value on feedback than those with less tenure.

Morrison and Weldon (1990) reported that individuals with assigned performance goals sought more feedback than those without such goals. Further, among the individuals who were assigned goals, those who sought feedback were more likely to achieve their goals. Morrison and Weldon suggested that the assigned goal increased feedback seeking because those individuals with goals valued attainment of the goals and could use the feedback to accomplish that. This reasoning is consistent with the view of Ashford and Cummings (1983) that feedback can be a resource for the individual work performer.

The impact of additional characteristics of individuals and feedback systems on feedback seeking were studied by Northcraft and Ashford (1990). They obtained results that varied due to the type of feedback being sought. For feedback about one's personal performance (based on objective and absolute measures), it was found that individuals engaged in less feedback inquiry when performance expectations were low, when self-esteem was low, and when the feedback was to be delivered publicly (especially for those with low performance expectations). For social-comparison feedback (which compared the individual's performance to that of others), performance expectations had no effect on inquiry. Public feedback delivery decreased feedback inquiry in comparison to private delivery. Northcraft and Ashford speculated that the differences between personal performance and social-comparison information might be due to the perception of most subjects that the seeking of personal performance information would be viewed as appropriate (these were lab subjects performing a fairly novel task), but that seeking social-comparison information might be construed as excessively competitive. In any event, the results suggest that the calculation of costs and benefits of feedback information are likely to be complex and situationally dependent. They also indicate that individuals who may need (at least in terms of performance improvement) feedback the most, those with low performance expectations, are least likely to request it and, thus, less likely to improve.

In summary, the various studies that have looked at factors influencing feedback seeking offer general support to the propositions originally put forth by Ashford and Cummings (1983). Feedback seeking, both in terms of amount and mode, seems to be moderated by the individual's perceptions of the various costs and benefits to be derived from the information that might be obtained. However, we still do not have a complete picture of all the factors affecting those judgments nor how the individual combines these perceptions to make decisions regarding feedback seeking. Nonetheless, the data do suggest that individuals who are being formally assessed (e.g., in a selection or promotion situation) will be motivated to learn how well they have performed, whether on selection instruments (in the case of selection candidates) or on the current job (in the case of promotion candidates). Thus, the impact of feedback seeking on reactions to selection and assessment devices seems quite probable.

THE GIVING OF FEEDBACK

The previous material covered in this chapter has been concerned with feedback from the perspective of the work performer. Feedback can also be viewed from the standpoint of the potential feedback provider. As noted earlier, there are several different possible sources of feedback information; however, in this section only the manager as a source of informal feedback is considered. Larson (1984, 1989) has suggested a model of informal feedback giving that is quite compatible with the general orientation of this chapter. It examines the cognitive, affective, and situational antecedents that are likely to influence the manager's decision to give feedback to a work performer and also considers the cognitive and affective consequences that giving informal performance feedback can have for the manager. Larson (1989) has discussed the interplay between the employee's feedback-seeking behavior and the subsequent giving of feedback by the manager with focus on the case of the poor-performing employee. Of less interest to Larson are the effects of such feedback on the work performer's performance, although the employee's response to feedback is a part of the model. Figure 11.1 presents a simplified version of Larson's (1984) model of informal feedback giving; Fig. 11.1 also includes Larson's (1989) addition of employee feedback seeking to his earlier model. Larson's model is based on concepts of attribution theory that have already been discussed in some detail earlier in this chapter.

Antecedents of Feedback Giving

Rather than discuss in detail the rationale for the antecedents of feedback giving shown in Fig. 11.1, a summary of the major predictions of the model is given next (see Larson, 1984, 1989, for more details.) Additional references that support the predictions are provided where appropriate.

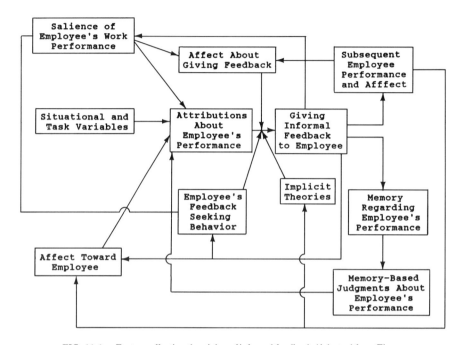

FIG. 11.1. Factors affecting the giving of informal feedback (Adapted from Figure 1 in Larson, 1984, including concepts discussed in Larson, 1989).

To summarize the antecedents of feedback giving shown in Fig. 11.1, a manager is more likely to give informal feedback to an employee following a particular behavior or performance if: (a) The manager views the behavior as important; (b) the performance level deviates from the typical one, especially if below standard (Hobson, 1986; Larson, 1986; Quinn & Farr, 1989); (c) the employee is viewed as being personally responsible for performance (and effort plays a major role in determining performance level); (d) the manager's own performance and rewards are dependent on the performance of the employee (Larson, 1986); (e) the organizational norms and particular role held by the manager encourage the transmittal of performance information; (f) the employee is well liked by the manager and the feedback is favorable; (g) the manager anticipates positive affect resulting from the giving of feedback; and (h) the manager believes that employees will respond in a positive manner to feedback.

Larson (1989) hypothesized that employees who believe that they are performing poorly often will initiate the inquiry mode of feedback seeking, directing the query at the manager. The prompting mode (Starnes & Farr, 1991) might be utilized also. The value to the employee of such inquiries or prompts is based on the well-established tendency of managers to distort feedback to poor performers in a positive direction (i.e., to provide feedback indicating that performance is better than it objectively is; Benedict & Levine, 1988; Fisher, 1979;

Larson, 1986; Longenecker, Sims, & Gioia, 1987). A direct query or prompt by a poor performer, prior to the giving of "spontaneous" feedback by the manager to the performer, may result in the manager indicating that the performance is adequate or involves only minor problems. (Such feedback seeking can be thought of a specific instance of impression management or influence tactics; see, for example, Schriesheim & Hinkin, 1990; Wayne & Ferris, 1990; Wayne & Kacmar, 1991.) Thus, the seeking of feedback may prevent the giving of more negative feedback. Supporting this prediction, Quinn and Farr (1989) found that high feedback seekers were given more total positive feedback than low feedback seekers, controlling for the actual performance level of the performer.

Following the provision of feedback to the feedback seeker, the manager may also remember the feedback and not the actual, more negative, performance, leading to a more positive performance "record" for that employee in the mind of the manager. Thus, feedback seeking by the relatively poor employee may have both short- and long-term effects. The long-term effects may include better chances for positive assessments and subsequent promotions for those who more frequently inquire about and prompt performance feedback.

Consequences of Giving Feedback

As indicated in Fig. 11.1, a manager's giving informal feedback to an employee has several direct consequences that can also indirectly influence some antecedent variables. The giving of feedback may itself more directly influence certain other antecedent variables. Figure 11.1 denotes the dynamic nature of the feedback-giving process over time.

The very act of giving feedback influences the salience of the employee's performance by focusing attention on the behavior and by demanding the processing of information about the behavior. Particularly for less than adequate performance, the manager is more likely to pay attention to the employee's future performance if feedback has been given in the past, especially if the feedback has included performance goals or specific corrective actions to be taken by the employee.

In a related vein, giving feedback is likely to facilitate the manager's memory for past performance information through increased processing of performance-relevant information or through the increased availability of performance information (Larson, 1984). Memory-based judgments about the employee's performance may also influence future attributions. If the manager gives feedback only about poor performance, the manager's recall of performance information for the employee will be biased in the direction of greater unfavorability. These may lead to a judgment of consistently poor information and, thus, an internal and stable attribution regarding the causes of the employee's behavior (e.g., I remember only poor performance; therefore, this employee must not have the ability to do the job). As noted earlier, feedback seeking by the employee is likely to result in positively distorted feedback from the manager that, in turn, may similarly bias the recall of the employee's performance history. Also, Farr, Schwartz, Quinn, and Bittner (1989) found that high feedback seekers were rated as more highly task motivated than low feedback seekers. Such evaluations may influence later behavior and decisions of the manager concerning the employee.

The employee's subsequent performance and attitudinal responses to feedback are affected by the feedback given by the manager, but in potentially complex ways (e.g., Taylor, Fisher, & Ilgen, 1984). Of greater interest to Larson's (1984) model are the effects that such consequences have on prior variables. Employee responses to feedback impact on the manager's implicit theories about the effects of feedback by providing data relevant to such theories. These implicit theories are presumed to change rather slowly, although a particularly vivid single event could trigger a major change (Nisbett & Ross, 1980). Affect toward giving feedback and toward the employee are both influenced by the employee's reactions to the feedback. Employees who respond in line with the feedback and accept the feedback without defensive or negatively emotional responses are likely to be better liked. Favorable reactions will also tend to make more positive the anticipated effect resulting from the giving of feedback in the future.

Recent research on reactions to informal feedback suggest that the potentially destructive responses to negative feedback can be lessened. Baron (1988, 1990) has demonstrated that negative feedback that is harsh in tone, nonspecific, and focuses on the employee as the sole cause of the poor performance leads to greater employee anger and tension, lowered self-efficacy, and less willingness to collaborate or compromise. Baron has also found that if criticism is paired with apologies by the feedback giver concerning the feedback (e.g., "I'm sorry to have made you angry"; "I'm sorry that I had to be so harsh in evaluating your performance.") or if the giver indicates that there were no harmful intentions of the negative feedback, that many of the undesirable reactions of the work performer are minimized. Fedor, Eder, and Buckley (1989) also found that, if the intentions of the feedback giver were viewed as constructive and supportive of the employee, then negative feedback was reacted to in a more positive manner than if less favorable intentions were perceived.

Importance of the Feedback Giving Model

There has long been interest in developing better ways of presenting formal performance feedback, such as in performance appraisal interviews (e.g., Kay, Meyer, & French, 1965; Meyer, Kay, & French, 1965). However, prior to the work of Larson (1984), there has not been an attempt to develop a comprehensive model of giving feedback on an informal basis as a part of the daily process of supervising and managing others at work. The subsequent integration (Larson,

1989) of the feedback-seeking literature with the feedback-giving model adds to our understanding of these dynamic processes. It also suggests how the individual may influence assessment outcomes (and subsequent personnel decisions) that rely on judgments made by others in the work setting.

It seems clear that informal feedback by its potential frequency and temporal closeness to behavioral acts should be far more powerful as a mechanism for effecting change than formal performance-appraisal methods that typically occur once or twice per year. Larson (1984, 1989) has given us a good start in understanding informal feedback giving. However, there is still much to learn. We do not know if it is important whether feedback has been given spontaneously by the supervisor or has resulted from a query or prompt from the performer. In addition, Larson has only considered the supervisor or manager as the source of informal feedback, but co-workers certainly represent another source with great potential for providing such feedback. We need to examine factors likely to influence the decision of peers to give feedback or not to their colleagues. Also, Larson's model is concerned with the individual employee as the recipient of feedback. As work groups with interdependent roles and tasks become more prevalent in work organizations (see the chapter by Prieto, this volume), we need to be more concerned with giving feedback to groups (Nadler, 1979; Varca & Levy, 1984).

IMPLICATIONS FOR PRACTICE

In the previous sections of this chapter the concern has been primarily in terms of theory and research related to performance feedback. In this section the focus is on the implications of recent research and theory for practice, that is, how performance feedback can be more effectively given and received. Space does not permit a thorough discussion of all such implications; the following is a selective number of those highlighted by the material presented in this chapter:

1. Generally in work situations, individuals desire more feedback than they are currently receiving about their work performance. Although not a surprising conclusion, recent research on feedback seeking highlights an important consequence of a less than desired amount of feedback. In the absence of sufficient feedback, many work performers will search for or create feedback for themselves. They may interpret various actions and messages from managers, peers, and others as having performance-relevant information, even if such is not intended by the other person(s). This may lead to errors by the work performer in his or her understanding of how others evaluate his or her work performance. Research evidence suggests that individuals seek less feedback when their work role is not ambiguous, when the manager provides information about the relationships between performance and organizational rewards, and when the in-

dividual has been employed for a relatively long period of time (Ashford & Cummings, 1985). Thus, managers should be especially careful to provide feedback to organizational and work group newcomers (Miller & Jablin, 1991) and to those in positions that are not well defined or do not result in readily observable outcomes.

2. Several findings point to the importance of the type of information that is communicated to the work performer. Nadler (1977) and Baron (1988, 1990) noted that feedback should be relatively specific, based on particular behavioral events, and constructive in nature, that is, indicating ways in which the performance can be improved. Future performance goals should also be specified, and employee input into the setting of these goals is often useful for their acceptance and accomplishment (Ilgen et al., 1979; Latham & Wexley, 1981; Nadler, 1979). The specificity of goals serves well both the directing and motivating purposes of feedback. Research concerned with the role of attributions in motivating work performance suggests that managers should include feedback statements that encourage employees to make appropriate internal attributions (Parsons, Herold, & Leatherwood, 1985); for example, employees should be told that poor performance may be overcome by working harder, or that a task can be learned and performed well only after practice and early errors. Similarly, managers should indicate to employees after successful performance that their success was due to ability and effort. Feedback needs to include not only information about the outcomes of performance (that is, the overall or final success or failure), but also information about the effectiveness of process variables leading to the outcome (Jacoby, Mazursky, Troutman, & Kuss, 1984). Jacoby et al. found that better performers sought feedback of a cognitive, diagnostic nature and not outcome feedback (see also the work of Earley et al., 1990).

3. Informal or day-to-day feedback is more important than feedback that occurs during the annual or semiannual performance-appraisal session in terms of its impacts on work performance and attitudes. However, managerial training tends to focus on the formal feedback process. More organizations need to be concerned about developing the manager's ability and willingness to give informal feedback. Attention also needs to be given to the topic of training work performers to receive feedback in a nondefensive constructive manner.

4. Organizations must be concerned about the perceptions of employees concerning the fairness and accuracy of feedback and appraisal mechanisms (see Dickinson, this volume). The performance standards of the organization and manager must be reasonable, and there should be reasonable congruence between organizational and personal standards for effective performance (Taylor et al., 1984). Periodic attitude surveys concerning both performance evaluation methods and feedback processes are needed to monitor employee opinion and to identify problems before they become severe.

5. Individual differences among work performers require the provider of feedback to be sensitive to variations in interpretation of and reaction to performance information. Not enough is known about the specific links between individual characteristics and feedback-related behaviors and attitudes to be able to identify how certain types of individuals will respond to various kinds of feedback messages. What is important for the manager to understand is that one should not expect all employees to respond in the same way.

REFERENCES

Ashford, S. J. (1986). Feedback-seeking in individual adaptation: A resource perspective. *Academy of Management Journal, 29,* 465–487.

Ashford, S. J., & Cummings, L. L. (1983). Feedback as an individual resource: Personal strategies for creating information. *Organizational Behavior and Human Performance, 32,* 370–389.

Ashford, S. J., & Cummings, L. L. (1985). Proactive feedback seeking: The instrumental use of the information environment. *Journal of Occupational Psychology, 58,* 67–79.

Baron, R. A. (1988). Negative effects of destructive criticism: Impact on conflict, self-efficacy, and task performance. *Journal of Applied Psychology, 73,* 199–207.

Baron, R. A. (1990). Countering the effects of destructive criticism: The relative efficacy of four interventions. *Journal of Applied Psychology, 75,* 235–245.

Becker, T. E., & Klimoski, R. J. (1989). A field study of the relationship between the organizational feedback environment and performance. *Personnel Psychology, 42,* 343–358.

Benedict, M. E., & Levine, E. L. (1988). Delay and distortion: Tacit influences on performance appraisal effectiveness. *Journal of Applied Psychology, 73,* 507–514.

Bennett, N., Herold, D. M., & Ashford, S. J. (1990). The effects of tolerance for ambiguity on feedback-seeking behaviour. *Journal of Occupational Psychology, 63,* 343–347.

Dweck, C. S. (1986). Motivational processes affecting learning. *American Psychologist, 41,* 1040–1048.

Earley, P. C., Northcraft, G. B., Lee, C., & Lituchy, T. R. (1990). Impact of process and outcome feedback on the relation of goal setting to task performance. *Academy of Management Journal, 33,* 87–105.

Farr, J. L. (1991). Leistungsfeedback und Arbeitsverhalten [Performance feedback and work behavior]. In H. Schuler (Ed.), *Beurteilung und forderung beruflicher leistung* (pp. 57–80). Stuttgart: Verlag fur Angewandte Psychologie.

Farr, J. L., Schwartz, A. C., Quinn, J. C., & Bittner, K. L. (1989). *Consequences of feedback seeking on supervisory performance ratings and attributions.* Paper presented at the Fourth Annual Conference, Society for Industrial and Organizational Psychology, Boston.

Fedor, D. B., Eder, R. W., & Buckley, M. R. (1989). The contributory effects of supervisory intentions on subordinate feedback responses. *Organizational Behavior and Human Decision Processes, 44,* 396–414.

Fisher, C. D. (1979). Transmission of positive and negative feedback to subordinates: A laboratory investigation. *Journal of Applied Psychology, 64,* 533–540.

Greller, M. M., & Herold, D. M. (1975). Sources of feedback: A preliminary investigation. *Organizational Behavior and Human Performance, 13,* 244–256.

Hanser, L. M., & Muchinsky, P. M. (1978). Work as an information environment. *Organizational Behavior and Human Performance, 21,* 47–60.

Herold, D. M., Liden, R. C., & Leatherwood, M. L. (1987). Using multiple attributes to assess sources of performance feedback. *Academy of Management Journal, 30,* 826–835.

Herold, D. M., & Parsons, C. K. (1985). Assessing the feedback environment in work organizations: Development of the Job Feedback Survey. *Journal of Applied Psychology, 70,* 290–305.

Hobson, C. J. (1986). Factors affecting the frequency, timing, and sign of informal supervisory feedback to subordinates in a simulated work setting. *Multivariate Behavioral Research, 21*, 187–200.

Ilgen, D. R., Fisher, C. D., & Taylor, M. S. (1979). Consequences of individual feedback on behavior in organizations. *Journal of Applied Psychology, 64*, 349–371.

Jacoby, J., Mazursky, D., Troutman, T., & Kuss, A. (1984). When feedback is ignored: Disutility of outcome feedback. *Journal of Applied Psychology, 69*, 531–545.

Jennings, D. L., Amabile, T. M., & Ross, L. (1982). Informal covariation assessment: Data-based versus theory-based judgments. In D. Kahneman, P. Slovic, & A. Tversky (Eds.), *Judgment under uncertainty: Heuristics and biases.* Cambridge, UK: Cambridge University Press.

Kay, E., Meyer, H. H., & French, J. R. P. (1965). Effects of threat in a performance appraisal interview. *Journal of Applied Psychology, 49*, 311–317.

Kelley, H. H., & Michela, J. L. (1980). Attribution theory and research. *Annual Review of Psychology, 31*, 457–501.

Larson, J. R., Jr. (1984). The performance feedback process: A preliminary model. *Organizational Behavior and Human Performance, 33*, 42–76.

Larson, J. R., Jr. (1986). Supervisors' performance feedback to subordinates: The role of subordinate performance valence and outcome dependence. *Organizational Behavior and Human Decision Processes, 37*, 391–408.

Larson, J. R., Jr. (1989). The dynamic interplay between employees' feedback-seeking strategies and supervisors' delivery of performance feedback. *Academy of Management Review, 14*, 408–422.

Latham, G. P., & Wexley, K. N. (1981). *Increasing productivity through performance appraisal.* Reading, MA: Addison-Wesley.

Liden, R. C., & Mitchell, T. R. (1985). Reactions to feedback: The role of attributions. *Academy of Management Journal, 28*, 291–308.

Longenecker, C. O., Sims, H. P., Jr., & Gioia, D. A. (1987). Behind the mask: The politics of employee appraisal. *Academy of Management Executive, 1*, 183–193.

Meyer, H. H., Kay, E., & French, J. R. P. (1965). Split roles in performance appraisal. *Harvard Business Review, 43*, 123–129.

Miller, V. D., & Jablin, F. M. (1991). Information seeking during organizational entry: Influences, tactics, and a model of the process. *Academy of Management Review, 16*, 92–120.

Mitchell, T. R., Green, S. G., & Wood, R. E. (1981). An attributional model of leadership and the poor performing subordinate: Development and validation. In L. L. Cummings & B. M. Staw (Eds.), *Research in organizational behavior* (Vol. 3, pp. 197–234).

Morrison, E. W., & Weldon, E. (1990). The impact of an assigned performance goal on feedback seeking behavior. *Human Performance, 3*, 37–50.

Nadler, D. A. (1977). *Feedback and organization development.* Reading, MA: Addison-Wesley.

Nadler, D. A. (1979). The effects of feedback on task group behavior: A review of the experimental research. *Organizational Behavior and Human Performance, 23*, 309–338.

Nisbett, R., & Ross, L. (1980). *Human inference: Strategies and shortcomings of social judgment.* Englewood Cliffs, NJ: Prentice-Hall.

Northcraft, G. B., & Ashford, S. J. (1990). The preservation of self in everyday life: The effects of performance expectations and feedback context on feedback inquiry. *Organizational Behavior and Human Decision Processes, 47*, 42–64.

Parsons, C. K., Herold, D. M., & Leatherwood, M. L. (1985). Turnover during initial employment: A longitudinal study of the role of causal attributions. *Journal of Applied Psychology, 70*, 337–341.

Quinn, J. C., & Farr, J. L. (1989). *Antecedents to the delivery of informal feedback: The influence of feedback seeking, performance level, and gender.* Paper presented at the Annual Convention of the American Psychological Association, New Orleans.

Salancik, G. R., & Pfeffer, J. (1978). A social information processing approach to job attitudes and task design. *Administrative Science Quarterly, 23*, 224–253.

Schriesheim, C. A., & Hinkin, T. R. (1990). Influence tactics used by subordinates: A theoretical and empirical analysis and refinement of the Kipnis, Schmidt, and Wilkinson subscales. *Journal of Applied Psychology, 75*, 246–257.

Starnes, W., & Farr, J. L. (1991). *Prompting as a mode of feedback seeking.* Unpublished manuscript, Department of Psychology, Pennsylvania State University, University Park.

Taylor, M. S., Fisher, C. D., & Ilgen, D. R. (1984). Individuals' reactions to performance feedback in organizations: A control theory perspective. In K. M. Rowland & G. R. Ferris, (Eds.), *Research in personnel and human resources management* (Vol. 2, pp. 81–124).

Varca, P. E., & Levy, J. C. (1984). Individual differences in response to unfavorable group feedback. *Organizational Behavior and Human Performance, 33*, 100–111.

Wayne, S. J., & Ferris, G. R. (1990). Influence tactics, affect, and exchange quality in supervisor-subordinate interactions: A laboratory experiment and field study. *Journal of Applied Psychology, 75*, 487–499.

Wayne, S. J., & Kacmar, K. M. (1991). The effects of impression management on the performance appraisal process. *Organizational Behavior and Human Decision Processes, 48*, 70–88.

Weiss, H. M., & Shaw, J. B. (1979). Social influences on judgments about tasks. *Organizational Behavior and Human Performance, 24*, 126–140.

Zalesny, M. D., & Ford, J. K. (1990). Extending the social information processing perspective: New links to attitudes, behaviors, and perceptions. *Organizational Behavior and Human Decision Processes, 47*, 205–246.

III

Influence of the Social Context on Selection and Assessment: Introductory Comments

The chapters in this section address several important issues about which the interests of the individual and the organization may be in conflict, or which require consideration of the wider social context that surrounds the individual and the organization. One such issue is the fairness of selection procedures for all candidates. Organizations are typically interested in obtaining employees with the highest predicted job performance in order to maximize expected productivity. A societal goal may be the equitable (fair) treatment of minority group members in selection situations. Wigdor and Sackett in Chapter 12 discuss a recent examination of the General Aptitude Test Battery (GATB) by a committee appointed by the U.S. National Academy of Sciences. The GATB is administered to large numbers of job applicants who use the various state employment offices to seek positions. Wigdor and Sackett present data comparing various ways of referring (to organizations for hiring) candidates from rank-ordered (using GATB scores) lists of applicants. Their results support a *performance fair* approach to selection that results in equal proportions of *good* workers from various minority and majority groups in the referred sample.

Pearn in Chapter 13 provides the European perspective to fairness in selection and assessment. He details the development of equal employment legislation and practice, focusing on the United Kingdom but with information on the broader European context as well, and notes differences with the U.S. experience. Pearn also suggests a preliminary model for describing conditions that may lead to unfairness in organizational selection systems.

A shift from personnel selection based solely on factors related to an individual's ability to perform an independent task or job to selection that addresses the individual's ability to perform in a group setting on interdependent tasks is advocated by Prieto in Chapter 14. Prieto argues that interpersonal "fit" is an increasingly important factor in determining work team effectiveness. He describes a set of interpersonal proficiencies that he labels as the ASCII control codes for team proficiency that can be assessed using multiple methods and incorporated into a diagnosis of individual fit within a work group.

In Chapter 15 Ilgen notes that organizational decision makers, and industrial-organizational psychologists, have long pursued the goal of *accurate* performance appraisals; that is, the principal concern has been to obtain an assessment of the performance of an employee that reflects the actual current contribution of that employee to the organization and, then, to provide candid performance feedback to the employee. Ilgen argues that such a goal may often be misguided as it does not correspond to what is desired by either the evaluator or the employee. This is a provocative argument that challenges both conceptual models and organizational practice and may cause the reader to rethink many common assumptions about the value of accurate appraisal information.

The final chapter in this section by de Wolff also challenges industrial-organizational psychologists to expand their thinking beyond the usual prediction paradigm. The prediction paradigm emphasizes traditional empirical validity of selection procedures and a one-way approach to selection, that is, the organization demands certain information from applicants and then tells the applicants whether they will be hired or promoted. Although valid procedures are necessary, de Wolff notes that many situations do not allow for empirical validation for various reasons. Also, where the requirements of a position are dynamic and/or ambiguous, negotiation between the applicants and the organization may be necessary in order to yield the best choice for the job.

12

Employment Testing and Public Policy: The Case of the General Aptitude Test Battery

Alexandra K. Wigdor
National Research Council

Paul R. Sackett
University of Minnesota

In this chapter we present a description of a controversial employment testing program that illustrates the conflict between different perspectives on the role of testing. At issue is the tension between organizational goals of productivity maximization and societal goals of equitable treatment of members of minority groups. The authors served as the study director and as a committee member, respectively, of a U.S. National Research Council committee charged with an evaluation of the use of the General Aptitude Test Battery (GATB) by the U.S. Employment Service. We describe the social and political context in which controversy over the GATB arose and summarize the committee's finding regarding the GATB.

Over 3 million jobs in the United States are filled annually through the Public Employment Service, a cooperative federal–state employment agency that includes a network of 1,800 local employment offices administered by the states. The United States Employment Service (USES), a division of the Department of Labor and the federal partner in the Public Employment Service, has encouraged the states to experiment with a new referral system that uses the General Aptitude Test Battery to screen applicants for virtually all jobs. By replacing traditional interview procedures with a system that refers people to jobs in order of their scores on a standardized test, USES hopes to be able to provide employers with a more proficient group of candidates to consider for employment.

If this plan to use a general aptitude test to refer job seekers to all kinds of jobs is found legally acceptable under the civil rights laws, it is likely that employers will be drawn in great numbers to the Public Employment Service, hoping to cloak their hiring procedures in the protective mantle of a federally sponsored employment test.

THE LEGAL ENVIRONMENT

Despite language in Title VII of the Civil Rights Act of 1964 that explicitly permits employers to use any professionally developed employment test as long as it is not "designed, intended, or used to discriminate," the courts have tended to find challenged employment tests, particularly paper-and-pencil aptitude or ability tests, to be discriminatory. The reason for this outcome is plain: The minority groups on whose behalf the Civil Rights Act was passed have significantly lower average scores on cognitive tests than the majority group. As a consequence, members of these groups are hired or promoted in much lower proportions than they are present in the applicant pool when test scores are determinative. Whereas a claim of discrimination can be countered by evidence that the selection device in question is in fact job related, many employers do not have such evidence available, and others find the evidence they provide subject to a set of standards that are difficult to meet.

As long as these group differences in test scores persist, it is a given that the use of employment tests will generate charges of discrimination. Because test scores are highly correlated with economic, social, and educational status, cognitive tests can quite rightly be viewed as a tool to continue the historical disadvantage visited on Blacks and certain other minority groups, even if, from another perspective, such tests are seen to promote productivity in the work place and to reward achievement.

In addition to outlawing employment discrimination, which is essentially a Thou Shalt Not commandment, the federal government has also encouraged, and for public agencies and government contractors required, employers to take "affirmative action" to redress past discrimination against minorities and women. Affirmative action is an explicitly race- and gender-conscious policy and for that reason has been controversial. Hiring or promotion plans that dilute the influence of test scores or other objective criteria by combining them with considerations of the racial or gender mix of the existing work force have frequently raised the charge of reverse discrimination.

In 1979 the Supreme Court upheld the legality, in carefully circumscribed circumstances, of voluntary affirmative action programs to benefit members of minority groups under Title VII (*United States Steelworkers v Weber*, 443 U.S. 193). However, the climate of judicial opinion in the late 1980s has apparently brought this cautious endorsement of affirmative action into question.

Consider, for example, the case of the city of Birmingham, Alabama, and its fire department. In 1974 seven Black individuals brought suit under Title

VII alleging discriminatory hiring and promotion practices. Before the trial was completed, the city entered into a consent decree with the plaintiffs that set up an extensive remedial program, including interim and long-term annual goals for hiring Blacks as firefighters and for promoting Blacks within the department. The consent decree was challenged at the time by seven White firefighters who claimed that it would discriminate against them. The court ruled against them. However, the Supreme Court recently upheld the right of a new generation of White firefighters, hired since the consent decree was entered into, to sue the city of Birmingham on the grounds that the court-approved promotion plan preferred less qualified Blacks in violation of Title VII (*Martin v Wilks*, Slip Opinion No. 87-1614, June 12, 1989).

This decision paves the way for challenges to voluntary and court-approved affirmative action programs more generally and leaves employers as vulnerable to reverse discrimination suits as they are to discrimination suits under the adverse impact doctrine. Employers are, as the saying goes, between a rock and a hard place.

THE EFFECTS OF FEDERAL EEO POLICY

The federal government's attempts to deal with the realities of pervasive discrimination in the work place have had an enormous impact on the way firms hire and promote people, on the expectations of those in whose behalf the Civil Rights Act was passed, and, not least, on employment testing.

Many testing professionals would agree that the pressure of federal civil rights policy has had a number of salutary effects on the science and practice of employment testing. The job-relatedness doctrine enunciated by the Supreme Court in *Griggs v Duke Power* (401 U.S. 424) has forced employers to take a more critical look at their procedures. Most sizable companies have committed greater resources to personnel matters, hiring trained personnel managers, undertaking validation studies to support their use of tests, and, of necessity, documenting their procedures.

Despite new vitality in the theory and practice of employment testing, however, the overall impact of federal civil rights policy has not been salutary. There are destructive—and thus far intractable—tensions in federal policy, tensions between free market principles of maximizing productivity and freedom of employer choice and the desire to bring minorities and women into the mainstream economy. Even stickier are the tensions between affirmative action policies, which many believe are necessary to any substantial improvement in the economic position of Blacks, women, and others traditionally denied access to most jobs, and the fundamental principle that all citizens should be treated equally under the law.

Many observers are concerned that the contradictions in federal equal employment opportunity policy are forcing employers to seriously compromise, if not abandon, their interest in worker quality at a time when our faltering competitive position in world trade already threatens American business and industry. The fate of employment testing certainly supports that contention. Even cognitive tests with a substantial research base supporting them have generally failed to survive legal challenge because of enormous imbalances in the rate at which majority and minority applicants are hired and promoted when test scores dominate the decision—as has been the case, for example, in federal, state, and municipal merit systems. The federal government decided to abandon its own Professional and Administrative Career Examination (PACE), the screening tool for entry-level civil servants, as part of a consent decree early in the decade because of its adverse impact on minority applicants.

Caught between the twin specters of discrimination and reverse-discrimination suits, many employers, both public and private, have turned away from objective selection procedures in order to avoid legal challenge. This has to have an effect on work-force efficiency that the individual employer, to say nothing about the society as a whole, can ill afford.

In an opinion handed down in 1988 (*Watson v Fort Worth Bank & Trust*, Slip Opinion No. 86–6139, June 29, 1988), Justice Sandra Day O'Connor recognized that the inevitable focus on statistics in disparate or adverse impact cases could put undue pressure on employers to adopt what she called inappropriate prophylactic measures: "If quotas and preferential treatment become the only cost-effective means of avoiding expensive litigation and potentially catastrophic liability, such measures will be widely adopted" (p. 12). Justice O'Connor decries this outcome as clearly contrary to congressional intent, which no doubt it is.

Unfortunately, federal policy has provided no clear alternative course of action. The fundamental purpose of the Civil Rights Act of 1964 was to extend to Blacks the fruits of citizenship that they had long been denied. By failing to face forthrightly the extreme long-term disadvantage produced by centuries of denying Blacks (and to a far lesser extent women) virtually all chance to compete as equals for education, economic opportunity, and social status; and by denying the need to explicitly provide for some period of preferential treatment in the present to combat the cumulative effects of past law and policy, federal policy has placed the societal interest in economic productivity in direct competition with the equally compelling interest in integrating Blacks and other disadvantaged minorities into the larger society.

The threat to productivity is not, however, the most dangerous side effect of the federal government's failure to develop a coherent policy for bringing disadvantaged minorities into the economic mainstream. The strength of the social contract lies in the belief of a preponderance of citizens that the system is essentially fair and evenhanded. This conviction has been dangerously eroded.

THE CASE OF THE GATB

The recent history of the Department of Labor's General Aptitude Test Battery (GATB) illustrates the complicated interplay of scientific and policy issues that surround employment testing. Developed by the U.S. Employment Service in the 1940s, the GATB is a general test of cognitive functioning similar to what used to be called IQ tests. The GATB is a bit unusual because it also includes a number of psychomotor subtests to assess manual and finger dexterity. Until 1980 the GATB had an unassuming career in the state-administered local Employment Service offices as an aide to vocational counseling and as a tool for referring job seekers to employers with openings in a limited number of jobs for which the predictive validity of the test was established over the years. Typically, only about 8% of applicants were tested; most referrals were made on the basis of brief interviews and the assignment of job codes according to each applicant's work experience and training.

The interview is known, however, to be a quixotic means of choosing among job candidates. There is a large research literature that demonstrates the greater predictive power of well-developed ability tests (e.g., Hunter & Hunter, 1984). In an atmosphere of declining American competitiveness and in response to the business orientation of the Reagan Administration, the Department of Labor in 1980 took a new look at the GATB. Encouraged by developments since 1975 in the theoretical underpinnings of psychological testing, the staff of the U.S. Employment Service proposed that the GATB be adopted throughout the Employment Service system to screen applicants for virtually all jobs.

Approximately 19 million people pass through the 1,800 local offices annually, and about 3.5 million of them are actually placed in jobs. If even a third to a half of all registrants were given the GATB, this would be by far the largest testing program in the country. In comparison, about 2 million high school seniors take the two major college admissions tests—the SAT and the ACT—annually.

The U.S. Employment Service's plan to use the GATB to refer people to all kinds of jobs was made possible by advances in a new field of analysis called validity generalization (VG). This is a type of meta-analysis, a system for combining the results of many separate studies of the predictive validity of a test (Hunter & Schmidt, 1990).

Test validity research studies are commonly plagued by a number of errors: the idiosyncrasies of small samples, measurement error, and restriction in the range of ability found in the group of people tested as compared with the total relevant population. The problem of using small unrepresentative samples is that the validity relationships found across studies will vary dramatically. Until recently, this effect led most testing professionals to argue that a test should be validated for each substantially new use—for every new job, for every job in a new location, and if the population of test takers deviates from the sample used in validating the test. In other words, professional opinion traditionally emphasized the situational specificity of tests, and, in accordance with the conventional wisdom, the GATB was used only sparingly.

The theory of validity generalization is in the process of turning the conventional wisdom upside down. VG analysis attempts to estimate the "true validity" of a test, that is, to estimate how accurately the test would predict job (or school) performance if we had data for the entire relevant population (e.g., all people who would be likely to apply for the kind of job in question, etc.) rather than just a small and/or unrepresentative sample of that group. The major contribution of VG analysis has been to show that the appearance of tremendous variance across studies in the size of validity coefficients is due in large part to sampling error (i.e., to the use of small samples). Evidence that the "true variance" across studies is relatively small once sampling error is adjusted for supports the new proposition that test validities can be generalized to jobs, locations, and populations not studied. Hence, the USES staff concluded that the GATB is a valid predictor of performance in many—Department of Labor technical reports claim all—of the 12,000 jobs in the U.S. economy, not just the 500 for which it has been specifically validated.

DESIGN OF THE USES TESTING PROGRAM

The U.S. Employment Service (USES) designed its new VG–GATB testing program (the designation reflects its reliance on validity generalization analysis) to balance two goals: first, to offer employers the maximum possible productivity gains from improved employee selection, and, second, to comply with federal nondiscrimination law, that is, to avoid adverse impact on minority clients.

In order to get the greatest possible economic benefit from testing, the VG–GATB program was set up so that people would be referred to jobs in order of test score. Because the probabilities are that the higher test scorer will also be the better performer on the job, this top-down method of choosing from among the applicants on file would give the employer that subset of available job seekers with the greatest expected performance.

However, USES recognized that referral in strict order of test score would also make the employer—and the Employment Service—vulnerable to charges of discrimination under Title VII. The research staff had evidence that the mean GATB score for Black applicants falls about one standard deviation below the mean score in the White group (the mean for Hispanics is halfway between). In practical terms, this meant that if 25% of the majority group were referred, only 5% of the Black group would be referred to a typical job handled by the Employment Service. It was felt that this disparity in referral rates would be sufficient to establish a strong legal case against any employer who hired from the resulting referral pool—and against the Department of Labor's 50 partners in the Employment Service system, the states.

To prevent this from happening, USES sought a compromise between the governmental interest in promoting economic productivity and the equally compelling interest in helping disadvantaged minorities into the economic mainstream. The solution employed was to compute each registrant's GATB score as a percentile score within his or her own racial or ethnic group (Black, Hispanic, and other).

This strategy retains the top-down approach to referral, but in a qualified way. It effectively wipes out the average score differences among the groups, because Black, Hispanic, and White candidates assigned a given percentile score—let us say the 70th percentile—would be referred at the same time even though their raw scores on the GATB would be substantially different. In general, employers would receive a more qualified group of applicants to look at than the old Employment Service system provided, when referrals were based on brief interviews by the local office staff, and in accordance with Federal EEO goals. In the new system, those referred from the available pool of applicants would be the Black, Hispanic, and White applicants with the highest predicted performance in their respective groups. At the same time, minority applicants would be referred, on average, in numbers proportionate with their presence in the applicant pool, thus avoiding the exclusionary effect that testing would otherwise cause.

Many employers were very enthusiastic. In part employers responded positively because they saw results in reduced training time, better performance, and less turnover. But there was also enthusiasm because an agency of the federal government was sponsoring a testing program that solved their EEO problems.

Or so they thought.

ENTER THE DEPARTMENT OF JUSTICE

In the fall of 1986, William Bradford Reynolds, then Assistant Attorney General for Civil Rights in the U.S. Department of Justice and one of the most formidable critics of any kind of preferential treatment, challenged the VG–GATB referral system because of the within-group scoring strategy. In a letter to the director of the U.S. Employment Service, he urged that all states that had adopted the procedure be notified to cease and desist under threat of legal action.

In Mr. Reynolds' view, computing test scores by racial and ethnic subgroups constitutes an illegal and unconstitutional violation of an applicant's rights to be free from racial discrimination. The scoring strategy classifies Employment Service clients by race or national origin, which in his view is a contravention of the equal protection clause of the 14th Amendment to the Constitution as well as Title VII of the Civil Rights Act of 1964. And because the effect of the score adjustments is to raise the scores of Blacks and Hispanics, Mr. Reynolds found that it advances the interests of one group at the expense of another, and as such "constitutes intentional racial discrimination," in this instance what is commonly called reverse discrimination.

Cease and desist orders were not in fact issued. Recognizing the importance and the extreme complexity of the issues raised by the VG–GATB referral system, officials of the Labor and Justice Departments agreed to disagree until a study could be conducted by outside experts. That task was undertaken by the U.S. National Research Council (NRC), the working arm of the U.S. National Academy of Sciences, and a report presenting the study committee's findings and recommendations was recently published under the title *Fairness in Employment Testing: Validity Generalization, Minority Issues, and the General Aptitude Test Battery* (Hartigan & Wigdor, 1989).

PRODUCTIVITY AND FAIRNESS
CAN BE COMPLEMENTARY GOALS

The federal government can use the DOL–DOJ conflict of opinion over the VG–GATB as an opportunity to work out a more effective public policy on employment testing—one that simultaneously advances the economic goal of increasing work-force efficiency and the statutory goal of bringing Blacks into the economic mainstream instead of keeping the two at loggerheads. *Fairness in Employment Testing* makes it clear that—given the present state of the testing art—the two goals are not mutually exclusive. The crucial issue is to find a way to use the GATB so that it will not screen out virtually all Black and Hispanic job seekers on the one hand or unduly abridge the rights of majority-group job seekers on the other.

The Department of Labor's within-group scoring procedure struck the Department of Justice in 1986 as an infringement of the rights of nonminority Employment Service clients. Based on its analysis of GATB validities and of the joint distributions of group status, test score, and job performance, the National Research Council committee of experts has concluded that score adjustments are essential if the GATB is going to be used as a primary referral tool. But the committee is recommending a system of score adjustments to federal policy makers that is responsive to changes in the accuracy of the test and is more evenhanded, because it extends to Black, Hispanic, and White applicants who are at the same level of job performance an equal probability of being referred.

The policy recommendations of the *Fairness* report derive from two central findings about the GATB: (a) All things being equal, use of the VG–GATB referral system could provide individual employers with meaningful performance gains over the existing referral system (given certain essential improvements in the test and the research base); and (b) use of unadjusted test scores to refer Employment Service applicants would mean that a Black worker at the same level of job performance as a White worker *would not* have the same chances of being referred to a job. An explication of these findings follows.

THE RESEARCH BASE FOR THE GATB

The NRC committee's findings about the efficacy of test-based referral are based on its reanalysis of the entire corpus of 755 studies of the predictive validity of the GATB. The committee's work replicated and extended the work of Hunter (U.S. Department of Labor, 1983a, 1983b), which served as the original basis for the VG–GATB system. Accepting the basic premises of validity generalization theory, the committee estimated conservatively that the "true validity" of the GATB for the 500 jobs studied ranges from .20 to .40, with an average figure of .30.

The committee felt that it would be inappropriate to report a single set of figures as representing the validity of the GATB. We outline here three critical choices that will have an effect on the conclusions one would draw about the magnitude of test validity.

The first is a decision as to which set of studies should serve as the basis for conclusions. One troubling issue is that more recent studies tend to produce lower validity coefficients. Three sets of studies can be proposed as the basis for conclusions. The first is the original set of 515 studies used by Hunter in the creation of the USES–GATB validity generalization system. This set of studies produces the highest validity coefficients. The second is the complete set of 755 studies that result from adding the studies done since Hunter's analysis to the database. This results in lower mean validities due to the inclusion of the newer studies that have generally lower validities. The third is the set of 240 studies done since Hunter's analysis. Based on the argument earlier studies should be discarded because recent studies produce different findings, one might select this database.

As an illustration, consider the use of the General–Verbal–Numerical (GVN) composite for jobs in the compiling–computing job family for predicting job proficiency. The Hunter data produces a mean observed validity of .27; the data set combining the Hunter data and the new data produces a mean of .23; and the set of new studies alone produces a mean of .21.

The second decision involves the correction of the observed validity coefficients for measurement error in the criterion measure. The concept of correction for unreliability is not controversial, and the application of corrections in situations in which data on the degree of unreliability in a study is available is straightforward. However, in the GATB database criterion reliability data are not available for all studies. Thus corrections are made based on assumptions about the likely degree of unreliability. Hunter assumed that the typical reliability of criterion measures was .60 and made corrections using this value (corrected validity equals mean observed validity divided by the square root of the reliability coefficient). Whereas this figure of .60 has not been challenged in the published literature, many psychologists report obtaining interrater reliabilities of around .80 in applied work. Noting that the lower the reliability estimate, the higher the corrected value, one might argue for a more conservative correction, such as .80, rather than Hunter's .60.

Continuing the preceding illustration, let us apply these two different corrections to the mean validity figures:

	Hunter studies	All studies	New studies only
mean observed validity	.27	.23	.21
mean corrected validity, using .60 correction factor	.35	.30	.27
mean corrected validity, using .80 correction factor	.30	.26	.23

Thus, depending on one's choices as to the appropriate set of studies on which to base one's conclusions and on the choice of a correction factor for criterion unreliability, estimates of the mean validity range from .23 to .35.

The third critical choice involves the issue of correction for restriction of range. As with the case of correction for unreliability, the notion of correcting a validity coefficient when it is based on a sample with less variability than in the population of interest is not controversial. In a given study, if one knows the test standard deviation in the applicant pool and in the sample used to compute the validity coefficient, the ratio of these two standard deviations forms the basis for the range restriction correction.

In the USES databases, data on the applicant pool for each validity study are unavailable and thus must be estimated. As an estimate of the applicant pool standard deviation, Hunter computed the pooled standard deviation across all the studies in the GATB database. Conceptually, this is intended to represent the standard deviation of test scores among applicants in the U.S. economy at large, as Hunter argues that the sample of studies represents the economy at large. It is important to be very clear as to the meaning of validity coefficients corrected for restriction of range in this fashion: These corrected validities represent the degree of validity that would be obtained if (a) the applicant pool for every job was a representative sample of job applicants in the U.S. economy (e.g., the full range of ability was represented), and (b) no prescreening was done by USES or by the employer using any screening device correlated with ability (e.g., education). We doubt that either of these requirements is met. First, there is surely self-selection in terms of the ability level of individuals applying for highly skilled versus unskilled jobs. In fact, the GATB database shows that the range of ability within each job family is smaller than the range in the full GATB database. Second, the operational system proposed by USES does not preclude screening at the employer's request on the basis of factors such as education, experience, or possession of specific skills prior to GATB-based referral, thus restricting the effective applicant pool for the job in question.

An alternative view is to make no correction for restriction of range and to view the validity data as an indicator of the incremental validity of GATB screening in addition to the selection criteria already in place. Most studies in the GATB database represent the use of a concurrent validation strategy (i.e., the GATB was administered to current employees and, thus, was not part of the hiring decision). Thus, individuals included in the studies were those who met a particular employer's standards, and the validity coefficients computed on such samples indicates the incremental value of the GATB above and beyond the screening system already in use by the employer. Correction for range restriction would be inappropriate if the individuals hired and, thus, available for inclusion in the concurrent validity study constitute a representative sample of applicants meeting the employer's existing education, experience, and other standards. (Note that this discussion has focused on range restriction on the predictor. It is possible that range restriction on the criterion has taken place, e.g., low performers have been dismissed and high performers promoted. Even if this was the case, it is our sense that this form of range restriction is likely to have a very limited effect on validity in the studies in question.)

We see three approaches to range restriction correction. The first, following Hunter, produces a validity estimate that we feel can only be viewed as hypothetical: the validity that would be obtained if all applicants in the work force were viewed as candidates for every available job and if no screening on other criteria took place prior to GATB referral. This approach leads to the use of the most substantial correction factor. Recall that estimates of GVN validity for the job family in question range from .23 to .35; applying Hunter's correction raises to lower bound estimate from .23 to .33 and raises the upper bound estimate from .35 to .51.

The second approach involves obtaining data on the range of test scores in actual applicant pools for various jobs and making corrections based on these data. This is clearly the preferred approach; however, such data were not available to the committee. We feel quite confident in projecting that, if such data were available, the result would be a substantially smaller correction than that used by Hunter.

The third approach is based on the view that the question of interest is the incremental validity of the GATB above and beyond screening systems in use by employers. It can be argued that validity results from concurrent studies give a good estimate of this incremental validity and that range restriction corrections are not appropriate. For example, a high school diploma requirement will restrict the range of ability in an applicant pool, as ability and high school graduation are correlated. If the question of interest is "what is the incremental value of the GATB in this prescreened pool," correcting the GATB validity to the full range of ability found in an unscreened pool simply does not answer the question. Using this approach, the GVN validity estimates, which ranged from .23 to .35, would not be adjusted.

Thus, uncorrected GVN validity estimates for this job family range from .21 to .27 as a function of which of three databases are chosen as the basis for one's conclusions. Applying either of two criterion reliability corrections to any of the three databases results in validity estimates ranging from .23 to .35. Applying either Hunter's range restriction correction or adopting the "incremental validity" approach and not adjusting validities for range restriction results in a range of estimates from .23 to .51.

Where in this range does the true value lie? Choices are based on conceptual arguments as to the appropriateness of various corrections; we find ourselves unable to resolve this issue based on data available at present. We do note that the largest contributor to this range in estimates is the range restriction correction, and we feel that the Hunter correction, which produces the values at the upper end of the range, is not conceptually appropriate for answering the question of the operational value of GATB use. Thus, we lean toward the lower, rather than the upper, end of the range of validity estimates; hence our conclusion the GATB validities are "modest," though potentially useful to individual employers.

The committee also concluded that its estimate of the true validity of the GATB (i.e., validity corrected for sampling error) can be expected to hold more generally for the kinds of jobs handled by the Employment Service—jobs such as auto mechanic, medical technician, machine operator, administrative specialist, and other jobs in the semiskilled, skilled, and administrative occupations. However, the committee stopped well short of endorsing the use of the GATB to refer people to all 12,000 jobs in the United States economy, as U.S. Employment Service literature does.

What do these validity estimates mean in terms of gains to the employer? Obviously, validities averaging .30 are modest, but they indicate a stronger relationship than is found for the commonly used unstructured interview. Individual employers can reap substantial benefits even from selection instruments of such modest pretensions, assuming of course that there is a large enough pool of job seekers to permit selectivity and that the employer is offering attractive conditions of labor.

Psychologists have in recent years tried to translate the performance gains derived from selecting employees on the basis of test scores into a dollar metric. Indeed, the U.S. Employment Service commissioned such a study and has since advertised its conclusion that use of the GATB throughout the system for all referrals could produce increases in work-force productivity totalling almost $80 billion dollars.

Questions about the USES claims for gains in work-force productivity fall into two categories. One set involves questions about the mathematical model used to assess utility; the other involves questions not about the model per se, but about the way in which parameters of the model are estimated. Several examples follow. First, the USES model requires an estimate of average job tenure. The USES estimate of this parameter is the average tenure in the entire U.S. work force; given the number of low-level and short-term jobs filled through USES, it is likely that this is a potentially large overestimate. Second, the USES model requires an estimate of test validity; our earlier discussion suggests that the USES estimate of .50 is overly optimistic. Third, the USES model requires an estimate of the value of differing levels of performance (technically, an estimate of the standard deviation of performance in dollars). USES used 40% of salary as the estimate of this parameter. However, this estimate is based on averaging performance variability estimates across a wide variety of jobs, whereas a focus on the type of job filled through USES produces a much lower estimate. Fourth, the USES model requires an estimate of the degree of selectivity available to an employer. Their model assumed that all employers are able to select the top 10% of the applicant pool. Clearly, this is not possible: Although some employers with reputations for high wages and good working conditions may be able to attract only individuals in the top 10%, at an aggregate level, the hiring of high ability applicants by one employer reduces the talent pool available to other employers. In short, one can very easily obtain dramatically different estimates of the gain in work-force productivity from those presented by USES. Thus the committee rejected the USES $80 billion claim as highly exaggerated and incapable of proof. It went further and recommended that the Department of Labor and the Employment Service avoid making such dollar estimates given the present state of the art.

QUESTIONS OF FAIRNESS

Until now, policy debate on the issue of fair use of tests has been dominated by test scores. Many proponents of meritocratic principles and those who value economic competitiveness above all argue for strict adherence to top-down selection. From this point of view, the job applicant with the highest test score deserves to be hired first, the second highest second, and so on. At least superficially, top-down selection makes qualifications the determining factor in hiring and thus fulfills one common definition of equity.

On the other hand, those whose social sympathies turn in the direction of getting rid of barriers to the advancement of Blacks and other minorities interpret group differences in test scores as evidence that ability tests are racially or culturally biased and that tests ought, therefore, to be eliminated.

Neither position is sound, either from the position of science or of public policy.

As the earlier discussion of GATB validities indicates, an overly literal attachment to test scores is misguided. Although it makes sense to take advantage of whatever predictive power inheres in the GATB, there is no merit in a public policy that sanctifies such scores when it is known in advance that doing so will systematically deprive Black Americans of virtually all chance at the jobs they aspire to.

Likewise, to dismiss tests as hopelessly biased because there are group differences in test scores is misguided. The preponderance of evidence, for the GATB and for other tests of cognitive functioning, documents that group differences in test scores are accompanied by group differences, albeit smaller group differences, in educational and job performance; to pretend that such differences do not exist may be more comfortable than facing the difficulties of overcoming longstanding patterns of low achievement, but it makes for ineffective public policy.

IT'S TIME TO FOCUS ON JOB PERFORMANCE

The crucial point that both sides in this argument miss is that test scores do not tell the whole story. They are only an imperfect indicator of what we are really interested in, and that is job performance. By shifting its attention from test scores to realized job performance, the committee came to very different conclusions about fairness in the use of employment tests.

At the heart of the committee's fairness analysis is the following proposition: *Employers should place equal value on Black and White workers who do equally well on the job.*

The problem is that employers do not know at the point of hiring how well each applicant will actually do. Employers could hire all applicants for 6 months and then select the best workers for retention, but this is a very costly way to do business. Employment tests offer the employer a shortcut.

The critical question is whether employment tests, which we adopt for the sake of convenience and efficiency, lead the employer to place equal value on Black and White applicants who will turn out to be equally good on the job. The answer for the GATB, as for any test of less than perfect validity, is no. Group differences in job performance are substantially smaller than the difference in average test scores between Blacks and Whites: There is about a .3 to .4 standard deviation difference in job performance as compared with a 1 standard deviation difference in average test score (Ford, Kraiger, & Schechtman, 1986).

The 200 or so GATB validity studies that report results separately by race document the point. They record test scores earned by workers already on the job, whose performance was also rated by their supervisor using a special rating form developed for research purposes. Black and White workers who are rated as equally proficient on the job do not have the same distribution of test scores; as a consequence, they would not have had the same chance of being referred or hired had their employer hired on the basis of GATB scores.

What this means is that if unadjusted test scores are used as the basis for referring job seekers, Black Employment Service clients will be subject disproportionately to false rejections; that is, a greater proportion of the Blacks who could have performed successfully on the job will be screened out than Whites who could have performed successfully. Consider as an illustration a GATB validity study that included 45 Black and 45 White carpenters.[1] The committee's analysis shows that 50% (8 of 16) of Black carpenters who were rated good workers would have failed the test and thus would not have been referred to the employer. In contrast, just 14% of the White carpenters who were rated good workers (5 out of 35) would have been falsely rejected on the basis of their test scores (see Fig. 12.1).[2] Note that the converse applies to false positives. To wit, 40% of the poor-performing White carpenters passed the test (4 out of 10) as compared with 17% of the Blacks rated as poor performers (5 out of 24).

This outcome does not result because GATB scores mean something different for Blacks and Whites. The test is not biased in that sense. Rather, the disproportionate rejection of able Blacks results from the interplay of two factors: the modest validity of the test and the lower average test scores of Blacks as a group. Because of prediction error, in every group there will be some people who could perform successfully on the job, but whose low test scores will keep them from being referred. Because Blacks score lower on average, a greater proportion of Black applicants than of White applicants will be falsely rejected. Conversely, a greater proportion of the White group will benefit from the other type of prediction error, false acceptance; that is, they will score well on the test but not perform satisfactorily on the job. Figure 12.2 illustrates the effects of the interaction of prediction error and group differences in average test scores. Sector D represents false rejections and Sector B false acceptances.

It was the committee's carefully considered judgment that fair test use requires at the very least that the inadequacies of testing technology should not be visited on the social groups already burdened with the effects of past and present discrimination.

This way of looking at fairness has proven to be controversial. We describe here how and why this approach differs from approaches commonly taken by psychologists. As noted earlier, Black–White differences in criterion performance are considerably smaller than Black–White test differences. If one gave all applicants a job tryout and kept the highest performers (i.e., hiring on the basis

---

[1]For ease of communication the numbers have been standardized. In the actual study there were 91 White carpenters and 45 Black carpenters.

[2]These figures provide evidence of group differences in successful job performance as well as the disproportionate rate of false rejections that able Black carpenters would suffer if selection was by test score.

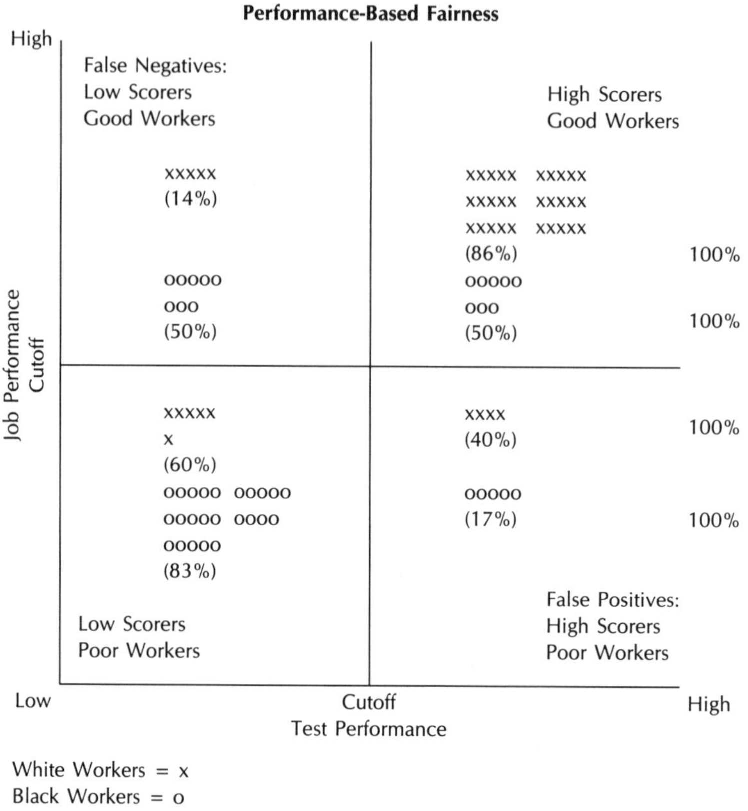

Performance-Based Fairness

High

False Negatives:	
Low Scorers	High Scorers
Good Workers	Good Workers
xxxxx	xxxxx xxxxx
(14%)	xxxxx xxxxx
	xxxxx xxxxx
	(86%) 100%
ooooo	ooooo
ooo	ooo
(50%)	(50%) 100%

Job Performance Cutoff

xxxxx	xxxx
x	(40%) 100%
(60%)	
ooooo ooooo	ooooo
ooooo oooo	(17%) 100%
ooooo	
(83%)	
	False Positives:
Low Scorers	High Scorers
Poor Workers	Poor Workers

Low   Cutoff   High
                          Test Performance

White Workers = x
Black Workers = o

FIG. 12.1. Frequency counts showing the joint distributions of test performance
and job performance for 45 White and 45 Black workers, and the proportions of
each group subject to false rejection and false acceptance.

of what is the criterion in the typical validity study), one would retain considerably more Blacks than would be hired using the present test. This observation
is at the heart of the committee's adoption of an approach that focuses on the
probability of selection given a specified level of job performance, rather than
the focus on the probability of a specified level of job performance given selection. In contrast, most psychologists have long argued that because only test
performance is known prior to hire, fairness models should focus on success
given selection, rather than selection given success. Some psychologists have
also argued that because this phenomenon is not explicitly racial (with a less
than perfectly valid test, any lower scoring group with a larger difference from
the majority group on the predictor than the criterion will produce this result),
it is not appropriate to remedy the unfairness for a racially defined group. In
other words, proponents of this position can accept that *all* low scorers will

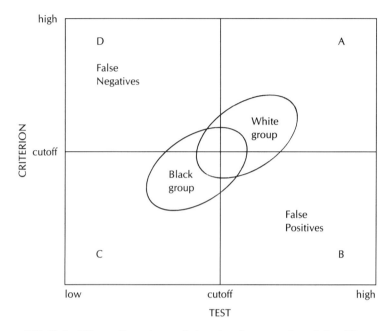

FIG. 12.2. Effects of imperfect prediction when there are subpopulation differences in average test scores.

be subject to disproportionate rates of false rejection in order for employers to enjoy the benefits of testing, but not that *some* low scorers (i.e., Blacks) should be spared the effects of imperfect prediction.

In our opinion, it is important to differentiate between fairness as a characteristic of a test and fairness as a characteristic of a selection system. The committee's focus is the latter; the focus in psychology has concentrated on the former. Imagine the following scenario: Two uncorrelated traits (sociability and conscientiousness) each have a squared correlation of .50 with performance: Thus, these two factors completely explain performance. Assume Blacks and Whites differ by 1 SD in sociability and by 0 SD in conscientiousness; in this situation the Black–White difference in job performance would be .7 SD. Now assume a researcher sets out to develop a selection system for this job. The researcher attempts to measure only sociability: No attempt is made to measure conscientiousness. The researcher finds that the sociability test is valid, finds that Black performance is not underpredicted, and concludes that the test is fair. Yet the committee's approach would find this unfair, as the Black–White difference in job performance is much smaller than the Black–White difference in test performance. The researcher's approach is appropriate in determining whether there is something wrong with his or her measure of sociability; the researcher has properly determined that the sociability measure is not unfair in the sense of being a more accurate predictor for one group than another.

Yet by failing to include other aspects of the predictor domain that are also important for job performance and on which Black–White differences are smaller, the end result is a system in which Blacks who would have been high performers if hired are less likely to be hired than Whites who would be high performers if hired. As the committee's report concludes, the burden of the limitations of testing technology falls more heavily on Blacks than Whites; hence the recommendation of score adjustment.

It is important to note the context in which the committee endorsed score adjustments, namely, one in which the GATB would be used by the Employment Service as a screening device. The top-scoring applicants on this device would be referred to the hiring organization, which would then further screen the applicants using any of a wide variety of selection techniques. The committee was concerned about the exclusion of a high proportion of the minority applicant pool on the basis of a single factor—GATB scores—when it is very clear that other factors are also relevant for job success. In endorsing *referral* on the basis of adjusted scores, the committee sought to extend to minority applicants the opportunity to have their job-relevant characteristics recognized, and to reserve to the employer the capacity to look at minority and majority job seekers in terms of the specific characteristics that are important in the employer's firm. For example, in some jobs punctuality and regular attendance are critical; in many firms the ability to work in small interactive groups is critical; and in many jobs sociability is fundamental. The GATB does not purport to measure any of these characteristics. Does this mean that the GATB is of no value? Obviously not. GATB abilities, however imperfectly measured, are also related to successful job performance. Adjusting scores so that Blacks and Whites who perform equally well would have the same referral chances means that GATB information can inform the employer's decision but will not overwhelm it to the exclusion of all other relevant factors.

PRESCRIPTION FOR A FAIR REFERRAL SYSTEM

The Department of Labor can create a referral system based on the use of the GATB that offers individual employers a more proficient pool of applicants to choose from and that extends to *equally able* Black, Hispanic, and White workers the same chances of referral. The goal of such a "performance fair" selection system is to compute test scores so that people with a given level of performance on the job will have the same distribution of test scores no matter which population subgroup they belong to. When that situation obtains, a referral rule that selects workers in order of test score will select the same proportion of good workers in each population subgroup—not the same proportion of workers in each subgroup, as some have misread the *Fairness* report to say, but the same proportion of *good* workers.

In practical terms, a performance fair referral system will require that the scores of Black, Hispanic, and White applicants be computed separately. More specifically, it will require that the raw scores (number of right answers) of Black and Hispanic test takers be adjusted upward so that workers of equal proficiency in the several groups have the same distribution of test scores and, thus, the same chance of selection.

One of the attractions of the performance fair strategy is that it is flexible, responsive to the accuracy of the test being used and to the temporal position of the population groups. The size of the appropriate adjustment depends on two factors that can be empirically determined: the size of the score difference between the groups and the degree of prediction error in the test. The basic formula is the higher the validity of the test, the smaller the needed adjustment. With current GATB validities of about .3 the appropriate adjustment would be sizeable, approaching one standard deviation for Black test takers and half that for Hispanics.

COSTS AND BENEFITS OF PERFORMANCE
FAIR REFERRAL

No policy is without costs. A system designed to prevent damaging prediction error from falling more heavily on Blacks and Hispanics than on others will mean that the employer receives a somewhat less proficient pool of job candidates. By equalizing the percentages in each group subject to false rejections through score adjustments, we also equalize the percentages of false acceptances. In other words, to give able Black workers an equal probability of being selected, we will have to increase the chances of the employer choosing Black workers who "pass" the test but perform poorly on the job.

How great is the cost compared with other referral strategies? Table 12.1, which is based on 72 of the GATB validity studies that report data separately by race, tells the story. A strict top-down referral system using raw scores results in the highest expected performance, in this data set a very modest .22 correlation between test score and job performance. The performance fair strategy produces a slight drop in correlation (.20). In contrast, a minimum competency system that referred at random from the top 70% of applicants would result in dramatic declines in predictive accuracy and, therefore, in the expected proficiency of the people referred to employers. The performance fair strategy performs very similarly to the within-group percentile strategy in this example. Note, though, that the two approaches will diverge in the case of selection devices of higher validity. The performance fair system is explicitly linked to the validity of the selection system, whereas the within-group approach is independent of selection system validity.

At validities of .20 to .40, the productivity costs of performance fair referral

TABLE 12.1
Effects of Referral Rules

Applicant Population = 30% Black
If 20% of Whites are Referred:

Referral Rule	Correlation of Corrected Score with Job Performance*	Minority % Referred
Raw Score	.22	4
Within Group Score	.20	20
Performance Based Score	.20	19
Minimum Competency Score (> 30%)	.13	8

*Based on 72 studies that contain 50 Black and 50 nonminority workers. Note that the average value for these studies is at the lower end of the range of validities found for all 755 studies.

are relatively modest. Look now at the relative effects of the various strategies on the percentage of Blacks referred. If 20% of White clients are referred, use of the strict top-down system based on raw scores will mean that just 4% of the Black clients are referred. Yet, when the validity is modest, as it is for the GATB, many of the minority applicants excluded would have performed better than many of the Whites included. The performance-based score adjustment would, at these low validities, place 19% of Blacks in the referral group. For its part, the performance fair strategy will have the effect of referring Blacks whose expected performance is below that of some Whites not referred (thus the drop in validities).

CODA

Testing is a probabilistic science and, in the present state of the art, can only be perceived as fair if one is willing to think in aggregate terms. It helps us make better decisions about allocating educational and employment opportunities than we otherwise can. But all low scorers are at risk. Some of them will miss out on opportunities because of prediction error when they could have performed as well or better than others with higher scores.

Given the concern of the Civil Rights Act of 1964 to extend the guarantees of equality for the first time to Black Americans, a performance fair testing policy makes a good deal of sense. There is no doubt that it will be extraordinarily difficult to change the terms of debate on the fair use of tests and equal employment opportunity as they have been etched into the public consciousness and worked out in the case law. But we have as a nation reached a deadlock. Employers are hard pressed to defend their procedures from charges of discrimination and/or reverse discrimination. Both majority and minority workers feel that the system is loaded against them. In deciding on a future course of action with regard to the General Aptitude Test Battery, the Departments of Labor and Justice have the opportunity to advance a definition of fairness that links directly to job performance. A referral system designed around the performance fair use of tests assures Black and White Employment Service clients who would perform at the same level on the job that they will have equal chances of being referred.

For here and now, the recommended formula for adjusting the GATB scores of Black and Hispanic job seekers for purposes of identifying the pool of applicants to refer to an employer[3] reconciles the governmental interests in productivity and equality. It makes qualifications an important factor in employment decisions and, in extending to Black and White workers who would perform equally well an equal chance of being referred, it fulfills the constitutional promise to all citizens of equality under the law.

A final postscript, added as this volume goes to press: The score adjustment procedures discussed in this chapter have been made impermissible in the United States by the recently enacted Civil Rights Act of 1991. One provision of this Act prohibits score adjustment or differential test cutoffs by race. In the eyes of Congress, score adjustment was seen as violating principles of fairness: Two people with the same number of correct answers should receive the same test score. Many state employment services have suspended the use of the GATB screening program subsequent to the Civil Rights Act, and the Department of Labor is undertaking a major research effort aimed at producing an improved testing system. For the present, the result is a difficult situation for employers with serious interests in both employee productivity and workforce diversity. Without score adjustment, the adverse impact produced by ability tests has such severe consequences for achieving diversity goals that the use of such tests becomes untenable, thus depriving employers of the productivity gains that could result from the use of the tests. Thus, the search for mechanisms for reconciling diversity and productivity goals will continue.

REFERENCES

Ford, J. K., Kraiger, K., & Schechtman, S. L. (1986). Study of race effects in objective indices and subjective evaluations of performance: A meta-analysis of performance criteria. *Psychological Bulletin, 99,* 330–337.

---

[3]For purposes of reporting test scores where the interest is in permitting employers and applicants to make correct inferences about likely job performance, the committee recommends that two test scores be used: a within-group score (with the group identified) to permit comparisons with others in the same racial or ethnic group; and a total-group expectancy score that shows the individual's chances of being a better than average worker in comparison to all other candidates regardless of racial or ethnic identity.

Hartigan, J. A., & Wigdor, A. K. (1989). *Fairness in employment testing: Validity generalization, minority issues, and the General Aptitude Test Battery.* Washington, DC: National Academy Press.

Hunter, J. E., & Hunter, R. F. (1984). Validity and utility of alternative predictors of performance. *Psychological Bulletin, 96,* 72–98.

Hunter, J. E., & Schmidt, F. L. (1990). *Methods of meta-analysis: Correcting error and bias in research findings.* Newbury Park, CA: Sage.

U.S. Department of Labor (1983a). *Overview of validity generalization for the U.S. Employment Service* (USES Test Research Report No. 43). Division of Counseling and Test Development, Employment and Training Administration. Washington, DC: U.S. Department of Labor.

U.S. Department of Labor (1983b). *Test validation for 12,000 jobs: An application of job classification and validity generalization analysis to the General Aptitude Test Battery* (USES Test Research Report No. 45). Division of Counseling and Test Development, Employment and Training Administration. Washington, DC: U.S. Department of Labor.

Fairness in Selection and Assessment: A European Perspective

Michael Pearn
Pearn Kandola Downs
Oxford, United Kingdom

Formal research on fairness in selection and assessment, and associated debate both public and academic, dates back to the late 1960s with the publication of a book (Kirkpatrick, Ewen, Barret, & Katzell, 1969) reporting a research study that investigated the social and technical problems associated with the fairness and validity of selection tests for different ethnic groups. The study stimulated the first phase of the debate about differential validity and differential prediction, which continued well into the next decade, leading to large numbers of published studies (see Arvey & Faley, 1988) claiming both the existence of differential validity and the opposite, that it was a statistical artifact.

The resolution of this debate had more than academic interest. There are major implications for the policy and practice of employing organizations. In addition, it affects the guidelines and advice given by official and semiofficial bodies involved in upholding equal opportunity legislation. The dilemma posed was that the use of predictively valid tests (i.e., higher scoring people tend to do better on jobs and therefore should be selected) would result in the perpetuation of disadvantage for groups who were already socioeconomically disadvantaged.

American society committed itself to a policy of equality with the Civil Rights Act, 1964, and subsequent equal opportunity legislation, and so did the European Community by the Treaty of Rome, 1957, which committed Member States to create national legislation to ensure the equal treatment of men and women in employment.

The possible conflict between efficiency of selection and the perpetuation of inequality was well described in the National Research Council study of validity generalization and the General Aptitude Test Battery. Hartigan and Wigdor (1989) stated:

> In order to provide employers with the maximum benefits of testing, the Employment Service would need to refer applicants in order of test score. Such a policy, however, would severely reduce the employment opportunities of lower scoring applicants, particularly of minority job seekers, who have lower average test scores as a group than the majority.
>
> What is the appropriate balance between anticipated productivity gains from better employee selection and the well-being of individual job seekers? Can equal employment opportunity be said to exist if screening methods systematically filter out very large proportions of minority candidates? (p. vii)

As Hartigan and Wigdor pointed out, such a situation would leave the employer, or the users of such tests, vulnerable to charges of unfairness under equal opportunity legislation not only in the United States but in the United Kingdom and several European countries.

In recent years much energy has been devoted to research and debate about the nature of validity, models of test fairness, the validity as well as the potential for adverse impact of particular selection methods, and the adequacy of guidelines by official and semiofficial law enforcement agencies (see Schmitt, 1989). In practical terms, the outcome of all the research and debate, both public and academic, primarily in the United States and to a lesser extent in the United Kingdom and Europe (see Pearn, Kandola, & Mottram, 1987) can be summarized as follows:

- Validity generalization is, on the whole, an acceptable way of justifying the use of a selection instrument.
- Criterion-referenced validation studies can lead to serious underestimation of the predictive potential of selection instruments.
- Meta-analysis of the validity of selection methods provides a reasonable basis of confidence that certain methods have sufficient predictive validity.
- The potential of some selection instruments to produce adverse impact on minority groups has been established.

The best assessment methods that combine higher predictive validities with minimal adverse impact are:

- assessment centers (relatively expensive to set up, limited application)
- work sample tests (expensive to develop but cheap to operate)
- peer evaluations, especially assessment for promotion (wide application)
- aptitude or cognitive ability tests (wide application, relatively cheap)

- structured criterion-based interviews (wide application, relatively cheap).

The methods that may have relatively low adverse impact but frequently low predictive validities are:

- personality questionnaires
- interest inventories
- self-assessments

Although there is growing evidence of an increased use of techniques such as assessment centers and aptitude tests (Robertson & Makin, 1986), the majority of employers in the United Kingdom still rely almost exclusively on unstructured interviews, the validity of which has been shown to be very low.

The overall impression, when reviewing this period of research in the 1970s and 1980s, is that a great deal has been learned. We appear to have a better understanding of the nature of validity (e.g., there is no such thing as *the* validity of an instrument; instead there are as many validities as there are sources of evidence justifying inferences from performance on the test): We have systematic and reliable evidence on the generalizability of the validity of instruments and their potential for adverse impact on minority groups; and a better feel for the relationship between those models of selection fairness where the only consideration is accuracy of prediction (over or underprediction) as opposed to models that take into account the potential impact on society's goals for a more equitable distribution of its resources between subgroups (see Schmitt, 1989).

Although it is fair to conclude that much has been learned, it is also reasonable to ask how much has been achieved. In order to answer this question, it may be useful to examine in more detail what has happened in the United Kingdom over this period. To do this a brief review of the history of the legislation is required (see Fig. 13.1).

Treaty of Rome 1957 and associated EEC Directives on Equal Treatment

Race Relations Act 1965 (repealed)
Race Relations Act 1968 (repealed)
Race Relations Act 1976

Sex Discrimination Act 1975, 1986

Fair Employment Act (Northern Ireland) 1976
Equal Opportunities Act (Northern Ireland) 1976
Fair Employment Act (Northern Ireland) 1988
Disabled Persons Employment Act 1944, 1947

FIG. 13.1.   Equal opportunities legislation in the United Kingdom.

As a colonizing power for several hundred years, it was not surprising that over a long period of time people from Africa and other parts of the British Empire have settled in the United Kingdom. However, it was not until the late 1950s and 1960s when Britain was experiencing a severe shortage of labor that formal attempts were systematically made to encourage immigration and settlement from what was then called the New Commonwealth (viz the Indian subcontinent, Black Africa, and the Caribbean). During this period organizations such as the Health Service and employers in transport and heavy manufacturing systematically encouraged people from these areas to come and work in Britain. In some cases they even set up recruiting offices in these countries. Consequently, there was a relatively large influx over a period of 10 years of people from the New Commonwealth (Rose, 1969).

During the early 1960s it became apparent that some of these colored people, as they were then called, were subject to various forms of ill-treatment and discrimination. Various attempts were made in Parliament to introduce legislation but these failed. However, 1 year after the introduction of the 1964 Civil Rights Act in the United States, Britain created its first domestic legislation on race relations in its legal history (Lester & Bindman, 1972).

The first Race Relations Act 1965 was very modest. In effect, it made unfavorable treatment on grounds of race (i.e., acts of discrimination) unlawful in public places only (e.g., refusing someone a table in a restaurant or a room in a hotel on grounds of their race). The Act also created, for the first time, the criminal offense of incitement to racial hatred. The Act did not apply to employment or to education. This came a few years later with the passing of the 1968 Race Relations Act. For the first time ever, the employer's right to choose freely whom to appoint, promote, or dismiss was constrained by law. It did not matter on what grounds an employer made a selection decision as long as it was not directly influenced by the race of the candidate. As in other countries, the anomalous situation arose where it appeared not to matter how arbitrary or capricious an employer was in relation to job candidates or employees as long as what was done was not attributable to the person's race.

The 1968 Race Relations Act coincided with a tightening up of immigration policy, particularly in relation to the New (i.e., non-White) Commonwealth. Nonetheless, for the first time legislation existed and a law enforcement body (the Race Relations Board) was created that had the exclusive responsibility for taking race cases before the courts. The legislation had been passed in response to evidence from surveys that showed that New Commonwealth workers, as they were called then, experienced higher levels of unemployment, were concentrated in lower status jobs, and were also concentrated in sectors of the economy that were more vulnerable to decline and/or had lower status in terms of pay and conditions (McIntosh & Smith, 1974).

Britain's legislative development closely followed American experience. In 1976 a new Race Relations Act was introduced that strengthened the enforcement powers of a newly created Commission for Racial Equality and also introduced the concept of indirect discrimination. This followed the American concept of discrimination in effect (Griggs v Duke Power), and a growing body of research that confirmed in the United Kingdom that Black workers, as they were now called, continued to experience higher levels of unemployment, on average earned lower hourly wages than the White population, and were concentrated in lower status jobs and in sectors of the economy that were more vulnerable to decline, poorer working conditions, and so forth.

As a result of Britain's entry into the European common market, under the Treaty of Rome (1957), Britain as a Member State of the EEC was required to have national legislation on the equal treatment of men and women at work (as well as other areas outside the scope of this chapter). This led to passing, for the first time in the United Kingdom, legislation making unlawful direct and indirect discrimination on grounds of gender and marital status (Sex Discrimination Act, 1975). It also brought into operation, again for the first time in the United Kingdom, legislation on equal pay that had initially been introduced in 1970 (Equal Pay Act 1970).

At the same time, the first legislation on avoidance of discrimination on grounds of religious and political belief was passed in Northern Ireland in 1976 but, as such, had no direct application to the United Kingdom. Consequently, it was and still is unlawful in Northern Ireland to discriminate on grounds of religion but not unlawful in the United Kingdom. To this day it is not unlawful to discriminate on grounds of race in Northern Ireland, but it is in the United Kingdom. Both Northern Ireland and the United Kingdom have comparable legislation that outlaws discrimination based on gender and marital status. Consequently, in the United Kingdom there is antidiscrimination legislation on race, color, nationality, ethnic and national origins, gender, and marital status. There is no antidiscrimination legislation on sexual orientation, age, disability and handicap, class, and religion except in Northern Ireland.

Despite this 20-year-old legislative background, a lack of political will and the lack of a coordinated strategy have resulted in a perpetuation of the severe imbalance between Britain's Black and White population (Brown & Gay, 1985). The Labour Force Survey (Employment Gazette, 1991) reveals that 4.7% of the working age population, or 1.6 million people, were from ethnic minority groups. In terms of type of work done, 29% of ethnic minority men were employed in distribution, hotels, catering, and repairs, compared with 16% of White men. Ethnic minority men were also strongly represented in metal goods, engineering and vehicles (13%) and other manufacturing (also 13%), and transport and communication (10%). Ethnic minority women were mainly employed in distribution, hotels, and catering (25%), and in other manufacturing (11%).

In terms of occupational distribution the overall proportions of ethnic minority men in nonmanual (47%) and manual (53%) occupations were the same as for White men. However, there are considerable differences in distribution. West

Indian and Pakistani–Bangladeshi men are severely under-represented in supervisory, managerial, and professional occupations.

The picture for women continues to provide cause for concern. Women continue to be severely under-represented in management. The occupational distribution of women is very different from that of men. Women are still concentrated in sectors of the economy that reflect the traditional roles of women (care of children, health and welfare, textile and food manufacturing, support services, etc.). Women's average earnings continue to be only approximately 75% of the average weekly hourly earnings for men, despite 15 years of equal pay legislation.

THE EUROPEAN CONTEXT

All 12 Member States of the European Community are required, in the form of Directives under the Treaty of Rome, to have legislation on equal pay and equal treatment between men and women (see Fig. 13.2). There is, however, no requirement under the Treaty of Rome for Member States to have national legislation on racial discrimination. The Commission for the European Community in Brussels commissioned the Runnymede Trust (1987) to prepare a study of racism and xenophobia and to make recommendations for new approaches to the legal protection of European Community citizens and that aliens working in the EEC be legally protected from racism and xenophobia.

The main Directives are:

Directive 75/117/EEC concerning the principle of equal pay for men and women

Directive 76/207/EEC concerning the implementation of the principle of equal treatment for men and women as regards access to employment, vocational training and promotion and working conditions.

Directive 79/7/EEC concerning the implementation of the principle of equal treatment for women and men in matters of social security

Directive 86/378/EEC concerning equal treatment in occupations, pension schemes for employees and self-employed people

Directive 86/613/EEC concerning equal treatment for self-employed men and women and women in agriculture

Directive 76/207/EEC prohibits any discrimination, direct or indirect, on the basis of sex, marital or family status and provides for the possibility of positive action in favor of women.

FIG. 13.2.   Directives on equality (under the Treaty of Rome, 1957).

Few of the Member States have developed comprehensive systems of civil remedy for racial discrimination. Limited systems exist in the Netherlands, Belgium, Luxembourg, and Denmark, but only in the United Kingdom is there a system of laws that offers minorities legal protection from discrimination and that also gives the individual a private right to bring a case. Although the Netherlands does not have formal antidiscrimination legislation, there are constitutional rights provided for the equal treatment of all persons on Dutch territory that forbids discrimination based on religion, mental outlook, political views, race, gender, or any other grounds. There is a general protection under the European Convention of the Protection of Human Rights and Fundamental Freedoms that covers race and nationality (Article 14), but only in the United Kingdom is there a formal legislative framework that is comprehensive in scope. The Runnymede Trust argued in 1987 that, despite its limitations, the United Kingdom model could provide the basis for recommendations to Member States.

The European Commission and Parliament are currently debating a strategy for countering racism and xenophobia in Europe. On the one hand, the Council of Ministers has argued for a cooperative education-based and voluntary approach, but the Commission and Parliament are beginning to argue in favor of stronger protection for the approximately 5 million non-EEC nationals. The Commission for Racial Equality in the United Kingdom has called for EEC-wide legislation on racial discrimination as neither the Treaty of Rome nor the Single European Act, 1987 that creates the Single Market in Europe after 1992 requires Member States to legislate on racial discrimination.

The European Social Charter is a development that will have important implications for the legal protection of minorities against unfair treatment. The Social Charter arises from the so-called ''social dimension'' in the 1992 program to create a single market under the Single European Act, 1987 (Rajan, 1990). The industrial restructuring of the EEC that will result from the Single Market (as part of the move toward full economic union) will cause considerable unemployment and hardship in the short term. The social dimension is designed to build and extend on the social traditions that were partially created in the Treaty of Rome, 1957, by adding elements that would help to ensure and smooth the way for orderly social and economic change as a result of the Single European Act.

At another level, the social dimension can be seen as a necessary set of considerations to ensure that social progress in Europe occurs in parallel with economic and political progress toward a more united Europe. The most important official document specifying the appropriate response of Member States is the Social Charter. In effect, the Social Charter extends the binding provisions on Member States under the Treaty of Rome. The social dimension is seen as crucial to the success of the Single Market as an instrument for the development, deployment, and management of know-how in the Community's work force. Market forces that will drive the large-scale industrial restructuring will be balanced by the social dimension, which will not only operate as a palliative but also as a mechanism for contributing to the speedy training and channeling of surplus labor into alternative uses. The Social Charter does not specifically focus on the need to avoid discrimination but does create 12 specific rights. Under current U.K. law there is legal protection only for people who have suffered from discrimination based on race or gender. There is no right to protection from unfavorable treatment, per se. In other words, an employer is not under any obligation to take action to prevent such discrimination occurring. As the law stands, they are only liable if they are found to have contravened the legislation. The Social Charter is important because it creates a new framework of rights and expectations. The 12 rights are listed in Fig. 13.3.

The Social Charter can be seen as a vision of a new Europe. The eventual recognition of a right to equal treatment is far more powerful than the protection under present laws of specific occurrences of discrimination. One consequence will be the removal of the anomaly that an employer should avoid unfair discrimination in selection on grounds of gender and race but is entirely free to discriminate unfairly on grounds of age and other considerations that are not related to job requirements.

The combination of economic need and political idealism is likely to ensure that the Social Charter will have significant impact on the thinking, policies, and practices of employers across Europe. It is even possible that European debate and achievement will supersede American achievement in this area. The United States' constitution, in addition to federal legislation, has provided a powerful basis for bringing about change in the United States but equally, and particularly in recent years, has also operated as a brake to progress. The social dimension and the associated Social Charter in Europe is likely to provide a highly focused and consistent pressure toward change in a less unpredictable way than has been the case in the United States. Nevertheless, only time will tell whether the promise of the Social Charter will manifest itself in concerted action and progress toward social and economic change in Europe.

- Right to freedom of movement
- Right to fair treatment
- Right to improvement of living and working conditions
- Right to social protection
- Right to freedom of association and collective bargaining
- Right to vocational training
- Right to equal treatment
- Right to information, consultation and participation of workers
- Right to health and safety protection at the workplace
- Rights for children and adolescents
- Right to decent standard of living for the elderly
- Right to integration for people with disabilities

FIG. 13.3.   The European Social Charter: 12 rights.

But where does this leave the large body of research on fairness in selection, and what are the implications for the future? In the past, there has been a preoccupation with research on, and evaluation of, selection methods per se. This has resulted in focusing on effects of average differences in group performance with the associated concerns for over or underprediction of performance on job- or training-related criteria (Pearn, 1978). There has also been a preoccupation with content bias and differential validity. Research has investigated variables that affect performance on assessment instruments, such as unfamiliarity, anxiety, and expectation of failure. By contrast, there has been less emphasis on the impact or effect on equal opportunity goals of the persistent use of specific selection methods.

There is a need for a more integrated, multifactorial approach to the understanding of fairness in selection, as distinct from bias in assessment methods. If fairness in assessment is based on the reliability and validity of the assessment devices, including distinctive subgroups by reference to age, gender, race, and so on, then it can be argued there is already a sufficient stock of knowledge to draw reasonable conclusions. At the simplest, it can be seen that structured criterion-referenced interviews carried out by trained interviewers are going to be fairer to everyone than the use of unstructured interviews by untrained interviewers with ill-defined criteria. Similarly, it can be shown that, despite the initial development costs, assessment centers, when correctly designed and implemented, appear not only to have minimal adverse impact on subgroups (Iles, 1989) but are also predictive to an acceptable level and more than repay their development costs in terms of monetary gain to the user (Woodruffe, 1990). It has been shown that trainability assessments, work sample questionnaires, and carefully constructed biodata questionnaires can be fair in their assessment of candidates.

A TENTATIVE MODEL OF UNFAIRNESS IN SELECTION

The aim of this model is to help explain why the extensive body of research on selection fairness appears to have little impact on organizations, at least in the United Kingdom.

A critical difference between concern for "fairness in assessment" and fairness of selection lies in the decision-making process that results from the assessment, but also from other decisions that both affect and reflect the way an organization operates. A number of factors need integrating, and a suggested model relating the factors is presented in Fig. 13.4.

Tolerance of segregation and acceptance of inequality are two attributes of key decision makers in an organization that directly lead to a resistance or reluctance to change practices on policy with a view to overcoming either segregation or inequality in the organization.

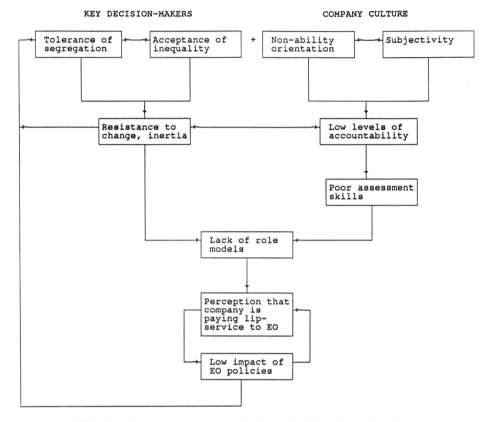

FIG. 13.4. A tentative model to explain the relatively low impact of equal opportunity policies.

Tolerance of the Segregation

Many senior officials in public sector organizations and managers in private companies in the United Kingdom are aware that large percentages of women are concentrated in low paid, low status work from which there are few, if any, career prospects. They can see in many organizations that the large proportion of ethnic minority workers are concentrated in lower status, lower paid occupations or are concentrated in some departments within the organization and are conspicuously absent from other parts of the organization. Awareness of this situation, when combined with a decision that no action is required, is itself a factor to be understood. Admittedly, some of the inequality in employment is the result of historic factors going back over years if not decades, but, none-the-less, the tolerance and acceptance of systems of recruitment, assessment, and selection that perpetuate this pattern seem to warrant investigation and research.

Acceptance of Inequality

At a more general level, given the evidence that has been accumulated and reinforced over 20 or 30 years, there is still a failure by the majority of employers, senior managers or senior public officials, to recognize that large sectors of the working population are being underutilized. With a few conspicuous exceptions, managers prefer to accept the status quo.

Resistance to Change

Most organizations can be scaled on a dimension of high resistance or inertia in relation to change, to a readiness and adaptiveness to respond to changes both in the external and internal environment. Organizations that are slow to respond to change are almost certainly going to be slow to introduce alternative ways of attracting and selecting candidates. Consequently, they may either rest content with methods that have high adverse impact or minor changes that do not result in significant changes in the proportion of minority people being recruited, or promoted.

Some of the resistance to change may be the result of tolerance of segregation and inequality (which may reflect both individual as well as corporate values).

Three aspects of organizational culture also contribute to the low impact of equal opportunities policies on selection and recruitment practices (viz., subjectivity, a nonability orientation), and low levels of accountability for decision making.

The Nonability Orientation

Experience in many organizations confirms the belief that a great deal of decision making about people is based on subjective and often inconsistent grounds. Over 20 years ago Quinn, Tabor, and Gordan (1968) carried out a study that showed that employers could be divided into those that were largely "nonability orientated" and those that were "ability orientated" in terms of the ways they made decisions about the selection and advancement of personnel. It was found that nonability-oriented organizations tended to have fewer women in management and generally fewer minorities in employment. There does appear to be a significant cultural factor whereby a high commitment to the objective recognition and assessment of ability results in a reduction of stereotypical employment patterns in relation to women and minorities.

High Level of Subjectivity

Organizations can also be divided into those where most decisions are based on an open evaluation of relevant facts or data, and those where the personal judgment of an individual manager is sufficient. In this respect, organizations can be scaled in terms of their overall commitment to objective evaluation and systematic appraisal of evidence and data rather than the use of authority, personality, or individual values as a basis for decision making.

Low Levels of Accountability for Decision Making

Many organizations operate in a somewhat secretive manner when it comes to policy formulation and decisions about recruitment and promotion. It is not uncommon in many organizations that above a certain level of management there are no formal declared selection criteria for promotion and, equally, no formal assessment process, even though this might be elaborately developed at lower levels in the organization. The lack of openness and accountability at this level could contribute to high levels of subjectivity, indeed, arbitrariness, which can effectively eliminate the chances of women and minorities being recognized and selected.

Poor Assessment Skills

One of the practical consequences of an organization with nonability orientation and high levels of subjectivity is that assessment skills (especially interviewing) are unlikely to be developed to a high degree, if at all, among supervisors, managers, and others responsible for recruitment and promotion.

The notion of manager as assessor has been well described by O'Neill (1989) as a critical management competence. The development and application of good assessment skills will result in a higher level of consistency, accountability, and objectivity (given that criteria are well defined and communicated). It may not of itself bring about reductions in inequality or unfairness, but it is likely to minimize and reduce the effects of biases, stereotypes, unquestioned assumptions, and other forms of prejudicial thinking about minorities and women.

Organizations that have well-developed appraisal schemes with managers highly trained in appraisal skills, and that also make extensive use of assessment centers, are also likely to minimize or even eliminate barriers to the career advancement of women and minorities. The distinctive role that can be played by assessment centers in contributing to equal opportunity goals or, at the very least, minimizing the effects of subjective and biased assessment has been reviewed by Iles (1989).

Lack of Role Models

The combined effect of organization cultural and individual attitudes or values of key managers is that relatively few women will be found in nontraditional occupations at high management levels. This would also be true of ethnic minorities, the disabled, older workers, and other underutilized groups. One consequence would be the lack of role models to provide example and encouragement to others. The absence of women, ethnic minorities, and disabled people succeeding in nontraditional occupations and managerial roles has been well documented as an inhibiting factor with regard to the career progression and achievement of equal opportunity goals.

Perception That the Organization Pays Lip Service to Equal Opportunities

An integrating concept that helps explain inertia or an organization's failure to achieve significant results is "lip service." This was one of the factors identified by Quinn et al. (1968) as contributing to the failure of managers to take seriously the policy intentions of the organization. This holds true when the political will of the country to achieve significant change is low, which is the case in the United Kingdom and indeed in all other EEC Member States. Accordingly, equal opportunity policies, goals, and objectives were more talked about than actually achieved. A recent study by Kandola, Milner, Banerji, and Wood (1991) has revealed above-average levels of occupational stress in a representative sample of equal opportunity managers and advisers in the United Kingdom. Much of this stress was caused by the gap between the creation of a managerial role to advise on and implement effective equal opportunity policies and the inertia and sometimes open resistance within the organization, often exacerbated by a lack of top management support.

Low Impact of Equal Opportunities Policies

The combined effect of the factors is to contribute to the failure of many organizations to achieve significant change. Despite all the research that has been done both in the United Kingdom and in the United States on the fairness of selection methods, organizational culture inhibits the achievement of significant change. It seems that, in the absence of strong laws with vigorous enforcement and punitive settlements (as occurred in the United States in the 1970s and 1980s), the culture of most organizations will inhibit real change despite all that we know about selection fairness. There is an important lesson for EEC Member States here (McCrudden, Smith, & Brown, 1991).

One objective of this chapter has been to place the scientific findings of research on selection methods in the context of a broader framework within which the results of their research must be applied. There appears to be no legal obligation, at least within the United Kingdom, for employers to use, and only use, methods of selection that have maximum statistical predictive power for the majority group, regardless of whether this has a high adverse impact on minorities.

The general implication of the statutory definition of indirect discrimination, both within the Sex Discrimination Act, 1975, and the Race Relations Act, 1976, could mean that it may not be acceptable under the law for an employer to persist in using the statistically most efficient method of assessment if, at the same time, there is a high adverse impact on minorities or protected groups under the legislation. This is particularly the case where equally predictive (e.g., work sample tests, criterion-based interviews), or maybe even slightly less predictive methods, can be shown to exist that have much less predictive methods, can be shown to exist that have much less adverse impact on a minority group. Under United Kingdom law there is a requirement that the selection procedure be justified without reference to the race or gender of the affected groups. There is scope within the definition to allow sympathetic courts or tribunals to weigh the benefits to the organization of using the method against the potential detriment or cost to the groups that experience adverse impact. A deeper understanding of the factors contributing to organizational tolerance and perpetuation of inequality might lead to voluntary management decisions to work systematically toward equal opportunities goals through predictively valid and fair (low adverse impact) methods of assessment. However, in the absence of vigorous antidiscrimination legislation, this seems unlikely. This is one of the most important lessons to be drawn from a comparison of United Kingdom and United States' experience for equal opportunity in employment (Pearn, 1989).

The formal start of the Single Market in Europe on January 1, 1993, will bring about a new era in Europe. Large-scale industrial restructuring will be associated with large movements of industrial workers and occupational groups between the Member States. Under the Social Charter, new rights will be created and reaffirmed, many of them enshrined in national legislation. There is a growing likelihood of a pan-European race relations act to protect the non-EEC migrant workers or those who have settled in one Member State and who may wish to move to and work in other EEC countries. A continued preoccupation with statistical models of selection fairness and the predictive efficiency of selection methods is necessary within the European context but will fall far short of the kind of research and thinking that is necessary to ensure that selection and assessment processes, however valid they may be declared to be, are not used intentionally or inadvertently to perpetuate historic inequalities in Europe, or create new ones in the future.

REFERENCES

Arvey, R. D., & Faley, R. H. (1988). *Fairness in selecting employees.* Reading, MA: Addison–Wesley.
Brown, C., & Gay, P. (1985). *Racial discrimination: Seventeen years after the Act.* London: PSI.

Hartigan, J. A., & Wigdor, A. K. (1989). *Fairness in employment testing: Validity generalisation and minority issues, and the General Aptitude Test Battery.* Washington, DC: National Academy Press.

Iles, P. (1989). Using assessment and development centres to facilitate equal opportunity in selection and career development. *Equal Opportunities International, 8*(5), 1–32.

Kandola, R. S., Milner, D., Banerji, N., & Wood, R. (1991). *Equal opportunities are bad for your health.* Oxford: PKD.

Kirkpatrick, J. J., Ewen, R. B., Barret, R. S., & Katzell, R. A. (1969). *Testing and fair employment.* New York: New York University Press.

Lester, A., & Bindman, C. (1972). *Race and law.* Harmondsworth: Penguin.

McIntosh, N., & Smith, D. (1974). *The extent of racial discrimination.* Political & Economic Planning, Broadsheet S47.

McCrudden, C. J., Smith, D. J., & Bronn, C. (1991). *Racial justice at work.* London: Policy Studies Institute.

O'Neill, B. (1990). *Manager as assessor.* London: IPM.

Pearn, M. A. (1978). *Employment testing and the goal of equal opportunity: Lessons from America.* London: The Runnymede Trust.

Pearn, M. A. (1989). Fairness in employment selection: A comparison of UK and USA experience. In M. Smith & I. Robertson (Eds.), *Advances in selection and assessment.* Chichester: Wiley.

Pearn, M.A., Kandola, R. S., & Mottram, R. D. (1987). *Selection tests and sex bias: The impact of selection testing on the employment opportunities of women and men.* London: HMSO.

Quinn, R. P., Tabor, J. M., & Gordan, L. K. (1968). *The decision to discriminate.* Ann Arbor: Institute for Social Research.

Rajan, A. (1990). *1992: A zero-sum game.* London: Industrial Society Press.

Robertson, I., & Makin, P. (1986). Management selection in Britain: A survey and critique. *Journal of Occupational Psychology, 59,* 45–57.

Rose, E. J. B. (1969). *Colour and citizenship.* London: Oxford University Press.

Runnymede Trust (1987). *Combatting racism in Europe: A report to the Commission for the European Communities.* London: The Runnymede Trust.

Schmitt, N. (1989). Fairness in employment selection. In M. Smith & I. Robertson (Eds.), *Advances in selection and assessment* (pp. 133–154). Chichester: Wiley.

Woodruffe, C. (1990). *Assessment centres.* London: IPM.

The Team Perspective in Selection and Assessment

José M. Prieto
Universidad Complutense
Madrid, Spain

The selection procedure is a genuinely interactive process between an individual applying for a position and a member of the organization that is hiring. Among the selector's goals are: (a) gathering information about applicants that will provide the decision maker with a means whereby future job performance may be robbed of some of its surprises; (b) determining whether the "personal chemistry" between applicants and the incumbents with whom they will be working will be satisfactory.

The psychometric tradition assumes that the main purpose of recruitment and selection is to predict the individual's successful job performance. The personnel decision is, in principle, a matter of fitting the person to the job. Two major approaches have been produced: the effectiveness-oriented methods and the adjustment-oriented methods. Both involve the basic tenets of psychometrics and emphasize the use of quantitative techniques in a quasi-formula approach.

During the 1980s, effectiveness-oriented methods have received accolades from review studies that have applied meta-analysis to job performance predictions. By contrast, adjustment-oriented methods have been relegated to a secondary role due to the fact that often the criterion group is largely determined by situational factors.

On conceptual grounds, both methods are rooted in the idea that *the individual's performance* is the simpler behavioral criterion that might be approached in the theoretical spectrum. This is not the case if *the individual's contribution to work performance* in the department, the unit, or the team becomes the simpler behavioral criterion in the organizational milieu.

The latent idea behind the concept of *"individual's job performance"* is that each employee completes alone, and without help, each task determined in advance by management. The task idea was stated by F. W. Taylor as a core element in scientific management. It became significant for the emergence of industrial psychology in two ways (Hollway, 1991): It transferred control from the work force to management, and it provided an industrial relations strategy that changed the focus from workers en masse to workers as individuals.

As a consequence, work has been regarded as an individualistic goal-seeking activity because the management specifies what must be done and how it should be done. Applicants are hired because they are expected to have the skills required to perform the tasks allocated to the position.

In contrast, the concept of *"individual's contribution to work performance"* emphasizes the idea that each employee furnishes *along with others* an expected outcome. As a consequence, effective performance is understood as a constructive effort within the work group in the present job. Work is viewed as a collaborative goal-seeking activity. Applicants are hired because the personnel supervisor expects them to have the skills required to team up satisfactorily while working together for the unit's goals and purposes. The point at issue is the assessment of the degree of person–team match in the context of small-group activities at the work place (Cole, 1991). How to facilitate the work-group acceptance and integration of new-hires is the main question that may be answered through psychological research and actions.

The commonality of interests favors the development of continuous dialogue and exchange systems between formal and informal work groups (Wood, 1990). Workers clearly have strong feelings about what they do on the job and about the people they work with. Present positions in new technology-based organizations, for instance, demand an extensive collaboration and peer-group strategies to perform current tasks and solve real problems (Hurley, 1990). They acknowledge that they pass more time with their co-workers than they spend anywhere. Work performance is viewed as a positive-sum game. The group members work together on a continuous basis to coordinate different tasks, make decisions about how to do their work, and take responsibility for the total operation.

This chapter focuses some of the arguments and approaches dealing with the individual's contribution to work performance. The personnel decision is, also, a matter of fitting the person to the team of co-workers performing the job. It takes account of the person–job fit but is embedded in the context of designing effective work groups. Underlying this idea of exploring determinants of work-group effectiveness and strategies for designing adequate selection procedures are certain assumptions that are accepted as pertinent by practitioners but are rather absent in personnel psychology books (e.g., Levy-Leboyer, 1990; Smith, Gregg, & Andrews, 1989). Hackman and Morris (1975) said: "There is substantial agreement among researchers and observers of small task groups that something important happens in group interaction which can affect performance outcomes'' (p. 49).

Landy and Farr (1983) mentioned it as an aspect of the work setting. Smith (1976) did not include this issue in her three-dimensional framework of performance measures. Too often it is ignored that one of the most significant contributions to successful job performance is having the right persons teamed at the right time.

However, with assessment centers it is fairly common practice to study dimensions and exercises that relate to group work and interpersonal skills. But the approach has been used almost exclusively with management groups. This chapter emphasizes that this view must also apply to other occupational groups where actual performance requires joint work and joint decision making to cope with the work of the entire unit (Prieto, Blasco, & Quintanilla, 1991).

It is, perhaps, an alternate way of thinking about the validation of selection procedures to point out that group behavior is aimed at improving the work in which co-workers are engaged. The small-group activity represents an important criterion in determining accurate levels of individual effort and performance. Quite often, the isolation of employees in the workshop or in the office is not allowed nor reasonable.

INDIVIDUAL VERSUS TEAM PERFORMANCE

Managers attempting to organize information about productive work and overall performance are interested in: (a) actual yields that are directly produced over a given time, and, (b) actual outputs that are indirectly brought about when employees interact with each other or with clients, communicate, and work together in the organization.

Personnel psychologists prefer to concentrate on those behavior patterns that are exhibited through the whole process of executing certain job activities during a given period. They try to ensure that each dimension represents a single job activity instead of an aggregate of job activities and interplays among workmates. Such is the insularity of personnel analysts' approaches that standard practice manuals suggest that each rater only evaluates a ratee on a regular basis. Thus, individual performance becomes a construction by the job analyst. This approach needs to be adjusted to accommodate the multiple activities that describe everyday work situations. Ratees interact while performing the job and take the necessary measures to cope with the work of the unit. In this way, they create their competencies, reconciling time limits and task requirements that are currently used and those that ought to be used in working groups.

Emphasis is usually placed on categories of products or services (criteria) rather than on business systems (processes) depicting work flows and performance. Since Freyd's (1923) seminal article, criterion constructs and measures have been identified, developed, and validated as far as they have produced revenue earnings. So, according to Astin (1964), performance criteria have become "operational statements of goals and desired outcomes." They are considered evaluative standards to assess individual working and productivity indices (Blum & Naylor, 1968). Drenth (1984) divided goals of employee appraisals into four main categories: personnel management, guidance development, potential assessment, and criterion. Supervisors, peers, subordinates, the incumbent, or clients become the various sources of appraisal data. Broadly, their scheme of thought conveys only the individual's characteristics. Individual's job performance measures stand away from the strategic thinking of managerial actions on small groups and units.

As it happens, the individual employee's job performance appears as the most appropriate measure. Nevertheless, this assumption may be avoided from a conceptual and empirical perspective. It is accepted that individual levels of performance are affected by several conditions surrounding the position (Cascio, 1982) like organizational characteristics, environmental safety, life-span variables, job location, personal habits, commercial efficiency, or feasibility of goods and services, and so on.

The alternate framework implies another view of working life. Work in groups is commonplace at all levels in many organizations. Employees depend on each other to execute tasks successfully because they work for common purposes. The group works as a team under intensive socialization efforts. The effective team is one in which each member is, according to Bass (1982), "highly interdependent, coordinated and cooperative in their efforts" (p. 195). Applied psychologists are aware that team effectiveness arises out of matching role assignments with individual differences. Under such circumstances, functional specialization is of secondary importance. Very often, human resources issues may range from *"the right person at the right place"* to *"the right number at the right place."* A proactive role for personnel psychologists requires knowledgeable entry into these types of "flow planning and decisions." Every selector faces the challenge of helping develop an adequate approach to serve as the basis for setting up task-oriented and problem-solving teams.

Team performance has been explored through concrete models (Goodman, Ravlin, & Argote, 1986) that provide another frame of reference that seem absent elsewhere in personnel selection literature. Indeed, the main criterion for final acceptance, after a probation period of any applicant, derives from the supervisor opinion about the newcomer's ability to participate fully in team efforts. In a private Spanish bank, during 4 years, around 80% to 90% of supervisor's refusals to grant tenure to newcomers may be classified under this category. During this period 286 dismissals came as a consequence of this motive. Elsewhere, exit interviews at the bank also implicated person–team relationships as a major cause of turnover. The second most frequent reason for voluntarily leaving a tenured position mentioned an unacceptable climate or some unsatisfactory aspects of the existing work group.

In a case study, a group of seven competent candidates who had decided to quit their jobs after a short period was contrasted with another group of seven suitable candidates who remained in similar positions. They were randomly identified from personnel files of a psychological consulting firm in Barcelona. Their 16 PF profiles were compared statistically following the adjustment method. No significant differences were found. Their background data, as well as their previous turnover indices, were also very similar (Blasco, 1988). Again, the exit interview disclosed considerable discomfort with the work group.

In everyday practice, it is not easy to isolate individual performance from team performance. This contravenes the strenuous insistence of personnel psychologists on individual performance as the only pertinent criteria.

Other executives and middle managers do not pay too much attention to this. They look for capable, easygoing, and highly motivated subordinates who can function as a unit. They scrutinize newcomers in an attempt to learn if they may have the potential to do the job and to enrich the heterogeneity of other co-worker abilities. They also try to attract new employees as soon as they have tested their positive role affiliation and their supportiveness. They even emphasize that they prefer to sponsor training programs for unskilled but cooperative workers rather than accept skilled but stubborn and self-sufficient employees that do not contribute to team climate, communication patterns, and group adherence.

In Spain there is, for instance, an increasing demand to introduce in selection procedures measures of social intelligence and interpersonal insight. At first glance this is a reaction against those applicants who behave in an unusual way or have an unusual appearance. In fact, it is usually requested as a measure for setting aside odd applicants who cannot behave in a way that is socially correct and considerate of other people's feelings in face-to-face encounters.

Social sensitivity while interacting in the work group and person perception in meetings or teams are behavioral-cognition abilities (Guilford & Hoepfner, 1971), which are welcomed warmly by managers.

Levy-Leboyer (1989) has recently devised a selection procedure for an insurance company. The experimental battery included a leaderless group test where the group was in charge of writing a paper on "The Ten Commandments" of the insurance agent. A participation scale was produced by rating the involvement of candidates during the leaderless session. The "social quality" of applicants seemed to underlie the prediction of success in sales activity. This is an indirect way to test resourceful applicants while performing in work groups.

Organizations "in Search of Excellence" (Peters & Waterman, 1982) have decided not to pursue exclusively individual performance. Their personnel policies prefer patterns of behaviors that are thought to be successful only in the case that a majority of job incumbents become involved. They produce conditions that are imposed on the team through concrete designs and time schedules. New hires are selected not only on personal merits but on the extent to which they are likely to be easily assimilated into the organization, avoiding underproduction. Together they begin a training program aimed at developing and enhancing both group solidarity and consciousness. Their outstanding outcomes arise from team-building attitudes and from the quality of group problem-solving activities. So group process, social intelligence, and interpersonal skills are the criteria that are often demanded and rewarded in the context of team effectiveness. Such behavioral abilities forecast group-level outcomes of work groups with interdependent tasks. They have been linked to human resource planning approaches involving effectiveness and efficiency.

Team performance implies specific job behaviors performed by an employee as well as regular interaction and coordination among incumbents. Therefore, it is convenient to consider individual as well as work-group performance outcomes to ascertain actual criteria for selection purposes. Factors affecting individual performance on tasks have been a classic subject of study in personnel psychology (Fleishman & Quaintance, 1984). Nevertheless, team performance is crucially affected by several interpersonal skills and performance factors (Burack & Mathys, 1987; Guirdham, 1990; Robbins, 1989) such as:

person-interpretation skills, self-presentation, listening, communicating, and persuasion;

providing feedback, running a group meeting, problem analysis, stress tolerance, decisiveness, decision making;

flexibility and adaptability to deal with people's needs, failures or achievements, joint problem solving, understanding of goals, roles, norms, and conformity pressures.

Thus, the topic of performance raises its Janus head. There are, simultaneously, isolated task behaviors carried out by individuals *and* interdependent task-related behaviors that are meant only for the team. Both issues determine effective and meaningful job outcomes. Both perspectives are clearly rooted in management policies and thoroughly intertwined with their organizational significance. The implications of both views and the associated frame of reference have important repercussions on selection practices. Herriot (1984) said: "if individual's performance is not the sole criterion, measures of individual's characteristics should not be the sole predictors" (p. 12).

JOB SPECIFICATION
VERSUS FUNCTIONAL FLEXIBILITY

According to Algera and Greuter (1989), "By applying job analysis to personnel selection problems a specific goal is intended: as a result of job analysis, characteristics (behavior and ability requirements) must be laid down, which are typical of effective job performance'' (p. 8). The legitimacy of this approach lies on several assumptions:

There are specific jobs or job families.

Each employee performs only one job with differentiated tasks.

There are current and critical aspects of successful performance in a job.

Applicants are selected to perform a job.

There is a validated relationship between the candidate's characteristics and the available measures of performance on the job.

Those assumptions can be traced back to the job specialization principle. This view merits discussion. Certainly, there are distinct jobs and job families in public and private organizations. Nevertheless, at least in what concerns Spanish labor relationships, each employee becomes assigned to one occupational category and one wage level. It also seems to be the norm, not the exception, in European Community countries. A given category gathers together several jobs and positions. The same occupational category underlies different positions. Very often each position becomes redesigned, fitting the job to the person. Applicants are selected for a given category, for instance, administrative assistant. The assistant's duties are not identical at the aftersales service or at documentary reproduction service. The assistant's duties in a new unit are not the same as in a stable unit. In a new unit the new-hire deals with peer-group pressures. In a stable unit the supervisor looks at a novice workman and compares his results with those of an expert. In both cases, the assistant is a learner. The admission, relative status, and even the role of a younger or an aged overseer is perceived by the working group in a different way. Their wage structure and salary ranges are regulated by the collective bargaining.

Job analyses often ignore the social contexts of actions. For example, an office manager at headquarters may operate in a task-centered context, whereas an office manager in a rural milieu may operate in a neighbor-centered one. Similarly, the tasks of a secretary under an autocratic or a "laissez faire" supervisor are not identical. The content of both jobs are modulated by conditions external to the occupational category.

Therefore, it is necessary to know the job but also to know about the context. Who is the supervisor? Who are the fellow workers and subordinates? What is known about the prospective client? What are the sets of behaviors that incumbents expect from the newcomer to a given position? Role-making processes are involved in concrete job settings. They are absent in conventional personnel strategies mentioned throughout the available literature. A new competent employee may respond in dysfunctional manners by trying to modify the role definition or the existing interpersonal relations. Then he or she is fired during the probation period. The newcomer may be suitable from the personnel psychologist's frame of reference, but supervisors and fellow workers may argue that the candidate cannot fit the slot because he or she does not truly fit into the team.

In 1984, after a conventional selection procedure, a follow-up study was started on 26 new policemen in charge of deactivating bombs in Madrid, Bilbao, and Sevilla. Tests of aptitude (cognitive and psychomotor skills) and personality questionnaires were administered. These variables were established after the job analysis profile and the relationship between predictors and criteria was already validated. A year later, the procedure was revised. The psychologist avoided a new job analysis and decided to spend a day in each unit. He realized that the members of such a task force dedicated a great amount of time to talking, walking, doing physical exercises, playing cards, joking, visiting the cafeteria, and so forth while they were waiting for a decisive phone or radio call. The climate in each unit varied by leadership style and prevalent role-making choices among members. They used to distribute themselves in jeeps not haphazardly or by priorities, but mainly by friendship. The devised steps in manuals to deactivate a bomb are always incomplete, because reality is often more complex than expected. Delicate patterns of cooperation were requested. A warm climate of friendship and mutual trust improved this. Adequate selection and training were not enough. Person perception and social qualities, again, underlie the adaptable coping strategies. It was a very specialized job that could be solved successfully or unsuccessfully through differentiated work-group patterns of performance.

Once again, a very paradoxical situation was attained after a follow-up of the fire brigade's job analysis. At first glance, they have to deal successfully with fire calls. At the fire station, firemen are supposed to be used to waiting for fire alarms. This is not often the case. They do not feel like firefighters. Customarily, they mainly solve emergency situations that do not cause destruction by fire (rare events where children, aged or solitary people, or others are the source of the trouble). They have been employed and trained to extinguish fires or to assist people to escape safely from a burning building. Large fires only occur from time to time. So, job analysis indicates that the effective performance as firemen is related to nonfire incidents and situations. Nevertheless, as soon as the critical accident occurs, the successful performance requires differentiated skills as well as a climate of fellowship and comradeship. They become comrades in the fire station, while they share social activities that are unrelated to fire alarms. Here, again, this is a case of team performance and not of individual performance. A selection procedure focused exclusively on fire performance appears both meaningless and meaningful. This is a very traditional and specialized job!

During Franco's régime in Spain, policemen succeeded in quelling political riots. Afterwards, under the democratic régime, riots broke out again. It was decided to select and provide adequate training to a specialized new task force. There are now riots of pacifists, conscientious objectors, and even severely handicapped people. In such new situations, successful performance is not direct-ly related to the acquired training but to the flexible accommodation of the unit to each kind of rioter. At the end of the day, police officers, governors, politi-cians, as well as journalists value the unit performance and their unspecified accommodation to actual rioters. Everybody gives simpleminded opinions. Is it necessary to change predictors, criteria, or both?

These exemplars are not the exception. Delicate situations of this kind are the rule and are commonplace in many positions. They need very careful and tactful treatment. Again, incumbents have been selected for an occupational category whereas the job contents are broad and even diffuse. The working group redefines the rules that govern each member activities. If someone is absent or the group climate is unpleasant, the performance of an individual mem-ber is influenced by the group in a differentiated manner. There are, often, dis-approved or provocative behaviors that will be enhanced by the group and will be forbidden by the organization. Performance measurements almost never pay attention to such temporary behaviors, which are considered substandard. However, these behaviors may be regarded as the quid pro quo for the working-group cohesiveness and the team level of performance.

Recently, functional flexibility has become a fashion in the labor market of European Community countries. It consists "in manipulating the skill status of work, the multi-skilling of the workforce and, of course, their motivation" (Eu-ropean Foundation for the Improvement of Living and Working Conditions, 1988a). New kinds of work strategies and involvements have been brought about by technological change and industrial merging or restructuring. Even if special-ized jobs still exist, organizations now emphasize multivalency in jobs even in fairly independent occupational categories (Prieto, 1990; Prieto & Martin, 1990). The search for multiskilled and multirole employees or for integrated work groups by management is a feature of many new redesigned jobs and positions. High degrees of flexibility, expertise, working methods, and involvement from adapt-able incumbents are being demanded to cover a variety of tasks, accepted changes, widened responsibilities, and product qualities.

Flexible teams and semiautonomous production units are stressed in the new work force. Thus, occupational categories are retrieved and reinforced against old job contents or status. Continuous innovation is the leitmotif of the newly created flexible jobs that are central to sustaining production and quality con-trol. There is a redeployment of workers (European Foundation for the Improve-ment of Living and Working Conditions, 1988b).

Another example illustrates how the idea of functional flexibility operates. The trainer's profile indicates that the training and development function is not a unidimensional job. Conventionally, three major roles are involved (learning specialist, manager, and consultant) that demand quite independent competen-cies (Nadler & Nadler, 1989). Their evaluation requires, at the same time, in-formation about the trainer, trainees, available programs, staff, transfer, organizational benefices, and so on (Brinkerhoff, 1987; Kirkpatrick, 1987). Thus, it is necessary to consider separately each "ad hoc" training group to evaluate the effectiveness of a given skilled trainer. This is another example of group rather than individual performance used in obtaining criteria to validate further selection procedures.

Finally, during the 1980s, personnel psychologists in European Community countries have realized that they do not select applicants for a permanent job but for changing to new positions (Herriot, 1989). Even if employee career patterns vary considerably, success or failures are judged mainly by the incumbent, not by the normative, opinion of employers. Organizational commitment has acquired greater relevance than before. The self-concept, self-esteem, personal goals and values, the sense of personal efficacy, opportunity awareness, feelings toward work groups, role-related episodes and attitudes, transition learning, and so on are new behavioral repertoires introduced in selection schedules to reduce new-hires turnover. These constructs are not directly related to short-term performance. They point explicitly to long-term involvement and performance. Thus, practitioners look at career development within the company by "tracking" a group of similar applicants. Developments like equal opportunity legislation and affirmative-action programming are seen under a different light because they may lead to practical actions that are potentially harmful. They often provide sources of uncertainty for the human resources planning processes, especially in the context of organizational commitment.

In this context, the analysis of individual job performance is supported by the existence of job specifications. But as far as functionally flexible jobs determine the ground rules in personnel management, alternate frameworks must be developed to deal with contemporary personnel policies, upgrading *personnel specifications*, and *personal adjustment* methods to the new required standards. The sole criterion of individual performance should be regarded as only a "halfway house."

THE EFFECTIVE TECHNOSTRUCTURE

The available literature in personnel psychology pays considerable attention to individual performance because an efficient employee is considered a specialist in his or her job. The concept of technostructure alludes to the hierarchy of expert groups in any organizational system and the dominant role they play to ensure the productive capacity and fair trade through effective work-group performance and decision making. The production of standardized goods and services depends, for success, on the technostructure behind the personnel allocation plan. Galbraith (1973) stated: "The counterpart of specialization is always organization. Organization is what brings specialists, who as individuals are technically incomplete and largely useless, into a working relationship with other specialists for a complete and useful result'' (p. 81). The concept of techno-structure does not belong to the psychological and assessment realm. There-fore, it provides a coherent framework to the content of this chapter. The guiding mind of the business firm is not individual performance but the technostructural performance. As soon as an applicant becomes an employee, he or she becomes a member of the technostructure at any level. His or her individual performance is absorbed by the planning system in the organization. He or she belongs to a given unit where he or she will be evaluated after the synergistic performance of the work group. The power of the technostructure to accept or reject con-crete outcomes is extremely important. The candidate is hired, retained, promot-ed, transferred, or fired by the technostructure. The candidate will remain or quit the organization as a consequence of his or her involvement in the techno-structure.

The concept of technostructure is broader than work groups or teams. It alludes to the core of joint decision making and problem solving at each level of the organizational structure. Each person in his or her position is an active or passive actor of the technostructure.

Failures in personnel selection may be derived from the personnel psycholo-gist's complete or partial inability to capture the technostructure plans, priori-ties, and policies. The technostructure assures its existence through the work-groups' interactive efforts and achievements. The technostructure produces a setting where the emphasis is on the strategic aspects of human resources planning, linking these to strategic selection practices in the frame-work of business planning and policy capturing.

DEALING WITH PERSON-TEAM FIT

The technostructure welcomes suitable newcomers who know how to gain the group acceptance (A), to increase the group solidarity (S), to be aware of the group consciousness (C), to share the group identification (I), and to manage others' impressions (I) of him or her.

Team proficiency is built on these five functions. They represent the ASCII control codes of work-group performance. Simulations, group practices, reversed role playing, sociograms, open-ended exploration, group interviewing techniques, success stories, debriefing sessions, action plans, and so forth allow assess-ment of the behavioral repertoires and interactive actions. The basic procedures suggested by this approach can be summarized in this way:

1. The ASCII repertoires are specified in terms of observable behaviors or personal projects that must be displayed. Exercises and games are designed to assess the behavior and performance of the group of applicants as a whole and of each applicant influenced by that group.

2. When the small group of applicants begins the interaction, the initial and subsequent team attainments are assessed. Participants get feedback about the implications of their actions.

3. Participants' performances are monitored as they interact. The psychologist finds out what they are doing by obtaining data about individual contribution to team goals.

4. Objective and subjective observations are generated for evaluating ASCII role episodes. An assessment is performed to detect where deficits exist and to help in the determination of a suitable new-hire.

A systematic appraisal is made, soon afterwards, of on-the-work team performance on a before-and-after basis. The new employee, the supervisor, some subordinates, or peers are interviewed to find out teamed job performance and any symptoms of interpersonal or behavioral problems. If these problems arise, it may be convenient to run a counselling session. The purpose of the session is to spell out to the new employee the problems he or she is causing and the consequences of continuing the present behavior. Opinions and comments gathered are used as a trigger to discussion, not as a dissection statement. Internal and external causes behind behavioral, interpersonal, or job performance problems are analyzed.

Thus, during probation, individual and team performance become actual criteria in personnel decisions. Exit interviews and transfer interviews point out areas for improvement.

A statistical analysis is also carried out to compare the stability and competence of a work group before and after the introduction of new members. Objective measures include turnover, grievances, absenteeism, promotions, transfers, accident rates, injuries, group attendance rates, production wastes, complaints from clients, and so on.

Such sets of operational predictors and criteria outline several research designs for collecting performance data. Potential outcomes of such research include: Successful new employees express their understanding of what is to be done and of how it is to be done in the job. Personnel psychologists find themselves rewarded for helping to create efficient working groups in the technostructure.

ACKNOWLEDGMENT

The author acknowledges the kind comments and suggestions received from Dr. Mike Smith, who has improved the final English version of this chapter.

REFERENCES

Algera, J., & Greuter, M. A. M. (1989). Job analysis for personnel selection. In J. M. Smith & I. T. Robertson (Eds.), *Advances in selection and assessment* (pp. 7–30). Chichester: Wiley.

Astin, A. W. (1964). Criterion-centered research. *Educational and Psychological Measurement, 24*, 807–822.

Bass, B. (1982). Individual capability, team performances and team productivity. In M. D. Dunnette & E. A. Fleishman (Eds.), *Human performance and productivity: Human capability assessment* (pp. 179–232). Hillsdale, NJ: Lawrence Erlbaum Associates.

Blasco, R. (1988, April). *El fracaso en selección de personal realizado por medio de asesoria externa* [Failures in personnel selection practices in a consulting firm]. Unpublished paper produced for the II National Congress of Social Psychology, Alicante, Spain.

Blum, M. L., & Naylor, J. C. (1968). *Industrial psychology: Its theoretical and social foundations* (3rd ed., chap. 6). New York: Harper & Row.

Brinkerhoff, R. O. (1987). *Achieving results from training.* San Francisco: Jossey–Bass.

Burack, E. H., & Mathys, N. J. (1987). *Human resource planning: A pragmatic approach to manpower planning and development* (2nd ed.). Lake Forest, IL: Brace Park.

Cascio, W. F. (1982). *Applied psychology in personnel management* (2nd ed., chap. 6). Reston, VA: Reston.

Cole, R. E. (1991). *Strategies for learning: Small-Group Activities in American, Japanese and Swedish industry.* Berkeley: University of California Press.

Drenth, P. J. D. (1984). Personnel appraisal. In P. J. D. Drenth, H. Thierry, P. J. Willems, & C. J. de Wolff (Eds.), *Handbook of work and organizational psychology* (Vol. 1, p. 200). Chichester: Wiley.

European Foundation for the Improvement of Living and Working Conditions. (1988a). *The changing face of work* (p. 35). Luxembourg: Office for Official Publications of the European Communities. (SY-52-88-590-EN-C)

European Foundation for the Improvement of Living and Working Conditions. (1988b). *Participation in technological change.* Dublin, Ireland: European Foundation for the Improvement of Living and Working Conditions. (Working Paper Series: EF/WP/87/146/EN)

Fleishman, E. A., & Quaintance, M. K. (1984). *Taxonomies of human performance: The description of human tasks.* Orlando, FL: Academic Press.

Freyd, M. (1923). Measurement in vocational selection: An outline of research procedure. *Journal of Personnel Research, 2*, 215–249, 268–284, 377–385.

Galbraith, J. K. (1973). *Economics and the public purpose.* Boston: Houghton–Miflin.

Goodman, P. S., Ravlin, E. C., & Argote, L. (1986). Current thinking about groups: Setting the stage for new ideas. In P. S. Goodman (Ed.), *Designing effective work groups* (chap. 1, pp. 1–33). San Francisco: Jossey-Bass.

Guilford, J. P., & Hoepfner, R. (1971). *The analysis of intelligence* (p. 258). New York: McGraw-Hill.

Guirdham, M. (1990). *Interpersonal skills at work.* New York: Prentice-Hall.

Hackman, J. R., & Morris, C. G. (1975). Group tasks, group interaction process and group performance effectiveness: A review and proposed integration. In L. Berkowitz (Ed.), *Advances in experimental social psychology* (Vol. 8, pp. 45–99). New York: Academic Press.

Herriot, P. (1984). *Down from the ivory tower: Graduates and their jobs.* Chichester: Wiley.

Herriot, P. (1989). *Recruitment in the 90s.* London: Institute of Personnel Management.

Hollway, W. (1991). *Work psychology and organizational behaviour: Managing the individual at work* (chap. 1). London: Sage.

Hurley, J. (1990). The collaborative imperative of new technology organisations. *The Irish Journal of Psychology, 11*(2), 211–220.

Kirkpatrick, D. L. (1987). Evaluation. In R. L. Craig (Ed.), *Training and development handbook: A guide to human resource development* (3rd rev. ed., pp. 301–319). New York: McGraw-Hill.

Landy, F. J., & Farr, J. L. (1983). *The measurement of work performance: Methods, theory and applications.* New York: Academic Press.

Levy-Leboyer, C. (1989). A case study examining the accuracy of predictors. In M. Smith & I. Robertson (Eds.), *Advances in selection and assessment* (pp. 129–132). Chichester: Wiley.

Levy-Leboyer, C. (1990). *Evaluation du personnel; Quelles mèthodes choisir?* Paris: Les Editions D'Organisation.

Nadler, L., & Nadler, Z. (1989). *Developing human resources.* San Francisco: Jossey-Bass.

Peters, T. J., & Waterman, R. H. (1982). *In search of excellence: Lessons from America's best-run companies.* New York: Harper & Row.

Prieto, J. M. (1990). Incertidumbre laboral percibida a travès de las nuevas formas de empleo y autoempleo [Perceived job uncertainty through new forms of employment and self-employment]. *Psicologia e Lavoro, 19*(76-77), 6-12.

Prieto, J. M., Blasco, R. D., & Quintanilla, I. (1991). Recrutement et sélection du personnel en Espagne [Recruitment and selection in Spain]. *European Review of Applied Psychology, 41*(1), 47-62.

Prieto, J. M., & Martin, J. (1990). New forms of work organization. *The Irish Journal of Psychology, 11*(2), 170-185.

Robbins, S. P. (1989). *Training in interpersonal skills: Tips for managing people at work.* Englewood Cliffs, NJ: Prentice-Hall.

Smith, M., Gregg, M., & Andrews, D. (1989). *Selection assessment: A new appraisal.* London: Pitman.

Smith, P. C. (1976). Behaviors, results and organizational effectiveness: The problem of criteria. In M. D. Dunnette (Ed.), *Handbook of industrial and organizational psychology* (pp. 745-775). Chicago: Rand-McNally.

Wood, S. (1990). Tacit skills, The Japanese Management Model and new technology. *Applied Psychology, An International Review, 39*, 169-190.

15

Performance-Appraisal Accuracy: An Illusive or Sometimes Misguided Goal?

Daniel R. Ilgen
Michigan State University

BACKGROUND

Approaches to Performance Appraisal

There are few statements more central to the practice of industrial and organizational psychology than the adages to "know thy job" and "know thy people." In the latter case, the rule is often institutionalized in the form of formal performance-appraisal systems. The implicit goal of all such systems is to provide accurate appraisals of employee performance based on the judgments of one or more other persons who are also organizational employees.

Unfortunately, rarely if ever is anyone satisfied with such ratings. They never seem to meet anyone's expectations. Those being appraised are satisfied only if the appraisals match their often inflated beliefs about their own performance. Those who complete the evaluations find them time consuming, bothersome, and disquieting when they must provide performance feedback. Managers and others who look at the appraisal data of many employees often find them less than credible as they try to reconcile the apparent discrepancy between the glowing appraisal reports on file and their own personal beliefs about the level of performance in the work force.

Dauntless, we industrial and organizational psychologists see the problems not as debilitating limitations but as challenges to be met. Given our psychometric training and our knowledge, capabilities, and demonstrated success developing systems for assessing jobs and individual differences, our initial response to such problems was to assume that the limitations were rooted in rating errors and other manifestations of measurement problems. This led to extensive work on the definition of criteria of job performance and the development of measures of these criteria. Our early efforts were focused on three interrelated sets of issues. The first was the development and evaluation of scales for rating performance that were psychometrically sound. The second was training evaluators to use the performance-rating instruments effectively. Such training focused on insuring familiarity with the scales themselves, standardizing their use across raters in the sample of raters, creating an awareness of the types of errors to which raters often fall victim, and then providing ways to attempt to avoid these errors. Finally, at the system level, policies and practices complete with manuals, schedules of when to appraise, and centralized procedures to keep track of the appraisal process were developed.

By almost any standard, our efforts were successful. We identified performance-appraisal scales that are better than others under particular conditions (Bernardin & Beatty, 1984); we learned how to train raters to reduce rating errors and improve their ability to use the performance-appraisal system (Wexley & Latham, 1981); and we established guidelines for the development and implementation of appraisal systems (see, for example, Bernardin & Beatty, 1984). In spite of these gains, the dissatisfaction with performance appraisals remained.

Landy and Farr, in their watershed 1980 *Psychological Bulletin* article, reviewed the literature on performance appraisal up to that time and responded to the criticisms by suggesting that attention shift from a concern for the rating scale, training, and appraisal practices related to using particular scales to that of understanding the judgment processes of raters. These authors suggested that work in the late 1970s combining cognitive processing with person perception provided provocative ideas about the ways in which persons who rate the performance of others may observe, store in memory, and recall social cues that form the bases for evaluations of others. At about the same time, Jack Feldman (1981) was even more specific in linking social cognition with performance appraisal. A flurry of research activity developed pursuing the understanding of the cognitive processes of performance appraisers. This research activity dominated performance appraisal research in the 1980s.

Almost without exception, the primary criterion of the recent research has been some index of the extent to which raters accurately report the behaviors of ratees or accurately evaluate ratee performance. That is to say, in earlier research, it was *assumed* that the goal of the appraisal process was to provide accurate observations and evaluations of employees, but research rarely addressed rater accuracy directly. If accuracy was addressed, the tendency was to assume that rating errors were indicators of accuracy or that interrater agreement represented accuracy. The work in the 1980s questioned both rating errors and interrater agreement as measures of rater accuracy, preferring instead the establishment of known standards of performance in which to compare raters' appraisals. To create conditions where the standards of performance were known, it was usually necessary to conduct research under far more controlled conditions than had been done for most performance-appraisal research prior to 1980. Much of the later research was done in the laboratory.

In a recent review and evaluation of the performance-appraisal literature of the 1980s directed at understanding factors affecting raters' ability to provide accurate ratings, Ilgen, Barnes-Farrell, and McKellin (in press) concluded that the research had contributed to a better understanding of four general issues related to the application of performance appraisals in organizations. These four related to: (a) the need to improve the raters' ability to obtain unbiased samples of ratee behaviors prior to making appraisal judgments, (b) the correction of misguided advice about the nature of rating scales and the ability of raters to observe events without simultaneously evaluating those events, (c) the importance of the frames-of-references of raters (called "schemas" in the jargon of social cognition), and (d) the need to be extremely cautious when using archival performance-appraisal ratings due to the effects of the purposes of ratings and other setting-specific variables on ratings that appear in personnel files.

Reactions to Performance Appraisals

Ironically, in spite of a number of major gains in the last 15 to 25 years in performance-appraisal technology, dissatisfaction with performance appraisals is no less today than it was in the past. If anything, criticisms have been more prevalent. For example, Longenecker, Sims, and Gioia (1987) reported the results of their lengthy interviews regarding performance appraisals with 60 executives representing 11 functional areas in 7 large corporations. The authors concluded that the political realities of corporate life supersede goals of accuracy and honesty when managers are asked to complete performance appraisals. Mohrman and Lawler (1983), commenting on the link between appraisals and pay, stressed that those who think that tying salary decisions to performance appraisals will decrease the probability of bad salary decisions soon find that both their salary structures and their performance evaluations are based on bad data. Banks and Murphy (1985) criticized much of the performance-appraisal research of the 1980s for paying too little attention to the practitioner concerns of (a) managerial commitment to the appraisal process, (b) the nature of communications between supervisors who serve as raters and their subordinates, (c) supervisors' performance feedback skills, and (d) their ability to clarify objectives for others. Finally, I was struck by the invariance of the complaints over time when I attended a panel discussion at the annual conference of the Society of Industrial and Organizational Psychology held in Boston in April of 1989. The panel discussion was entitled, "Real World Performance Appraisal: What do Scientists have to Offer?" Of the four panelists, two were from academia and two were employed in corporations where they developed or were involved with the operation of the performance-appraisal systems. The concerns that the organizational representatives raised about the lack of help that they saw coming from research on performance appraisal could just as easily have been raised in 1949 as in 1989, in spite of the fact that performance-appraisal scales, rater training, and operational procedures are considerably better today than at that time.

The cursory historical review just outlined presents a curious phenomenon. Research and development regarding employee performance-appraisal systems document real improvements over the years, and yet, in spite of the improvements, the perceptions of those who use such systems have not changed; the same old problems that plagued the systems from their inception exist today with little change in magnitude. Why?

Three explanations come to mind. The first of these is that the advancements that have been made in performance-appraisal systems by those who do research on the systems have not been incorporated into systems in use. Without a doubt, there are a number of systems in operation that have serious technical flaws. It is not hard to find systems with graphic rating scales having no anchors other than the endpoints, and these scales are being used for general performance outcomes such as "overall job performance" or for a list of ill-defined traits. Even in cases where the systems have been very carefully defined and introduced into the organization, often they are poorly maintained so that, over time, new raters are required to use the systems with inadequate training. Unfortunately, complaints about the systems are not limited to settings where the systems have not applied state-of-the-art procedures. Under the best of conditions, the concerns that were raised earlier prevail.

A second explanation is that with improved techniques also come rising expectations. Dissatisfaction could exist in the face of improved practices if the persons using the systems had expectations that remained some constant level above what the system could deliver, regardless of the fact that the system might deliver more at time $t + 1$ than at time t. Although this explanation cannot be ruled out, it also seems unlikely. First of all, those who have introduced improvements in rating scales, rater training, and other components of performance-appraisal systems, in general, have tended to show a prudent respect for the limits of their techniques. Furthermore, the content of the issues addressed by the technologically focused improvements are often independent of the issues with which complaints are raised. For example, improvements in rater training may focus on reducing rating errors, but the concerns of the users may be with the political factors that dictate the use of the rating scale.

A third possibility is that those who are most interested in designing research on performance-appraisal systems may have looked at too narrow a domain for addressing the problems of these systems. For the most part, the researchers have been industrial and organizational psychologists or human resource management persons oriented toward microindividual-level views of the appraisal process. Given this orientation, it is easy to understand why such persons would look to the nature of measurement instruments, scaling, rating errors, and training to attempt to "fix" the system. Likewise, when the limits of these approaches were addressed and alternatives suggested, it is understandable that researchers, drawn from this pool, look to other psychological literatures, in this case social cognition, to move from the limited effectiveness plateau. I suggest that it is time to redefine the problem from a different perspective and to explore whether such a redefinition will lead to possible changes in approaches to performance-appraisal systems that address some of the concerns that have remained with us over the years.

A Functional Perspective on Performance Appraisal

A Description of Functions.   Rather than search our psychological roots for explanations of performance appraisals, let us ask a more basic question. Why establish a performance-appraisal system in the first place? Table 15.1 provides one way to answer this question. The answer is based on the assumption that performance-appraisal systems are designed to meet the needs of particular constituencies, and that there are certain functions served by performance appraisals for these constituencies.

It is suggested in Table 15.1 that the constituencies served by a formal performance appraisal can be clustered into two mutually exclusive categories. The first represents the organization's goals. It is labeled *organizations*. Next, there are the persons whose performance is appraised. This set is labeled *individual appraisees*. The functions that the appraisal system serves the organization are again clustered into two sets. The first of these deals with the need to encourage

TABLE 15.1
Potential Constituencies and Functions of Formal Performance Appraisal Systems

Constituencies	*Functions*
I. Organizations	A. Control through Human Resource Management
	1. Communicate Performance Standards
	2. Administer Rewards
	3. Discipline & Dismissals
	B. Data for System Level Decisions
	1. Criteria for:
	Selection
	Training Evaluation
	2. Needs Analyses
II. Individual Appraisee	A. Learn
	B. Obtain Rewards
	C. Avoid Negative Sanctions

reliable behavior from organizational members. This function typically is called control (Lawler, 1976). Although the specific methods of control vary a great deal, three general classes of variables are suggested. The first of these is informational. Performance-appraisal systems provide an opportunity to communicate the standards of job performance to job incumbents. The other two of these involve the establishment and communication of contingencies between standards of performance and outcomes. In Table 15.1 the outcomes are clustered in terms of their value or valence to the recipients.

The second cluster of functions of performance-appraisal systems for organizations does not deal directly with individual employees; it deals with information that makes possible the evaluation of organizational systems. Such information is for the establishment and operation of essential organizational practices, but it is not necessary that employees evaluated by the performance appraisal system be aware of the results of their own evaluations in order for the evaluations to be useful for system evaluation purposes.

Turning to individual employees who are evaluated by the performance-appraisal system, three sets of functions are listed. Obviously, in order to meet these functions, the evaluated employee must be aware of his or her evaluation. The first of these functions involves learning the tasks involved in the job. Ideally, performance-appraisal systems with feedback not only communicate to the employees what it is that they are supposed to do but also inform them of the degree to which they have met the standards over the time period covered by the appraisal.

The other two functions are based on the hedonistic assumption that employees will want to obtain rewards and avoid punishments. To the extent that performance appraisals convey knowledge about the contingencies between performance of the job and the attainment of rewards and the avoidance of punishments, they serve employees' desires and have the potential of influencing future employee behaviors. I would contend that, to the extent that appraisals aid in learning and provide for the attainment of valued outcomes along with the nonattainment of negative outcomes, they serve the functions of the employees.

The Functional Role of Appraisal Accuracy. Note that we mentioned earlier that the underlying assumption regarding performance-appraisal systems is that their fundamental purpose is to provide a valid and reliable measurement of employee job performance. That is to say, the system is a measurement system that should be an accurate reflection of how employees perform their jobs. However, also note that when we ask another basic question, "What do we hope to accomplish for whom with a performance system?," we have generated a set of functions served by the systems without mentioning accuracy. In some cases, this may be because accuracy was simply assumed. Certainly, if organizational decisions are going to be made on the basis of data generated by appraisal systems, we would hope that the data on which the decisions are based are accurate. Likewise, if individuals are to learn how to do their jobs from the system, accuracy is important. On the other hand, is it necessary that appraisal information be accurate to control employee behavior or to provide the employees with means to obtain rewards and avoid negative sanctions? The answer to this question is less clear. In fact, it is sufficiently unclear to me that it makes me a little uneasy to even ask it, because, in asking it, I feel compelled to consider the alternative that there may be cases when inaccurate appraisals serve functions that seem quite legitimate. At this point, let us tuck this thought away but not forget it.

Performance-Appraisal Options

Performance-appraisal systems vary a great deal in the way in which they are conducted. In order to address the functions served by appraisals, we must first consider how these functions might be met. For purposes of discussion, consider the following general practices.

Coach and Consequences. In most all-inclusive performance-appraisal systems, information is gathered in the system that is communicated to employees and also becomes part of their personnel record. The data in the system are then used for both individual- and system-level decisions. Individual ones involve such outcomes as salary, promotions, job assignments, and dismissals. The performance evaluations are also fed back to the employees to provide them with a basis for maintaining behaviors that were valued and change those that were seen as in need of improvement. Such information is also useful for setting future performance objectives.

Coach. A second common use of performance-appraisal information is directed primarily at the coaching function. In this case, the information is decoupled from administrative functions. It is used primarily to provide feedback for self-evaluation and for setting future performance goals. Two slightly different modifications of the coaching practice address the way in which the data are handled once they have been used for coaching. Most frequently, the data are maintained at the unit supervisor level and not shared with others in the organization. Another alternative is to place the data in a file that can be accessed for making system-level decisions but not individual-level ones. In this case, the data could be used to evaluate training programs or validate a selection system, but the data would not be placed in the employee's personnel file. These two variations are labeled Coach Only and Coach and Store, respectively.

Research Only. Performance-appraisal data can also be collected only for use regarding organizational-system decisions. The most common of these uses is in validating selection systems. The appraisals serve as the criteria against which tests, interviews, and other selection materials are evaluated. Data collected for research purposes are also useful for inventorying the performance levels of employees when needs analyses for training are conducted. The common characteristic of the research-only option is that the data are not shared with the employees, and they are not inserted into their personnel records for access regarding individual personnel decisions.

No Performance Appraisal. For completeness, there is one other option regarding performance appraisals. This option is not to do them. Although those of us who are involved with the many facets of human resource management are loathe to consider this option, managers and workers are not so committed to the appraisal process. Therefore, we need to consider this option as we lay out possible responses regarding performance appraisal.

Matching Functions and Options

Table 15.2 combines the functions of performance-appraisal systems with the options. The ''X''s in the table indicate the functions that are typically believed to be addressed by the particular option that is used.

TABLE 15.2
Functional Objectives of Performance-Appraisal Options

	Organizational					Individual		
	System Level Evaluations		Control					
Appraisal Option	Crit.	Needs A.	Comm.	Rew.	D & D	Learn.	Rew.	Sanc.
Coach & Consequ.	X	X	X	X	X	X	X	X
Coach & Store	X	X	X			X		
Coach Only						X		
Research	X	X						
No P. A.								

Abbreviations:
Crit.   = Criteria
Needs A. = Needs Analysis
Comm.   = Communicate Performance Standards
Rew.   = Administer Rewards
D & D   = Discipline and Dismissals
Learn.   = Learning
Rew.   = Obtain Rewards
Sanc.   = Avoid Negative Sanctions
Consequ. = Consequences
P. A.   = Performance Appraisal

In Table 15.2, the first option, Coach and Consequences, is described as all things to all people. The performance-appraisal system is administered to provide information for the organization to guide system-level decisions regarding the validation of selection procedures, training evaluation, and other practices of human resource management, as well as to control individuals by communicating standards and administering rewards and sanctions. Likewise, the individual is to receive individual feedback and experience the motivational value of contingent rewards and sanctions. If this sounds like too much of a good thing, it is. Although this option is the most frequently attempted option, using appraisals to accomplish all these ends is asking the system to deliver more than it is capable of doing (DeVries, Morrison, Shullman, & Gerlach, 1986). As a result, using the coach and consequences option creates many of the complaints to which we have already alluded among those who use and are affected by the system.

There are two ways to respond to the inability of the Coach and Consequences option to deal with many of its problems. One is to attempt to remove some of the conditions that lead to problems and still try to maintain all the functions. There have been many attempts to do this. Increasing managerial commitment to the system (Banks & Murphy, 1987), creating an attitude of support and constructive feedback (Burke & Wilcox, 1969; Maier, 1958; Solem, 1960), involving ratees more in the system through participation (Mohrman & Lawler, 1983), and numerous other attempts to address variables both within and outside the system (see, for example, Beatty & Bernardin, 1984; Wexley & Latham, 1981) have been used to reduce problems with the system and yet still maintain all desired functions.

A second position is to question whether any performance-appraisal system can be expected to accomplish all the ends outlined in Table 15.2. Such a line of questioning leads to the exploration of conditions that would limit any system that attempts to be all things to all people. The early work at General Electric by Herb Meyer and his colleagues (Meyer, Kay, & French, 1958) recognized the fact that the goal of evaluation for organizational decisions was incompatible with coaching and learning when it was advocated that these two functions be separated. More recently, Longenecker et al.'s (1987) position is that, because organizations are political systems, any performance appraisal tied to individual outcomes will be influenced by political forces to the detriment of rating accuracy.

The preponderance of the data would imply that no system can do all that the coach and consequence option demands (DeVries et al., 1986). Furthermore, when systems try to do it all, the result is likely to be that the data collected by such systems are not likely to serve any of the functions very well. More than likely, the data (ratings) will be distorted (Mohrman & Lawler, 1983).

If a system cannot meet all objectives, an alternative strategy would be to focus on only some objectives. Table 15.2 suggests that there are three limited objectives. The most common of these is the Coach Only option. Here appraisals

are conducted and the information shared in a performance-appraisal review between the appraiser and the appraised. This information is kept confidential between the appraiser and appraisee. Such systems can be valuable for working
with employees at the individual level. The limitations that do exist are due to
the fact that the employee may not see the appraisal interview as truly independent of the appraisal with consequences. The idea of separating the appraisal interview for consequences from that with only coaching functions, as suggested by Meyer et al. (1958), underplays the fact that the employee is still aware
that the same person giving the coaching feedback may also evaluate him or
her later (Ilgen & Feldman, 1983). The result of this realization is that the ties
to evaluation still influence ratings and responses to them in the coaching setting.

Another coaching option suggested in Table 15.2 is to store the coaching
information, but only as criterion data for organization needs, not at the individual
level. To my knowledge, this is not frequently done. This may be due, in part,
because systems developed for coaching purposes try to avoid any distribution
of information beyond the level of the supervisor. Certainly to do so must involve careful assurances of confidentiality and guarantees that the data would
never be used for individual personnel decisions. Another limitation may be that
the types of ratings and information most useful for coaching may not be the
types that best serve the validation of a selection system or the assessment
of training needs. It would seem that both the usage problem and that of the
nature of the information could be addressed and would be valuable for increasing the use of the data, whereas at the same time not creating conditions that
are likely to conflict in such a way as to lead to distortions of the ratings.

A third option mentioned in Table 15.2 is that of using the performance-
appraisal data only for research purposes. There is a great deal of evidence that
performance evaluations gathered only for research purposes are of higher quality
than those gathered for other purposes (Padgett, 1988). Presumably, the higher
quality is due to the fact that the confidentiality of the ratings removes any felt
need to distort the data on the part of the raters.

To my knowledge, data gathered for research purposes in the past have only
been collected on a single case basis; that is, the research purpose goal of performance evaluations has not been institutionalized. Ratings are not obtained
on a regular basis only for research. If the research option is to be considered
one of several for performance-appraisal systems and is to be depended on to
generate data necessary for criterion development and needs analyses on a regular basis, it would be necessary to institutionalize this process. The advantage
of a regular collection of such data under the protection of anonymity is that
it would provide a database that is likely to be more accurate and valid than
other methods of generating performance data. The disadvantage is that the
users of such systems may feel that the time and effort needed for establishing
the criterion dimensions, training on the use of the system, and completing the
evaluation is not worth it if the data are not used for other purposes; that is,

the disadvantages are likely to be motivational with respect to the raters, not the ratees.

The fourth and final option listed in Table 15.2 is one that those of us involved in developing and implementing performance appraisal systems are loathe to consider—the option of no performance appraisal. For medium-to-large-sized organizations, I believe that it is unwise to have no performance-appraisal system, and I would like to think that this belief is based on more than self-serving biases. On the other hand, if the organization is unwilling to put forth the effort to develop and maintain a good system leaving only a system that is mistrusted and produces ratings of questionable validity, then the option of a no-rating system may be preferable to the one in use, but not to a properly designed and maintained one.

Another option for the lack of use of performance appraisals is to suggest that when, at the organizational level, a performance-appraisal system is in use, there still may be conditions under which performance appraisals should not be used. Let me suggest several such conditions.

In most organizations, there are a number of jobs on which there is very little opportunity for individual differences in job performance. Under such conditions, performance appraisals have little or no value for controlling behavior, nor do they provide much information about job performance over and above what is known from the fact that the person is in attendance and not disrupting the performance of the unit. Furthermore, in such conditions, the employee is likely to gain little or no additional information about his or her performance from the ratings. Therefore, for such jobs, the system is redundant and unnecessary.

In other situations, rather than be redundant, performance-appraisal systems may be disrupting. Consider the situation in which the typical raters of performance (supervisors) do not have the opportunity to observe the performance of subordinates or do not know the jobs well enough to provide the level of evaluation demanded by the performance-appraisal system. Under such conditions, the supervisors lack credibility, and the evaluations that they generate may be more disruptive than valuable. Unless one can change the reporting process or alter the structure of the evaluation process, it is unlikely to be of much value to attempt to fine tune the performance-appraisal instrument or to train the raters.

Work teams provide another challenge for performance-appraisal systems. By their very nature, performance appraisals are individually oriented; they map evaluations onto individuals (Ilgen, 1988). When team performance becomes the primary unit of analysis, the issue of individual performance in the team often becomes difficult to judge. In addition, it may also be detrimental to emphasize individual differences in these types of work relationships. It is this latter process issue that is often emphasized by those who advocate teamwork and the Japanese norms of team over individual orientations as a reason not to do individual performance appraisals in teams. Although the positions tend to be based more on general reactions than on data, I do think it is premature to dismiss the fact that individually driven performance appraisals, under some types of teamwork structures, may be detrimental.

As one final situational condition that may lead to questioning the use of performance appraisal, let me raise the issue of multiple performance dimensions where some of the dimensions are very concrete and others are much more abstract or difficult to quantify. Under such conditions, the more concrete standards are likely to dominate behavior; that is, because performance can be measured more easily on the concrete dimensions, it will be easier to agree about the extent to which a person has done well or poorly on these dimensions. Thus, if the person has to perform on a number of dimensions, some of which are concrete and others less so, it is likely that the person will "play" to the concrete ones to the detriment of the others. The latter is particularly true if valued rewards are tied to the appraisal system. If successful performance of the job demands spending a great deal of time and effort working on the less concrete dimensions, the existence of a performance-appraisal system may decrease the frequency of the less concrete dimensions.

The conditions just mentioned questioning the use of performance appraisals have all focused on the work setting. Let me suggest that there also may be conditions within the person that suggest that particular persons be excluded from a regularly scheduled performance appraisal. Consider one condition that I contend is not all that rare. This is the condition of an employee who, over time, maintains a relatively constant level of performance; the person has been an outstanding performer for years or even a very satisfactory one. Assume that this employee then performs considerably worse than his or her previous, well-established, pattern of performance. Also assume two other conditions. The first is that there is a readily available reason for the lower performance such as the need to cope with a serious personal problem such as a spouse who is fighting a substance abuse problem or the employee's own physical illness. Second, assume that the employee is well aware of his or her drop in performance over the time period. Under these conditions, if there is a regularly scheduled performance appraisal for the person, it usually is necessary to appraise the person along with all others. The appraiser is then faced with a dilemma; should he or she appraise the person at the level the ratee performed during the time period, or should the appraisal be based on the employee's "normal" performance? Most appraisers would alter the rating in order to protect the employee if the rater believed that the current level of performance was an aberration. However, to do such simply puts into the appraisal system ratings that are less accurate than the rater is capable of producing. Furthermore, if the data are to be used as criteria for organizational decision making, these manipulated data may not serve very well as criteria. I suggest that, rather than leave the rater only the alternative to distort the rating in order to protect an employee in whom the rater has a great deal of confidence regarding the employee's future performance, it might be more reasonable to create an evaluation system that allows the rater the option to skip an appraisal cycle for the employee.

The combination of issues raised regarding times when appraisals may not be reasonable suggests the incorporation of the option to omit appraisals when it is likely that the appraisal data will not be accurate or when accurate appraisals may have detrimental effects on individual or unit performance. From the perspective of an individual's employment with an organization over time, any particular individual in such a system could be missing an appraisal during any particular cycle, either because he or she was on a job where conditions were not good for appraisals or because of some personal characteristics that justified exclusion. To the extent that the appraisal system was used for making individual-level decisions about reward allocations, promotions, and other decisions, procedures would have to be developed to deal with "missing data." At first glance, such missing data seem disconcerting. However, it should be kept in mind that the missing data exist because the alternative is to get bad data. I suggest that having the option to remove persons from the appraisal process for reasons of the job or of the person himself or herself has the potential for increasing system-level accuracy. The latter should increase the usefulness of performance-appraisal data for both organizational and personal functions. Whether this indeed occurs waits for empirical verification.

RESEARCH IMPLICATIONS OF A FUNCTIONS OPTIONS PERSPECTIVE

Earlier in this chapter, I mentioned that when problems arose with performance-appraisal systems, the initial response was to rely on our psychological roots and search for solutions among those psychological processes that we understood best. In particular, we looked to our knowledge of scaling to provide the answers and relied on our knowledge of training and other methods of influencing human behavior to put our scaling knowledge to work. When that failed, we again turned to psychological zeitgeist to suggest ways to proceed. This led us to focus on the rater as a judge.

If we begin with the point of view that there are several goals to be met with performance-appraisal systems and that there are a limited set of options for meeting these goals, then the search for solutions to problems is broadened. It leads one to ask what critical functions are to be addressed and what mix of options might meet these functions. In the exploration of answers to these questions, the range of relevant issues expands from those of psychological processes. In particular, I believe that the perspective immediately forces one to consider the conditions of the environment in which the systems are to be placed. At this time it is too early to say exactly how this environment should be construed. However, let me give you one example of the way in which one might approach the problem.

Margaret Padgett (1988), a recent PhD from Michigan State University, looked at the kinds of factors that might lead people to report ratings on the formal appraisal forms that were not in agreement with their best judgments about the person's actual performance. To gather such data was not easy. It required that she put in a great deal of time and effort to gain the confidence of the people so that they would be willing to report discrepancies between how they rated subordinates and how they felt about them. She met with over 100 supervisors individually to discuss the project and gain their commitment to rate a recently appraised employee on a research instrument. The supervisors also provided responses to a number of other variables and gave permission for us to access the rating of one particular employee selected by the researcher. The supervisors also

Without going into great detail, I have presented the model that she tested in her dissertation and the best fit model that resulted from using a LISREL analysis. Figure 15.1 is the predicted model for a number of factors that she believed would affect the extent to which raters would bias their reported performance evaluations in the positive direction compared to what they really believed was the employee's performance level. According to the model, the most salient factor was the extent to which the raters believed they could be honest in their evaluations. This belief was predicted to be a function of the rater's desire to be liked by the ratee, ability to document his or her rating, expected reaction of the ratee to the rating, and the extent to which the employees were

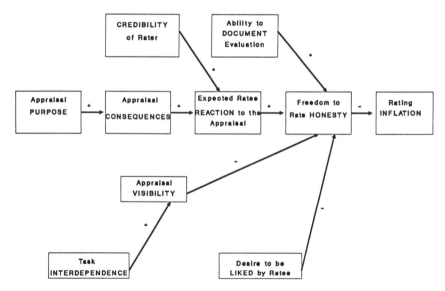

FIG. 15.1.   Padgett's (1988) initial model for factors affecting rater motivation to provide accurate performance evaluations.

likely to share their evaluations with others (Appraisal Visibility). Expected reactions, in turn, were expected to be a function of the credibility of the rater, the sharing of the ratings with others, and whether or not there were or were not positive or negative consequences associated with performance evaluations. Finally, the purpose was believed to be associated with the consequences.

Figure 15.2 presents the final structural model. To go into great detail describing this is beyond my purpose here. My point is not so much in the findings as in the approach. What I am suggesting is that research needs to address the contextual factors influencing performance appraisal. Through a better understanding of context along with clearly specifying the functions we want the appraisal to serve, we should be more aware of the fact that no appraisal system is likely to be able to serve all the functions that we have been typically asking it to serve. Once we understand these limits and understand the options available regarding appraisals, perhaps our research will learn more about mix of performance-appraisal options that will meet a more realistic set of functions.

CONCLUSION

Performance appraisals have been with us a long time. Over that time period, those concerned with developing and refining these systems have made a lot of gains. At the same time, criticisms and dissatisfaction have plagued the use of these systems from their inception. It has been argued here that, in spite of the changes, criticisms have changed little in either level (frequency and intensity) or content; complaints that were heard years ago are still echoed today.

Frustrations with some of the limitations with performance appraisals at the end of the 1970s led Landy and Farr (1980) to suggest a change of course in our efforts to improve such systems. This suggestion was heeded, I suspect, far beyond their expectations. The result was a surge of research effort directed at the rating process.

As I survey the performance-appraisal landscape more than 10 years later, I see little reason to be much less frustrated than were Landy and Farr. There has been some progress, as I have mentioned, but the sources of frustration have changed little. Thus, I too would like to suggest that we alter or change, somewhat, our path in pursuit of the perfect appraisal. The suggestions that I have may seem radical to those of us, myself included, who have come to be interested in performance appraisals from a broader concern with the psychological processes important at work or from a human resource management view of human behavior that looks to the microprocesses of human knowledge, skills, abilities, and attitudes to structure appraisal systems. I have two suggestions.

First, unlike past corrections that turned from one psychological path to another, in my opinion, needed today is a course less dominated by psychologi-

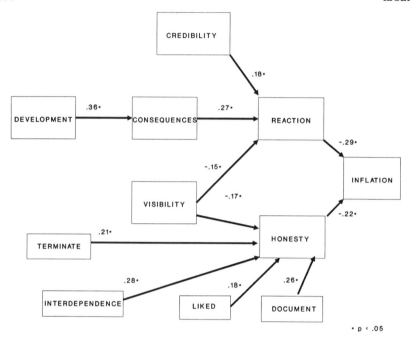

FIG. 15.2.   Structural parameters for Padgett's final model of rater motivation.

cal or psychologically-oriented domains. At the theoretical level, the issues involve the nature of the social milieu in which appraisals operate. Practically,
the issues are more managerial than technical; that is, the issues may not be
so much developing the technical features of the system as they are managing
the system so that it can operate effectively. For example, consider the issue
of managerial commitment to accurate appraisals. All would agree that such commitment is a necessary condition in order for a performance-appraisal system
to operate effectively. However, once managerial commitment has been identified as an important variable, making an appraisal system work in a particular
setting is less of a technical issue than a managerial one of establishing policies
and practices that will create and maintain commitment. Thus, establishing a
new performance-appraisal system will require not only the usual practices of
obtaining approval for the system, developing scales, and training users, but
it will also require months of "campaigning" for the system prior to its implementation, working to establish ways to reward good appraising behavior, and other
efforts far beyond the boundaries of duties and responsibilities of those who
developed the appraisal system in the past.

My second suggestion is that the analogy of a path to the perfect appraisal
is incorrect. We should be open to the possibility that there is not one path and
to the possibility that some paths lead to no appraisals at all. Even worse from
our proappraisal bias, I think we should be open to the possibility that perform-

ance appraisals may actually inhibit effective individual or unit performance. If this is the case, then we must be open to the possibility of recommending that appraisals should not be used. From the standpoint of research, our task becomes that of discovering those situations when appraisals are not appropriate as well as identifying ways to make them work better when they are used.

Incorporating the two previous suggestions into the total domain of performance appraisal in organizations creates a two-pronged attack on performance evaluation. The first of these focuses on the technological issues of the past. I have stated all along that we know a great deal about how to construct performance-appraisal scales and train people to use them. We should not forget or ignore this knowledge and should continue to expand it.

Our second focus must be on the context in which appraisals are placed. We must work to understand this context and then work to change or modify the context so that it is possible for the appraisal system to function appropriately. We may also need to fit the appraisal system into the context in a way that the system is most likely to provide meaningful performance-evaluation data in that context. The task of understanding the context is primarily one for the researchers. That of changing and modifying the context goes beyond that of knowledge and expertise to that of power, persuasion, and influence in the organizational system in which the appraisal is to be embedded. The final result will be fitting and modifying the appraisal system and also fitting and modifying the organization in order to create a good match. In that matching process, it should be kept in mind that the modifications of the appraisal system may lead to a complex appraisal system that excludes some jobs and some people from the appraisal process at particular times. The approach is one of discovering boundary conditions for performance appraisals; also it is one that goes beyond the simple discovery of boundaries and then copes with them, suggesting that the boundaries themselves may need to be shaped and molded.

REFERENCES

Banks, C. G., & Murphy, K. R. (1985). Toward narrowing the research-practice gap in performance appraisal. *Personnel Psychology, 38,* 335–347.

Bernardin, H. J., & Beatty, R. W. (1984). *Performance appraisal: Assessing human behavior at work*. Boston: Kent.

Burke, R. S., & Wilcox, D. S. (1969). Characteristics of effective employee performance and development interviews. *Personnel Psychology, 22,* 291–305.

DeVries, D. L., Morrison, A. M., Shullman, S. L., & Gerlach, M. L. (1986). *Performance appraisal on the line*. Greensboro, NC: Center for Creative Leadership.

Feldman, J. M. (1981). Beyond attribution theory: Cognitive processes in performance appraisal. *Journal of Applied Psychology, 66,* 127–148.

Ilgen, D. R. (1988). Small groups and teams in work organizations: Barriers to successful use. In R. S. Schuler, S. A. Youngblood, & V. M. Huber (Eds.), *Readings in personnel and human resource management* (3rd ed., pp. 340–349). St. Paul: West.

Ilgen, D. R., Barnes-Farrell, J. L., & McKellin, D. B. (in press). Performance appraisal research in the 1980s: What has it contributed to appraisals in US. *Organizational Behavior and Human Decision Processes.*

Ilgen, D. R., & Feldman, J. (1983). Performance appraisal: A process approach. In B. M. Staw & L. L. Cummings (Eds.), *Research in organizational behavior* (Vol. 5, pp. 349–380). Greenwich, CT: JAI Press.

Landy, F. J., & Farr, J. L. (1980). Performance rating. *Psychological Bulletin, 87,* 72–107.

Lawler, E. E., III. (1976). Control systems in organizations. In M. D. Dunnette (Ed.), *Handbook of industrial and organizational psychology* (pp. 1247–1292). Chicago: Rand McNally.

Longenecker, C. O., Sims, H. P., Jr., & Gioia, D. A. (1987). Behind the mask: The politics of employee appraisal. *The Academy of Management Executive, 1,* 183–193.

Maier, N. R. F. (1958). *The appraisal interview: Objectives, methods and skills.* London: Wiley.

Meyer, H. H., Kay, E., & French, J. (1958). Split roles in performance appraisal. *Harvard Business Review, 43,* 123–129.

Mohrman, A. M., & Lawler, E. E., III. (1983). Motivation and performance appraisal behavior. In F. J. Landy, S. Zedeck, & J. Cleveland (Eds.), *Performance measurement and theory* (pp. 173–188). Hillsdale, NJ: Lawrence Erlbaum Associates.

Padgett, M. Y. (1988). *Performance appraisal in context: Motivational influences on performance ratings.* Unpublished dissertation. East Lansing: Michigan State University, Department of Management.

Solem, A. R. (1960). Some supervisory problems in appraisal interviewing. *Personnel Administration, 31,* 853–888.

Wexley, K. N., & Latham, G. P. (1981). *Developing and training human resources in organizations.* Glenview, IL: Scott, Foresman.

16

The Prediction Paradigm

Charles J. de Wolff
Universiteit Nijmegen, The Netherlands

In the past 50 years the literature on selection has been dominated by the prediction paradigm. Textbooks on the subject describe at length how psychologists should do validation studies and how decisions about hiring employees should be based on the prediction of future performance.

This approach was developed in the United States and proved to be highly successful in World War II for the selection of pilots (Thorndike, 1949). At that time there also was another approach, the clinical one, which was widely used in Europe. The publications of the Army Aviation Psychology program aroused much enthusiasm among psychologists, not only in the United States but also in Europe. The prediction paradigm was adopted by the scientific community as the only suitable one. Expectations at that time were high; selection had become a science.

Now, some 40 years later, expectations are different. There have been traumatic experiences during the 1960s and the 1970s, and the optimism that was so strong during the 1950s has disappeared. Although the paradigm still has a strong position, practitioners still continue to use clinical methods. Even projective tests are still in use.

Articles have appeared adopting other approaches (e.g., Herriot, 1989). In this chapter I argue that the prediction paradigm is useful under certain conditions but might be less adequate in other situations.

EXPECTATIONS

The prediction paradigm concentrates on prediction only. Other aspects of personnel selection are not taken into consideration. Applicants do, however, have expectations about selection procedures, or at least they feel that procedures should meet certain demands. Implicitly, psychologists assumed that recommendations about hiring or nonhiring of applicants would be appreciated, not only by the management but also by applicants. As long as they could demonstrate that such recommendations were based on valid predictions, they thought that this was in the interest of the applicants also.

In the late 1960s and 1970s it became apparent that expectations and demands of applicants clashed with the ideas of psychologists. This led to government intervention and often traumatic experiences of psychologists. Many psychologists turned their attention to other subjects, which was quite detrimental to personnel selection.

Some psychologists were aware of this issue. In 1950 Bingham wrote "Persons or Guinea pigs?" The applicant should not be treated as an object but as a subject. In the early 1960s books were published wherein selection methods were confronted: "The brain watchers" (Gross, 1962); "The naked society" (Packard, 1964). Psychologists were seen as "Peeping Toms" (Washington Post, July 4, 1965). Numerous books appeared portraying testers and interviewers as "brain watchers" or "brain washers" with some pathological interest in prying into other persons' affairs (Amrine, 1965). Psychologists had to defend themselves in Senate and House hearings in the United States (November issue, "American Psychologist," 1965). Dozens of pickets stood in front of APA headquarters to protest against psychological tests.

Although the Senate and House hearings concentrated on the selection of government employees, much of what the committee members said made clear that they thought psychologists should not just make predictions. Psychologists have a wider responsibility toward applicants.

Brim summarized it earlier in 1965 in an article on "American attitudes towards intelligence tests": Testing does not occur in isolation; there is always a social context. Test scores have a social meaning. They have impact on one's self-esteem; they influence one's life's chances; they engage one's deepest political and social attitudes. These forces must be understood as part of the social setting in which intelligence testing is carried on.

Also in the 1960s the discussions on discrimination started. The Civil Rights Act of 1964 included a paragraph on Equal Employment Opportunities (EEO). New guidelines on testing promulgated by the Equal Employment Opportunity Commission (1970) and the Office of Federal Contract Compliance, which carried the threat of legal and economic sanctions against employers who used biased tests, raised enormous problems for psychologists (Bray & Moses, 1972). They were embarrassed. All of a sudden applicants filed complaints. Ash and

Kroecker (1975) mention that in the early 1970s the extent of involvements of legal process in selection procedures and policies broadened enormously. Psychologists were ill prepared, because they had not realized that such issues were involved.

There were also discussions on these issues in Europe. Drenth addressed privacy issues in his inaugural address in 1967. In 1971 questions were asked in the Dutch parliament, and the minister of social affairs appointed a committee on selection practices (The Hessel Committee). Critical reports were published by unions (SWOV, 1973; Association of Banking, Insurance, and Administrative Personnel, 1973).

Jansen (1979) summarized the complaints. Applicants want to be treated with care and on the basis of equality. They complain about ambiguity, lack of openness, and lack of carefulness on the part of psychologists.

The Hessel Committee (Commissie Hessel, 1977) formulated the rights of applicants. They summarized their report in two principles: Selection should be based on the applicant's suitability for the job, and all parts of the selection procedure should be consistent with human dignity.

There were problems in other European countries also. In Italy psychologists' interest in selection virtually disappeared. In general, there was much avoidance. Many psychologists directed their attention to other subjects. At universities the subject more or less disappeared, and it was only during the 1980s that it re-emerged. At present some 10% of university psychology departments in Europe see personnel selection as one of their major research interests (de Wolff, 1985).

The basic issue in this period of contestation was human dignity. Applicants felt "processed" by selection procedures. They felt that work psychologists had their loyalty entirely with the organization. They thought procedures should be more open, and organizations should be more considerate and should deal with applicants more on an equal basis. They also felt they needed more information for their own decision-making process. So there is a need for restructuring selection procedures to meet demands of applicants and governments.

ASSUMPTIONS

There are not only problems related to dignity but also other problems. The prediction paradigm is based on a number of implicit or explicit assumptions. These appear, however, not to be realistic in all cases. Four problems deserve special attention in this respect: (a) Is the criterion known? (b) Can the decision-making process be isolated? (c) Is performance determined by traits? (d) Are validation studies always feasible?

The Criterion.   The paradigm is based on predicting future performance. So it is assumed that requirements are known. Thorndike (1949) already realized that this is a difficult assumption. He wanted to predict "the complete final goal'' but realized that this would probably never be available. So he accepted ''intermediate'' criteria. In the case of pilot selection, such criteria were obtainable. Today, the situation is more complicated. Organizations have to operate in a turbulent environment and have to accommodate. Individuals have to meet new demands and have to acquire new knowledge and different skills. In many cases we do not know what demands there will be in the future.

In Japan new employees are not hired for specific positions. They become members of a team, and it is the team that specifies what the task will be. In Western countries teamwork also becomes more important and is having an impact on task specifications.

The prediction paradigm appears to be applicable in a closed system. It is probably also useful for positions in the core technology that is sealed off from environmental influences (Thompson, 1967). This means the paradigm can be used for production workers. It is, however, less applicable for boundary spanning jobs.

In Western society, moving into the direction of postindustrialism, the number of positions that can be approached in the classical way is diminishing. But the number of positions where demands change, due to a turbulent environment, is increasing.

The Decision-Making Process.   In the classical approach the psychologist is only involved in the decision about hiring. What occurs before and after that decision is supposed to be independent of that decision. That appears not to be true. What occurs before may have clear consequences for the size and quality of the number of applicants. And what happens during the selection process may have a clear impact on performance on the job and willingness to accept an offer, or to stay with the organization. Staffing has become a complex process, and the different steps should be seen in their interrelationships and their consequences for future action. Psychologists should not restrict themselves to predictions on the basis of traits but should also be aware of the implications of other steps.

To give some idea about the different steps, whenever there is a vacancy many organizations will first ask themselves if that vacancy should be filled. An organization that wants to ''downsize'' might decide to restructure, to make that position redundant.

If one feels the vacancy should be filled, there are many ways to do so. Today the labor market is rather segmented, and it is not easy to decide about the category of workers where one will try to find applicants: internal or external, temporary or permanent, part-time or full-time, shift work or normal office hours. There are also categories like minorities, long-term unemployed, handicapped, and females, where it is felt that individuals should have better chances for employment, and where there might be special programs to stimulate employment.

Another step has to do with the selection of a recruitment procedure: Should the organization advertise or use internal means to announce the vacancy; should an employment agency be used or a headhunter; should there be campus recruitment? All these decisions have large consequences for the size and quality of the group of applicants.

The selection process is also related to what occurs afterwards. During the selection procedure there is intense interaction between applicants and officials like managers and personnel officers. Hiring is the beginning of a socialization process and of a career. In European countries it is quite common that people stay with a company for a long time. For example, in a large Dutch steel company the average period of employment is 12.1 years. So the interaction during the selection process is used to acquire an idea about future cooperation. The selection procedure can be used to build up involvement. If an applicant feels treated with care and consideration, perceives he or she is treated on an equal basis, and there is mutual decision making, it will contribute to increasing involvement and will shape expectations about future cooperation. This in turn will affect the acceptance of job offers, future performance, and the willingness to stay with the organization. The definition of involvement implies such a relationship.

So selection should not be isolated from other aspects of the staffing process. There are clear interrelationships, the selection process should not only aim at deciding who should be hired but should also be tailored in such a way that involvement is increased.

Is Performance Determined by Traits?   The prediction paradigm assumes that outcomes are determined by traits. Psychologists measure aptitudes and personality characteristics and expect that on the basis of test scores future performance can be predicted. Research has shown that performance is based on many aspects, not only on traits but also on situational variables. In a recent study Greuter (1988) showed that situational variables can be included in a prediction model. This makes the validation process, however, very complicated. Performance is also related to training and to motivation.

In recent discussions about validity generalization, it is assumed that performance is particularly related to general intelligence (Greuter, 1988). This assumption is controversial. Others point out that experience and motivation should be taken into account. Many positions do not only require specific aptitudes but also specific experience and education. In selection procedures managers spend quite some efforts in assessing to what extent experience could be contributing to successful operating. It is widely accepted that experience is an essential factor in job success.

Motivation (e.g., job involvement) is thought to be important for the decision to accept a job offer and is thought to effect the length of stay with an organization. It is also thought to have an impact on quality and quantity of performance.

Are Validation Studies Always Feasible?   The prediction paradigm assumes that the personnel psychologist can do a validation study. There are, however, technical and financial problems. A validation study can only be done on a sample that is sufficiently large. In many cases this is not possible because there are only a few positions and there is only a small number of applicants. Test construction, performance measurement, and validation studies can be very costly. It requires considerable resources, and many organizations and practitioners are not prepared to commit such resources. So organizations restrict themselves to selection interviews.

The Availability of Other Approaches.   Performance can be improved in many ways. Concentrating on personnel selection is one way, but one can also try to improve training, leadership, participation, organizational structure, communication, working conditions, and many other activities. Which approaches need priority and how resources are allocated is not usually the decision of the personnel psychologist. This is a responsibility of the management. The decision is highly dependent on conditions. In some organizations one might work to invest in selection, but in others concentrating on training could be a better choice. So organizations may choose not to invest in the technology of the prediction paradigm, but to direct their resources elsewhere.

UNDERLYING BELIEFS

In 1964 Leavitt wrote a paper on underlying beliefs in approaches to organizational change. He recognized that consultants base themselves on very different belief systems. He made a distinction between "technical," "structural," and "people" approaches (Leavitt, 1964). It appears that the same approaches can be found in personnel selection. Those who favor the prediction paradigm clearly fall in the technical category. Leavitt gives the example of scientific management.

He sees as the main characteristic the faith in the ultimate victory of better problem solutions over less good ones. The technical approach is first of all a rational approach. Leavitt (1964) said that the weakness of technical approaches (as perceived by people-oriented practitioners) is the "sheer naivete about the nature of man . . . they can point, in evidence, to a monotonously long list of cases in which technological innovations, methods or changes . . . have fallen short because they ignored the human side of enterprise" (p. 62). Leavitt wrote this in 1964, when most of the discussions on fairness and discrimination had still to come!

The structural approach attempts to improve performance through clarifying and defining the jobs of people and setting up appropriate relationships among jobs. It concentrates on legal aspects and responsibilities.

This is an approach that is not popular with psychologists. They think it to be too formal and too legalistic and poorly anchored in empirical data. It is an approach favored by lawyers and government officials. One tries to regulate behavior through laws, contracts, and ethical codes. It is clear that much of what occurred during the 1970s has to do with this approach.

Finally there is the "human" approach. It concentrates on the relationships between individuals. Its central concept is "involvement." Only when individuals are "involved" can a project be successful. From this point of view selection procedures should concentrate on building up involvement, both on the part of the employee as well as on the applicant. Such programs do exist. An early example is the LIAMA (1968) program for selecting life insurance agents, whereby the different demands of the job are discussed with applicants to find out to what extent they expect they can meet such demands. In this program mutual exploration and joined decision making are the key words. Other examples can be found in the literature on career development, in which placement is extensively discussed with employees.

Leavitt (1964) argued that each approach has its merits, but also its limitations. He suggests there should be a kind of melange. For selection this might mean that a particular approach might be useful under certain conditions, but also that a combination can be used (e.g., prediction and joined decision making).

SOME CONSEQUENCES

Staffing is today a rather complex decision-making process. One has to be well aware about the labor market, governmental regulations, and selection methods. Most managers are only occasionally involved in this activity. So there is a great need for expertise, to avoid the many pitfalls and to do an effective job. Psychologists can offer expertise. They should, however, make up their minds about the kind of services they want to offer. When they base themselves solely on the prediction paradigm, this appears to be too limited. There is need for a broader approach.

The position of the psychologist in personnel selection has changed. Some 20 years ago he had a well-accepted position and there was little competition. Others who offered their services, like graphologists, were considered to be less qualified or were even seen as quacks. Today that is different. There are now head hunters, employment services, and agencies for interim managers. Although some psychologists are involved in these activities, most of the individuals engaged in this type of work are nonpsychologists. They all advise management about hiring decisions. In the late 1970s, where there was a shortage of work psychologists (at least in the Netherlands), organizations who used to employ work psychologists for personnel selection hired clinical psychologists. So there are now different kinds of professionals offering their services to organizations. There appears to be little colleague surveillance. This looks to be a situation where similar problems can arise as occurred in the late 1960s.

Whatever approach psychologists will select for personnel selection, this might be different in different parts of the world, due to differences in socioeconomic systems. The United States has detailed legislation on Equal Employment Opportunities, and due to many court cases there is now ample jurisprudence on personnel selection practices. In Europe legislation has concentrated more on industrial democracy to guarantee workers some influence on decision making. Jurisprudence on personnel selection is quite different.

Nevertheless, there is a substantial knowhow on personnel selection that has been developed by psychologists. And it is in the interest of society and of psychologists to make proper use of this knowhow. One should not base oneself entirely on the prediction paradigm.

The prediction paradigm seems particularly suited for situations where the criterion is well known and stable, and where there are large numbers of applicants. This is often the case with training programs (e.g., pilot training). When the criterion is less known, and where work experience becomes important and involvement is a key factor, other approaches will be more useful. This is the case with the selection of executives. In such cases selection is more a kind of negotiation process between two parties, trying to reach an agreement.

The psychologist has quite a repertoire to assist the parties. He or she can make a job analysis, to formulate job demands. He or she can assist in structuring the recruitment and selection procedure (e.g., the selection interview), can instruct managers about assessment, and can provide scales and scale anchors. Assessment centers are good examples. Psychologists should also try to make the parties aware of relationships between selection and other parts of the staffing process and career management. Selection should be seen as "organizational entry," and an introduction to a career. It is related to activities like training and appraisal interviews. Goal setting and performance management (Locke & Latham, 1990) are very relevant approaches in this respect.

Furthermore, psychologists should be aware about market differentiation. Many professionals offer their services as special kinds of positions, or special kinds of applicants (e.g., interim managers, part-time workers, temporary workers, executives, computer specialists). There appears to be a need for specialization, due to the fracturing of the job market. This might also mean that there will be more interdisciplinary approaches, whereby teams or specialists offer services (e.g., psychologists and lawyers). There is a need for more research on professional services. It appears to be time that some of the efforts that have been spent on validating predictions are now directed to this broader approach.

REFERENCES

Amrine, M. (1965). Special issue of the "American Psychologist" (review of the controversy over testing). *American Psychologist, 20*, 1965, 857–993.

Ash, P., & Kroecker, L. P. (1975). Personnel selection, classification and placement. *Annual Review of Psychology, 26*, 481–507.

Association of Banking, Insurance, and Administrative Personnel (1973). *Applicant, application, applying (Sollicitant, sollicitatie, solliciteren).* Utrecht: Author.

Bingham, W. V. (1950). Persons or guinea pigs? *Personnel Psychology, 3*, 395–400.

Bray, D. W., & Moses, J. L. (1972). Personnel selection. *Annual Review of Psychology, 23*, 545–576.

Brim, O. G., Jr. (1965). American attitudes towards intelligence tests. *American Psychologist, 20*, 125–131.

Commissie Hessel. (1977). *Een sollicitant is ook een mens* [The applicant, too, is a human being]. Den Haag: Staatsuitgeverij, Sociale Zaken, 5.

Conrad, H. S. (1966). Clearance of questionnaires with respect to invasion of privacy, public Equal Employment Opportunity Commission. *Guidelines on employment testing procedures*, Equal Employment Opportunity Commission.

Equal Employment Opportunity Commission. (1970). *Guidelines on employee selection procedures*, Federal Register.

Greuter, M. A. M. (1988). *Personeelsselectie in perspectief* [Personnel selection in perspective]. Amsterdam: Uitgeverij Thesis.

Gross, M. L. (1962). *The brain watchers.* New York: Random House.

Herriot, P. (Ed.). (1989). *Assessment and selection in organizations.* Chichester: Wiley.

Jansen, A. (1979). *Ethick en practijk van personeelsselectie* [Ethical and practical issues in personnel selection]. Davanter: Kluwer.

Leavitt, H. J. (1964). Applied organization change in industry: Structural, technical and human approaches. In W. W. Cooper, H. J. Leavitt, & M. W. Shelley (Eds.), *New perspective in organizational research.* New York: Wiley.

LIAMA (1968). *Agent selection kit.* Hartford, CT.

Locke, E. A., & Latham, G. P. (1990). *A theory of goal setting and task performance.* Englewood Cliffs: Prentice-Hall.

Packard, V. (1964). *The naked society.* New York: McKay.

SWOV (Stichting Wetenschappelijk Onderzoek Vakcentrales) (Unions' Foundation of Scientific Research) (1973). *De afhankelijke sollicitant (The dependant applicant).* Utrecht: Lumax.

Thompson, J. D. (1967). *Organizations in action.* New York: McGraw-Hill.

Thorndike, L. J. (1949). *Personnel selection: Tests and measurement technique.* New York: Wiley.

Wolff, Ch. J. de (1985). *Directory of work and organizational psychology.* University of Nijmegen.

Contemporary Approaches to Selection and Assessment—Some Examples: Introductory Comments

In this final section some contemporary approaches to selection and assessment are presented—reviews or empirical studies that demonstrate typical and innovative methods in personnel psychology. Some of them go beyond what is common in present selection within most organizations. New trends in this field may be in a better position than conventional approaches to include individual as well as organizational perspectives in their further development.

The first chapter is a review of emerging trends in computer-assisted assessment. Bartram examines current and future possibilities of using computers in personnel assessment. He distinguishes two main types of computer use: to obtain information about people (administration, scoring, and analysis), and to make use of the information gained (interpretation, feedback, and decision making). The author describes how these components influence each other (e.g., how computer technology affects test construction or the logistics of assessment). For each of the possible steps of computer-assisted assessment, he reviews present possibilities and foreseeable developments and demonstrates the wide range of procedures and techniques. Overall, one can get the impression that developments in psychology and psychometrics lie behind those in computer technology. This makes it hard to keep ahead and favors the danger of seemingly attractive but substantially useless or premature offers to those administering selection programs. Concerning the rights of the persons who are being assessed, Bartram points out the possibility of fairness control at the item level, and he contrasts the fear of an Orwellian future to the chance to better insure that it is the candidate who owns the data and to the opportunity for personnel selection to become a more interactive process of negotiation between applicant and organization.

Concerning application, a rather novel approach to computer-based testing is presented by Putz-Osterloh in the following chapter. She describes the process of problem solving in a complex and dynamic scenario and discusses whether this kind of simulation can be seen as an adequate tool for the assessment of those cognitive abilities that are especially useful in management tasks. Essential for such a scenario is that it is complex, that the system is nontransparent, and that it is dynamic and meaningful.

Scores in such a simulation are not restricted to a final result, but process measures are used such as gathering information, testing hypotheses, planning, decision making, and correcting decisions following feedback. Whereas other systems operate with automatic data registration, in the system described here process data are collected by having the subjects think aloud. Two systems are reported in detail. Psychometric data are encouraging, although in general there is still a lack of convincing evidence of the external validity of such systems. Among the variety of conceptual and methodological problems for most of these systems is the lack of standardization of each step in the process, except of the initial state and the psychometric problems connected herewith.

Trost and Kirchenkamp present an example from the senior author's extensive research on the prediction of academic and occupational success. In this case, subjective criteria of occupational choice and job success were chosen. The time-span covered a total of 11 years, and the predictors were aptitude and achievement measures as well as self-reports of students on study habits and extracurricular activities. Medium to high correlations were found between academic aspirations and later occupational decision; scholastic aptitude and satisfaction at the university were predictive for occupational choice in a medium range; low, however, were the correlations of all predictors with occupational success. This result may, in part, be due to the operationalization of the variables in this study but is not essentially different from our general knowledge of these relationships. Now that ability–performance relationships are fairly well researched, studies like the present one can contribute to our knowledge of self-selection and occupational choice.

In one of the most popular selection devices, the assessment center, the inherent lack of perfect standardization gives room for all kinds of rater effects, but also for direct effects of group composition on the behavior of participants. This may be not only a psychometric problem, but additionally a problem of fairness. In the last chapter of this section, Schmitt investigates whether the gender and race composition of an assessment center group affects participants' results. Analyzed for a rather large number of cases, the results indicate no support for the hypothesis that the ratings were affected by the demographic characteristics of the group members. There were, however, consistent differences between White and Black candidates (albeit without an indication of adverse impact). No differences were found for gender. As the centers in this study contained only one group interaction task, Schmitt recommends that further research be directed to situations in which interpersonal behavior is observed in group settings. For those who are concerned with legal and social responsibilities, the subgroup fairness observed in this study should be of interest nonetheless.

Emerging Trends in Computer-Assisted Assessment

D. Bartram
University of Hull, United Kingdom

This chapter examines some of the ways in which computers can be used in personnel assessment. To provide a framework for looking at the implications of automating assessment procedures, Bartram (1989a) divided the assessment procedure into seven main components:

1. Selecting an assessment instrument.
2. Administering the instrument.
3. Scoring it.
4. Analyzing the measures obtained.
5. Interpreting the measures.
6. Providing feedback to candidates.
7. Making decisions dependent on the results.

These seven components can be categorized into two main groups: those that are primarily concerned with obtaining data about people (administration, scoring, and analysis) and those that primarily concern how that information is used and why it is being collected. This division is only "rough" as, for example, feedback interviews often entail the collection of additional information.

The first component—selecting the assessment instrument(s)—is closely tied to the last—decision making. The purpose of an assessment is to obtain information that will help in the making of some decision (e.g., selection of a person for a training course). The nature of the decision and the information required to support the process of reaching it both help to define what assessment instruments to use.

Indeed, in temporal terms, instrument selection may occur as more than just the first step in assessment. There are many situations where it is desirable to "tailor" a battery of tests to an individual's needs or abilities, with this tailoring being dependent partly on the individual's performance during the testing procedure. Because of the inter-relationship between instrument selection and decision, these two components are discussed together.

The remainder of the chapter is divided into three main sections. The first looks at the impact of computers on procedures for obtaining assessment data; that is, tests and other assessment instruments. The second considers how developments in computer technology might affect the logistics of assessment. Finally, the third focuses on ways in which computers can support the process of aggregating and using assessment data.

OBTAINING THE DATA

In this section we see how computer-based assessment (CBA) has provided the means of moving from item-based tests that are fixed in their item content, item order, and duration, to the use of procedures that can generate items or tasks from algorithms, employ types of item or task that are dynamic rather than static in form, and that can be adaptive to the performance of the candidate. Whereas many traditional forms of test can be computerized, there is a growing range of new forms of computer-based tests that cannot be administered by people and can have no parallel noncomputerized forms.

In the following sections illustrations of some of the novel ways in which CBA can be used are taken from the present author's work on the Micropat test battery. This battery includes a range of "task-based" tests designed to assess both psychomotor coordination and information management skills (the system and the tests are more fully described in Bartram, 1987, 1989a; Bartram & Dale, 1991; Telfer, 1985).

Administration, Scoring, and Analysis

Administration can be broken down into a number of substages: (a) explaining what is required to the candidate (e.g., presentation of test instructions and example items); (b) the data collection process (e.g., administration of test items); (c) collection and recording of response information.

The level of expertise required for administration varies considerably from one instrument to another. However, in all those cases where administration can be separated from interpretation, the expertise required is essentially "technical'' and could be automated. In cases where some degree of judgment and interpretation is part of the administration procedures (e.g., administering the WAIS), automation will be far more difficult, if not impossible at present.

For many types of assessment, computers can carry out scoring both more quickly and more reliably than people. The fact that the computer can carry out scoring in parallel with item presentation has made possible the development not only of the tailored batteries of tests but also of adaptive tests where the selection of each item is some function of the respondent's performance on the previous items.

One of the most practical advantages of automation lies in the computer's ability to apply large numbers of algorithms to data (test results, rules, etc.) quickly, accurately, and consistently. Analyses, like the calculation of 30 or 40 specification equations and goodness-of-fit measures, which might take a person many hours to carry out by hand, can be carried out in seconds by computer. Although this kind of analysis software reduces the need for the user to have both computational skills and a lot of free time, it does not reduce the need for a good knowledge of the test and what the computed measures mean.

Modes of Automation in CBA

The relative importance of each component of the assessment process and the value of automating it (either wholly or partially) will vary from application to application. Bartram (1989a) defined four main alternative ''modes'' of automation for the administration, scoring, and analysis components (see Fig. 17.1).

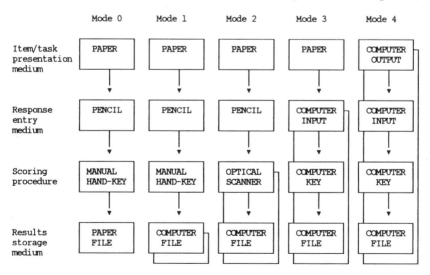

FIG. 17.1. Modes of computer-based test administration and scoring.

These vary from the off-line Modes 1 and 2 (where computers are used for scoring and/or data storage, analysis, and interpretation) to the on-line semi-automated Mode 3 and fully automated Mode 4. Traditional noncomputerized paper-and-pencil testing is referred to as Mode 0.

Where computerized versions of paper-and-pencil tests are concerned, both Modes 3 and 4 raise problems of equivalence (especially for speeded ability tests). Most paper-and-pencil "speed" tests have time constraints that are based not simply on how quickly a person can think but on how long it takes to respond (e.g., find the right cell on the answer sheet and black it in with a pencil). The poor ergonomics of most paper-and-pencil instruments makes the response process both slow and error prone (e.g., Hodgkinson, 1986). For a speed test, changes to the design of the interface could well influence the scores obtained. For this reason the issue of test equivalence is especially important here (Bartram, 1989a; Bartram, Beaumont, Cornford, Dann, & Wilson, 1987).

Mode 2 (and to a lesser degree, Mode 1) provides one solution for those who need to retain paper-and-pencil group testing but still want the advantages of computerized data handling (e.g., the development of a client database, the use of sophisticated analysis, and interpretation software).

We can illustrate the various modes in relation to the SCREENTEST test administration and data management system (Bartram & Phillips, 1989). SCREENTEST incorporates a number of test administration, results analysis, and results interpretation (i.e., report generator) modules. The 16PF is implemented as a Mode-4 test—with none of the conventional paper-and-pencil materials being used. The Graduate and Managerial Assessment tests (GMA; Blinkhorn, 1985), on the other hand, are implemented as Mode 3. These include some abstract reasoning and numerical reasoning items that would have been difficult to transfer from paper to the computer screen without serious risk of changing the test. An equivalence study of the two forms of GMA (Bartram, 1989b) showed that this form of automation was successful in maintaining equivalence. The data management part of the system allows for data to be entered as raw scale scores (with or without item data) either manually or by file—providing Mode 1 and Mode 2 options.

Computer-Guided Assessment

Whereas most of us would accept that specialized training is essential for those who are going to use psychometric tests, there is less consensus on the need for training assessors to make reliable use of checklists, behaviorally anchored rating scales, structured interviews, and other less "formalized" assessment methods. However, far more assessment is carried out using such informal procedures than is the case for more formal standardized tests and assessment procedures.

This "incidental" assessment role poses the following problems:

1. Carrying out assessments is likely to be an additional load on an assessor's normal job (line manager, supervisor, etc.).

2. The procedures typically used (e.g., in job selection, job competence assessment, performance appraisal) really require training analogous to that required for assessment center assessors.

3. Staff turnover rates make it difficult for companies to justify the investment in sufficient relevant training for people whose main function lies outside the personnel department.

4. Conventional assessment procedures involve considerable amounts of paper work: log keeping, form filling, reading manuals describing assessment procedures, and filling in rating forms.

One way of alleviating these problems is through the use of computer-guided assessment techniques: where the computer interface is between the assessor and the assessment procedures rather than between the candidate and the assessment procedure. In general, we can define computer-guided assessment as a procedure where the computer provides the assessor with: (a) a request for some information, (b) advice or instructions on how to obtain the relevant information, (c) a means of entering the information, and (d) a means of defining one's confidence in how accurate or reliable the information is.

A simple example might be the question, "Have you observed the candidate carrying out any tasks in the last 6 weeks that involved the use of a micrometer?" Such questions might be answered from the assessor's immediate knowledge, by asking the candidate, or by looking at some work records. Depending on the answer to this question, the assessor could next be asked either for evidence on the speed and accuracy with which the person used the micrometer or be given instructions on how to set up a simple practical test for the candidate.

Although this use of computers has been little developed, one obvious area of application is in situational interviews. Computer guidance could also be used to assist assessors in structuring conventional interviews. Having been primed with information about the candidate from application forms, tests, and so on, the computer could adaptively lead the interviewer through an oral assessment of the candidate—prompting the assessor with relevant open-ended questions and providing help with how to categorize responses. In the area of graduate and management selection, systems like PROMPT (produced by Psychometrics Research and Development Ltd, 1989) and SIGMA (produced by Saville and Holdsworth Ltd, 1990) provide selection interviewers with a clear structure for their interviews, a list of relevant areas and issues to explore, and guidance on how to evaluate information in relation to its job relevance.

Automated Item Generation

Test administration normally involves the presentation to the candidate of items that were written prior to the assessment procedure. Computer-based assessment makes it possible not only to decide which item to present as the test proceeds but also to write the items as well.

The traditional method of producing test items is to rely on people who are able to interpret what is required for a test and generate items to meet this need. This can lead to bias and idiosyncrasies in the item pool, and the utility of the test becomes highly dependent on the quality of the person who writes the items. Some of the problems associated with this have been outlined by Bormuth (1970). Items produced in the traditional manner do not necessarily have a logical relationship with what they are intended to assess: The item writer only produces items that he or she feels happy about; the way the items are phrased and the language used are left up to the item writer.

Various proposals have been made for item-generation algorithms, or procedures, to provide frameworks that constrain item production (e.g., Hively, 1974; Scandura, 1977). For conventional item-based tests, evaluations have suggested (e.g., Irvine, Dann, & Anderson, 1990; Roid & Haladyna, 1978) that there is little difference in the results obtained using algorithm-generated items and those developed in the traditional manner. This may not seem a very positive finding. However, if rule-based item generation is at least as good as the traditional procedures, that is a major advance—as we can concentrate the attention of item writers on producing good algorithms and rules that can then be used to generate very large numbers of items or sets of parallel versions of tests.

Irvine et al. (1990) described an item generation procedure that builds on Carroll's (1986) work on predictors of item difficulty. They developed four parallel versions of five tests using an item-generation technique whereby those aspects of the task that contribute to item difficulty (so-called "item radicals") are varied systematically within tightly defined parameters, whereas other components of the task are allowed to vary randomly. Their results showed that this approach does produce parallel tests with statistically invariant properties.

Item-generation techniques are not confined to direct "knowledge assessment." The present author's work (e.g., Bartram, 1987) on the Micropat battery of tests has involved the use of both task and item-generation algorithms for relatively complex performance tasks. For most of the tasks developed for Micropat, there are no prewritten sets of items. Each test or task contains a set of rules and constraints from which items are generated. These rules can either specify that the same set of items be generated every time, or that different (but equivalent) sets be generated for each candidate.

Rule-based item generation, whether carried out on line or off line, has a number of advantages over the use of predefined test items: (a) It does away with the need for many hours of work in designing items; (b) one can develop parallel versions of a test almost ad infinitum; (c) the psychometric properties of the test (assessed using samples of items from the domain defined by the rules) are domain specific rather than item specific. This last point is important. In principle, one could generate "random" samples of items from the domain defined by the generation rules and hence use item data to estimate the properties of the domain independently of the item content of any one particular "test."

Adaptive Testing

The general principle of adaptive testing is that the information contained in a candidate's responses is used to modify the test in such a way that the criterion (e.g., to obtain an accurate estimate of the candidate's ability) is reached as efficiently as possible. The procedures used to drive this modification process and the effect they have (varying difficulty, test duration, or both) vary considerably as a function of the underlying model.

The Micropat battery includes a number of different types of "adaptive" tasks. For example, performance on continuous pursuit tracking is assessed using a task that varies in difficulty as a function of the candidate's level of skill. The better the candidate, the more difficult the task becomes (and vice versa). During the first few seconds of each task, the system "finds" the optimal difficulty level for the candidate. From then on, in effect, the person is presented with a task whose difficulty is ideally matched to his or her ability.

A variant of this adaptive tracking task requires the candidate to control the adaptive parameter. Thus the candidate is given direct control over how difficult the task will be. Although there is a moderate correlation between the difficulty level reached with the machine-adaptive version and that which the candidate controls, there is also significant variance accounted for by individual differences in "error tolerance"; that is, candidates differ in the level of error they consider to be acceptable—some will "go for" a more difficult level at the expense of accuracy, whereas others will minimize error by keeping the difficulty level low.

A similar notion is explored by Rocklin and O'Donnell (1987), who compared self-adapted verbal reasoning tests with fixed difficulty "easy" and "hard" versions. In the self-adapted version, candidates were given feedback after each response and then chose the level of difficulty for the next item (from one of eight levels). Their results showed that the self-adapted version led to higher ability estimates and minimized the effects of test anxiety on performance without reducing measurement precision.

For item-based tests, one of the simplest adaptive procedures involves presenting items in a fixed order (as in conventional tests) with the number of items being tailored to the individual candidate using some stopping rule, such as Wald's (1947) sequential probability ratio test. One advantage of this technique is that it is relatively easy to implement and to explain to the person being tested. A number of other adaptive strategies have been described (e.g., McBride, 1979). One of the simplest is the two-stage adaptive test, where an initial "routing test" is used to select the correct level of achievement test. "Flexilevel" testing employs a fixed set of items, ordered by difficulty, with presentation commencing with the item of median difficulty. Items are then selected according to the person's performance so that by the end of the test a contiguous sequence of approximately half [$k/(2k-1)$, to be precise] the items in the set have been presented. In stradaptive testing (Weiss, 1973), items are arranged in "strata" of varying difficulty (usually nine strata) and ordered within each stratum by discrimination. When an item is answered wrongly, the next is picked from a lower stratum; when it is correct, the next comes from a higher stratum.

For most people, however, the term *adaptive test* has come to mean instruments that use an item-selection procedure based on one of the family of Item-Response Theory (IRT) mathematical models (Hambleton & Swaminathan, 1985; Lord, 1980). The essential logic followed by IRT adaptive testing is to select items for presentation that, at the time they are selected, provide the largest reduction in uncertainty about the individual's trait level. There are a number of strategies for carrying out this selection procedure. One of the most widely used is the maximum information search and selection technique developed by Brown and Weiss (1977) and implemented in the microcomputer package MICROCAT (see Weiss & Vale, 1987, for a brief description).

To assess how "informative" an item is, IRT needs to have prior estimates of certain properties of that item: (a) What are the chances of getting it correct by guessing? (b) how difficult is it (i.e., what is the relationship between achievement level and the chances of getting it right)? (c) how good is it at discriminating between people of differing achievement levels (i.e., how rapidly does the probability of getting it right increase as achievement level increases)?

One of the main practical problems of using IRT-based methods lies in the difficulty of obtaining these parameter estimates. Relatively large numbers of people are required in order to obtain initial estimates of these values. Once this initial calibration has been completed, however, there are procedures for calibrating new items against existing ones. Thus once set up, the item pool can be developed over time without requiring a complete restandardization. There are various options to the full three-parameter model. For example, simpler parameter estimation models (such as Rasch) have been widely used for many years in the United Kingdom for generating conventional paper-and-pencil tests from item banks.

Given the need for large amounts of data for parameter estimation, it is not surprising that the main developments in this area have tended to occur where large-scale testing is employed. One of the first adaptive batteries in operational use was CAST (Computerized Adaptive Screening Test), developed for the U.S. armed forces (Hakel, 1986). Trials of an adaptive version of the U.S. Armed Services Vocational Aptitude Battery (the CAT–ASVAB) suggest that candidates feel less pressured by the computer adaptive version and do not perceive any differences in either difficulty or fairness compared to the paper-and-pencil ASVAB. Furthermore, testing is completed more quickly (see Wiskoff & Schratz, 1989, for a recent review of work on the CAT–ASVAB).

By definition, the measure traditionally used in ability tests (number of correct items) cannot be used for tests where either the number of items presented or the difficulty of the items or both is varied across candidates. One of the major advantages of IRT-based methods of adaptation is that they produce a final estimate of trait level that is independent of the number and nature of items actually administered.

Adaptive testing techniques have been shown to be effective in reducing test length while obtaining good trait-level estimates (e.g., Bejar, Weiss, & Gialluca, 1977; Brown & Weiss, 1977). In general, positive results have been obtained for IRT-based tests both for reliability and comparability with their paper-and-pencil equivalents. The main advantages of CAT are seen as being better psychometric properties, better differentiation between candidates, a wider range of difficulty levels within one instrument, and a general increase in the quality and efficiency with which ability can be measured.

Automating Complex Scoring Procedures

Scoring procedures that involve a degree of expertise and judgment are more difficult to automate. For item-based tests, scores are usually simple to define (e.g., the sum of the correct items). A number of the Micropat tests are not item based: They present continuous tasks with which the candidate interacts to try to achieve some predefined goal. Two main methods have been used in the Micropat tests to "score" performance on such tasks.

Continuous Comparison Against an Optimal System

One of the dynamic Micropat tests (Schedule) presents the candidate with a continually changing array of five boxes (one in each of five columns). These boxes contain numbers (their "values") and have "lives" (boxes with a double outline have a value of twice the number they contain but only last, on average, for half the time of single boxes). These boxes appear at different distances from the top of each column. The candidate's task is to choose columns: In the most recently chosen column, a line moves down from the top toward the box. If the line reaches the box before the box's "life" expires, the candidate's score is incremented by the value of the box. Whenever a box's life expires or whenever it is reached by a line, everything in its column is erased and a new box is generated. Performance is measured against a simulation of an "optimal operator" that is run in parallel with the candidate. The optimal operator repeatedly carries out a cost-benefit analysis—looking at the likely outcome of choosing each of the five columns—and then looks to see if the real candidate is performing optimally or not.

Assessment by Scoring Rules
that Model Expert Judgments

For many tasks it is difficult, if not impossible, to specify the type of rules needed to define "optimal operators" (as in the Schedule task). One of the Micropat tests (Landing) requires the candidate to perform a complex time-dependent tracking and monitoring task leading to a final goal (obtaining a display that shows an aircraft symbol correctly aligned for landing). Whereas a large range of measures are generated by the program (speed of approach, various alignment measures, rate of descent, etc.), it is not obvious how one should combine these measures into a score that represents how well the candidate has met the task criteria.

One solution to this problem is to ask experts to provide ratings of a range of "landings." One can then statistically model these judgments using the measures available from the test. The resultant equations are then built into the test and used to generate the measures of test performance. (A more complete description of this approach is provided in Bartram, 1987.)

CHANGES TO THE LOGISTICS OF ASSESSMENT

We have so far said very little about the issue of how computer technology may affect the logistics of assessment. People often argue that CBA is all right for testing people one at a time, but it cannot be cost effective for group testing.

This view confuses a number of issues. First, the original rationale for group testing may well have been the need to minimize administration costs. With CBA one can allow people to be assessed at times convenient to them rather than altogether in one large group. Second, either a central facility containing a large number of computers or computers distributed in smaller numbers throughout the country can become highly cost effective for organizations involved in regular large-scale testing (e.g., the military, civil service, etc.). Third, it is only meaningful to make direct comparisons between paper-and-pencil and computer-based tests when the latter are computerizations of the former.

As we have seen, the real promise of CBA lies in the use of new approaches to assessment.

The Portable Computer

One technological development that will impact on the cost effectiveness and flexibility of CBA assessment procedures is the availability of cheap portable computers (which can be plugged into large-scale networks for programming or for data transmission). This portability provides the flexibility one would need for carrying out computer-guided assessment in the work place; administering tests to people working in "restricted" environments (such as underwater or in space, where it would not be possible to have a test administrator let alone traditional materials). Within the U.S. armed forces, serious consideration is being given to the use of CBA on small portable computers, as much of their testing is done by travelling recruiters.

Based on work carried out by Bittner, Carter, Kennedy, Harbeson, and Krause (1986), a system called APTS has been developed (originally for the portable NEC PC 8201A and now for IBM compatible portables). This has software for over 30 different ability tests and inventories. The low cost of systems such as this, together with their networking capability, make group assessment a real possibility. Their portability also makes them ideal for use in awkward or "hostile" environments, making it possible for assessment to be carried out under conditions where only CBA is practical.

SCREENTEST (Bartram & Phillips, 1989) provides a Mode-3 implementation of 16PF. Each candidate uses the conventional paper item booklet but enters his or her responses on a hand-held PSION Organizer II. This enables group administrations to be carried out cost effectively. Data from each PSION Organizer are then transferred directly into SCREENTEST using an RS232 cable connection. Saville and Holdsworth Ltd also have Mode-3 implementations of their Occupational Personality Questionnaires and interest inventories that use a Casio PD300 pocket computer.

The Promise of Large-Scale Networks

For the four Modes defined earlier (see Fig. 17.1) the computer involved may be local (i.e., "on-site") or remote (from a few yards to thousands of miles away); or there may be both a local and a remote device. If remote, it may be accessed in one of two ways: directly through a network link or via a telephone modem connection, or, in the cases of Modes 1 and 2 only, indirectly through mailing candidates' scores or answer sheets. Figure 17.2 shows some of the many possible configurations of local and remote devices. The configura-

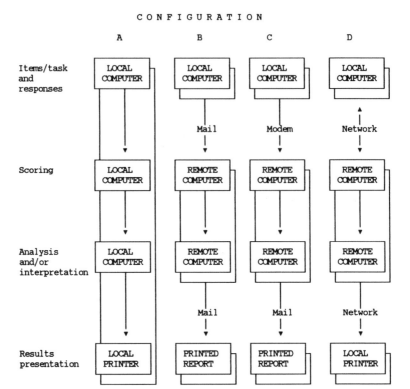

CONFIGURATION

	A	B	C	D
Items/task and responses	LOCAL COMPUTER	LOCAL COMPUTER	LOCAL COMPUTER	LOCAL COMPUTER
		Mail	Modem	Network
Scoring	LOCAL COMPUTER	REMOTE COMPUTER	REMOTE COMPUTER	REMOTE COMPUTER
Analysis and/or interpretation	LOCAL COMPUTER	REMOTE COMPUTER	REMOTE COMPUTER	REMOTE COMPUTER
		Mail	Mail	Network
Results presentation	LOCAL PRINTER	PRINTED REPORT	PRINTED REPORT	LOCAL PRINTER

Configuration A: All functions carried out locally.
Configuration B: Local administration with item responses mailed to a remote site for scoring, analysis and interpretation. Written report returned by mail.
Configuration C: Local administration with immediate transmission of item responses by telephone modem connection to a remote site for scoring, analysis and interpretation. Report returned by mail.
Configuration D: Local administration with immediate transmission of item responses by network to a remote site for scoring, analysis and interpretation. Report returned through the network for local printing or word-processing.

FIG. 17.2.   Some example configurations of local and remote devices.

tions shown in the Fig. 17.2 represent Mode 3 or 4 tests. In practice, configurations similar to these could be used with other modes. (For example, Configuration A: paper-and-pencil answer sheet mailed to a human expert for hand scoring, analysis, and the production of a written report, which is then mailed back.)

Configuration D illustrates the possibility of direct feedback from the remote to the local computer. This would enable on-line monitoring of test performance (with intervention by the assessor where necessary), interactive analysis and interpretation of results, and so on.

Of the assessment software products listed in *Psychware Sourcebook* (Krug, 1988), there is "teleprocessing" support (Configuration C) for about 10%, and "mail-in" (Configuration B) for about 31%. Eighty-five percent of the products are available in on-site (Configuration A) form.

Potentially, the most significant impact of computers on occupational assessment will come from the use of networking at the national level. Such large-scale networked systems were proposed some time ago as providing the medium for paperless application forms (e.g., the U.S. armed forces CENSUS system). However, few countries have, as yet, the necessary infrastructure required to implement such procedures.

One notable exception is the MINITEL system in France (where telephone subscribers are given a computer terminal instead of a traditional book-form telephone directory). Through this terminal, users can look up telephone numbers on a centralized up-to-date database of subscribers. The network supporting this can also be used for a wide range of other purposes. In 1989 MINITEL was first used for job applications. Applicants phone a number given in the job advertisement and the application form is then presented for completion on their computer terminal. This has been found to both increase the response rate (as less effort is required to make an application) and the speed with which applications can be obtained and sifted.

National networking provides enormous potential for the development of item banks. However, one can go further and envisage a situation where tests are only "published" in electronic format with strictly controlled access through a national network. This would provide a means for publishers and producers to control the use of their test materials and provide control over the use of personal data on test results. Essentially, the advent of "electronic tests" would lead to a complete change in the way tests are marketed. Apart from training courses and test manuals, there would be no "materials" to sell. Instead, people would purchase test results (i.e., they would pay for information).

The use of tests in graduate recruitment in the United Kingdom, for example, could be transformed into a situation where a standard range of ability biodata items were published on the network (see Fig. 17.3). Graduates would have access to these through terminals and be able (under the supervision of suitably trained personnel) to complete a range of the available tests during their final undergraduate year. They would also be able to specify which potential employers may have access to this information. In turn, these employers would be able to put their own specialized tests or "application forms" onto the system and be notified of any "applicants." They would then have the option of purchasing information about them.

The advantages of such a system are that publishers and developers would be able to ensure greater security for their products—with a resultant increase in standards and in test revenue and royalties. It would be possible to develop

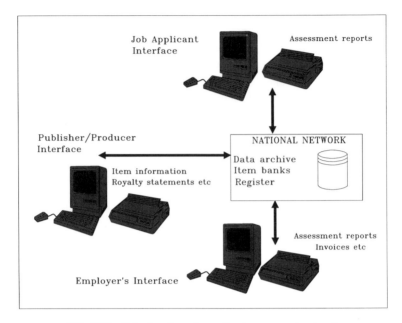

FIG. 17.3. Selection through a national assessment network.

new more powerful assessment instruments as item data would be automatically accumulated and would be obtained at much faster rates than is now possible. Those being assessed would have the freedom to take the tests when it suited them and would be able to exercise total control over who should and should not have access to their results.

For employers the costs of handling and sifting application form data would be massively reduced, as all the data would arrive already on computer (as on the MINITEL system). The smaller employers would be able to access highly sophisticated assessment procedures with minimal overhead and capital investment costs and would be able to carry out a more effective prescreening of candidates before the first interview. Finally, the data itself should be ''better'' as there would be control over how many times a candidate had taken a test.

AT&T is currently exploring the use of voice response technology in testing. Candidates would ''dial a test.'' The questions would be ''spoken'' to them and they would respond using the telephone keypad. Developments of such a scheme could utilize Mode 3 testing—where the candidates had a printed test booklet but keyed answers into the phone.

Systems such as these provide the opportunity to change the relationship between the individual test candidate, the test data, and the organization. At present, people are tested by the organization, and the organization tends to see the information obtained as its own. The proposed system, however, would reverse this. The test information would clearly be the property of the test candidate who would have control over who had access to it.

USING AND AGGREGATING ASSESSMENT DATA

There are two quite distinct aspects of the assessment process. We have already considered one of these (the process of obtaining measures of performance on various relevant tasks). The second is the process of aggregating and interpreting information about the candidate (wherever that information comes from). Computer-based assessment techniques—especially adaptive methods—have an important role to play in the latter as well as the former aspect of the assessment process.

Computer-Based Test Interpretation

Interpreting the results of an instrument requires a good specific knowledge of it plus the more general knowledge and experience necessary to draw psychologically valid conclusions from the results. The growing use of personality assessment in preselection screening, assessment centers, and career guidance has led to a growing demand for Computer-Based Test Interpretation (CBTI). Personality assessment software is by far the largest single category of products in the 3rd Edition of *Psychware Sourcebook* (Krug, 1988). Furthermore, the majority of products listed are for test interpretation rather than for test administration. Whereas CBTI offers some advantages over traditional methods of interpretation, it also poses some serious problems.

CBTI provides the potential for immediate written or oral feedback. Also by ensuring uniformity and consistency in how evidence is weighed, its use should lead to an increase in the reliability (though not necessarily the validity) of the interpretations. On the negative side, Matarazzo (1983, 1986) has pointed out the potential damaging effects of CBTI in the hands of those not qualified to understand it. Others have made similar points about the potential for misuse and the need for limiting access to such software (e.g., see Eyde & Kowal, 1987). It is generally agreed that the main safeguards are that use should be restricted to properly qualified users, and the software should be fully documented (i.e., details of the equations used to generate composite scores and the rule base should be accessible to the user). There is also a need for formal construct validation of the rule system and the interpretive text that these systems use (Matarazzo, 1986; Moreland, 1985, 1987).

CBTI's proper role is a decision support one for the trained interpreter—not as a replacement for the expert. Given this role, another major weakness of most CBTI systems is apparent: They lack interrogation facilities, whereby the user can ask the system why a particular judgment has been reached, they tend not to have been validated, and they tend to be poorly documented.

Feedback to Candidates

Feedback to the candidate is linked to many components of the assessment process. There is feedback during the assessment process, there may be simple "factual" feedback at the end ("Well done—you have passed"), or there may be a more interactive process of discussion with the candidate about his or her performance and its implications. Such feedback sessions often provide the assessor with valuable additional information about the candidate. The ability to provide feedback to candidates requires more than just experience and skill in test interpretation. It also requires the ability to communicate a valid interpretation of the results in terms comprehensible to and appropriate for the "lay" candidate, and, depending on the situation, some degree of counselling skill. Although computers can be used to generate CBTI reports, they are not yet able to negotiate with a candidate about the interpretation of their personality profile.

Computer-guided feedback, however, is a realistic possibility. In a manner analogous to that proposed earlier for computer-guided assessment, the computer could be used to assist the assessor in identifying areas that should be explored, provide prompts for possible questions, and so on. This is potentially a far more valuable use of CBTI technology than the production of "glossy" client reports.

Computer-Based Decision Support

Most of the applications of computer technology to interpretation and feedback can be described as "decision support." Ideally, the computer should neither dictate the "answers" to the assessor nor should it be totally nondirective. Rather, it should play a role of supporting the assessor in those areas where he or she is weakest: for example, aggregating information from many different sources, scanning large databases for similar patterns of results, and so on.

We can extend this notion of assessment support systems from test interpretation to the whole assessment procedure. For example, in work-place assessment, comparing the performance of individuals against nationwide standards poses considerable problems. Work-place assessments are not only subject to the problems of assessor unreliability but to variability associated with differences in the working environment from one location to another. Such differences will relate to a number of variables: the physical nature of the workplace and its ergonomics, the social networks, the opportunities afforded for the demonstration of various aspects of competence, and so on.

For reasons such as these, it would be quite impractical for competence assessment to be standardized for all people across all work places. Any practical procedure will have to be designed to take account of the local conditions and opportunities for assessment. Thus, from necessarily varied assessment procedures we need to be able to make inferences about common standards of competence. To do this we have to develop adaptive assessment procedures. The essential characteristic of adaptive assessment is that it provides a way of assessing the same characteristic in different people by using "methods" that are responsive to differences between the people and the conditions under which they can be assessed.

If we have obtained a certain amount of evidence about a person's competence at work or suitability for a new position and have some prior data on how useful further sources of evidence might be in improving that assessment, we could set up an adaptive system that would, in effect, select the next assessment procedure to provide the best and most practical source of new information about the candidate. This may be a checklist of questions about a person's performance in the work place or a formal psychometric "test." The method by which the data are obtained will differ, but the procedures used for analysis and aggregation can be the same.

The fact that we cannot always stipulate (for practical reasons) that everybody should have to supply the *same* information in order to be assessed along a common dimension implies that we will have to develop procedures for deciding when *sufficient* evidence has been accumulated about a person for a decision to be made (e.g., the person is or is not competent at their job; the person should or should not be selected for training; the person should or should not be promoted; etc.).

We can adapt the same kind of Bayesian logic used in adaptive testing to this process of decision support. The convenient point about Bayesian modeling is that all kinds of evidence can be combined. All we require is an estimate for each item of evidence of the probability of obtaining that evidence, given that the person has the criterion attribute and the probability of obtaining it, given that the person does not have the criterion attribute (e.g., competence, suitability, training success, or whatever). Where the criterion attribute is a continuously distributed trait, we have in effect a situation identical to that of adaptive testing (with item responses constituting evidential data).

A more detailed outline of this type of system is presented in Bartram (1990). In practice, the types of evidence it would need access to can be classified in terms of two main characteristics:

1. Who generates it (the candidate, the supervisor, the candidate's peers, an outside assessor, etc.).

2. What type of information it is (work-place observation checklist or rating data; simulation performance data; task-based test scores; computer-based adaptive knowledge elicitation; written tests; accredited prior learning; etc.).

Among the parameters the system would need to have about each source of evidence are:

1. Relevance—what is the relationship between the evidence and the performance criterion (i.e., what is its "validity")?
2. Dependability—how much reliance can be placed in the data; how much of it is needed? Cost—how difficult and expensive (in terms of time, money, manpower, and facilities) it is to obtain the information?
3. Complexity—how much expertise is needed by the assessor in order to obtain the evidence?

Why use a computer to do this data aggregation—why not rely on the assessors to decide what evidence to collect and to judge whether sufficient information has been obtained? Although it may seem unlikely that such a system could ever get as good as the people whose data it was based on—let alone becoming better than them—there is now overwhelming evidence to show that human assessors are not good at optimally weighting evidence in decision making. Dawes (1979) has argued that the optimum role of the human assessor lies in identifying what to assess, how to assess it, how to code the data, and to state how the data relates to the criterion. Having done these tasks, a computer should be allowed to integrate the data and assess the likelihood that the data do demonstrate competence.

Comparisons between computer-based and human judgments in a range of areas—from clinical psychology, through agriculture and geological prospecting, to medical diagnosis—have shown that "expert systems" tend to be more reliable, more consistent, and have a lower error rate than the experts they are derived from. This general phenomenon was well established some time ago in the area of clinical prediction (e.g., Dudycha & Naylor, 1966; Goldberg, 1970; Kleinmuntz, 1963; Yntema & Torgerson, 1961).

Human decision makers frequently employ heuristics that introduce systematic biases (Kahneman, Slovic, & Tversky, 1982; Tversky & Kahneman, 1974) into their estimations of probability. The problems of integrating sequentially presented evidence are made worse when the information is derived from a number of different sources (e.g., work samples, interview, application form, psychological tests). As more information is provided, so human decision makers tend to filter rather than aggregate it (Payne, 1980), with the filtering being done on the basis of salience rather than validity. In addition, people have increasing problems in taking reliability into account as the amount of evidence they have to deal with increases.

Thus, there is a strong case for providing some form of decision support, along the lines outlined previously, for those responsible for making decisions based on assessment data. In the United Kingdom, systems like PARYS (described in Randell & McKinnell, 1985) and Saville and Holdsworth's Intelligent Recruitment System (1991) represent significant moves in the direction of assessment support systems.

CONCLUSIONS

Computer-based assessment (CBA) is not a procedure or a technique. Rather it refers to a wide range of procedures and techniques, all of which have to some degree modified traditional assessment practices by introducing computer technology. We have seen that these effects can be found in various components of the assessment process—from data collection to data aggregation; from presenting items to candidates to guiding assessors through an interview; from a portable lap-top computer to a terminal on an international network.

To date, much CBA has been oriented toward replacing paper-and-pencil testing. This situation will only begin to change as the public begins to realize the assessment potential CBA affords, and as the system technology infrastructure required for CBA is developed. The concept of an "Intelligent Assessment System" able to manage all seven components of the assessment process was first outlined over 7 years ago in Bartram and Bayliss (1984). Despite its technical feasibility, however, it has not been implemented to any significant degree. Reasons can be suggested for this impasse. The rate of development in technology has outstripped developments in psychology and psychometrics. Many of the ideas discussed in this chapter will take years of research to bring to fruition. Where people have rushed early into the marketplace, the products may have looked impressive, but they have often left much to be desired in terms of validity, utility, and usability. Although the hardware may be inexpensive, the cost of developing high-quality assessment systems is considerable, and the development times are long. In addition, the market for assessment products tends to be conservative and traditional. It is more likely to accept a computerized version of an existing test than some novel type of assessment procedure. For the present, the Intelligent Assessment System remains a somewhat Utopian goal!

It will probably be the development of widely accessible national and international networks together with advances in adaptive testing that will have the most immediate impact on assessment—revolutionizing the use of tests in job selection. The traditional practice of using psychometric tests late in the selection process will change as it becomes possible to have access to test results either at the same time as or even before a job application is made. Indeed, the developments already happening in France presage a situation where there may no longer be a clear-cut distinction among application forms, interviews, test, and other assessment procedures. A growing demand for more structured and systematic work-place assessment should increase pressures for the commercial development of computer-based techniques that can provide a framework for such competence assessment.

Whereas all this may appear to portend a rather Orwellian future, this need not be the case. In fact, the kind of procedures outlined in this chapter give potentially more control to the person who is being assessed. The basic premise of the networked assessment system is that it is the *candidate* who owns the data—not the organization. Such a system additionally provides an opportunity for job selection to become a much more interactive process of negotiation between applicant and hirer: Such a system makes it as easy to provide applicants with answers to their questions (about the company, the nature of the work, etc.) as to provide the hirer with information about the applicants.

Each organization has, as a major goal, the need to optimize the productivity of its human resources. In a broader sense, the development of national economies depends on targeted investment in training and development programs. Individuals have goals that are complementary to these: to optimize their current or future potential job satisfaction; to spend their time on training courses that will enable them to work in areas where they are likely to succeed in both financial and personal terms. By being able not only to carry out assessment procedures but also to bring together information about candidates, specific job requirements, labor market needs, and so on, computerized assessment support systems should have significant medium and long-term benefits at the individual, organizational, and national levels.

REFERENCES

Bartram, D. (1987). The development of an automated testing system for pilot selection: The Micropat project. *International Review of Applied Psychology, 36*, 279-298.

Bartram, D. (1989a). Computer-based assessment. In P. Herriot (Ed.), *Handbook of assessment in organisations*. London: Wiley.

Bartram, D. (1989b). *Graduate and managerial assessment: Software documentation for the SCREEN-TEST test administration and profiler modules*. Windsor: NFER-NELSON.

Bartram, D. (1990). An appraisal of the case for the adaptive assessment of knowledge and understanding in the delivery of competence-based qualifications. In H. Black & A. Wolf (Eds.), *Knowledge and competence: Current issues in training and education* (pp. 55-65). London: HMSO, Careers, and Occupational Information Center.

Bartram, D., & Bayliss, R. (1984). Automated testing: Past, present and future. *Journal of Occupational Psychology, 57*, 221-237.

Bartram, D., Beaumont, J. G., Cornford, T., Dann, P. L., & Wilson, S. L. (1987). Recommendations for the design of software for computer-based assessment—Summary statement. *Bulletin of the British Psychological Society, 40*, 86-87.

Bartram, D., & Dale, H. C. A. (1991). Validation of the Micropat battery of pilot aptitude tests. In P. L. Dann, S. H. Irvine, & J. M. Collis (Eds.), *Advances in computer-based human assessment* (pp. 149-170). Dordrecht, Netherlands: Kluwer.

Bartram, D., & Phillips, R. (1989). *SCREENTEST assessment and data manager*. Windsor: NFER-NELSON.

Bejar, I. I., Weiss, D. J., & Gialluca, K. A. (1977). *An information comparison of conventional and adaptive tests in the measurement of classroom achievement* (Research report 77-7). Minneapolis: Department of Psychology, University of Minnesota.

Bittner, A. C., Carter, R. C., Kennedy, R. S., Harbeson, M. M., & Krause, M. (1986). Performance evaluation tests for environmental research (PETER): Evaluation of 114 measures. *Perceptual and Motor Skills, 63*, 683–708.

Blinkhorn, S. F. (1985). *Graduate and managerial assessment*. Windsor: NFER-NELSON.

Bormuth, J. R. (1970). *On the theory of achievement test items*. Chicago: University of Chicago Press.

Brown, J. M., & Weiss, D. J. (1977). *An adaptive testing strategy for achievement test batteries* (Research report 77–6). Minneapolis: Department of Psychology, University of Minnesota.

Carroll, J. B. (1986). Defining abilities through the person characteristic function. In S. E. Newstead, S. H. Irvine, & P. L. Dann (Eds.), *Human assessment: Cognition and motivation* (pp. 8–11). Dordrecht, Netherlands: Nijhoff.

Dawes, R. M. (1979). The robust beauty of improper linear models in decision making. *American Psychologist, 34*, 571–582.

Dudycha, A. L., & Naylor, J. C. (1966). Characteristics of the human inference process in complex choice behavior situations. *Organizational Behavior and Human Performance, 1*, 110–128.

Eyde, L. D., & Kowal, D. M. (1987). Computerized test interpretation services: Ethical and professional concerns regarding U.S. producers and users. *International Review of Applied Psychology, 36*, 401–418.

Goldberg, L. R. (1970). Man versus model of man: A rationale plus evidence for a method of improving on clinical inferences. *Psychological Bulletin, 73*, 422–432.

Hakel, M. D. (1986). Personnel selection and placement. *Annual Review of Psychology, 37*, 351–380.

Hambleton, R. K., & Swaminathan, H. (1985). *Item response theory: Principles and applications*. Boston: Kluwer-Nijhoff.

Hively, W. (1974). Introduction to domain referenced testing. *Educational Technology, 14*, 5–9.

Hodgkinson, G. P. (1986). An evaluation of the Vocational Preference Inventory answer sheet in the light of population stereotypes. *Ergonomics, 29*, 925–927.

Irvine, S. H., Dann, P. L., & Anderson, J. D. (1990). Towards a theory of algorithm-determined cognitive test construction. *British Journal of Psychology, 81*, 173–196.

Kahneman, D., Slovic, P., & Tversky, A. (Eds.). (1982). *Judgment under uncertainty: Heuristics and biases*. New York: Cambridge University Press.

Kleinmuntz, B. (1963). MMPI decision rules for the identification of college maladjustment: A digital computer approach. *Psychological Monographs, 77*(14, whole No. 477).

Krug, S. E. (1988). *Psychware sourcebook: Third edition*. Kansas City, Missouri: Test Corporation of America.

Lord, F. M. (1980). *Applications of item response theory to practical testing problems*. Hillsdale, NJ: Lawrence Erlbaum Associates.

Matarazzo, J. D. (1983). Editorial on computerized psychological testing. *Science, 221*(4608), 323.

Matarazzo, J. D. (1986). Computerized clinical psychological test interpretations: Unvalidated plus all mean and no sigma. *American Psychologist, 41*, 14–24.

McBride, J. R. (1979). *Adaptive mental testing: The state of the art* (Technical report 4237). Alexandria, VA: Army Research Institute for the Behavioral and Social Sciences.

Moreland, K. L. (1985). Validation of computer-based test interpretations: Problems and prospects. *Journal of Consulting and Clinical Psychology, 53*, 816–825.

Moreland, K. L. (1987). Computer-based test interpretations: Advice to the consumer. *International Review of Applied Psychology, 36*, 385–400.

Payne, J. W. (1980). Information processing theory: Some concepts and models applied to decision research. In T. S. Wallsten (Ed.), *Cognitive processes in choice and decision behavior* (pp. 95–115). Hillsdale, NJ: Lawrence Erlbaum Associates.

Randell, G., & McKinnell, J. (1985). PARYS: *Computer-based testing*. Paper presented at a British Psychological Society Standing Committee on Test Standards Workshop, London.

Rocklin, T., & O'Donnell, A. M. (1987). Self-adapted testing: A performance-improving variant of computerized adaptive testing. *Journal of Educational Psychology, 79*, 315–319.

Roid, G., & Haladyna, T. (1978). A comparison of objective-based and modified Bormuth item writing techniques. *Educational and Psychological Measurement, 38,* 19–28.

Scandura, J. M. (1977). Structural approach to instructional problems. *American Psychologist, 32,* 33–53.

Telfer, R. (1985). Microcomputer based psychological testing and record-keeping. *Defense Forces Journal, 54,* 57–61.

Tversky, A., & Kahneman, D. (1974). Judgment under uncertainty: Heuristics and biases. *Science, 185,* 1124–1131.

Tversky, A., & Kahneman, D. (1981). The framing of decisions and the psychology of choice. *Science, 211,* 453–458.

Wald, A. (1947). *Sequential analysis.* New York: Wiley.

Weiss, D. J. (1973). *The stratified adaptive computerized ability test* (Research report 73-3). Minneapolis: Department of Psychology, University of Minnesota.

Weiss, D. J., & Vale, C. D. (1987). Adaptive testing. *International Review of Applied Psychology, 36,* 249–262.

Wiskoff, M. F., & Schratz, M. K. (1989). Computerized adaptive testing of a vocational aptitude battery. In R. F. Dillon & J. W. Pellegrino (Eds.), *Testing: Theoretical and applied perspectives* (pp. 66–96). New York: Praeger.

Yntema, D. B., & Torgerson, W. S. (1961). Man–machine co-operation in decisions requiring common sense. *IRE Transactions on Human Factors in Electronics, 2,* 20–26.

18

Complex Problem Solving as a Diagnostic Tool

Wiebke Putz-Osterloh
Universität Bayreuth, Germany

The term *complex problem solving* has been created by Dörner (see Dörner & Reither, 1978) and refers to planning and decision making in complex computer-simulated task scenarios. In the technical domain similar research is done under the heading of *system control* (see Rasmussen, Duncan, & Leplat, 1987).

Typical research in this area exposes subjects to a "real-world-like" scenario where some input variables are allowed to take values according to the decisions made by the subjects, whereas the other output variables are influenced by these decisions as well as determined by the (preprogrammed) dynamism of the simulated scenario. The goal given to the subjects is to change or control in a specified direction a scenario for some time, by making decisions and simultaneously using feedback data in order to check out the effects of previous decisions. (For another research perspective, e.g., "dynamic decision making," see Kleinmuntz, 1985).

Using these complex scenarios, it is possible to identify individual differences in planning and decision making. It is also possible to evaluate the success of subjects' decisions as the states of the goal variables at the end of the simulated time intervals are objectively defined. (The approach outlined is therefore different from the simulation techniques used by Streufert, Pogash, & Piasecki, 1988).

This chapter discusses the reason why a simulated scenario of this kind seems to be an adequate tool for the assessment of cognitive abilities that are not measured by classical tests of intelligence. Specifically, scenarios of this kind can assess some aspects of management abilities that can be defined as coping efficiently with complex, dynamic, and uncertain situations. The arguments are based on a (preliminary) classification of cognitive demands realized by complex scenarios in contrast to classical paper-and-pencil tests. The criteria for classification of problem demands are derived from theories in problem solving (see e.g., Newell & Simon, 1972) and are to be distinguished from other taxonomies established by correlational analyses between task components and ability measures (e.g., Fleishman, 1975).

Empirical results from basic research are reported that give some support for the hypothesized external validity of the scenarios as demanding strategies critical for management efficiency. In the final section the results from a research project are summarized that demonstrate one possibility of operationalizing decision making as well as organizing ability by means of strategic parameters derived from observational data based on planning and decision making in two different scenarios.

PROBLEM DEMANDS
AND DEPENDENT STRATEGIES

Problem Demands

According to a problem classification system used in research on problem solving, almost all items of intelligence tests belong to the category "well-defined" problems (Newell & Simon, 1972). These problems have well-defined initial states and well-defined goal states (commonly only one state is the correct solution or goal state). The problem-solving procedures are often demonstrated by examples given in the instructions.

In contrast to these test items, the simulated scenarios can be defined as "ill-defined" problems: There is more than one correct solution and a sequence of responses is involved. Examples for these types of problems are an economic scenario in which textiles are produced and sold or a fire-fighting system in which a forest region is to be protected against fire. These two scenarios are described in a following section. Complex problems like these have the following demands in common (see Dörner, Kreuzig, Reither, & Stäudel, 1983):

1. The scenarios are complex. That means that they entail many variables that are connected by a relational network rather than by single unidirectional relations. For example, the economic system consists of 24 variables out of which 11 input variables can be manipulated directly by the subjects. While deciding on one input change, subjects have to consider not only one possibly positive main effect of an input change but also other side effects that may have negative consequences.

2. The systems are not transparent. That means that the relational network connecting the variables one to another is not shown to the subjects. Instead, the subjects have to generate hypotheses about the effects caused by their decisions that they should test by analyzing the feedback data if they want to reach the given states of the goal variables. The subjects are allowed to revise or correct their input changes if they wish, making possible the adaptation of decisions with respect to changed situational demands.

3. The systems are dynamic. That means that the variables change their state over time, even if no input change has been made. For example, in the economic system the production rate of machines goes down, which is to be compensated by heightening the costs of maintenance. As a consequence, subjects have to monitor the development of system variables that they did not change by decisions in order to be able to prevent undesirable system states.

4. The systems are meaningful. That means that the variables and their interrelations are implemented in a scenario corresponding to a domain of reality. Therefore the subjects can and should use their domain-related preexisting knowledge to generate hypotheses. Otherwise, the subjects would never be able to control a complex scenario according to the goals in such an efficient manner as is sometimes the case (see Hesse, 1982).

Control Strategies

In accordance with differences between these demands and the demands of the test items, it is expected and substantiated by empirical data that the performance in complex problem solving is not predictable by intelligence test scores (see Dörner, 1986; Dörner & Kreuzig, 1983; for controversial discussion see Funke, 1983, 1984; Putz-Osterloh, 1981b, 1983).

As Dörner (1986) argued, the strategies of system control are determined by a superordinate type of intelligence: the so-called "operative intelligence." This type of intelligence refers to the construction and adaptive use of subordinate processes and strategies such as gathering information, generating and testing hypotheses, analyzing data, planning, decision making, and correcting decisions in dependency on feedback data and unexpected situational changes. Domain-related knowledge as well as generalizable strategies are to be used in combination. That use of knowledge, so Dörner argued, is typical of many real-life situations. Therefore it is expected that the subjects' use of strategies in complex problem solving should be generalizable to their behavior in "real-life" situations. Or the other way round, the subjects who efficiently deal with complex situations should be differentiated from less efficient subjects in the strategies they used for planning and decision making.

To get data about strategies in problem solving, the subjects are asked to think aloud while planning and making decisions for a simulated scenario. The analyses of these data give evidence for large individual differences in strategies as well as in success while controlling a complex scenario. Strategic deficits reveal generalizable failures and weaknesses of human thinking when subjects are confronted with complexity, uncertainty, and dynamism (see Dörner et al., 1983). Parallels are plausibly found in institutionally or politically wrong decisions that may be explained by these general strategic deficits. Up to now, the empirical base of these explanations has been very small, especially with respect to the hypothesized validity and generalizability of the identified strategies.

Data About the External Validity of the Tasks

Up to now, simulated scenarios can be classified according to the global demands just outlined. There is a lack of a finer specification of problem demands. This finer specification would allow comparisons between different scenarios in order to deduce precise predictions about the kind of "real-life" situational demands that a scenario might represent.

There are two empirical studies in which positive evidence for the external validity of the tasks can be found. The first study examined whether experts in business science ($N = 7$ university professors and $N = 23$ selected postgraduate students) use more efficient strategies while controlling a simulated economic scenario and also while controlling a simulated ecologically based scenario (advising the government of a developing country) than unselected students (see Putz-Osterloh, 1987; Putz-Osterloh & Lemme, 1987). The expected differences in strategies and performance between the experts and the students were verified. Additionally, there were generalizable individual differences in problem-solving strategies across the two different scenarios confirming the existence of similar global demands.

In a second study, high-level industrial managers ($N = 44$) were compared to university students in controlling the ecological scenario (the same scenario as in the first study). Here the assumption was tested that these highly selected persons are often confronted with complex, dynamic, and new or uncertain situations for which their standardized strategies and their specific knowledge are not sufficient (Dörner, 1989). As expected, these subjects use systematically more efficient strategies in planning and decision making and are more successful than university students, despite their lack of specific ecological knowledge.

These data set up the starting point for a research project. In this project, strategies in complex problem solving are used to operationalize decision making and organizational ability that is to be tested during the selection of officer candidates for the German military forces. For the purpose of evaluation, these data are compared to corresponding abilities rated by observers in an assessment-like procedure.

TWO SIMULATED SCENARIOS

In our empirical studies, two different simulated systems have been used. The first simulates a small company where textiles are produced and sold. (For a detailed description, see Funke, 1986.) Three goals are given to the subjects: to make profit as often as possible, to heighten the capital value from the start to the end, and to pay as much wages to the workers as possible. These three goal variables are used in combination to rate the level of performance in system control. The subjects are asked to control the system for 15 simulated months, deciding for instance how much raw material has to be bought, whether the wages should be increased, or how much advertising should be done. An experimenter operates the computer. The subjects have to ask about the actual state of the variables and must communicate their decisions to the experimenter. So, thinking-aloud data can be gained in quite a natural manner.

The second system simulates a forest region in Corsica; it is called *fire fighting*. (The computer program has been written by Dörner who took over central ideas from Brehmer's DESSY, 1987.) The system is controlled by the subjects themselves. The subjects are asked to take the role of a fire chief, who protects the forest against fire by issuing instructions to 12 fire-fighting units. The forest, the units, and the fires are displayed on a graphics terminal in front of the subjects. Two goals are given to the subjects: The first is to prevent the fire from reaching a village in the middle of the forest and three stations, where the units can fill up new water. The second goal is to minimize the area that is burned down (see also Brehmer, 1987). Again, these two criteria are used to rate performance scores. The exercise has 100 simulated time intervals that last a maximum of 1 minute each. In contrast to the first system, there are only data about decision pattern, which are recorded automatically by the system.

Decisive and Organizational Ability Operationalized by Strategic Parameters

To estimate the control over subordinate processes, different parameters of these "subordinate" processes should be combined; for instance, the frequency of correct (according to the system) hypotheses as well as the scarcity of false or irrelevant ones. These parameters are analyzed and summed over subsequent time intervals to evaluate control and adaptation. It is assumed that complex abilities, especially organizing and decision-making ability, can be operationalized adequately by combining the following strategic parameters that can be identified with the help of the behavioral and the thinking-aloud data.

Ability to Organize. Ability to organize means that one is able to structure information with respect to goal-oriented actions (e.g., to distinguish between more or less important things to do). High organizing can be defined by frequent prospective decisions to prevent undesirable system states, rare false decisions, and the coordination of different decisions to achieve more than one goal.

In the economic system the following parameters are combined: the scarcity of isolated decisions, the frequency of central decisions, which directly influence one goal variable, and the frequency of coordinated (in relation to the goal variables) decision pattern over time. In the fire-fighting system, prevention is realized by the number of units distributed over the area before a fire is seen. False decisions mean forgetting to let the units seek and fight fire by themselves. Coordination is measured simply by the number of changes of commands in the face of new fires throughout the game.

Decision-Making Ability. Ability to decide means that one is able to transform efficiently and quickly the results of theoretical analyses and plans into actions. High decision-making ability can be defined as goal-directed planning and realizing decisions precisely and fast.

In the economic system the following aspects are combined: time to control the system, frequency of postulated correct effects of decisions, and rareness of decisions that do not work in the system.

In fire fighting, the speed and the accuracy of the decisions are rated in combination. That means the number of new fires that are dealt by precise commands are summed up and weighted by the average time lag between the time of fire and the time when the corresponding command is given. In the total exercise the system states are dependent on prior decisions. So these parameters are measured in the first 40 intervals when the situational variance between the subjects is not too large.

It is important that these abilities are defined a priori on a theoretical base instead of being inferred from a posteriori interpreted correlations or factors. The procedure used allows differential descriptions of individual strategies and, at the same time, the measurement of complex abilities.

EMPIRICAL RESULTS

Although it is slightly unusual, some results concerning the internal and external validity of strategies are summarized first and then estimations of reliability are reported.

Performance and Strategies

In complex situations, it should be established whether different subjects are aiming at comparable goals. If the goals are only vaguely defined, the subjects will probably define different specific goals for themselves. Different goals imply different strategies. So there is no justification to evaluate success and strategies in relation to common criteria. Consequently, in our studies, specific goal variables are given to the subjects that should be influenced in a specified direction. Additionally, the objectively defined performance scores are correlated to subjectively rated success. Only if there are systematic relationships between these two scores will the assumption that different subjects have used comparable strategies while aiming at common goals be valid.

In Table 18.1 rank-correlations are reported referring to both systems from two studies. All correlations are statistically significant. An important characteristic of performance in system control is its partially ambiguous meaning. As it can be shown even for the solution procedures of intelligence test items (Hunt, 1974; Putz-Osterloh, 1981a), performance level in system control is not equivalent to a single aspect of problem-solving strategies. Rather, there are several strategic differences in planning, information gathering, quality, dosage, and sequential ordering of decisions that may underlie identical performance levels. That does not mean that successful strategies can not be discriminated from unsuccessful ones. Instead, there are families of efficient strategies that are different from inefficient ones. But it does mean that descriptions of strategies can tell us more about individual differences than the performance level alone.

Following these arguments, the internal validation of identified strategies should be the proof that strategic differences are systematically related to the performance level, whereas different strategic measures should not be correlated too highly one to another. One may disagree with the view that the strategies must correlate with the performance because strategies represent partial solutions. This argument is not valid because performance refers to the effects of planning and decision making, whereas strategies—as operationalized previously—cover behavioral aspects that are not specific to content- or scenario-dependent effects of that behavior.

In our studies there is clear evidence that differences in strategies are systematically related to performance even if the correlations are not impressively high. There are differences between the studies concerning the amount of common variance. Taking the economic example, correlations between measures

TABLE 18.1
Rank-Correlations Between Objectively Defined Performance
in Problem Solving and Subjectively Rated Success

		N	r
Economic system	Sample A	100	.52*
	Sample B	48	.48*
Fire system	Sample C	28	.33*
	Sample D	50	.75*

*: $p < .05$.

TABLE 18.2
Rank-Correlations Between Strategic Measures and
Performance Level in System Control

Economic System	N	r (Organizing)	r (Decision Making)
performance	32	.44*	.43*
	48	.50*	.28
	100	.13	.20*
Fire Fighting			
performance	30	.67*	.48*
	50	.66*	.58*

*: $p < .05$.

of strategies and performance are replicated in three studies, ranging from .20 to .50 with two exceptions (see Table 18.2). For fire fighting the correlations are higher.

Further issues concern interdependency between the two strategic measures. If they are correlated too highly, the validity of operationalizing two different abilities must be severely questioned. Taking the economic example, no systematic correlations between decision-making and organizing ability is found, whereas in the fire-fighting example, there is either no relationship or there is no more than 9% common variance between the two measures (see Table 18.3).

Strategies in Complex Problem Solving Compared to Ratings of Abilities Based on an Assessment Center-Like Procedure

In our research project, two samples of officer candidates are rated by observers according to 14 traits and aptitudes including organizing and decision-making ability in an assessment center-like procedure as it has been used in the German military selection procedure. The candidates were afterwards confronted with one of the two systems so that comparisons could be made between the

TABLE 18.3
Rank-Correlations Between Decision Making and Organizing

	N	r
Economic system	100	.12
	48	.22
Fire fighting	30	.24
	48	.30*

*: $p < .05$.

different data sets. Ratings are based on standardized tests, school marks, interviews, and unstandardized situational tests. Groups of four to five applicants each are rated by an observer group consisting of a psychologist and two military experts.

From literature it would be expected that one global factor explains the main variance in the rating data. In two independent studies ($N = 100$, $N = 25$), this expectation is substantiated by data: The ratings are explained by one global factor. Furthermore, no systematic correlations were established between the rating scores and the performance or strategies in system control. These results give support neither to the rating nor the strategic data, even if the difference between the 14 rated abilities is proved to be an artifact.

On the other hand, the difference between decision-making and organizational ability (as measured by strategic parameters) for system control is supported by the data. Furthermore, the validity of the ratings is unclear, as can be seen from correlations with intelligence test scores. Whereas, in one study, the sum of ratings is systematically correlated with intelligence ($r = .59$, $N = 100$), in another, there is no systematic relation ($r = -.29$, $N = 25$). There are no systematic differences in the distribution of test scores that could explain that lack of agreement.

Generalizability of Performance and Strategies in System Control

Despite overt differences between the economic and the fire-fighting exercises, such as time pressure (low vs. high), control activity (via experimenter vs. direct manipulation), and quality of feedback (verbal vs. graphic), there are similarities between the systems with respect to the global problem demands. They are complexity, dynamism, and opaqueness. Although there are no specific predictions, it should be tested empirically, whether the similar demands are efficient.

Table 18.4 gives correlations between the two scenarios for performance scores and the two strategic measures of two groups and the whole sample of $N = 50$ university students. Group F controls the fire fighting system first,

TABLE 18.4
Estimations of Generalizability (Rank-Correlations) of Performance and Strategies Between Two Systems (Economic and Fire Fighting System)

	T-Group (N = 23)	F-Group (N = 25)	Whole Sample (N = 48)
Performance	.11	.50*	.33*
Organizing ability	−.03	.55*	.26*
Decision-making ability	.14	.09	.10

*: $p < .05$.

and afterwards the economic system. Whereas Group T has a reversed order.

It can be seen that there is a clear sequence effect: If subjects work on the fire-fighting exercise first, they seem to transfer their strategies to the economic exercise, whereas subjects working on the economic exercise first do not show generalizable behavior. A post hoc interpretation may be that the fire-fighting exercise is subjectively more demanding so that the following economic exercise via an experimenter seems to be relaxed, and strategies are transferred. For the other group the fire-fighting exercise may seem extremely different from the first exercise encountered. Maybe some subjects transfer their strategies, whereas others change their behavior in an unpredictable direction. In a further study the sequence effect has been partially replicated even if the economic exercise has been presented in a comparable mode (subjects interacted with the computer directly). The assumption is that time pressure is one crucial difference between the two scenarios.

Despite these ambiguities, the evidence for generalizability, even between overtly different systems, justifies the assumption that behavior in system control is determined by generalizable individual differences. The lack of correspondence between the two measures in decision making may be attributed to differences between the way data is collected (e.g., thinking-aloud data vs. behavioral data).

Data on Reliability

Last but not least, some data on reliability needs to be considered. Concerning the economic exercise, retest between different trials of system control seems to be inappropriate. Content-related changes in strategies are to be expected such as, "In the last trial I lowered the prices, now I only want to manipulate advertising." These changes may influence performance without being attributable to a lack of reliability. Empirical results for two studies show moderate levels of stability of strategies, but stability in performance is variable (see Funke, 1983; Strohschneider, 1986). Indirect evidence of reliability is given by replicability of results in independent studies.

Taking the fire-fighting exercise, content-dependent changes in strategies are not expected. In an experimental study, two versions of system parameters were constructed differing in amount and timing of new fires. Subjects had to control each version for three trials, so that stability can be estimated ($N = 50$ university students).

Between the first trials the correlations are lower than in the latter ones. Between the last two trials all correlations are higher than .80, referring to the performance as well as to the strategic parameters. Even between the two versions the correlations are all systematically above chance (see Table 18.5). These high reliabilities are replicated in a new study with modified instructions in which

TABLE 18.5
Estimations of Retest Reliability for Performance Scores and
Strategic Measures in the Fire-Fighting Scenario

(Rank-Correlations, N = 50)	r	Mean r
Performance/between two trials (first variant)	.60	
(second variant)	.89	
between the two variants	.56	.72
Organizing/between two trials (first variant)	.74	
(second variant)	.81	
between the two variants	.60	.72
Decision making/between two trials (first variant)	.75	
(second variant)	.88	
between the two variants	.64	.77

the system has to be controlled for three trials only (N = 80 university students, all correlations higher than .75). Additionally, in this study, a high level of stability of the strategies is accompanied by significant gains in strategies as well as in performance.

CONCLUSIONS

The conclusions of our studies are:

1. There are individual differences in complex abilities that are not testable by usual tests of intelligence. These differences are of interest for personnel selection if one wants to test, for example, organizing and decision-making ability.

2. Simulated systems produce complex demands that are standardized and replicable. Therefore the systems offer great advantage over the more or less unstandardized complex tasks that are used in assessment center approaches in order to assess complex abilities in planning and decision making (see Jeserich, 1981). For example, in group situations neither individual goals are controlled nor can problem demands be standardized because demands are influenced strongly by behavior of the group.

This conclusion is supported by an empirical comparison between the ratings based on observations (in an assessment center approach) and the strategic measures derived from decision-making behavior (in a simulated scenario). The latter data can be recommended to be used in addition to traditional tests in order to assess organizing and decision making for selection of officer candidates.

3. Individual differences in strategies of system control can be identified that are related to success. These individual differences are reliable if subjects are allowed to control a system in repeated trials.

4. There is some evidence for external validity of the tasks and for generalizability of strategies and performance in system control. Further theoretical and empirical work has to be done to specify the demands of different simulated scenarios and to analyze their relationships to demands of real-life situations.

ACKNOWLEDGMENT

The projects were supported by grants from the Ministry of Defense of the Federal Republic of West Germany.

REFERENCES

Brehmer, B. (1987). Development of mental models for decision in technological systems. In J. Rasmussen, K. Duncan, & J. Leplat (Eds.), *New technology and human error* (pp. 111–142). Chichester: Wiley.

Dörner, D. (1986). Diagnostik der operativen intelligenz (Diagnosis of operative intelligence). *Diagnostica, 32,* 290–308.

Dörner, D. (1989). *Bericht über arbeiten im rahmen des forschungsprojektes "heuristisches wissen"* (Research report: Heuristic knowledge). Universität Bamberg: Lehrstuhl Psychologie II.

Dörner, D., & Kreuzig, H. W. (1983). Problemlösefähigkeit und intelligenz (Competence in problem solving and intelligence). *Psychologische Rundschau, 34,* 185–192.

Dörner, D., Kreuzig, H. W., Reither, F., & Stäudel, T. (1983). *Lohhausen. Vom umgang mit unbestimmtheit und komplexität* (Dealing with complexity and uncertainty). Bern: Huber.

Dörner, D., & Reither, F. (1978). Über das problemlösen in sehr komplexen realitätsbereichen (Problem solving in very complex domains of reality). *Zeitschrift für Experimentelle und Angewandte Psychologie, 25,* 527–551.

Fleishman, E. A. (1975). Toward a taxonomy of human performance. *American Psychologist, 30,* 1127–1149.

Funke, J. (1983). Einige bemerkungen zu problemen der problemlöseforschung order: Ist testintelligenz doch ein prädiktor? (Some notes about problems in research about problem solving or: Are intelligence test scores even predictive?). *Diagnostica, 29,* 283–302.

Funke, J. (1984). Alles bestätigt? Anmerkungen zum kommentar von Wiebke Putz-Osterloh (Anything verified? Notes to the comment of Wiebke Putz-Osterloh). *Diagnostica, 30,* 104–110.

Funke, J. (1986). *Komplexes problemlösen: Kritische bestandsaufnahme und weiterführende perspektiven* (Complex problem-solving: Some critical comments to its actual state and future perspectives). Berlin: Springer.

Hesse, F. W. (1982). Effekte des semantischen kontextes auf die bearbeitung komplexer probleme (Effects of a semantic cover story on complex problem solving). *Zeitschrift für Experimentelle und Angewandte Psychologie, 29,* 61–91.

Hunt, E. (1974). Quote the Raven? Nevermore! In L. Gregg (Ed.), *Knowledge and Cognition* (pp. 129–157). Hillsdale, NJ: Lawrence Erlbaum Associates.

Jeserich, W. (1981). *Mitarbeiter auswählen und fördern.* (Selecting and promoting personnel). Assessment-Center-Verfahren. München: Carl Hanser.

Kleinmuntz, D. N. (1985). Cognitive heuristics and feedback in a dynamic decision environment. *Management Science, 31,* 680–702.

Newell, A., & Simon, H. A. (1972). *Human information processing.* Englewood Cliffs, NJ: Prentice-Hall.

Putz-Osterloh, W. (1981a). *Problemlöseprozesse und intelligenztestleistung* (Problem solving processes and performance in intelligence tests). Bern: Huber.

Putz-Osterloh, W. (1981b). Über die beziehung zwischen testintelligenz und problemlöseerfolg (On the relation between performance in intelligence tests and success in problem solving). *Zeitschrift für Psychologie, 189*, 79–100.

Putz-Osterloh, W. (1983). Über determinanten komplexer problemlöseleistungen und möglichkeiten zu ihrer erfassung (Determinants of complex problem solving and methods of assessment). *Sprache & Kognition, 2*, 100–116.

Putz-Osterloh, W. (1987). Gibt es experten für komplexe probleme? (Are there experts for complex problem solving?). *Zeitschrift für Psychologie, 195*, 63–84.

Putz-Osterloh, W., & Lemme, M. (1987). Knowledge and its intelligent application to problem solving. *The German Journal of Psychology, 11*, 286–303.

Rasmussen, J., Duncan, K., & Leplat, J. (1987). *New technology and human error*. New York: Wiley.

Streufert, S., Pogash, R., & Piasecki, M. (1988). Simulation-based assessment of managerial competence: Reliability and validity. *Personnel Psychology, 41*, 537–557.

Strohschneider, St. (1986). Zur stabilität und validität von handeln in komplexen realitätsbereichen (Stability and validity of decisions in complex domains of reality). *Sprache & Kognition, 5*, 42–48.

Predictive Validity of Cognitive and Noncognitive Variables With Respect to Choice of Occupation and Job Success

Günter Trost
Institute for Test Development and Talent Research
Bonn, Germany

Thomas Kirchenkamp
Bodan Software GmbH, Markdorf, Germany

THE PROBLEM

The predictability of occupational success has been the topic of a great number of empirical studies (see e.g., the reviews and meta-analyses presented by Ghiselli, 1966, 1973; Hunter & Hunter, 1984; O'Leary, 1980; Reilly & Chao, 1982; Schmitt, Gooding, Noe, & Kirsch, 1984; Schuler & Funke, 1989). Most of these studies have two features in common: They are restricted to one occupational area or a small number of areas each, and they cover a short time span of one or only very few years between the assessment of the predictor data and the assessment of the criterion data.

In the study presented here, the predictive validity of a set of somewhat general predictors with respect to criteria of success in occupations of all kinds is examined. The predictor data were obtained on an unselected national sample of upper secondary school pupils, partly at the beginning of their 13th school year, partly during and after the end of their higher education. This design also allowed for an investigation of the determinants of the choice of occupation. The time span between the first assessment of predictor data and the assessment of the data on choice of occupation and job performance is 11 years.

The central question answered by this study is: "What are the relations between aptitude and achievement measures as well as self-reports of work habits and extracurricular activities obtained at the end of secondary school and during higher education on the one hand, and the choice of occupation together with some criteria of job success and satisfaction on the other hand?"

THE STUDY

The Institute for Test Development and Talent Research is conducting a longitudinal study that was launched in 1973 on a sample of about 9,000 West German secondary school pupils in their 13th school year. Information on biographical and educational data and the pupils' performance in a general scholastic aptitude test was collected. (For more details of the initial assessment of data, see Trost, Pauels, and Schneider, 1976.) Five and 11 years later, the subjects were asked to report on their progress and success in tertiary education or vocational training and their success and satisfaction with the careers they had chosen (see Table 19.1).

Sixty-four percent of the original sample (a total of 5,643 persons) for which complete predictor data are available participated in all the three assessments of data. They are fairly representative of the 1973 population of West Germany's students in the 13th school year. First results of the longitudinal study are reported in Leferink (1988) and in Trost (1987). Further follow-up studies are planned.

For the analyses reported here, we selected 3,528 persons who, in the winter of 1984–1985, had a full-time job. Their average age was 29 years. Sixty-eight percent of them were males, 32% females. On average, they had had 2.5 years of job experience. Four out of 5 subjects had attended a university.

PREDICTOR AND CRITERION VARIABLES

Table 19.2 shows the predictor and criterion variables used for the present study. For the predictors the data were mainly collected in the years 1973 and 1978. In 1973 a 3-hour scholastic aptitude test with a verbal and a quantitative section was administered in the classrooms. Further, the pupils filled in a questionnaire concerning extracurricular interests and activities as well as work habits at school, career plans, and aspirations. Five years later subjects were mailed another questionnaire investigating average mark in the school-leaving certificate (Abitur) and self-ratings of study habits in university, progress, and satisfaction in higher education.

In 1984–1985 information was obtained both on the results of the final academic examinations and on the criterion variables "choice of occupation," "oc-

TABLE 19.1
Participants in the Follow-up Study

	1973	1978	1984/85	Subjects with Full-time Jobs 1984/85
Sample size	8,775	7,000	5,634	3,528
Percent of the original sample	100%	80%	64%	40%

TABLE 19.2
Predictor and Criterion Variables

Predictor Variable	Number of Items	Criterion Variables	Number of Items
1973:		*1984/1985:*	
Total score in a general scholastic aptitude test (TAB)	1		
		choice of occupation	1
Study habits at school	3		
Extracurricular activities	21		
Career plans and aspirations	2	occupational position (only employees)	1
1978:			
Average mark in the school leaving certificate (Abitur)	1	amount of responsibility	1
Self-ratings of study habits, progress and satisfaction at university	8	monthly income	1
1984/1985:			
Results of final academic exams	2	overall job satisfaction	1

cupational position," "amount of responsibility," "monthly income," and "overall job satisfaction." "Choice of occupation" was assessed by means of an open-ended question; the responses were categorized into 11 major domains on the basis of a job classification system developed by the Federal Ministry of Labor. "Occupational position" was assessed by self-ratings on a scale also provided by the Federal Ministry of Labor; the responses were later assigned to a 4-level rating scale. "Amount of responsibility" was defined by means of a 5-point rating scale with verbally described categories (lowest category: "My tasks are prescribed by others in detail, execution is largely determined"; highest category: "I act completely on my own responsibility"); this item was scored only for those who were employed in an organization. "Monthly income" was assessed by a 9-point rating scale (only for those with full-time jobs). "Overall job satisfaction" was assessed by a 5-point rating scale.

PREDICTION OF CHOICE OF OCCUPATION

In a first approach we selected six areas of occupation that (a) were represented by more than 100 subjects each, (b) were each well defined (i.e., the various jobs could be easily categorized), and (c) covered, as a whole, a wide range of activities.

The following areas met these requirements:

- teachers at all school types except secondary school (N = 205).
- medical professions (physicians, dentists, veterinary surgeons) (N = 270).
- research–teaching staff (at university or in other research institutions) (N = 188).
- computer science professions (N = 133).
- legal professions (lawyers, attorneys, judges) (N = 119).
- businessmen or economists (N = 121).

The independent variables for which the analyses of variance or the chi-square analyses yielded highly significant results (p < .001) are listed in Table 19.3; they are arranged (a) according to the year the data were assessed and (b) according to the contingency coefficients indicating the closeness of the relations.

Table 19.3 shows medium to high coefficients for the relation between the subjects' career preferences and aspirations at the age of 18 to 19, as well as their overall performance in upper secondary school and the occupations they have actually chosen 11 years later. The high coefficient representing the correspondence between the subjects' preferences of areas of study at a university and their later occupations might have been expected. The relation between the score in the scholastic aptitude test and the given criterion is moderate. Very weak but still highly significant relations are found between some extracurricular activities during the last years of school and the future choice of occupation.[1]

Some self-ratings of progress in the chosen study courses and of aspects of satisfaction in higher education are moderately correlated with occupational choice. The comparatively high values for the predictive power of the average mark in the final examination are partly an artifact because differences in the grading levels between the faculties do exist.

The finding that people in the medical field had obtained the highest average marks in secondary school is explained by the fact that in the 1970s the selection for admission to courses in medicine, dentistry, and veterinary science was very rigorous and based mainly on the average marks in the school-leaving certificate.

Those who have become members of the research or teaching staff at a university or in other research institutes had generally scored highest in scales that represent intellectual activities and academic achievement.

---

[1]Coefficients reported in the tables do not necessarily indicate causal relations between the predictor variables and the criterion measures. The finding, for instance, that inclinations to musical activities during adolescence tend to be correlated to the subsequent choice of an occupation in the medical field may be due to a third variable, such as family tradition or parental educational attitudes.

TABLE 19.3
Predictive Value of Academic and Nonacademic Variables with Respect
to Choice of Occupation (N = 1,036)

Predictor Variable	Year of Assessment	Contingency Coefficient	Occupational Group(s) with Highest Scores
Preferred area of study at university	1973	.73	–
Level of *academic aspiration*	1973	.54	research, med.
Working-speed at school work (self-rating)	1973	.25	med., comp.
Total score in the *scholastic aptitude test* (TAB)	1973	.35	comp./research
Extracurricular activities:			
Experimenting on one's own or collecting objects in the area of natural sciences	1973	.19	research
Reading non-fiction literature	1973	.19	research
Playing one or several instruments/participation in choir or orchestra	1973	.18/.16	med.
Occupation with technical problems	1973	.17	research
Giving private lessons (coaching)	1973	.16	med.
Learning foreign languages outside school	1973	.16	med.
Participation in correspondence courses or pupils' competitions	1973	.14	comp./research
Average mark in the *school leaving certificate* (Abitur)	1978	.55	med.
Study habits and satisfaction at university:			
Satisfaction with chosen area of study	1978	.33	med.
Congruence of aptitudes and requirements of studies	1978	.27	med.
Self-rating of proceeding in studies	1978	.26	research
Congruence of preferences/interests and content of studies	1978	.24	med.
Personal enrichment through studies	1978	.23	med., teach.
Results in university exams:			
Average mark in final exam ("Staatsexamen"): medical, law studies, teacher training	1984/85	.72	teach.
Average mark in final exam ("Diplom")	1984/85	.61	research

PREDICTABILITY OF OCCUPATIONAL POSITION

The first indicator of job success selected was "occupational position." The analyses were based only on the data of those 1,876 subjects who were in full-time paid employment. Four levels of positions were defined, from "simple functions" (e.g., as a typist) to "comprehensive responsibilities" (e.g., as a managing director). Due to the rigid West German salary scales for university graduates,

63% of our subsample are placed in Category 3, a fact that certainly lowers the expectation concerning the discriminative power of the self-rating scale in our analysis.

The contingency coefficients and tau values are indeed fairly low (see Table 19.4 that again contains only those variables for which the results of chi-square analyses and/or the tau coefficients were significant on the .001 level). The level of academic aspiration and the study preferences during the 13th school year, the average mark in the school-leaving certificate, and the self-rating of the individuals' progress in university studies make the relatively largest contribution to the prediction of the criterion in question. The scholastic aptitude test ranks somewhat lower.

The chi-square analyses yielded highly significant results for only 5 out of the 21 variables of extracurricular activities—they are related to interests in academic matters, leadership, and sports; the contingency coefficients range from .08 to .16.

The students' self-reports on some aspects of their study progress and their overall satisfaction with the chosen area of study are significantly correlated to

TABLE 19.4
Predictive Value of Academic and Nonacademic Variables with Respect to
Occupational Position ($N = 1,876$)

Predictor Variable	Year of Assessment	Contingency Coefficient	Kendall's Tau B
Level of *academic aspiration*	1973	–	.26
Preferred area of study at university	1973	.26	–
Total score in the *scholastic aptitude test* (TAB)	1973	–	.14
Working-speed at school work (self-rating)	1973	–	.13
Extracurricular activities:			
Reading non-fiction literature	1973	.16	–
Giving private lessons (coaching)	1973	.10	–
Activities in extracurricular sports	1973	.09	–
Activities in pupils' committees	1973	.09	–
Participation in correspondence courses or pupils' competitions	1973	.08	–
Average mark in the *school-leaving certificate* (Abitur)	1978	–	.18
Study habits and satisfaction at university:			
Self-rating of proceeding in studies	1978	–	.18
Self-rating of working-speed in studies	1978	–	.13
Satisfaction with chosen area of study	1978	–	.13
Congruence of aptitudes and requirements of studies	1978	–	.10
Average mark in *final exam* ("Diplom")	1984/85	–	.09

the criterion; the coefficients, however, only range from .10 to .18. The relation between the average mark in the final examination and the occupational position is still highly significant, yet the tau coefficient only amounts to .09.

In general, the findings suggest there is a low but significant correlation between aptitude and achievement variables measured before the end of secondary school and during higher education, respectively, and the occupational position the former pupils have attained 6 and 11 years later, respectively.

PREDICTABILITY OF OTHER CRITERIA OF JOB SUCCESS AND JOB SATISFACTION

The results of three more analyses using three different criteria are briefly reported. The criteria were: amount of responsibility in the present job (5-point rating scale), actual average income per month (9-point rating scale), overall job satisfaction ("If you had the chance to start anew, would you choose your present occupation again?"; 5-point scale).

All the predictor variables used in this study were checked for possible relations to the three criteria. In the case of the extracurricular activities and other questionnaire data assessed in the year 1973, none of the obtained contingency coefficients exceeded .11, although some of the chi-square values were highly significant.

The remaining predictor variables as well as the three criterion measures have at least the quality of ordinal scales. For the sake of comparison, in all cases Kendall's tau coefficient was computed for the relation between the predictor and the criterion variables. Table 19.5 shows those values that are significant on the .001 level.

None of the predictor variables we used for these analyses is closely correlated with any of the three criteria. In comparison, the overall satisfaction with the chosen occupation can be best predicted, particularly by measures of satisfaction with the chosen area of study: The respective tau coefficients amount to .24 for the predictor variable "overall satisfaction with the chosen area of study," to .18 for the self-rating on the "congruence of preferences and interests with the content of studies," and to .15 for the self-rating on the "congruence of aptitudes and requirements of study." The validity coefficients regarding the criterion "monthly income" were generally even lower; the relatively highest predictive value was found for the predictor variable "level of academic aspiration" (.11). In view of the criterion "amount of responsibility," the highest coefficient was .10 (for the predictor "self-rating of proceeding in academic studies"). Neither the average mark in the school-leaving certificate nor the average mark in the final university examination proved to be substantially correlated with one of the criteria in question (maximum tau value: .10 for the correlation between average school mark and monthly income).

TABLE 19.5
Correlations Between Academic Predictors and Three Measures
of Occupational Success and Satisfaction (Kendall's Tau B) (N = 3,528)

Predictor Variable	Amount of Responsibility	Monthly Income	Overall Job Satisfaction
Level of academic aspiration	.05	.11	.08
Average mark in the school leaving certificate (Abitur)	–	.10	.08
Total score in the scholastic aptitude test (TAB)	–	.09	–
Working-speed at school work	–	.08	.05
Self-rating of proceeding in studies	.10	.10	.11
Self-rating of working-speed in studies	.08	.07	.08
Congruence of preferences/interests and content of studies	.04	–	.18
Congruence of aptitudes and requirements of studies	.06	.07	.15
Personal enrichment through studies	–	–	.07
Satisfaction with chosen area of study	.05	.08	.24
Average mark in final exam ("Staatsexamen"): medical, law studies, teacher training	.08	.06	–

DISCUSSION

The growing importance of "human resources" as a vital factor of a company's success has been emphasized in recent German literature (e.g., Atteslander, 1989; Johansson, 1990; Weber, 1990). However, the forthcoming decrease in the number of school and university graduates and hence the declining number of qualified candidates for certain jobs increases the need of improved procedures of selection and placement (Wottawa, 1990, p. 158).

As, in turn, more and more candidates will be in a position to select among jobs offered by several companies, assessment procedures will have to take account of the candidates' preferences, aspirations, interests, and values to a greater extent.

The present study provides some hints that even with regard to predictive validity measures of such "noncognitive" variables can be useful. One of the central findings is the medium to high correlation between certain aspects of academic aspirations and achievements on the one hand and later occupational decisions on the other hand. Somewhat lower coefficients in the range of the mid-20s to the mid-30s were found for the relations between scholastic aptitude as well as self-ratings of satisfaction at the university and the choice of occupation. The correlations between extracurricular activities in a variety of areas during upper secondary school attendance and the occupational decision are weak but still highly significant. All these relations deserve closer investigation because they can be used for counselling and placement purposes.

In general, the prognostic values of our predictors with respect to four criteria of occupational success (occupational position, amount of responsibility, monthly income, and overall job satisfaction) are much lower than those we found regarding the criterion of choice of occupation. The (uncorrected) coefficients do not exceed the value of .26. Among the four criteria, "occupational position" could be relatively best predicted. Of all the predictor variables used, the measures of academic aspiration and academic achievement turned out to be the most predictive for three of the four criteria; the criterion of overall job satisfaction, however, can be best predicted by self-ratings of satisfaction with the chosen area of study in higher education.

Due to the specific design of this study, its results cannot be compared with those of other studies without reservation. Yet as far as the prediction of occupational success on the basis of school marks, the total score in a scholastic aptitude test, biographical data, and marks in higher education is concerned, we can at least take a look at meta-analyses and reviews of studies that used similar predictors.

The coefficient we found for the predictive validity of the average mark in school with respect to occupational position is close to the mean coefficients reported by O'Leary (1980), Reilly and Chao (1982), and Samson, Graue, Weinstein, and Walberg (1984); its predictive validity with respect to the other three criteria of job success, however, is lower.

For the predictive power of scholastic aptitude tests regarding success in the professions, Klitgaard (1985) summarized empirical data that are hardly more encouraging than ours.

In many studies, biographical data have proved to be more predictive than the information on extracurricular interests and activities we used in our investigation (Funke, Krauss, Schuler, & Stapf, 1987; Hunter & Hunter, 1984; Reilly & Chao, 1982; Schmitt et al., 1984; Stehle, 1986).

Generally low, but still somewhat higher than in our study are the coefficients reported in the literature for the correlation between performance in college or university and success in the professions (Hoyt, 1965; Klitgaard, 1985; O'Leary, 1980).

Our data yields fairly low coefficients for the correlation between the predictor variables and the measures of occupational success and satisfaction both from an absolute point of view and in comparison to results of other studies. This may be due to the following features of the present study:

The time span between the assessment of most of the predictor data and the criterion data was unusually long: 11 and 6 years, respectively.

Both the predictors and the criteria were "weak" in the sense that (except for the scholastic aptitude test) each variable was represented by a single item and all the information was collected by means of questionnaires (self-reports and self-ratings); no correction for limited reliability was applied.

A wide variety of occupations was amalgamated when the criteria of occupational success and job satisfaction were assessed.

At the first stage of the longitudinal study, the instruments of assessment had not primarily been chosen to predict occupational success; the main goal of the study was to investigate the determinants of academic success.

Most subjects had only a few years' occupational experience. At the very start of a career it is more difficult to differentiate between people with regard to criteria of job success such as monthly income and amount of responsibility.

Besides these specific features there are some general problems inherent in criterion-oriented validity studies that set limits to the predictability of occupational success.

One interfering factor is the kind of selection procedures the organizations apply (e.g., Sussmann & Robertson, 1986). Obviously, a company's decision of accepting or rejecting an applicant is not only determined by the candidate's abilities and personality but as well by the employer's criteria and practices of selection. As only data on the job success of those who have been hired are available, effects of restriction of variance in the criteria of success on the outcome of validity studies are unavoidable. Yet, predictive validity studies are less susceptible to these effects than concurrent validity studies (Guion & Cranny, 1982).

Self-selection among potential candidates is another interfering factor that must be kept in mind (Eckardt & Schuler, 1988, p. 454; Nerdinger, v. Rosenstiel, Spiess, & Stengel, 1988). Self-selection can be based on self-perceived aptitudes as well as on interests and values and on the "fit" between these individual characteristics and the candidate's information and ideas about the organizations in question.

All these factors lower the general expectation with regard to the coefficients of predictability of occupational success. In the context of the present study, however, a clearer picture of the predictability of success in the professions may emerge as a result of a further follow-up when criterion variance is larger, when more differentiated criterion scales of achievement and satisfaction can be applied to allow for multivariate analyses, and when more homogeneous subgroups such as persons working in certain job clusters can be defined.

William James once wrote (Fincher, 1985): "We need not write biographies in advance. We need to leave something unaccounted for." The data that are presented here give little reason for us to worry about that. Indeed, they strongly support the assumption that an ample part of the variance of job performance will always remain unaccounted for.

REFERENCES

Atteslander, P. (1989). Personalpolitik wird zur Unternehmenspolitik [Personnel policy becomes company policy]. *io Management Zeitschrift, 58*(9), 32–34.

Eckardt, H. H., & Schuler, H. (1988). Berufseignungsdiagnostik. In R. S. Jäger (Hrsg.), *Psychologische diagnostik: Ein lehrbuch* [Assessment of vocational aptitudes. In Jäger, Psychological assessment: A textbook] (pp. 451–467). München/Weinheim: Psychologie Verlags Union.

Fincher, C. (1985, June 27 to July 2). *The assessment uses of the Scholastic Aptitude Test (SAT) in a statewide system of public higher education.* Paper presented at the 11th Annual Conference of the International Association for Educational Assessment, Oxford, Great Britain. Oxford: International Association for Educational Assessment.

Funke, U., Krauss, J., Schuler, H., & Stapf, K.-H. (1987). Zur prognostizierbarkeit wissenschaftlich-technischer leistungen mittels personvariablen: Eine metaanalyse der validität diagnostischer verfahren im bereich forschung und entwicklung [Predictability of performance in science and technology on the basis of personal variables: A meta-analysis of the validity of diagnostic instruments in the area of research and development]. *Gruppendynamik, 18*, 407–428.

Ghiselli, E. E. (1966). *The validity of occupational aptitude tests.* New York: Wiley.

Ghiselli, E. E. (1973). The validity of aptitude tests in personnel selection. *Personnel Psychology, 26*, 461–477.

Guion, R. M., & Cranny, C. J. (1982). A note on concurrent and predictive validity designs: A critical reanalysis. *Journal of Applied Psychology, 67*, 239–244.

Hoyt, D. P. (1965). *The relationship between college grades and adult achievement. A review of the literature* (ACT Research Report, No. 7). Iowa City: American College Testing Program.

Hunter, J. E., & Hunter, R. F. (1984). Validity and utility of alternative predictors of job performance. *Psychological Bulletin, 96*, 72–98.

Johansson, B. (1990). Human resources management wird pflichtfach für jedes unternehmen [Human resources management becomes obligatory for every company]. *io Management Zeitschrift, 59*(2), 43–54.

Klitgaard, R. (1985). *Choosing elites: Selecting the ''best and the brightest'' at top universities and elsewhere.* New York: Basic Books.

Leferink, K. (1988). *Geschlechtsunterschiede im ausbildungs- und berufsweg* [Gender differences in education and in professional careers]. Frankfurt: Peter Lang.

Nerdinger, F. W., v. Rosenstiel, L., Spiess, E., & Stengel, M. (1988). Selektion und sozialisation potentieller führungskräfte im zeichen gesellschaftlichen wertwandels [Selection and socialization of potential managerial personnel in a period of changing social values]. *Zeitschrift für Arbeits- und Organisationspsychologie, 32*, 22–33.

O'Leary, B. S. (1980). *College grade point average as an indicator of occupational success: An update* (Personnel Research Report 80–23). Washington, DC: U.S. Office of Personnel Management.

Reilly, R. R., & Chao, G. T. (1982). Validity and fairness of some alternative employee selection procedures. *Personnel Psychology, 35*, 1–62.

Samson, G. E., Graue, E. M., Weinstein, T., & Walberg, H. J. (1984). Academic and occupational performance: A quantitative synthesis. *American Educational Research Journal, 21*, 311–321.

Schmitt, N., Gooding, R. Z., Noe, R. D., & Kirsch, M. (1984). Meta-analysis of validity studies published between 1964 and 1982 and the investigation of study characteristics. *Personnel Psychology, 37*, 407–422.

Schuler, H., & Funke, U. (1989). Berufseignungsdiagnostik [Assessment of vocational aptitudes]. In E. Roth (Hrsg.), *Organisationspsychologie. Enzyklopädie der Psychologie*, Themenbereich D, Serie III, Band 3 (281–320). Göttingen: Hogrefe.

Stehle, W. (1986). Personalauswahl mittels biographischer Fragebogen [Personnel selection by means of biographical questionnaires]. In H. Schuler & W. Stehle (Hrsg.), *Biographische Fragebogen als Methode der Personalauswahl* [Biographical questionnaires as a method of personnel selection] (pp. 17–57). Stuttgart: Verlag für Angewandte Psychologie.

Sussmann, M., & Robertson, D. U. (1986). The validity of validity: An analysis of validation study designs. *Journal of Applied Psychology, 71,* 461–468.

Trost, G. (1987). Hochbegabte und eine repräsentativgruppe deutscher abiturienten in elfjähriger längsschnittbeobachtung: Vergleich der studien- und berufswege. Ein Zwischenbericht [A sample of highly gifted and a representative sample of German graduates from upper secondary school in an 11 year follow-up study: Comparison of educational progress and professional careers. An intermediate report]. *Empirische Pädagogik, 1,* 6–26.

Trost, G., Pauels, L., & Schneider, B. (1976). *Repräsentativerhebung an deutschen abiturienten* [Study on a representative sample of German graduates from upper secondary school]. Bericht Nr. 2 des Instituts für Test- und Begabungsforschung der Studienstiftung. Bonn.

Weber, W. (1990). Personal wird zum überlebensfaktor [Personnel becomes a factor of survival]. *Gablers Magazin, 2,* 10–15.

Wottawa, H. (1990). Umsetzung von situationsdiagnostischen erkenntnissen in personendiagnostische überlegungen [Transformation of knowledge about situational assessment into considerations on personnel assessment]. In W. Sarges (Hrsg.), *Management-Diagnostik* (pp. 143–160). Göttingen/Toronto/Zürich: Hogrefe.

Group Composition, Gender, and Race Effects on Assessment Center Ratings

Neal Schmitt
Michigan State University

Use of assessment centers to select personnel for managerial positions has spread rapidly since the first report of its application in industry (Bray & Grant, 1966). Moreover, assessment centers are now used for many purposes other than selection such as career management, development, and training. Teachers, engineers, school administrators, salespersons, military and police personnel, and others have been assessed. This popularity is certainly partly due to encouraging evidence regarding the criterion-related validity of the assessment center. Gaugler, Rosenthal, Thornton, and Bentson (1987) reported a meta-analysis of 50 assessment center studies in which the average validity across various performance criteria was .37.

Data regarding the reliability of assessor ratings (Schmitt, 1977) and the incremental validity (Huck & Bray, 1976) of center ratings (relative to paper-and-pencil tests of cognitive ability) have also been highly encouraging. Moreover, subgroup mean differences in assessment center performance have either been nonexistent (in the case of men and women candidates; Moses & Boehm, 1975) or smaller than those for traditional ability tests (in the case of Black–White differences; Huck & Bray, 1976). One of the purposes of the current chapter is to readdress the possibility of subgroup differences with a much larger sample of both candidates and assessors.

Aside from study of the predictive validity and reliability of assessment center ratings, industrial–organizational psychologists have also used the assessment center as a vehicle for studying broader scientific issues of interest to the field of psychology as a whole. One example is the literature on the construct validity

315

of assessment center ratings (e.g., Sackett & Dreher, 1984). A relatively robust finding is that center ratings of behavior within an exercise are more highly correlated than ratings of the same construct rated on the basis of different exercises. Other researchers have been interested in studying the raters' judgment process as it occurs during the center's operation (Russell, 1985; Sackett & Wilson, 1982). Still a third issue has been addressed by Schmitt and Hill (1977). These authors were interested in determining whether the gender and race composition of the group in which individual candidates are assessed would affect their ratings. They found evidence that some ratings were affected; for example, leadership ratings of women candidates were lower when they were assessed in groups that were largely male. However, the number of groups in their study was small; hence most observed relationships were nonsignificant.

The second purpose of the research reported in this chapter is to replicate the Schmitt and Hill research using a much larger number of candidates and groups. Before doing so, however, the social psychological research relevant to the group composition hypothesis is reviewed.

Kanter's (1977) description of the effect that is the focus of this study is perhaps the best. She states that the behavior, evaluation, and interactions between men and women may vary depending on the proportion of men to women in an organization or group. She also proceeds to characterize groups or situations as belonging to one of four types based on the different proportions of people of one gender, age, or ethnic group. Uniform groups have only one type of person. Skewed groups have a large majority of one type of person over another; for example, 85% to 15%. Tilted groups still have clear majority and minority components, but the distribution is less extreme (perhaps 65% to 35%). The balanced group has an approximately even distribution of persons of different status. Whereas introduced in connection with behavior in an organization or department, it seems that similar effects may occur in small interactive groups such as those that are evaluated in an assessment center.

Very few direct tests of this group composition hypothesis have been undertaken. The Schmitt and Hill (1977) study was mentioned. In a similar study on age, Cleveland, Festa, and Montgomery (1988) varied the composition of an applicant pool for the job of computer programmer to determine the degree of age bias in simulated personnel decisions. Hiring recommendations and ratings of the potential to advance were systematically lower as the proportion of older (age 60 or 61 versus 27 or 28) applicants in the pool was lowered.

The program of research of Heilman and her colleagues is relevant to both objectives addressed in this chapter. They have studied in a programmatic fashion the subtleties of bias that often enter decisions about members of different gender subgroups. For example, Heilman and Saruwatari (1979) found women who were attractive seemed to be disadvantaged by their appearance when they applied for managerial positions. This attractiveness disadvantage was even more pronounced when the work of managerial women was evaluated and recommendations for organizational rewards were set (Heilman & Stopeck, 1985a). Further, the success of high-level corporate personnel was more likely to be attributed to the ability (as opposed to luck or circumstances) of attractive men than it was to attractive women's ability (Heilman & Stopeck, 1985b). Heilman and Martell (1986) also demonstrated that gender discrimination in traditional male occupations can be overcome *provided* there is previous exposure to multiple women in the occupation for which personnel evaluations are being made. The conditions that determine the evaluation of women were further explored by Heilman, Martell, and Simon (1988). The results indicate that competent women applicants for extremely male sex-typed jobs were overvalued relative to men applicants. Outside of these rather restrictive conditions, women candidates were undervalued relative to men. Heilman's work is relevant to the research reported here because it underscores the subtleties of bias and the importance of the context in which ratings are being made. My position is that the group in which one is evaluated is an important determinant of the perceptions of member's behavior and, perhaps, the behavior itself.

Kraiger and Ford (1985) conducted a meta-analysis of ratee race effects in performance ratings. They found mean correlations between ratee race and ratings given by White and Black raters of .183 and .220, respectively, indicating that members of both groups assigned slightly higher ratings to members of their own race than to persons of the other race. Of more relevance to the current study was the fact that ratee race effects were more likely to be found in field studies in which Blacks constituted a small percentage of the work force.

Both rater and ratee race and gender effects on assessment center ratings are examined in this chapter. In the performance-appraisal literature there is a great deal of research exploring the influence of rater and ratee gender and the stereotype of the job (i.e., as one that is primarily male or female) on the performance ratings of individuals in those jobs. Rater gender does not typically influence ratings; when it does it seems that female raters may be more lenient (e.g., Bartol & Butterfield, 1976; Hamner, Kim, Baird, & Bigoness, 1974; London & Poplawski, 1976). Research investigating the hypothesis that ratee gender and the gender stereotype of the job interact to influence ratings has been mixed (Bartol & Butterfield, 1976; Jacobson & Effertz, 1974; Mobley, 1982; Rosen & Jerdee, 1973). Field studies have typically not found ratee gender effects (Pulakos & Wexley, 1983; Thompson & Thompson, 1985). One consistent finding is that same gender rater–ratee combinations do not result in higher ratings for these ratees than do rater–ratee combinations of differing gender (e.g., Izraeli & Izraeli, 1985; Mobley, 1982; Pulakos & Wexley, 1983).

Rater and ratee race effects on performance ratings have also been investigated and the results are similarly ambiguous. Some studies have indicated no rater race effects (Schmidt & Johnson, 1973), whereas others have (Campbell, Crooks, Mahoney, & Rock, 1973). Similarly, conflicting results have been reported for ratee race. Across studies, there does seem to be a small interaction of rater and ratee race as was found in Kraiger and Ford's (1985) meta-analysis already mentioned.

Recently, Pulakos, White, Oppler, and Borman (1989) presented an analysis of rater and gender effects on performance ratings in a very large sample. Results of tests of interactions between rater race and gender, ratee race and gender, and the job type revealed significant main effects and interactions, but the variance accounted for by all these effects combined was relatively insignificant (less than 1%). They were also able to identify a sizable number of instances in which a ratee was rated by both a Black and a White rater. Repeated measures analyses of these pairs of ratings allowed the investigators to separate the effects of rater bias and actual performance differences. These analyses also revealed minimal effects due to race and gender and the various interactions.

The present study represents a replication of the Pulakos et al. (1989) study of race and gender effects in the assessment center context. As stated earlier, some evidence exists that assessment center ratings exhibit minimal race and gender effects (Huck & Bray, 1976; Moses & Boehm, 1975), but there have been no previous studies in which simultaneous examination of both gender and race of candidates and assessors and the interaction of these variables were undertaken.

METHOD

Sample

The sample included 2,910 persons who were assessed as candidates for school administrator positions in 25 different centers located in various places across the United States. Most of these persons were teachers at the time of assessment, although some already held administrative positions as department heads or directors of special programs. The sample sizes for various analyses reported next vary because of missing data on one or more variable. Further, the analyses for race and gender of rater and ratee include many more cases because six raters provided ratings on each of the candidates in a center.

Assessment Center Dimensions and Administration

The assessment center was developed for the National Association of Secondary School Principals (NASSP) in 1975–1976 with the voluntary help of the APA Division of Industrial and Organizational Psychology (see Jeswald, 1977; Moses, 1977). Since that time NASSP has provided a staff consultant to provide advice and assessor training to interested school districts. A job analysis conducted prior to the development of the center indicated that 12 dimensions of behavior were important for successfully working school administrators. It was felt that these dimensions could be assessed in an assessment center. These dimensions and their descriptions are listed in Table 20.1.

In addition, a summary placement recommendation was also made. This was an overall rating made at the conclusion of the assessors' integration session and represented the assessors' overall appraisal of the candidates' potential as school administrators. Assessing these dimensions involved the use of two in-baskets, a semistructured interview, a fact-finding and decision-making simulation with an oral presentation, and an analysis and group discussion of a case study. All ratings were made on Likert-type 5-point scales. Consensus ratings of the skill dimensions as well as the placement recommendation were completed after a 2-day discussion of candidates by the assessor team. It should be noted that only in the case study exercise were the candidates (in groups of 6) observed by the raters interacting as a group. A total of 12 candidates was assessed at a time; occasionally illness or some other unavoidable occurrence meant that one or two less candidates were assessed.

Interrater reliabilities for each of the 13 assessment center ratings were com-

TABLE 20.1
Assessment Center Dimensions and Descriptions

1. *Problem analysis*. Ability to seek out relevant data and analyze complex information to determine the important elements of a problem situation; searching for information with a purpose.
2. *Judgment*. Skill in identifying educational needs and setting priorities; ability to reach logical conclusions and make high-quality decisions based on available information; ability to critically evaluate written communications.
3. *Organizational ability*. Ability to plan, schedule, and control the work of others; skill in using resources in an optimal fashion; ability to deal with a volume of paper work and heavy demands on one's time.
4. *Decisiveness*. Ability to recognize when a decision is required and to act quickly (without an assessment of the *quality* of the decision).
5. *Leadership*. Ability to recognize when a group requires direction, to get others involved in solving problems, to effectively interact with a group, to guide them to the accomplishment of a task.
6. *Sensitivity*. Ability to perceive the needs, concerns, and personal problems of others; tact in dealing with persons from different backgrounds; skill in resolving conflicts; ability to deal effectively with people concerning emotional issues; knowing what information to communicate and to whom.
7. *Range of interests*. Competence to discuss a variety of subjects (educational, political, economic, etc.); desire to actively participate in events.
8. *Personal motivation*. Showing that work is important to personal satisfaction; a need to achieve in all activities attempted; ability to be self-policing.
9. *Educational values*. Possession of well-reasoned education; philosophy; receptiveness to change and new ideas.
10. *Stress tolerance*. Ability to perform under pressure and opposition; ability to think on one's feet.
11. *Oral communication skill*. Ability to make a clear oral presentation of ideas and facts.
12. *Written communication skill*. Ability to express ideas clearly in writing; to write appropriately for different audiences—students, teachers, parents, other administrators.

puted by correlating the ratings given by different raters. Computation of coefficient alpha for the composite of these ratings indicated all 13 were measured with high interrater reliability ($\alpha > .90$).

Assessors were chosen by the local administrators but were trained by NASSP staff. The NASSP trainers could, and did frequently, recommend that assessors not be used because they failed to make the observations and/or ratings necessary to insure an appropriate assessment of candidates' skills.

Data Analyses

Tests of the group composition hypothesis required the computation of a group composition measure. For each group, four such scores were computed: the proportion of males in each group, the proportion of females in the group, the proportion of Whites in the group, and the proportion of Blacks in the group. These scores were then assigned to each member of that group. The group composition scores were then correlated with their ratings (a composite of the 6 assessors' ratings) on each of the 12 skill dimensions as well as the placement recommendation.

Analyses of mean ratings of Black and White candidates by Black and White assessors consisted of $2 \times 2 \times 2 \times 2$ (gender and race of candidate and gender and race of assessor) analyses of variance for each of the skill dimensions and the placement recommendation. There were minority candidates who were not Black, but their numbers were not large enough to justify separate analyses of these groups. Hence, they were dropped from these analyses. These 13 ANOVAs were not independent, as the ratings of all skill dimensions were correlated between .40 and .70.

RESULTS

The results of the group composition analyses are presented in Table 20.2. In the bottom two rows of this table we present the mean proportion of the group that was of a particular subgroup status when a member of that race–gender combination was a candidate in a given center. Because there were typically 12 candidates in a center, the White male mean proportion of .52 means that 6 of the 12 candidates were typically White males. A standard deviation of .18 is approximately equal to 2 candidates. Likewise mean Black male and female proportions are roughly equal to 2 of the 12 candidates. Of course, there were many assessment center groups that contained no minority members, and hence the proportions for minorities are overestimates of their representation in the total candidate group.

Of the 52 correlations presented in Table 20.2, only 4 were statistically significant ($p < .05$) and none exceeded .20. The significant correlations indicated

TABLE 20.2
Group Composition—Skill Dimension Correlations

	Proportion of White females & ratings of White females[a]	Proportion of Black females & ratings of Black females[b]	Proportion of White males & ratings of White males[c]	Proportion of Black males & ratings of Black males[d]
Problem analysis	− .06	− .01	− .06	− .07
Judgment	− .08	.02	.00	.02
Organizational ability	− .00	.10	− .01	− .01
Decisiveness	.04	.16*	.00	− .06
Leadership	− .04	− .06	− .01	.03
Sensitivity	− .05	.04	− .05	− .03
Range of interests	− .02	.03	.01	.19*
Personal motivation	− .05	− .06	.04	.12
Educational values	− .07	− .02	− .06	− .05
Stress tolerance	.09*	− .01	.00	− .02
Oral communication	− .00	− .02	.00	− .18*
Written communication	− .07	− .03	.04	− .10
Placement recommendation	− .04	.04	.01	− .04
$\bar{X}_{prop}$	.43	.20	.52	.20
SD_{prop}	.15	.09	.18	.11

*$p \leq .05$; [a]N of White females ranged from 505 to 515; [b]N of Black females ranged from 128 to 134; [c]N of White males ranged from 609 to 624; [d]N of Black males ranged from 91 to 97.

that (a) White females received higher Stress Tolerance ratings as the proportion of White women in the assessment center group increased; (b) Black females received higher ratings on Decisiveness with increases in the proportion of Black females in their group; and (c) Black males received higher ratings on Range of Interest and lower ratings on Oral Communication as the proportion of Black males with whom they were assessed increased. Overall, however, there is little evidence that group composition had any effect on the ratings of any of the four demographic subgroups.

Mean Ratings as a Function of Rater and Candidate Race and Gender

The results of analyses of the effect of candidate gender and race on composite ratings are shown in Tables 20.3 and 20.4. Table 20.3 presents the means and standard deviations of the composite skill ratings by candidate gender. Most notable in this table are the significant differences between males and females on all the composite skill ratings and placement recommendation. Without exception, female candidates received higher composite ratings than male candidates. The largest difference between male and female candidates occurred on the Written Communications and Personal Motivation dimensions. Although all

TABLE 20.3
Means and Standard Deviations of Composite Skill Ratings by Candidate Sex

	Male		Female	
	Mean	*SD*	*Mean*	*SD*
Problem analysis*	3.06	.63	3.22	.66
Judgment*	3.06	.63	3.17	.65
Organizational ability*	3.22	.73	3.41	.74
Decisiveness*	3.73	.76	3.85	.75
Leadership*	3.36	.79	3.47	.80
Sensitivity*	3.30	.62	3.39	.60
Range of interests*	3.39	.73	3.50	.73
Personal motivation*	3.72	.68	3.88	.72
Educational values*	3.35	.62	3.48	.64
Stress tolerance*	3.53	.62	3.60	.62
Oral communication*	3.62	.63	3.77	.62
Written communication*	3.29	.74	3.69	.69
Placement recommendation*	3.17	.74	3.35	.77
Sample size (low to high)	1428–1481		1296–1350	

*The mean rating of female candidates was significantly higher than that of male candidates, $p < .01$.

TABLE 20.4
Means and Standard Deviations of Composite Skill Ratings by Candidate Race

	White		Black	
	Mean	*SD*	*Mean*	*SD*
Problem analysis*	3.16	.63	2.72	.61
Judgment*	3.13	.62	2.75	.60
Organizational ability*	3.35	.71	2.82	.64
Decisiveness*	3.77	.71	3.38	.81
Leadership*	3.44	.80	3.00	.78
Sensitivity*	3.34	.62	3.17	.55
Range of interests	3.41	.71	3.43	.76
Personal motivation	3.75	.71	3.82	.68
Educational values	3.41	.62	3.36	.62
Stress tolerance*	3.53	.61	3.43	.61
Oral communication*	3.67	.60	3.44	.61
Written communication*	3.50	.72	3.03	.72
Placement recommendation*	3.29	.75	2.81	.74
Sample size (low to high)	1737–1801		318–337	

*The mean rating of White candidates is significantly higher than the mean rating of Black candidates, $p < .01$.

differences are statistically significant, it is important to note that the difference between male and female Placement Recommendations was only .18, which is a little less than one quarter of a standard deviation. Because sample size was very large, even very small differences were statistically significant.

White candidates received significantly higher mean composite ratings than Black candidates on Problem Analysis, Judgment, Organizational Ability, Decisiveness, Leadership, Sensitivity, Stress Tolerance, Oral Communication, Written Communication, and the Placement Recommendation. Most differences were equal to one half to two thirds of a standard deviation. The difference on the Placement Recommendation, for example, was .48, equal to .63 standard deviation units.

Table 20.5 presents the mean composite ratings received by the different race–gender groups of candidates. Black males score lowest whereas White females score highest, indicating the same trends that were obvious in Tables 20.3 and 20.4. Only one statistically significant gender by race interaction was found. Examination of the mean ratings for this dimension, Stress Tolerance, indicated that, whereas there were no differences between White and Black males, White women did significantly better than Black women. As elsewhere, the sample size is large, producing statistically significant differences in the presence of relatively small (.28) mean differences. Further, 1 significant result out of 13 is not much more than what would be expected by chance ($p < .05$).

TABLE 20.5
Means and Standard Deviations of Different Candidate Race–Sex Groups
on the Composite Skill Ratings

	White				Black			
	Males		Females		Males		Females	
	Mean	SD	Mean	SD	Mean	SD	Mean	SD
Problem analysis	3.06	.61	3.27	.63	2.68	.58	2.75	.63
Judgment	3.06	.61	3.22	.62	2.72	.59	2.77	.61
Organizational ability	3.24	.69	3.47	.71	2.73	.66	2.89	.62
Decisiveness	3.70	.70	3.84	.70	3.23	.82	3.50	.79
Leadership	3.36	.80	3.52	.81	2.92	.82	3.07	.74
Sensitivity	3.29	.63	3.39	.60	3.14	.56	3.20	.54
Range of interests	3.35	.71	3.49	.69	3.43	.77	3.43	.75
Personal motivation	3.67	.69	3.85	.71	3.78	.66	3.85	.70
Educational values	3.32	.62	3.50	.62	3.32	.68	3.39	.57
Stress tolerance*	3.48	.61	3.58	.61	3.47	.61	3.40	.61
Oral communication	3.59	.60	3.76	.59	3.37	.64	3.50	.57
Written communication	3.29	.72	3.74	.65	2.84	.74	3.18	.67
Placement recommendation	3.18	.73	3.42	.75	2.76	.80	2.84	.70
Sample size (low to high)	935–974		802–827		137–148		181–189	

*The interaction between candidate race and sex was statistically significant ($p < .05$).

In conclusion, there are race and gender differences among candidates, but there is little indication that race and gender interact to form a higher or lower scoring gender–race subgroup.

Assessor Gender and Race

The results of analyses of the effect of assessor gender and race on composite ratings are shown in Tables 20.6 and 20.7. Table 20.6 presents the means and standard deviations of the composite skill ratings by assessor gender. Two composite ratings for each skill dimension and placement recommendation corresponding to average male and female assessor ratings were computed for every candidate. Table 20.6 shows that there are no significant differences between composite male and female assessor ratings. Table 20.7 illustrates the means and standard deviations of the composite skill ratings by assessor race. These composite scores were calculated in the same manner as the male and female assessor composite ratings described earlier. Although several composite White assessor ratings are significantly higher than the composite Black assessor ratings, the differences are very small in standard deviation units. For example, the largest difference is on organizational ability, where a difference of .12 in the mean composite ratings is only .15 of a standard deviation unit. The Placement Recommendation difference between White and Black raters was only .08, about .10 of a standard deviation.

Interaction of Assessor Gender and Race and Candidate Gender and Race

Although the previous analyses provide a picture of the main effects, the most important summary of the data includes the interactions of rater and ratee race and gender effects. Table 20.8 provides the means and standard deviations of the skill ratings assigned by male, female, White, and Black assessors to male, female, White, and Black candidates. Composite ratings were not calculated here because it would be impossible to combine a candidate's assessors by their gender and race simultaneously. For example, Black assessors may be male or female. It was impossible to compute a composite Black assessor rating and assign a gender code to this rating. Therefore, interactions between assessor and candidate gender and race were calculated utilizing the separate ratings provided by each of the six assessors for every candidate. The large number of ratings results in powerful analyses with the ability to detect statistically significant differences even when the actual difference between the scores in two or more groups is very small.

The $2 \times 2 \times 2 \times 2$ ANOVAs yielded the main effects for assessor race and candidate gender and race just described, but only 13 of 143 interactions

TABLE 20.6
Means and Standard Deviations of Composite Skill Ratings by Rater's Sex

	Male		Female	
	Mean	*SD*	*Mean*	*SD*
Problem analysis	3.13	.68	3.13	.71
Judgment	3.12	.66	3.09	.70
Organizational ability	3.31	.75	3.30	.78
Decisiveness	3.79	.76	3.79	.81
Leadership	3.43	.82	3.39	.88
Sensitivity	3.34	.63	3.33	.69
Range of interests	3.46	.75	3.42	.80
Personal motivation	3.79	.72	3.77	.76
Educational values	3.43	.66	3.40	.71
Stress tolerance	3.56	.66	3.54	.70
Oral communication	3.69	.65	3.68	.70
Written communication	3.48	.74	3.46	.78
Placement recommendation	3.23	.78	3.22	.81
Sample size (low to high)	2338–2445		2197–2316	

TABLE 20.7
Means and Standard Deviations of Composite Skill Ratings by Rater's Race

	White		Black	
	Mean	*SD*	*Mean*	*SD*
Problem analysis*	3.15	.66	3.10	.75
Judgment*	3.14	.65	3.07	.73
Organizational ability*	3.35	.74	3.23	.81
Decisiveness*	3.83	.76	3.72	.82
Leadership*	3.45	.82	3.35	.88
Sensitivity*	3.38	.62	3.32	.71
Range of interests	3.49	.73	3.47	.82
Personal motivation	3.83	.70	3.83	.78
Educational values*	3.46	.66	3.37	.76
Stress tolerance*	3.58	.65	3.52	.74
Oral communication	3.70	.65	3.68	.72
Written communication	3.50	.74	3.46	.76
Placement recommendation*	3.25	.79	3.17	.84
Sample size (low to high)	2028–2130		898–1043	

*The mean rating provided by White raters was significantly higher than the mean rating provided by Black raters, $p < .05$.

TABLE 20.8
Means and Standard Deviations on the Composite Skill Ratings by Candidate and Assessor Sex and Race

	Male Candidate								Female Candidate							
	Male Assessor				Female Assessor				Male Assessor				Female Assessor			
	White Cand.		Black Cand.		White Cand.		Black Cand.		White Cand.		Black Cand.		White Cand.		Black Cand.	
	White AS.	Black AS.	White AS.	Black AS.	White AS.	Black AS.	White AS.	Black AS.	White AS.	Black AS.	White AS.	Black AS.	White AS.	Black AS.	White AS.	Black AS.
Problem analysis[1]	3.04	3.05	2.63	2.70	3.05	3.14	2.53	2.71	3.28	3.22	2.75	2.82	3.28	3.27	2.72	2.78
	.69	.69	.62	.75	.70	.74	.66	.72	.72	.64	.70	.86	.73	.73	.75	.67
Judgment[2]	3.03	3.04	2.63	2.87	3.05	3.07	2.56	2.71	3.25	3.26	2.76	2.91	3.19	3.17	2.71	2.69
	.70	.61	.65	.85	.69	.75	.61	.81	.71	.66	.64	.84	.73	.75	.69	.69
Organizational ability[1]	3.24	3.13	2.67	2.82	3.23	3.24	2.61	2.84	3.51	3.37	2.91	2.86	3.50	3.42	2.84	2.78
	.76	.70	.72	.88	.75	.83	.72	.77	.78	.66	.65	.82	.81	.84	.68	.70
Decisiveness[3]	3.70	3.79	3.18	3.29	3.67	3.71	3.10	3.40	3.84	3.85	3.49	3.63	3.83	3.80	3.52	3.59
	.76	.75	.85	.75	.80	.79	.93	.96	.77	.70	.80	.87	.78	.78	.88	.93
Leadership[1,3]	3.39	3.44	2.80	3.12	3.38	3.39	2.74	3.03	3.57	3.50	3.14	3.22	3.60	3.48	3.00	3.06
	.88	.82	.89	1.07	.91	.90	.86	.94	.88	.81	.80	1.00	.91	.88	.90	.90
Sensitivity[3]	3.32	3.23	3.05	3.20	3.27	3.33	3.00	3.19	3.42	3.30	3.19	3.36	3.40	3.37	3.22	3.21
	.71	.72	.62	.58	.75	.75	.67	.66	.68	.65	.64	.78	.74	.72	.66	.76

Range of interests	3.39	3.46	3.27	3.56	3.32	3.38	3.18	3.25	3.53	3.44	3.48	3.64	3.47	3.51	3.43	3.47
	.80	.78	.83	.72	.80	.84	.79	.87	.77	.70	.85	.85	.78	.83	.87	.89
Personal motivation	3.68	3.75	3.74	3.82	3.64	3.74	3.71	3.87	3.85	3.91	3.90	3.92	3.79	3.92	3.82	3.83
	.77	.75	.75	.65	.80	.84	.74	.86	.80	.62	.74	.90	.82	.82	.77	.81
Educational values[4,5]	3.33	3.39	3.33	3.40	3.29	3.31	3.11	3.29	3.52	3.65	3.38	3.62	3.53	3.48	3.35	3.23
	.73	.66	.87	.73	.74	.82	.90	.94	.75	.60	.66	.78	.78	.77	.64	.69
Stress tolerance	3.48	3.47	3.48	3.43	3.47	3.52	3.36	3.56	3.58	3.47	3.40	3.39	3.59	3.60	3.39	3.39
	.72	.72	.78	.58	.70	.77	.76	.92	.73	.64	.71	.69	.74	.75	.68	.81
Oral communication	3.58	3.66	3.38	3.58	3.53	3.59	3.35	3.45	3.73	3.78	3.47	3.62	3.74	3.77	3.48	3.50
	.68	.67	.76	.77	.69	.74	.88	.92	.62	.64	.65	.81	.71	.70	.71	.72
Written communication[5,3]	3.28	3.27	2.96	2.91	3.24	3.30	2.83	3.21	3.75	3.66	3.20	3.27	3.66	3.71	3.14	3.16
	.76	.70	.78	.71	.77	.80	.87	.81	.70	.70	.76	.74	.75	.73	.76	.74
Placement recommendation[1,3]	3.16	3.11	2.58	2.86	3.13	3.12	2.50	2.76	3.42	3.31	2.77	2.94	3.42	3.25	2.77	2.76
	.79	.78	.87	.78	.80	.86	.93	.96	.82	.78	.75	.81	.86	.87	.86	.73
Sample (low to high)	2581–	184–	209–	22–	1209–	339–	125–	54–	2105–	129–	386–	54–	1114–	340–	191–	104–
	2733	193	245	24	1280	353	143	59	2206	133	411	58	1115	353	208	106

[1]Indicates a statistically significant interaction between race of assessor and sex of candidate, $p < .05$.
[2]Indicates a statistically significant interaction between sex of assessor and sex of candidate, $p < .05$.
[3]Indicates a statistically significant interaction between race of assessor and race of candidate, $p < .05$.
[4]Indicates a statistically significant interaction between sex of assessor and race of candidate, $p < .05$.
[5]Indicates a statistically significant interaction between sex and race of assessors, $p < .05$.
[6]Indicates a statistically significant four way interaction between assessor and candidate race and sex, $p < .05$.

(11 interactions multiplied by 13 ratings) were statistically significant ($p < .05$). These significant interactions are indicated in the footnotes to Table 20.8. None of these interactions accounted for even 1% of the variance in ratings. Candidate race differences by contrast explained 5% of the variance. Of those interactions that were statistically significant, four involved the race of rater by race of candidate interaction—the same interaction reported in the Kraiger and Ford (1985) meta-analysis referred to before. In each of these four instances, the mean differences between White and Black raters of White candidates were virtually zero ($< .02$), whereas Black raters rated Black ratees more highly than did White raters.

Four other significant interactions involved the race of assessor and gender of candidate. In these cases, both Black and White assessors were rating women candidates higher than men, but the difference for White assessors was greater. In the case of all these interactions, the mean differences like the estimates of variance accounted for were small (less than one-third standard deviation).

DISCUSSION

The results of the analyses of the group composition effect indicate no support for the notion that assessment center ratings are affected in any way by the demographic makeup of the group in which one is assessed for any of the four race–gender groups studied. Previous studies of these effects in the field have also reported marginal group composition effects (Schmitt & Hill, 1977). In a simulation of a job application situation, Cleveland et al. (1988) reported mixed support for effects due to the age composition of the group. If group composition effects do occur, they appear to be quite subtle. One possibility is that such effects would occur only when members of different subgroups interact as in group discussions. The NASSP assessment center included only 1 exercise of this type, and conduct of that exercise included only 6 of the 12 candidates at a time. If any additional research on group effects is to be conducted, it might be best directed to situations in which interpersonal behavior is observed in a group setting.

As to gender and race effects on assessment ratings, the most important variable appears to be candidate race. Statistically significant mean differences favoring White candidates over Black candidates were observed for 10 of 13 rating dimensions. These differences were about two-thirds to three-fourths of a standard deviation in magnitude; hence they are practically as well as statistically significant. There is not a great deal of available published literature on mean differences in assessment center ratings between racial groups. Huck and Bray (1976) reported differences equal to .5 to 1.0 standard deviations between Black and White women on Administrative Skills, Sensitivity, and Effective Intelligence. Organizations that look to assessment centers as a means of eliminating adverse impact in selection procedures will be disappointed if our results and those reported by Huck and Bray (1976) generalize. However, it is important to point out that there were also performance differences between the Black and White subgroups that were the subject of this study, and that there was no evidence of differential prediction (see Schmitt & Cohen, 1990). This lack of differential prediction is also consistent with previously published (Huck & Bray, 1976) and unpublished (Byham, 1980) research.

There were also statistically significant gender differences in ratings. Previous research on male–female differences has also focused on differences in validity but Moses and Boehm (1975), who also reported the distributions of male and female center ratings, clearly did not find mean differences. The differences we found favoring women may reflect the greater acceptance of women in education than in management (Moses & Boehm's sample were AT&T applicants for managerial positions). In any event, the differences we report are very small (about one quarter of a standard deviation) and probably lack practical significance in most instances. Analyses of differential prediction (Schmitt & Cohen, 1990) indicated no evidence of slope or intercept bias for or against either gender subgroup.

Tests of the interaction of rater and ratee gender and race effects revealed some evidence that two interactions occur with more than chance frequency, although even these interactions accounted for a small portion of the variance, and examination of the mean differences between relevant subgroups indicated very small differences. The finding of a significant race of rater by race of ratee interaction is consistent with past research (Kraiger & Ford, 1985), but the form of the interaction reported here is different than that reported in the Kraiger–Ford meta-analysis. They reported evidence that both Black and White raters rated members of their own subgroup more highly than did members of another subgroup. In the present study, only Black candidates were differentially rated by White and Black raters.

The second interaction that was statistically significant across a number of rating dimensions indicated that the difference between male and female ratings was greater for White raters than Black raters. I do not know of any previous report of this race of rater by gender of ratee interaction, nor is there any readily apparent theoretical reason for this interaction.

Our results regarding interactions are consistent with those of Pulakos et al. (1989), who examined similar interactions for performance ratings in the military. Their sample sizes were even larger (nearly 40,000) than those reported here, so many interactions were statistically significant. All, however, were considered practically trivial. The results of these large field studies seem inconsistent with the laboratory work cited in the beginning of this chapter. Even in the laboratory work, however, it is rare to find a main effect for gender or race on ratings. Usually gender effects are more subtle in that they interact with physical attractiveness or job type, neither of which it was possible to evaluate in the current study. Pulakos et al. (1989) did have data on job type, but the proportions of variance accounted for by job type and its interactions with other variables were so tiny that it was excluded from most of their analyses.

Assessment centers have been generally well received by candidates who experience the center (Dodd, 1977; Schuler & Fruhner, this volume; Thornton, this volume; Thornton & Byham, 1982). This favorable reaction is likely due to what has been called social validity (Schuler, 1990). The data discussed in this chapter should do little to dampen enthusiasm for the procedure. Even the relatively large differences across race subgroups are smaller than those reported for most other selection procedures (see Schmitt & Noe, 1986). Further, there is little evidence that being observed and rated by a member of one subgroup versus another has any significant effect on one's evaluation. These data regarding the subgroup fairness of the center are obviously also important to organizations that are concerned with legal and social responsibilities (Pearn, this volume; Schmitt, 1989).

If more field research is to be conducted on rater and ratee demographics, it should be directed to the interaction of gender and race with other factors. These studies will also likely prove most useful if they are based on theoretically defensible hypotheses, such as those tested by Heilman and her colleagues.

REFERENCES

Bartol, K. M., & Butterfield, D. A. (1976). Sex effects in evaluating leaders. *Journal of Applied Psychology, 61*, 446–454.

Bray, D. W., & Grant, D. L. (1966). The assessment center in the measurement of potential for business management. *Psychological Monographs, 80* (17, Whole No. 625).

Byham, W. C. (1980). *What do we know about assessment centers?* Unpublished technical report. Pittsburgh, PA: Development Dimensions.

Campbell, J. T., Crooks, L. A., Mahoney, M. H., & Rock, D. A. (1973). *An investigation of sources of bias in the prediction of job performance: A six-year study* (Report No. PR-73-27). Princeton, NJ: Educational Testing Service.

Cleveland, J. N., Festa, R. M., & Montgomery, L. (1988). Applicant pool composition and job perceptions: Impact on decisions regarding an older applicant. *Journal of Vocational Behavior, 32*, 112–125.

Dodd, W. E. (1977). Attitudes toward assessment center programs. In J. L. Moses & W. C. Byham (Eds.), *Applying the assessment center method* (pp. 161–184). New York: Pergamon.

Gaugler, B. B., Rosenthal, D. B., Thornton, G. C. III, & Bentson, C. (1987). Meta-analysis of assessment center validity. *Journal of Applied Psychology, 72*, 493–511.

Hamner, W. C., Kim, J. S., Baird, L., & Bigoness, W. J. (1974). Race and sex as determinants of ratings by potential employers in a simulated work-sampling task. *Journal of Applied Psychology, 59*, 705–711.

Heilman, M. E., & Martell, R. F. (1986). Exposure to successful women: Antidote to sex discrimination in applicant screening decisions. *Organizational Behavior and Human Decision Processes, 37*, 376–390.

Heilman, M. E., Martell, R. F., & Simon, M. C. (1988). The vagaries of sex bias: Conditions regulating the undervaluation, equivaluation and overvaluation of female job applicants. *Organizational Behavior of Human Decision Processes, 41*, 98–110.

Heilman, M. E., & Saruwatari, L. R. (1979). When beauty is beastly: The effects of appearance and sex on evaluations of job applicants for managerial and nonmanagerial jobs. *Organizational Behavior and Human Performance, 23*, 360–372.

Heilman, M. E., & Stopeck, M. H. (1985a). Attractiveness and corporate success: Different causal attributions for males and females. *Journal of Applied Psychology, 70*, 379–388.

Heilman, M. E., & Stopeck, M. H. (1985b). Being attractive, advantage or disadvantage?: Performance based evaluations and recommended personnel actions as a function of appearance, sex, and job type. *Organizational Behavior and Human Performance, 35*, 202–215.

Huck, J. R., & Bray, D. W. (1976). Management assessment center evaluations and subsequent job performance of Black and White females. *Personnel Psychology, 29*, 13–30.

Izraeli, D. N., & Izraeli, D. (1985). Sex effects in evaluating leaders. *Journal of Applied Psychology, 70*, 540–546.

Jacobson, M. B., & Effertz, J. (1974). Sex roles and leadership perceptions of the leaders and the led. *Organizational Behavior and Human Performance, 12*, 383–396.

Jeswald, T. A. (1977). A new approach to identifying administrative talent. *NASSP Bulletin, 61*, 79–83.

Kanter, R. M. (1977). *Men and women of the organization*. New York: Basic Books.

Kraiger, K., & Ford, J. K. (1985). A meta-analysis of ratee race effects in performance ratings. *Journal of Applied Psychology, 70*, 56–65.

London, M., & Poplawski, J. R. (1976). Effects of information on stereotype development in performance appraisal and interview contexts. *Journal of Applied Psychology, 61*, 199–205.

Mobley, W. H. (1982). Supervisor and employee race and sex effects on performance appraisals: A field test of adverse impact and generalizability. *Academy of Management Journal, 25*, 598–606.

Moses, J. L. (1977). Developing an assessment center program for school administrators. *NASSP Bulletin, 61*, 76–79.

Moses, J. L., & Boehm, V. R. (1975). Relationship of assessment center performance to management progress of women. *Journal of Applied Psychology, 60*, 527–529.

Pulakos, E. D., & Wexley, K. N. (1983). The relationship among perceptual similarity, sex, and performance ratings in manager–subordinate dyads. *Academy of Management Journal, 26*, 129–139.

Pulakos, E. D., White, L. A., Oppler, S. H., & Borman, W. C. (1989). Examination of race and sex effects on performance ratings. *Journal of Applied Psychology, 74*, 770–780.

Rosen, B., & Jerdee, T. H. (1973). The influence of sex-role stereotypes on evaluations of male and female supervisory behavior. *Journal of Applied Psychology, 57*, 44–48.

Russell, C. J. (1985). Individual decision processes in an assessment center. *Journal of Applied Psychology, 70*, 737–746.

Sackett, P. R., & Dreher, G. F. (1984). Situation specificity of behavior and assessment center validation strategies: A rejoinder of Neidig and Neidig. *Journal of Applied Psychology, 69*, 187–190.

Sackett, P. R., & Wilson, M. A. (1982). Factors affecting the consensus judgment process in managerial assessment centers. *Journal of Applied Psychology, 67*, 10–17.

Schmidt, F. L., & Johnson, R. H. (1973). Effect of race on peer ratings in an industrial setting. *Journal of Applied Psychology, 57*, 237–241.

Schmitt, N. (1977). Interrater agreement and dimensionality and combination of assessment center judgments. *Journal of Applied Psychology, 62*, 171–176.

Schmitt, N. (1989). Fairness in employment selection. In M. Smith & I. Robertson (Eds.), *Advances in selection and assessment* (pp. 133–154). New York: Wiley.

Schmitt, N., & Cohen, S. A. (1990). Criterion-related validity of the assessment center for selection of school administrators. *Journal of Personnel Evaluation in Education, 4*, 203–212.

Schmitt, N., & Hill, T. E. (1977). Sex and race composition of assessment center groups as a determinant of peer and assessor ratings. *Journal of Applied Psychology, 62*, 261–264.

Schmitt, N., & Noe, R. A. (1986). Personnel selection and equal employment opportunity. In
    C. L. Cooper & I. Robertson (Eds.), *International review of industrial and organizational psy-
    chology* (pp. 71–116). London: Wiley.
Schuler, H. (1990). Personalauswahl aus der sicht der bewerber: Zum erleben eignungsdiagnostischer
    situationen [Personnel selection from the applicants' view]. *Zeitschrift für Arbeitsund Organisa-
    tionspsychologie, 34,* 184–191.
Thompson, D. E., & Thompson, T. A. (1985). Task-based performance appraisal for blue-collar
    jobs: Evaluation of race and sex effects. *Journal of Applied Psychology, 70,* 747–753.
Thornton, G. C. III, & Byham, W. C. (1982). *Assessment centers and managerial performance.* New
    York: Academic Press.

21

Individual and Organizational Perspectives on Personnel Procedures: Conclusions and Horizons for Future Research

Mike Smith
University of Manchester, United Kingdom

James L. Farr
Pennsylvania State University

Heinz Schuler
Universität Hohenheim, Stuttgart, Germany

A FRAMEWORK FOR ANALYSIS

A book of this kind contains many research findings and theoretical perspectives. The danger is to focus on one finding or one set of findings and to miss the general pattern that emerges. If the general picture is to emerge, the use of some kind of framework is indispensable. As Schuler, Farr, and Smith show in Chapter 1, the use of a clear framework has the enormous additional advantage of allowing the identification of gaps in the research effort. To encompass the range of material covered in this book, a very wide framework is needed. One particular framework, the general selection paradigm (Smith & Robertson, 1993), is readily available (see Fig. 21.1). It shows the classic conceptualization of the selection process and is implicit in work in the subject. The general selection paradigm is an idealized view that envisages the process as six main phases. The paradigm was developed from a technocratic view and represents a kind of flow chart designed to improve the accuracy of selection. As Schuler and de Wolff have pointed out in this book, the technocratic view is important but perhaps narrow. Nevertheless, it might be helpful to use the paradigm to organize the findings from the organizational and individual perspectives.

Before this is attempted, the organizational and individual perspectives themselves need some analysis. The organizational and individual perspectives are not themselves unitary concepts but are composed of many levels. Perhaps the most obvious levels to consider are perceptions, reactions, and outcomes.

Individual and organizational perceptions are easy to define. They are the "pic-

333

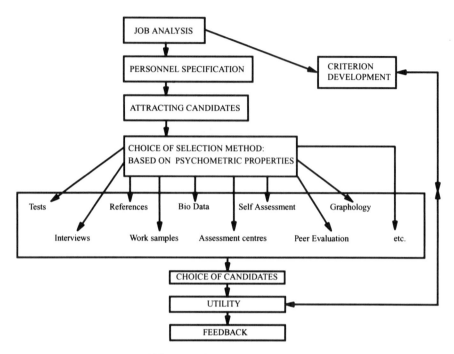

FIG. 21.1.   The selection paradigm.

tures'' or, in Kellian terms, the ''cognitive maps'' that people and organizations have about the phases of selection. Superficially at least, they are easy to study. A questionnaire asking respondents for their perceptions is all that is needed. The main problem lies in obtaining a ''real'' stimulus for people to perceive and obtaining a relevant sample of people to do the perceiving. The danger is that the results from students' perceptions of simulations are wrongly generalized to phenomena ''in the real world.''

Of course, matters rarely cease at the perceptual level. Most individuals and organizations react on the basis of what they see. These reactions can be positive, for example, greater motivation, increased self-confidence, or greater amenability. The reactions to perception can also be negative and result in stress, sabotage, or withdrawal from the selection process. These reactions are difficult to study because they may involve emotions and have a long latency before they manifest themselves.

The final level is the outcome level. Perceptions and reactions may have little or no relationship to the behavioral or economic consequences. A candidate may be enthusiastic about a recruitment procedure, but he or she may still reject the job offer. To a large extent these outcomes are the ''bottom line'' of the individual and organizational perspectives. They are also particularly difficult to measure and investigate.

Using the two axes, selection phase and level, it is possible to construct a systematic matrix within which the contents of this book can be organized.

INDIVIDUAL AND ORGANIZATIONAL
PERSPECTIVES OF JOB ANALYSIS

The individual and organizational perspectives of job analysis are the subject of Chapter 6 by Frank Landy. It shows that the importance of individual reactions was recognized from the very early days in the work of Viteles. More recent work has shown that individual perspectives differ and that they have a pervasive (but not uniform) effect on the outcomes—the job analyses themselves. Probably the strongest effect is the difference between men and women. Female job analysts, for example, seem to be more accurate and give lower ratings on most of the dimensions in the job analysis. On the other hand, it would seem that race and education do not produce differences in job analysis. Landy also draws attention to the fact that the outcomes of job analysis may be influenced by financial motivation. He presents data to suggest that getting one's job regraded to a higher category brings a higher increase in salary than achieving a merit increase, and this may explain the common finding that incumbents generally give higher ratings on job analysis questionnaires than their superiors do.

The chapter on job analysis is unusual in two ways. First, it goes beyond simply reporting the statistical significance of an effect. It actually goes on to quote an effect size that is an invaluable aid in helping the reader to estimate the practical importance of the research finding. Second, Landy was able to use the research findings to suggest ways of controlling the unwanted influences of individual perspectives.

Assuming that Chapter 6 is an accurate review of the field, it is possible to evaluate the progress that has been made. Although our knowledge is not complete, we already know a substantial amount about the influence of individual perspectives on the outcomes of job analysis. Because, in the context of job analysis, perceptions and outcomes are almost synonymous, we also know a great deal about perceptions too.

However, there are some areas where little research is reported. We seem to know little or nothing about people's reactions to job analysis. We do not seem to know the answers to basic questions such as do they prefer some forms to other forms, or does a job analysis promote or reduce stress? We also know little about the organizational influences on job analysis. Does the type of organization influence the type of job analysis, or even does the type of organization determine whether a job analysis is conducted in the first place.

INDIVIDUAL AND ORGANIZATIONAL
PERSPECTIVES OF CRITERIA

Three chapters (14, 15, and 16) are specifically concerned with the criteria used in selection and assessment. The chapter by José Prieto makes a strong case for changing the unit on which criterion information is collected from the results obtained by an individual to the results obtained by a group. This would not be a trivial adjustment because it would have important consequences on the predictors we would use in selection and assessment. In order to predict variance in group performance, we might need to use measures involving group processes and group composition. In theory at least, a part of this would be easy enough— instead of measuring, say, the personality of the applicant, it would also be necessary to measure the personality of all the group members in order to establish how the applicant would fit in. On the other hand, the search for predictors of group performance may lead us to develop new selection methods that involve some form of group activities. Both of these approaches may present considerable difficulties, but the work of Belbin (1981) shows promise and suggests that the approach can be made to work in practice.

The chapter by Dan Ilgen addressed another major issue concerning criteria: the effort to find ways of improving the ratings, usually provided by a superior, which the large majority of validity studies use as criteria and which form the bedrock of most appraisal systems. However, Ilgen pessimistically notes that a review of the research "presents a curious phenomenon. Research and development regarding employee performance appraisal systems document real improvements over the years, and yet, in spite of the improvements, the perceptions of those who use such systems have not changed; the same old problems that plagued the systems from their inception exist today with little change in magnitude. Why?" He suggests three possible explanations. First, the research findings have been ignored. Second, expectations have risen to exceed accomplishment. Third, the psychologists and researchers have maintained a narrow technocratic focus and have ignored the wider functions that are important from the organizational and individual perspective. From the organizational perspective, criteria are also used for functions such as communicating expected standards of performance, discipline, or training evaluation. From the individual perspective, criteria help individuals learn their job and, at a political level, survive and prosper within the organization. Perhaps the most important point that emerges is that, if the individual and organizational perspectives are ignored, dissatisfaction will continue and may reach the level where the use of a selection and appraisal system is threatened.

The points about using team performance as criteria and the importance of looking at the wider organizational perspective is reinforced by de Wolff's more controversial chapter on "The prediction paradigm." Indeed, he implies that the demonstrations against testing that took place in front of the APA headquarters in the 1960s were a direct result of psychologists being ill prepared to deal with the issues involved. It may be suggested that we were particularly ill prepared in terms of our organizational integrations and our knowledge of what constituted "best criteria."

Assessing the progress in establishing the individual and organizational perspectives of criteria in selection and assessment is not too difficult, at least as far as the criteria of subjective ratings are concerned. Traditional textbooks contain volumes of information on phenomena such as halo effects, leniency effects, and contrast effects. Ilgen's chapter adds a number of more recent themes such as the importance of raters' frames of reference. Ilgen also provides some data on the reactions and outcomes of using ratings as criteria in selection and assessment. Perhaps a balanced judgment would be that good progress has been made, but further research is needed in some areas—especially at the outcome level.

INDIVIDUAL AND ORGANIZATIONAL PERSPECTIVES ON PRODUCING PERSONNEL SPECIFICATIONS

A judgment on the progress of work in this area is easy because there has been little or no work. None of the contributors to this book makes any substantive reference to the individual or organizational perspectives on the production of personnel specifications. This is probably a reflection on the fact that, even in the selection context, the way that we deduce the skills, knowledge, and competencies needed to do a job is also a neglected area. Nevertheless, it means that we simply do not know what perceptions, if any, people have of personnel specifications. We know very little about how they react to them, and we do not know whether the presence or style of a personnel specification has any positive or negative impact.

INDIVIDUAL AND ORGANIZATIONAL PERSPECTIVES ON ATTRACTING A FIELD OF CANDIDATES

A great deal is known about the individual and organizational perspectives on attracting a field of candidates. The topic is a substantive part of Rynes' chapter, "When recruitment fails to attract," and Thornton's chapter on the "Effect of selection practices." Rynes indicates that the timing of search, the nature and type of information about the vacancy, and the feedback given to candidates does not have significant effects. The role of interviewers or other organizational representatives seems to be particularly crucial, and that applicants prefer warm enthusiastic recruiters who have high status, a background similar to the candidate, and who give the candidate detailed information. Rynes also presents data that suggest that recruiters rarely meet these requirements. Again, research seems to have reached the point where specific pointers can be given to solutions to practical problems. Thornton also emphasizes the particular importance of recruiter behavior, as well as the impact of Realistic Job Previews (RJPS) and reports the interesting finding that personalized job previews produced no improvement over ordinary job previews.

An evaluation of work in this area is fairly clear cut. Our knowledge of individuals' perceptions and their reactions to these perceptions is reasonably substantial. However, there seems to be a dearth of research dealing with actual practical outcomes in realistic selection situations: We may know what applicants think and feel about the efforts made to attract them, but we do not know whether it actually alters their decisions to accept an offer of employment.

INDIVIDUAL AND ORGANIZATIONAL
PERSPECTIVES ON PSYCHOMETRIC PROPERTIES

When psychologists consider psychometric properties of measures, the concepts of reliability and validity are often the first to spring to mind. However, as de Wolff implies in Chapter 16, these concepts rarely arise spontaneously from individuals or nonselection specialists in organizations. However, reliability and validity have direct consequences on both the individual and the organizations and these consequences are perceived. This is most clearly seen in Chapter 3 by Latham and Finnegan. They compared perceptions of traditional interviews that typically have poor reliability and validity with the perceptions of situational and patterned interviews that typically have much better psychometric properties. The results indicate that the interviews with better psychometric properties are viewed as being more practical by all three groups of subjects (applicants, managers, and attorneys). In addition, the interviews with better psychometric properties were also thought to be more defensible in court. However, there is some evidence that applicants prefer a nonstructured interview because it gives them greater freedom to say what they wish and because they feel the outcome will be based on their abilities rather than on the skill of the interviewer. This raises the strong possibility that individuals may choose the less structured and organized methods of selection.

Trost and Kirchenkamp (Chapter 19) look at validity in terms of the desirable outcomes from the perspective of the individual: making a good career, reaching a high occupational level, having a responsible and well-paid job, and being satisfied in one's job—which for individuals are more important than predicting job performance. Their investigation found that predictors, such as scores on general scholastic tests, study habits at school, career plans, and exam results, were quite good predictors of occupational choice (about .34). However, validity in terms of predicting subsequent occupational level was much lower and yielded correlations of about .14. Validity in terms of predicting occupational success was about .08, and validity in terms of predicting occupational satisfaction was about .12. The average of all the validity coefficients given by Trost and Kirchenkamp is about .17. This figure needs confirmation by other research and more rigorous statistical analyses using Fisher's r to Z transformation rather than simple averaging, but, for the moment, it is possible to contrast them with validities of about .40 that are obtained for biodata items and job performance. Thus, it may be possible to conclude that we find it less easy to predict the outcomes that are important from the individual perspective.

A particularly interesting aspect of validity is lying and dissimulation. Seisdedos, in chapter 7, presents a wealth of data and argues that "faking good" should be seen in a totally new light as a personality characteristic in itself. He argues that a high score on "lie scales" should not be construed as an attempt to mislead but as a stable characteristic—the willingness to assume a style that is socially acceptable in certain circumstances—in a way that is analogous to putting on one's best suit on Sundays. It could be an enduring predisposition to engage in impression management and use certain self-presentation skills. If this is true, then the variance is genuine and not error variance, and validity is not diminished.

The psychometric property of fairness is perhaps closer to the surface in the perceptions of individuals and organizations. A major concern is the fairness of different methods of selection. The chapter by Neal Schmitt (Chapter 20) presents the results from a series of 25 assessment centers designed to measure the suitability of teachers for positions of School Administrators. The sample sizes were quite large (male 1,428, female 1,296), and it was possible to examine the effects of race and gender. Schmitt found that the most important variable was candidate race. White candidates obtained ratings that were about two thirds to three fourths of a standard deviation higher than Black candidates. Women candidates obtained ratings that were about one fourth of a standard deviation higher than men. However, these differences did not imply bias because previous research had also found performance differences between the subgroups, and there was no evidence of slope or intercept bias. Schmitt noted three very interesting interactions that may have implications for validity. First, there was a small but statistically significant tendency for both Blacks and Whites to give higher ratings to their own subgroup. Second, White raters tended to show a larger difference between the ratings they gave to women applicants and men applicants. Third, the composition of the assessment center group had no effect on the ratings of participants.

Pearn's chapter also looked at the concept of fairness but from an entirely different viewpoint—a legal and European perspective. He noted that, although based on American experience, events have taken a different path in Europe. Only in the United Kingdom is there a system of laws that give minorities legal protection from discrimination and the right to bring a case to law. However, limited systems exist in the Netherlands, Belgium, Luxembourg, and Denmark. In addition, there is a range of relevant directives enshrined in the 1957 Treaty of Rome. The development of the European Social Charter promises to provide 12 social rights that will have the impact of strengthening the protection available to minority groups. Pearn notes that there has been a change in emphasis. Initial concerns were about the fairness of different methods of selection, content bias, and differential validity. He suggests, however, that the future perspective will focus on other issues such as the tolerance of segregation, the acceptance of inequality, the resistance to change, and other attitudinal and decision-making issues.

Some of the legal issues of current interest in the United States are covered in Widgor and Sackett's chapter (Chapter 12). They outline an evaluation by a committee of the National Research Council of the General Aptitude Test Battery (GATB) used by the U.S. Employment Service. This evaluation is particularly important because only a few members of the committee were organizational psychologists. The results suggest that the validity of GATB has, in the past, been overestimated because recent studies have produced lower estimates of validity and that, in the past, corrections for criterion unreliability have been too generous. Nevertheless, it was still concluded that individual employers can reap substantial benefits even from selection instruments of such modest pretensions. But, some major issues of fairness remain. Black candidates seem to obtain scores on the GATB that are about one standard deviation lower than those of White candidates. The actual performance of Black candidates is, however, about one half a standard deviation lower. This means that if the same norms are used, "good Black workers" would not have an equal chance of being offered employment. This outcome focuses on an essential difference between the employer's perspective (emphasizing minimizing the errors of predicting job performance) and the employee's perspective (emphasizing minimizing the errors of classification). Thus it becomes important to differentiate between the fairness of a measure (e.g., GATB) and the fairness of a selection system. From the individual perspective, it is not enough to determine that one component of the system is fair: It is the global impact of the system that is important. Using arguments of this kind, the committee went on to make the controversial recommendation in favor of upward score adjustments for minority groups.

Clearly, the psychometric issues from the individual and organizational perspective are important topics, but, based on the evidence of the material cited and given in this book, they have received a high level of attention—especially the psychometric issue of fairness.

METHODS OF SELECTION

Many methods of selection are available but none of the chapters in this volume seeks to establish which methods are used in practice. Fortunately, for many countries, these data are available elsewhere (e.g., Bruchon-Schweitzer &

METHOD OF SELECTION	GB	F	D	IS	N	NL	ALL
Interviews	92	97	95	84	93	93	93
CV/Application letter	86	89	92	72		63*	80*
Medical Examination			50			71	61
Experience			40			63	52
References/recommendations	74	39	23	30		49	43
Diplomas and certificates				44		28	36
Cognitive Tests	11	33	21		25	21	22
Performance evaluation			19				19
Preliminary test						19	19
Personality Tests	13	38	6		16		18
Discussion Groups			15				15
Trainability Tests	14						14
Graphology	3	52	2	16	2	4	13
Work Sample	18	16	13			5	13
Assessment Centres	14	8	10		3		8
Bio data	4	1	8		1		4
Astrology	0	6			1		2

(Column group header above GB–ALL: "COUNTRY")

FIG. 21.2. The use of various methods of selection in six countries. (Numbers refer to the percentage of maximum possible usage: * indicates minimum value.)

Lievens, 1991; Schuler, Frier, & Kauffmann, 1991; Smith, 1991). Smith and Abrahamsen (1992) have attempted to collate the information and present the use of selection methods in six countries (see Fig. 21.2).

The most striking thing about these data is the similarity between countries even though differing methods of collecting the data would be expected to reduce the apparent similarity. Generally, the most frequent methods of selection and assessment are interviews and application forms. The least frequent tend to be astrology and biodata. The main exceptions to the general pattern are that graphology is used more widely in France and references are used more widely in the United Kingdom.

Many chapters in this volume contain information about the individual's perceptions and reactions to different methods of selection. For example, Schuler, Latham, and Finnegan and Thornton consider various aspects of the most frequently used selection method, the interview. Two chapters of this volume deal explicitly with "new" predictors using computer techniques.

Bartram's chapter (Chapter 17) outlines some of the changes brought about by computers—particularly the availability of cheap computers and widespread use of computer networks that will bring organizations advantages in administration, scoring, and analysis. It also highlights the organizational advantages that might accrue from using computers to generate dynamic and adaptive tests and items. From the perspective of the individual, a particularly striking possibility is using large-scale computer networks such as the MINITEL system in France, where telephone subscribers are given a computer terminal rather than a traditional book-form telephone directory. As well as looking up telephone numbers, the terminal can be used for other purposes such as selection. Applicants are able to phone a number given in an advertisement and, on screen, complete an application form or a biodata questionnaire. In certain circumstances, they could also be given some kind of screening test. Developments such as these have been found to increase response rate and the speed of the selection process. These systems could change the relationship between the candidate and the organization—the answers would be given on the candidate's "home ground" and would be seen to be owned by the candidate rather than by the organization.

The potential of computers in selection and assessment is further underlined by Putz-Osterloch, who presents candidates with a computer simulation of the task of commanding a squad of fire fighters. The scenario is less artificial than many conventional tests. It is dynamic and depends on a complex web of relationships among the component parts of the scenario and, in addition, the abilities measured (decision-making and organizing ability) are less evident. It could certainly be postulated that, from the viewpoint of the individual, techniques of this kind are enjoyable and have greater face validity. Schuler and Fruhner's chapter also gives information about the way that candidates perceive aspects of assessment centers: Intelligence tests were regarded as the most stressful component of the center, and, on average, candidates were pessimistic of their performance on this measure. Of the measures included, interviews were seen as giving the best measure of their ability, produced positive feelings, and gave them one of the greatest opportunities to influence the results. Most candidates seem to believe they had performed fairly well at their interviews. Personality tests were thought to be transparent in their intentions but poor measures of their ability and were not susceptible to their powers of influence. In general, the candidate's opinions of personality tests were even poorer than their opinions of intelligence tests.

Although some perceptions of methods of selection have been established, there is much less work on the reactions that these perceptions produce. An exception is the chapter by Schuler and Fruhner (Chapter 8), which reports investigations of the impact of various aspects of assessment centers on self-perception. According to the data presented by Schuler and Fruhner, there were significant changes during an assessment center in candidates' self-concepts of their emotions, mathematical ability, problem solving and creativity, perceived intelligence, relationships with same-sexed peers, and "state" self-concept. In comparison, the control group showed changes only in general self-concept and emotional self-concept.

Reviewing, the whole topic of methods of selection from the individual and organizational perspective is difficult. Certainly with some methods such as interviews, the individual's perceptions and reactions are mapped out in a fairly detailed way. However, with other measures such as biodata, astrology, and graphology, data at even this perceptual and reaction level are missing. Furthermore, there is little information concerning the practical outcomes of using various selection methods. Is there any evidence, for example, that using tests either attracts or repels certain types of candidate? Is there any evidence, for example, that using biodata techniques has any influence on the likelihood of candidates accepting a job offer? Perhaps the only island in this sea of ignorance concerns situational interviews. If situational interviews could be regarded as realistic job previews, they could be expected to produce the practical consequence of reducing the turnover of employees once they have accepted a job offer.

ESTABLISHING THE MONEY VALUE OF SELECTION

One of the most conspicuous lacunae from the perspectives of the individual and the organization is the absence of any analysis of the monetary value of selection from the viewpoint of the individual. Utility analyses from the company viewpoint are well established and have been available for more than a decade (e.g., Cascio & Silbey, 1979; Hunter & Schmidt, 1982). These analyses have reached considerable sophistication, taking into account additional marginal costs, discount rate, and sensitivity analyses (Boudreau, 1989). Utility analyses are available to help organizations estimate the likely benefits of alternative recruitment strategies. Boudreau and Rynes (1985), for example, were able to contrast the strategy of newspaper advertisements and effective selection with the strategy of using a recruitment consultant and then using a poor method of selection. Indeed, in the United States and the United Kingdom, clients often insist that consultants include utility analyses as a part of a proposal.

In this volume, the chapter by Wigdor and Sackett (Chapter 12) suggests that when applied at national level traditional methods of calculating utilities of selection devices often overestimate the money value. In a single organization, the worst candidates can be selected out. In the economy as a whole, this is only marginally possible. Even in times of high unemployment, over 90% of the economically active population are at work. At best, the utility of selection is limited to the advantages obtained from differential placement. At worst, selection merely shifts the static pool of talent in favor of organizations who have efficient selection systems—without any net gain to the economy as a whole.

However, there is nothing in this volume to even hint at parallel developments from the perspective of individuals. Consequently, the following is an embryonic attempt to outline an approach that could be developed further.

Perhaps the best way to construct a utility analysis from the individual perspective is to simulate the simplest situation where there are only two applicants for each job, each of which is drawn at random from a large applicant pool. In order to establish the general "laws," this specific selection situation was simulated 1,000 times. Two sets, each of 1,000 random numbers that were normally distributed, were generated. These represented the applicant's "true scores" on their ability to do the job. In a perfect selection system the applicant with the higher of these scores would be offered employment. However, in all practical selection situations these true scores are "disturbed" by a random component. The less valid the measure, the greater the random element. The random element was simulated by generating two additional sets of normally distributed random numbers. The observed scores were obtained by combining the "true" scores with the random element to various degrees. A combination of 4% true score and 96% random element is equivalent to a validity of .2. A combination of 36% true score and 64% random element is equivalent to a validity coefficient of .6.

In practice, of course, individuals are not selected on the basis of their true scores and the random element in their observed scores will mean that, sometimes, the applicant with the lower true ability is hired. For the sake of simplicity the outcomes can be divided into four main categories:

1. Hits: The individual with the highest true score is offered employment.
2. Near misses: the wrong person is offered employment but the gap between the two applicants is small—say, less than half a standard deviation of true ability.
3. Clear misses: The wrong person is offered the job and the discrepancy in true ability is large—say, between one half of a standard deviation and a standard deviation.
4. Travesties: The wrong person is offered the job and the discrepancy in ability is huge—say, over a standard deviation.

The frequencies in which these outcomes occur can be obtained from the 1,000 simulations, and the results are given in Fig. 21.3.

	VALIDITY				
SCENARIO	.0	.1	.3	.5	.7
Hit	.539	.547	.574	.642	.784
Near Miss	.087	.087	.087	.087	.087
Clear Miss	.110	.110	.106	.098	.067
Travesty	.264	.256	.233	.173	.062

FIG. 21.3. Frequencies of four selection outcomes for various levels of validity.

The money value of each of these outcomes can, in principle, be allotted a monetary cost. No doubt future research will establish these costs empirically in the way that techniques for establishing the money value of selection from the organization's viewpoint were developed. Here, we will make speculative estimates in order to see how the method might develop. For each outcome, the utility for two people, the winner and the loser, needs to be considered.

The utility of the first outcome, "hits," is easiest to determine. Each candidate has borne the costs of producing a resume (CV) and devoting a day to the selection procedure—a cost of, say, 400 European Currency units (ecus) each. For the rejected candidate there are also the costs of disappointment. We will assume that the disappointment is not too great and can be overcome by an evening out with his or her partner at a further cost of 100 ecus. The successful candidate, on the other hand, is exhilarated, and the degree of exhilaration is equal to a night out with his or her partner (worth 100 ecus). In addition, the successful candidate obtains a raise of 5,000 ecus and earns commission of 4,000 ecus for each of the 5 years he or she stays in the job. So, in the hit situation the costs are 500 ecus for the rejected applicant and a benefit of 44,700 ecus for the accepted applicant.

The same kind of calculation can be made for the "near miss" situation except, because the successful candidate is not the best candidate, the work is not quite as good and consequently a lower bonus of only 2,000 ecus per year is earned. So the benefit to the successful applicant is only 34,700 ecus.

The calculations for the "clear miss" scenario are similar except that because the successful candidate is markedly poorer, he or she rarely earns commission that totals only 500 ecus in the total of the 5 years he or she stays in the job. Thus the net benefit to the successful candidate is 27,200 ecus.

The final scenario, the "travesty," is very different. The person selected is unable to do the job, is fired after 3 months, and spends the next 2 months without employment. The salary raise for 3 months is 1,250 ecus. But, the 2 months unemployment means that he or she forgoes the 5,833 ecus that would have been earned had he or she remained in the previous job that paid at a rate of 35,000 ecus per year. In addition, it is necessary to attend a further six interviews at a cost of 400 ecus each before obtaining suitable employment. Further, the traumas of failing in a job and being fired produce a feeling of depression that can only be dispelled by a walking holiday in the hills around Glossop in the British Peak District—at a cost of 2,000 ecus. The total costs to the "successful" applicant are therefore 9,783 ecus.

Figure 21.4 gives the outcomes for each scenario. It shows that the scenario does not make much difference to the costs for the unsuccessful candidate. However, the scenario does make substantial differences to the outcome for the successful candidate. With these estimates in mind, it is possible to return to the frequencies with which the scenarios occur and, by multiplying the frequencies by the costs or benefits, work out the average utility for the individuals that are produced by selection systems of different levels of validity. The results are given in Fig. 21.5. The utilities from the individual perspective may be compared with those obtained for the organizational perspective using the following parameters:

- selection ratio (p)   .5
- ordinate of normal curve at p (θ)   .3989
- validity coefficient   as in table heading
- annual salary   40,000 ecus
- standard deviation of performance (sd)   40% salary
- length of service (t)   5 years
- costs of selection (c)   500 ecus

The formula for utility per individual is:

$$U = (p/\theta \times r \times sd \times t) - c$$

The results are quite clear, for both the individual and the organization, the utilities increase with the validity of the selection device. Validity is good for all. However, it is also apparent, at least for the scenario envisaged in this chapter, that the utilities for the organization are considerably larger, usually more than 10 times larger than the average utilities for candidates. Indeed, a marginal increase in validity brought about by a method that is costly in candidate's time may well eliminate any utility from the candidate's perspective.

SCENARIO	SUCCESSFUL APPLICANT	UNSUCCESSFUL APPLICANT	BOTH APPLICANTS
Hit	44,700	− 500	44,200
Near Miss	34,700	− 500	34,200
Clear Miss	27,200	− 500	26,700
Travesty	− 9,783	− 500	− 9,783

FIG. 21.4.   Costs associated with four possible outcomes of selection.

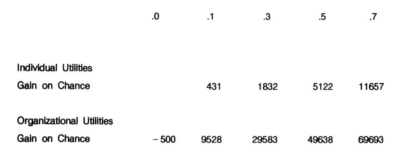

	.0	.1	.3	.5	.7
Individual Utilities					
Gain on Chance		431	1832	5122	11657
Organizational Utilities					
Gain on Chance	− 500	9528	29583	49638	69693

FIG. 21.5. A comparison of individual and organizational utilities in selection. Note: the organizational utilities are slight overestimates because service costs are not included (i.e., good employees cost more in terms of equipment and supplies and this should be deducted from the value of the extra production).

However, some cautions are vital. This embryonic attempt at utility analysis from the individual's perspectives suffers two, very major, limitations. First, many of the values of the parameters are mere "top of head" estimates. A whole genre of research could be instituted to establish the major parameters:

The costs to wrongly rejected candidates. The model suggested here suggests that the costs do not vary according to the correctness of the outcome: The cost to a rightly rejected candidate is equal to that of a wrongly rejected candidate. This may be acceptable in external recruitment situations when the candidates cannot judge the decision. But is it accurate when the rejected candidate knows that the candidate who has been accepted is quite incompetent?

The emotional costs of the outcomes. This model attributes certain values to the emotional outcomes of decisions. A negative decision is attributed a value of − 100 ecus. A positive decision is attributed a value of + 100 ecus. A dismissal for incompetence after 3 months is attributed a value of 2,000 ecus. These values used here are largely arbitrary. But, it is not beyond the capabilities of psychometric scaling to obtain more objective values.

Our categorization into "hits," "travesties," and so on is also arbitrary. But, empirical categorization is not impossible. Research could establish the point, in sd units, where dismissal for incompetence becomes an unacceptable probability. Similarly, the points at which earnings from commission decline by 50% or 75% could be established empirically rather than assuming that these levels occur when there is a difference of up to .5 or 1.0, respectively. Indeed, from the individual perspective, it would be worth exploring the utilities in jobs that pay commissions and jobs that pay flat rates provided minimum competence is provided.

Other aspects that need empirical verification are the average length of tenure and the salary increment that accrues to a successful application for a new job.

Second, the simulation is far too simple. The situation where there are only two candidates is quite rare. Usually, there are six or more plausible candidates. The likely effect of additional candidates is to increase the costs that are borne by unsuccessful candidates.

INDIVIDUAL AND ORGANIZATIONAL PERSPECTIVES OF FEEDBACK

Perhaps it is not surprising that a great deal is known about the individual and organizational perspectives of feedback because it is probably the most "candidate centered" phase of the general selection paradigm. Terry Dickinson's chapter outlines some important aspects of performance appraisal and formal feedback. Apparently, supervisors tend to distort feedback in a positive direction, and the traditional strategy of giving positive feedback first followed by any negative feedback tends to increase the perceived accuracy and acceptance of the feedback. Long-standing research also shows that feedback should be specific and attempt to influence motivation by emphasizing goals, rewards, and appropriate responses. Generally, feedback should be given in a way that generates a sense of personal control and accomplishment.

Dickinson also gives details about the way in which an individual's personality can influence his or her reaction to feedback. For example, when the self-concept is threatened, protection of the self-concept is a probable reaction, and consequently the strength of the self-concept is an important determinant of the reaction. It also appears that some individuals consistently seek more feedback than others, and this may be related to their motivations for achieving competence and enhancing their self-esteem. Another possible mediator of the reactions to feedback is age, with some studies showing that more senior employees have less favorable attitudes toward new performance-appraisal systems.

A totally different facet to feedback is the organizational characteristics and contexts in which feedback takes place, but little empirical work exists. However, Dickinson describes a study by Greenberg on the determinants of perceptions of fairness. Two factors accounted for 95% of the variance in perceptions of fairness—the procedures used and the relation between an appraisal rating and subsequent administrative action such as a salary increase or promotion. Dickinson also covers other aspects concerning individual perspective of feedback such as the training of those giving feedback, the motivation of managers to give feedback, and the standardization of feedback. It is clear that this field of research is well developed. Indeed, it is now at the point where models of feedback effectiveness can be formulated.

Dickinson and many other writers have focused on the formal feedback of appraisal and selection information. However, it can be argued that the majority of feedback is by informal means. The chapter by Farr (Chapter 11) reminds us that a considerable amount is also known about informal feedback. We already know the main types, sources, and modes of informal feedback. Again it is noted that people with poor self-concepts are most at risk in reacting to feedback in a negative way, and that various aspects of personality and biographical background are also likely to mediate the effects of feedback. Again, research has developed to the point where explicit models can be constructed. Indeed, research in this area has reached the point where the probable short- and long-term effects on ''poor'' employees can be suggested together with ways of ameliorating some potentially destructive responses to negative feedback. Clearly, feedback is a comparatively well-mapped domain.

A SATELLITE'S-EYE VIEW OF THE INDIVIDUAL AND ORGANIZATIONAL PERSPECTIVES ON SELECTION AND ASSESSMENT

Figure 21.6 draws together the conclusions made earlier in the chapter to provide a large-scale map from which a global evaluation can be made. Of course, some of the categorizations are tentative. The figure shows that perceptions of individuals and organizations have had the greatest coverage, and the outcomes in terms of changes in behavior have received the least attention. Particular lacunae concern the individual and organizational perspectives on personnel specifications and utility. In these areas, work seems to be either nonexistent or embryonic. Perhaps these areas might be the growth points for future research.

SELECTION AND ASSESSMENT FROM THE SELECTORS' PERSPECTIVES

Perhaps it is apposite to end this book with a complete change of focus and to suggest an entirely new perspective from which selection and assessment can be viewed—the perspective of the selectors themselves. We simply do not know even the basic demographic characteristics of the people who perform the function of selecting others for jobs. We certainly know very little about their psychological qualities such as mental ability, personality, and interests. However, the issues involved are very broad and they are perhaps best left as the subject of another book.

	PERCEPTIONS	REACTIONS	OUTCOMES
JOB ANALYSIS	Considerable	Meagre	Considerable
CRITERIA	Considerable	Some	Some
PERSONNEL SPECIFICATIONS	None	None	None
ATTRACTING CANDIDATES	Considerable	Considerable	Little
PSYCHOMETRICS & FAIRNESS	Some	Considerable	Considerable
METHODS OF SELECTION	Patchy; considerable for interviews and assessment centers	Patchy; considerable for interviews and tests	Patchy
UTILITY	None	None	Embryonic
FEEDBACK	Considerable	Considerable	Considerable

FIG. 21.6. The global picture of degree of research on the individual and organizational perspectives.

REFERENCES

Belbin, R. M. (1981). *Management teams: Why they succeed or fail*. London: Heinmann.

Boudreau, J. W. (1989). Selection utility analysis: A review and agenda for future research. In J. M. Smith & I. T. Robertson (Eds.), *Advances in selection and assessment* (pp. 227–258). Chichester: Wiley.

Boudreau, J. W., & Rynes, S. L. (1985). The role of recruiting in staffing utility analysis. *Journal of Applied Psychology, 70*, 354–366.

Bruchon-Schweitzer, M., & Lievens, S. (1991). Le recruitement en Europe: Researches et pratiques. *Psychologie et Psychometrie, 12*(2), 1–71.

Cascio, W. F., & Silbey, V. (1979). Utility of the assessment center as a selection device. *Journal of Applied Psychology, 64,* 107–118.

Hunter, J. E., & Schmidt, F. L. (1982). Fitting people to jobs: The impact of personnel selection methods on national productivity. In M. D. Dunnette & E. A. Fleishman (Eds.), *Human performance and productivity* (Vol. 1, pp. 233–284). Hillsdale, NJ: Lawrence Erlbaum Associates.

Schuler, H., Frier, D., & Kauffmann, M. (1991). Use and evaluation of selection methods in German companies. *European Review of Applied Psychology, 41,* 20–25.

Smith, J. M. (1991). Recruitment and selection in the UK with some data on Norway. *European Review of Applied Psychology, 41,* 28–34.

Smith, J. M., & Abrahamsen, M. (1992). Patterns of selection in six countries. *The Psychologist, 5,* 5, 205–207.

Smith, M., & Robertson, I. T. (1993). *The theory and practice of systematic personnel selection.* Chichester: Wiley.

Author Index

Subject Index

A

Ability, 76–77, 82, 85, 86–87
  processing of information and low, 66
Academic self-concept, 112, 114–116, 120
Acceptance, false, 197–199, 201
Accuracy
  of performance appraisals, 143–144,
    148–149, 153–154
Achievement tests
  predictability of occupational success and
    aptitude and, 303–305, 306–309,
    310–311
Adaptive testing
  flexilevel, 274
  item-based, 273
  Item Response Theory (IRT) models,
    274–275
  stradaptive, 274
  two-staged, 274
Adjustment-oriented methods, 221
Administration
  substages of, 268–269
Affirmative action programs, 184–185
  effects on applicants' perception of organi-
    zation, 64
Age
  as individual characteristic of performance
    appraisal, 152–153
  motivational distortion and, 103–104

Ambiguity, tolerance for, 170–171
  job-related vs. problem-solving, 170–171
Analysis
  computerized, 269
  utility, 343–348
Anonymity
  validity of questionnaires and, 92
Anxiety, 34
  and issue of timing in recruitment, 29–30
  processing of information and, 66–67
Applicants, *see also Individuals; Performance, job*
  effects of selection practices on their per-
    ceptions of organization, 57–67
  experience of
    acceptance of personality questionnaires
      and, 17–18
    in using interview methods, 50, 52–53
  growth in interest in perspective of, 11–12
  individual and organizational perspectives
    on attracting, 337–338
  individual reactions to personnel proce-
    dures, 71–73
  and interview questionnaires
    developing for, 44–47
    rating of, 49–50
  perception of, 7–9
  prediction paradigm and expectations about
    selection procedures, 254–255
  preferences of
    concerning contact with potential peers
      and co-workers, 32